A Sociology of Education

A Sociology of Education
Access to Power and Privilege

Mark A. Chesler

William M. Cave

University of Michigan

Macmillan Publishing Co., Inc.
New York
Collier Macmillan Publishers
London

LC
191
.C373

Macmillan Publishing Co., Inc.
866 Third Avenue, New York, New York 10022

Collier Macmillan Canada, Ltd.

Library of Congress Cataloging in Publication Data

Chesler, Mark A
    Sociology of education.

    Includes bibliographies and index.
    1. Educational sociology. I. Cave, William M.,
joint author. II. Title.
LC191.C373   370.19   80-15478
ISBN 0-02-322150-X

Printing: 1 2 3 4 5 6 7 8   Year: 1 2 3 4 5 6 7 8

PREFACE

The broad purpose of this book is to help readers reexplore their understandings of schools and school life. We say reexplore because all of us have already explored schooling as we passed through and continue to pass through these public institutions. Often, however, we move through schools without really seeing them, without penetrating the cloak of mystery and awe with which children and adults perceive the world. But the experience of schooling marks each of us, sometimes in ways we barely understand, and sometimes in ways we may not be able to control. Our purpose in writing this book is to help readers tag those marks, and to expand those understandings, through a reexploration of the constant and systematic operations of schools and schooling.

In the first section of this book (Chapters 1, 2, and 3) we examine the societal context of schooling in this country. The nature of the North American culture, and our political-economic system, help determine the shape of schools, and also shape the lives and backgrounds of people who live and work in schools—students, teachers, administrators, custodial and service personnel, and the like. Changes in the American society are reflected in the schools, and in Chapter 3 we examine some ways in which schooling has responded to the changing character of our society. In reexploring the ideas in this section, each of us should understand the ways our lives (and our schooling experiences) are embedded in the larger social world.

In the second section of this book (Chapters 4, 5, 6, and 7), we examine the organizational and institutional structures and processes of contemporary schooling. The community, the local school building, the professional organization of staff members, and common procedures for dealing with students are all key components of modern schooling. The community represents the most local external context of the school: it decides on policy, allocates financial resources, and lends moral support, although, in many cases it does not do those things very well. The local organization of the school building—staff and structures—interacts most directly with students, providing them with a direct taste of educational authority and the possibilities of educational liberation. The school and its students are often caught in a web of conflicts—disagreements about wants and needs, about ways of being together, and about appropriate ways of operating. But not only students are engaged in this conflict; the general citizenry and the professional staff of the school also struggle for their own way of seeing and conducting education. In reexploring the ideas in this section, each of us should become more precise about our understandings of the ways in which we live and work in educational institutions, and the ways we relate to others working in these settings.

In the third section of this book (Chapters 8, 9, and 10) we examine patterns of school outcomes, the ways in which the fruits of education are distributed or allocated throughout the population. Here, the problem of goals and goal measurement are paramount, and the discussion of outcomes begins with an attempt to survey various definitions of school outcomes, both conceptually and operationally, thereby to see how these outcomes are assessed. The messages are undeniably clear that schooling benefits whites more than blacks, Hispanics, and other minorities; relatively affluent youth more than nonaffluent or poor youth; and males more often than females. Why is this so? Here again we call for reexploration of our own perspectives and ideologies. Each of us carries various interpretive frameworks with which we analyze and make sense out of the data reported in Chapters 8 and 9. We ask the reader to reexplore her or his framework and to consider carefully the twin frameworks presented for understanding and making sense out of all these data. If, indeed, schools are partly responsible for teaching us how to make sense out of the world, we should see one of the outcomes of schooling reflected in the very frameworks we utilize to make sense out of the materials in these chapters. We invite the reader to reeducate himself or herself by reexploring the frameworks each of us use.

Throughout this book, we have tried to point the reader to the existence of discrimination and differential access to opportunity and privilege that exists in North American society, and to the school's role and procedures for reflecting and maintaining (some would even say creating) these differences. In the final section of this book (Chapter 11), we examine various ways in which people in local communities and schools have tried to alter these facts of life and to change the structure and character of schooling itself. In reexploring the ideas presented we invite the reader to think about those strategies that make sense to him or her, and which might be effective in altering the objectionable aspects of schools and schooling that each of us has experienced.

A book is a living thing. We have written it one way. A reader who carefully reexplores the ideas presented will read (and perhaps write) his or her own understanding of the operations of American schooling. A careful reader always reworks the material, and an active encounter with written materials should take us beyond those materials into a new understanding of ourselves and our world. To encourage this transformation of the book itself, we have provided the reader with a variety of exercises and encounters with himself or herself and the material. In this effort, we hope to help make this book a living thing, and to promote a practical and dialectical encounter between the readers and ourselves. Out of this encounter comes knowledge and learning, and not merely the acquisition of prepared information.

M.A.C.
W.M.C.

CONTENTS

1

THE SOCIOCULTURAL CONTEXT OF SCHOOLING

Educational experiences are universal phenomena in organized societies. The content and character of these experiences vary tremendously in different cultures, but they exist nevertheless. The universality of educational experiences can be attributed to the need for all human societies to preserve their cultural heritage, and to inculcate their young into the ideas, customs, and standards of that culture. The process by which the young learn these traditional ways is called *enculturation*. At the same time, all members of a society must learn how to adapt to constant changes in the culture. The process by which the young (or the old) learn these new and/or emerging customs and values is called *acculturation*. These two processes ensure cultural continuity, since all societies must maintain some stability while they continually undergo change. All people in a society must adapt their established patterns of behavior and modes of thinking to new or emerging values or risk conflict and stagnation. The rate and intensity by which these modifications occur vary enormously among and between cultures. But no matter what the particular level of a society, whether literate, preindustrial, "developed," or postindustrial, the cultural processes that govern the education and socialization of the young must deal with the same problems and processes.

Some scholars who are concerned with culture and schooling limit their use of the term *education* to the formal schooling apparatus, and utilize *socialization* as a broader term encompassing all that is learned. The culture seeps through both socialization and education processes, since these processes cannot be abstracted from the embracing culture and social structure; rather they can best be understood as part and parcel of the culture. The formal process of schooling is generally overt; it is visible to all and is usually well organized. But

1

both education and socialization occur informally and covertly as well, with little conscious awareness on the part of the individual.

In some societies, for instance among most tribal groups, and indeed in much of the underdeveloped Third World, the education and socialization of the young take place without extensive and formal learning networks. Nevertheless, the process of "schooling" is virtually ubiquitous, and it is almost impossible for one to avoid attending a school of some sort, whether the individual resides in a city or a village, lives in the jungle or the desert, is assigned to military duty, or is incarcerated in a prison. The universal nature of schools and schooling is illustrated in the following quotation:

> In America, and in all industrial societies, there are schools of six major kinds: (1) compulsory schools for that general transformation of youth into a qualified citizenry which occupies the childhood and adolescence of most young persons; (2) degree-granting schools (generally called colleges and universities) for advanced and specialized training of young adults; (3) religious (or political) schools for young and old; (4) military schools; (5) vocational and job-training schools; and (6) a vast miscellany of schools which impart what may be described as occasional knowledge of such widely various subjects as first aid, Zen Buddhism, and the manufacture of compost. Even in the most primitive societies, where schools of a kind familiar to us would be difficult to maintain, schools there are nonetheless, of a particular kind: the mystery schools. Mystery schools would seem to be three main types: the "bush schools" which indoctrinate pubescent males and females with the secret lore of adults; the religious and the professional schools which instruct young shamans in the arts of their profession. These schools have developed out of rites of passage, particularly initiation schools; they elaborate their socially useful function around joints in the tree of maturation, and always retain as much interest, if not more, in testing and celebrating the human transformation as in shaping the transformation itself. But they fit the definition: they are definite in place and time and membership, and concerned with communicating in symbols their definite bundles of information. Our schools differ from the primitive schools, apart from obvious discrepancies in size and plant, in the degree to which they are divorced from the process of celebrating the more or less spontaneous transformation of human experience, and in the extent to which they aggressively produce the transformations necessary to cultural continuity. Our schools profess, at least, to teach us almost everything we know. [1]

The universality of schooling is not an accidental occurrence, nor is the institution of education. At stake is the preservation of the cultural heritage and the process of societal continuity. Clearly, the manifest aim of education everywhere is to produce human beings who will perpetuate and improve the present society; failing that, it is hoped that they will not destroy the society's values and structures. The emergence of formal schooling has been largely a response to the growing complexity of the social order, reflecting a need for continuity, predictability, and social control over the impending threats of discontinuity and instability. No society consciously tolerates the systematic education of rebels and radicals that would radically alter the social institutions and structures upon which that society is based. Thus, all educational institutions are, by definition, conservative in nature.

At the same time, schools must deal with the fact that changes occur in cultures and societies, and that common historic meanings and values must adapt to the discontinuity of change. It is possible to view schools not only as conservers of societal tradition and transmitters of the cultural heritage but, under certain conditions, as "liberating" forces as well. Thus, we have a continuing debate whether the "true purpose" of education is to teach about the past or to prepare for the future, whether schools are conservers of historic tradition or agents of change. Probably either of these choices is more or less satisfactory depending upon our particular biases at the moment. We all want some things to change and others to stay the same.

WHAT IS A CULTURE?

Culture can be characterized as a uniquely human aspect of social interaction. Culture consists of material artifacts (such as buildings, railroads, cars) and symbols (such as ideas, cherished values, the flag, art forms) that have meaning for persons. The material goods of a society are not complete in themselves; they carry meanings associated with their function as well as fashion and design. Thus, private automobiles have a different meaning in the United States than in China. In China, private cars do not exist; in Russia they are the possessions of a privileged few and a symbol of elite status; in the United States they are the possessions of all but the poorest underclass, evidence of private property that is available to the masses. The particular fashion and design of American cars, with their high horsepower, chrome, and glass, symbolize something very different than do low-horsepower foreign cars. Major symbol systems, such as language and art and music, obviously communicate the hopes and fears and ideas of the society. As members of a society understand together the meaning of symbols and goods they take on shared regularities in thought as well as in deed. Outsiders do not know all the meanings and functions attached to these cultural artifacts, and thus may not know how to use them, appreciate them, or behave in their presence.

Some of the most important aspects of any culture are its accumulated belief systems, notions of appropriate behavior, and definitions of the "good life." Schools are one of the major carriers of the culture, one of the major institutions through which the young are prepared to take on the ways of the adult society. The church and the family play a similarly important role in cultural tradition and development, but the public responsibility of the school makes it a formal reservoir and transmission belt for the official culture. More particular cultures, or subcultures, are likely to be shared and shaped by persons of different racial groups, religious or ethnic groups, and local families. These particular cultural variations generally are codified and transmitted by private agencies such as churches, clubs, and kinship systems.

At any historic moment, every culture has its own definition of what it means to be human, no less what it means to be "American" or "Rhodesian" or "Cambodian." Sometimes this definition contains plural possibilities, and sometimes only very narrow tolerance exists. Whatever the leeway, this particular definition, with its concomitant rules and roles, must be passed on. What is transmitted, and therefore learned, may vary considerably according to the particular culture or the subculture observed.

In any society, the socialization and education processes help create these common definitions, rank alternatives in order of priority, and pass on traditions regarding the acceptable artifacts and symbols. In advanced industrial societies, such as in the United States, formal schooling officially has been charged with the responsibility for the mass transmission of the dominant culture. Some of the most explosive issues confronting American education relate to the nature of this content. Difficult and searching questions often are reduced to: Who decides what culture is "the culture"? Whose heritage is dominant and should thus be transmitted? What general values should be taught and what specific skills should be learned? Do nondominant cultures or subcultures deserve similar respect? Should they also be transmitted?

The mechanisms by which schools transmit this material are also the focus of much public debate and controversy. Some obvious and important questions in this regard are: How is specific material best transmitted? How is this material best learned? Where is the focus of decision making for education in a local community? What can the schools do that parents and churches cannot do, and vice versa? The fact that Americans have relied primarily upon a mass, public, and universal system of education indicates our commitment to the preservation of our culture in ways that attempt to unify our diversity and stabilize our changing society. How can this preservation be assisted through schooling?

SOCIALIZATION INTO SOCIETY

In the broadest sense of the terms *socialization* and *education*, education is the society's formal mechanism for aiding the process of socialization. Despite the wide variety of human cultures, and despite considerable variance within any society, this appears to be an omnipresent mechanism. For the society, the schools preserve the cultural heritage; for the individual, the schools transmit information and create commitment to the dominant pattern. Thus, the broad meaning of education is in many ways similar to the meaning of socialization, the process whereby persons are enculturated into human culture—the particular society.

The socialization of the young requires, in part, that they learn to appreciate the shared meanings and values that exist in the culture at large, and that they internalize these beliefs and values as guides for the conduct of their own lives.

The process of *imitation* has been used to describe some of the earliest learning of this sort; it involves the young child in copying or imitating behavior it sees being performed by mother or father or by a close sibling. Thus, the child first learns to relate to other people and objects (blankets, bed, bottle, breast) as it sees others doing. The process of *reinforcement* has been used to describe other significant learnings acquired by the young child. As the milk bottle produces food satiation, and as a mother's arms produce warmth and nurturing comfort, the young child learns to produce those behaviors (crying for the bottle, reaching out for mother's arms, smiling) that will gain it those rewarding or reinforcing responses from the environment.

As the young child grows, it utilizes *role learning* to learn what to expect from other people, and how to produce for them what is expected of children. To recognize and respond to the shared meanings implicit in human interaction the child must first learn to imagine the nature and elements of others' behaviors and engage in imagining the others' concept of the child and its behavior. Questions such as the following must be answered: "What did he mean by that?"; "What would I have meant by that had I been in his shoes?"; "How would I feel if that had happened to me?"; "How does she feel about what I did?"; "Does she know what I meant by that?" With the answers to these questions the child is able to see himself or herself from the other's vantage point. The illustration of the "looking-glass self" has been used to describe this process by Charles Horton Cooley [2]. According to Cooley, children begin to "see" themselves by perceiving how others treat them, developing an image or picture of themselves consistent with how they feel they are treated by others. Over time, young persons develop a coherent concept of "the self," a concept developed by peering into the "looking glass" of others' behaviors.

Another important concept used to describe this process is the "significant other," discussed by George Herbert Mead [3]. Mead indicates that young children seek the approval of other people who are close to them and important to them—people who provide reinforcement, for instance. In order to get this approval young children do what they think these significant others want and expect, and by so doing they learn appropriate ways of behaving in that family or culture. Over time, the combination of many significant others grows into a concept of the "generalized other," whereby children imagine, on the basis of their past experience, what other peeple in general or the society at large expect of them. The ability to imagine correctly what others expect, and how others will interpret one's behavior, is the basis of organized role behavior, sets of behaviors consistent with one's status and station in a given situation or in life in general. As one learns a role well, one is able to interact with others playing other roles and to engage in reciprocal role interaction over time.

The development of these skills in human interaction requires young persons to learn the ways of their immediate culture—what is expected of them and how to meet others' expectations. By understanding others' expectations and perceptions, young people are able to learn self-reflective behavior, the key to sustained and successful human interaction. By learning how to behave in ways consistent with others' considerations and roles, young people learn to behave in orderly and obedient ways, contributing further to the maintenance of a coherent and stable culture and to social order and control in general.

The length, intensity, and formality of this socialization process varies génerally with the complexity of the society in question. In nonliterate and most preindustrial societies, the relative simplicity of the social structure and homogenity of the population are such that there is little need for formal schools and professionally trained teachers. The job can be done by parents, siblings, peers, and certain elders. In her penetrating study of the Manus people of New Guinea, Margaret Mead describes the processes whereby the young are prepared for that culture.

> As soon as the baby can toddle uncertainly, he is put down into the water at low tide when parts of the lagoon are high and others only a few inches under water. . . . Swimming is not taught: the small waders imitate their slightly older brothers and sisters, and after floundering about in waist-deep water begin to strike out for themselves.
>
> The departments of knowledge which small children are expected to master are spoken of as "understanding the house," "understanding the fire," "understanding the canoe," and "understanding the sea." Understanding the house includes care in walking over uncertain floors . . . remembering to remove a slat of floor for spitting or urinating . . . not bringing mud or rubbish into the house. A child's knowledge of a canoe is considered adequate if he can balance himself, feet planted on the two narrow rims, and punt the canoe with accuracy, paddle well enough to steer through a mild gale, run the canoe accurately under a house platform without jamming the outrigger, extricate a canoe from a flotilla of canoes crowded closely about a house platform or the edge of an island, and bale out a canoe by a deft backward and forward movement which dips the bow and stern alternately. . . . Understanding of the sea includes swimming, diving, swimming under the water, and a knowledge of how to get water out of the nose and throat by leaning the head forward and striking the back of the neck. *Children of between five and six have mastered these four necessary departments.*
>
> *There is no belief that it is necessary to give a child formal teaching,* rather chance adult play devices are enlisted. . . . Here in Manus are a group of children, some forty in all, with nothing to do but have a good time all day long . . . The adult world is confronted by an unassimilated group, a group which speaks its language with a vocabulary for play, which knows its gods but gives them slight honor, which has a jolly contempt for wealth getting activities. [4]

The utter simplicity of the induction process, taking place under such seemingly primitive conditions, obscures a very complex series of events. Through interaction and imitation, the culture heritage of the society is being transmitted to the young. In the formal sense, there are no teachers and no schools; yet, there is a great deal of teaching going on and children are being "schooled" in the society's basic departments of knowledge. The abruptness of childhood is demonstrated by the expectation that children will master the necessary cultural learnings by the age of six, thereby signifying their readiness for transition into adulthood. As the adults in a society come to feel that the amount of learning required increases, so will the length of the socialization period.

In the case of the Manus society, the principal content of the socialization process would seem to be obvious. The young are taught what the culture regards as "important."

> The Manus child would probably be killed trying to cross a street where there was a traffic light; an American child of comparable age probably would drown playing with the Manus children. But the education of each *in its cultural setting* is reasonably efficient. The Manus child learns the Manus language, although he never sees a book, a dictionary, or an alphabet—he does not need them. The Manus child, like our own, learns a religion, a moral code and a system of etiquette, adequate to his needs and those of his society. To facilitate economic security, the Manus youngster learns sailing and fishing for precisely the same purpose as our children learn bookkeeping, farming, or law. Fundamentally, the purposes and outcomes of Manus education and American education are the same: to condition the plastic growing human so that he/she will be able to function in a society made up of similarly conditioned people. [5]

Oral and Written Cultures

Social scientists generally make distinctions between the modes by which the cultural heritage and practical knowledge of a culture are codified and transmitted to succeeding generations. Those societies that are characterized by an oral cultural tradition are referred to as *nonliterate*, whereas those characterized by a well-developed written language are termed *literate*. Although the fundamental processes and basic objectives of cultural learning bear marked similarity, some distinctive differences exist between the educational systems of nonliterate and literate societies in the degree of formality with which they approach their task. Among the Manus, there was relatively informal effort to educate the children: imitation of adult behavior was the primary medium of learning to meet societal expectations. By contrast, in literate societies there is a formal effort to teach areas of knowledge—the medium generally being teachers. The key differences involve the degree of formality in the system and the distinction between learning the culture by imitation and learning by deliberate instruction. This is a matter of degree, to be sure, because a great deal of learning occurs through informal and imitative means in our society as well.

Great differences also exist between literate and nonliterate societies in the quantity of formal education experienced. The more technologically advanced societies, such as Japan, the Soviet Union, Canada, the United States, and the nations of western Europe, have developed educational systems that tend to maintain control over students for a longer period of time. The infusion of more departments of knowledge (curricular areas) that the young are expected to master, the almost universal acceptance of a minimum compulsory school-age law, and the age-grade membership criterion represent a systematic effort to lengthen the socialization process and thus extend the period of childhood and adolescence under institutional surveillance. In the Manus society, children of five and six years of age have mastered the necessary departments of knowledge and are considered ready for passage into adult society. We do not assume that process to be complete until the age of fourteen or sixteen, at least. Although these differences reflect the relative complexity of the two societies and the amount of knowledge considered necessary for effective functioning, they also indicate different views of the extensiveness of the socialization process and the need for social control over the education of children. Among the Manus, almost all of the people appreciated their goods and symbols in the same way, and the one definition of a "good life" was agreed to be in common by all. But in a complex, widely dispersed, and heterogeneous society such as ours, the teaching of "*a* religion," "*a* system of etiquette," or "*a* moral code" inevitably encounters the existence of multiple religions, multiple etiquette systems, and multiple moral codes. Is one right and others wrong? Should we teach one "right way" or the multiplicity and pluralism of moral codes and cultural symbols? Private families can do as they wish, but as organs of the official government, schools must defend themselves against charges of religious, moral, cultural preference or partisanship and bias.

The differences between oral and written cultures can be characterized in many ways, and the differences in their educational traditions and mechanisms are also subject to different understandings. Oral cultures generally are less complex, smaller, more homogeneous, and provide clear and unambiguous expectations and rules for all members. Relations among persons in these cultures are highly personal and informal, often with substantial loyalty and affection. Sociologists and anthropologists have referred to these relationships as *primary relations*, and to the group or culture as *gemeinschaft*. In our highly industrialized and complex society we still find areas in which these traditions dominate: for instance, in the family and in close friendship groups. These are the first relationships we form, and in time and intensity they are primary. Written cultures are generally more complex, larger, and more widely dispersed geographically. They are also more heterogeneous, and have multiple and often ambiguous expectations and rules for their members. One of the reasons a written language develops in these cultures is to create regularity and a clear code for behavior in the face of diffusion and dispersion. Relations between persons in these cultures are less personal and often quite formal, with adherence to formal rules and roles. Sociologists and anthropologists have referred to these relationships as *secondary relations*, and to the group or culture as *gesellschaft*. Formally organized institutions are the model for these relations in our society, institutions in which people follow written rules for their behavior and relate to one another in limited and prescribed ways.

In most societies, with or without schools, a variety of groups or organizations are responsible for preparing the young for their entrance into the general culture and their adoption of a particular subcultural tradition. Generally, these institutions intervene between the larger elements of the total society, such as the polity and economy, and the individual's immediate environment. Lippitt has referred to those groups and persons that link the interests and needs of society and the actual learning activities of the young as the *socialization community*.

> The key elements in this total process of "raising the young" are the institutions and individuals who frequently interact with the young. These individuals and agencies are the links between the interests and needs of society and the actual learning activities of the young. We have called this cluster of influences the *socialization community*. [6]

The contexts of the socialization community are shown in Figure 1—1.

FAMILY AS A SOCIALIZING MEDIUM

A key mechanism of socialization in all human cultures is the family. Here the issues of transforming the young animal to a member of a human community are presented by intimates—people we know well and are close to. The family is the first prolonged and intimate interaction system the individual encounters. It is a "primary group," typically with personal loyalty, affection, and close relations among all members. In this context the child discovers humanness and moves from primitive biogenetic instincts to learned social responses. In the family are learned the rudiments of social interaction and role behavior, the content of one's culture. Here is also learned the lesson of

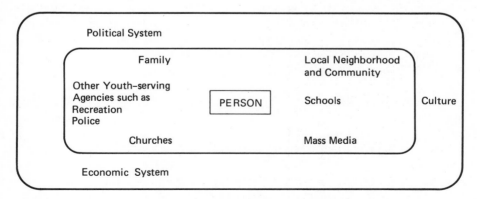

FIGURE 1—1. The societal contexts of the socialization community.

personal uniqueness and the lesson of group commonality, along with the interfaces between these two realities of human existence.

Historically, there is little we know with greater certainty about mankind's social background than that humans nearly always lived and learned together in biologically derived aggregations called families. In every age and in almost all known societies, families have been the initial and universal units of social experience. The enduring importance of families may largely result from the very diversity and versatility of the highly personal services they have been able to perform for their members. Families are the arena within which "legitimate" procreation and creation take place and they are sites for initial survival/safety training.

Nuclear families have held a virtual monopoly of this function in some societies. In other societies, kinship patterns are well enough integrated— physically and culturally—for the "extended" family to be so responsible. In either case, the family is the carrier of the local culture and the social unit through which unique or particular versions of this culture are interpreted and passed on to a new generation.

The things that members of a given family *wish to teach* or learn are limited by that family's unique historical and societal experience. In American society, the sharpest definers of each family's relation to a unique subculture are those of race, economic class, religion, and ethnicity. As a result of these differences we see familial differences in child-rearing practices as well as attitudinal or behavioral outcomes regarding social relationships and skills. Each child is more or less uniquely prepared for the cultural reality his or her own family experiences or wishes to experience.

Families always also have performed key political functions, helping to develop skills in group living, decision making, obedience to authority, and the like. As a local unit within which important decisions are made, the family functions itself as a micropolitical system. Here young people first learn how power is exercised, and how it may be confronted/challenged, bargained with, or subverted. Here also, young people learn the different forms and amounts of power available to men, women, elders, and youth. The value of obedience to parental authority helps develop a fear of rebellion and resistance that most of us carry into schools and society in general. At the same time, we learn to transfer that fear to people with whom we have progressively weaker affective ties.

In addition, families have always performed key economic functions as both producing and consuming units for goods and services. Within these intimate circles, children learn the attitudes and skills necessary to play a role in the production and consumption of goods and services. Each family adopts a division of labor regarding family tasks, and prepares its young for the notion of work, and the relation between work and appropriate rewards.

One interesting example of the family's early socialization efforts regarding economic skills is provided in the following series of excerpts from a biographical study of the Rockefeller family through several generations. First, we introduce the patriarch of the family, the senior Rockefeller, who founded the family's vast fortune and holdings and established the economic socialization patterns that were to influence the succeeding generation. Then, we introduce in succession the key actors of three generations of Rockefellers and the sustained efforts of each one to pass on the heritage and its concomitant skills. John D. Rockefeller, Sr., learned some key economic skills in the following manner:

> He wrote down, day by day and to the penny, the income and expenses, the saving and investment, the business and benefactions of his life. Besides the modest $1 for a week's room and board, there might be 75 cents for the Mite Society and 5 cents for Sunday School at the Erie Street Baptist Church, or 10 cents for the poor and 10 cents for foreign missions. The church was his only recreation, almost his only connection with the world outside the commission merchant trade. The total of the gifts he made was almost invariably 10 percent of his $3.50 weekly income. Other than grudging purchases of clothing, there was little else besides this disciplined giving. Ledger A was as close to keeping a diary as Rockefeller ever got; the figures recorded there were his autobiography. [7]

John D. Rockefeller, Jr., born into the same cultural tradition, was taught by his father to replicate these practices as follows:

> He worked hard to keep the money at bay. His father helped him, insisting that the fortune had been put in their custody by the Lord and was a special trust not to be wasted. He showed Junior how to keep accounts in a ledger book that mimicked his own Ledger A. It was one thing to keep such accounts if you were an eighteen year old bookkeeper setting out to make your way in the world, however, and quite another if you were the crown prince to the throne of Standard Oil. Junior must have suspected that his entries were a parody of his father's: "Practicing the violin at $.05 per hour; drinking hot water at $.05 per glass; killing flies at $.02 per fly." But the form was more important than the content; he kept his accounts as the sort of chastening experience he would later require of his own children, as if by meticulous, scientific accounting of the money he could exorcise the taint that contaminated its spirit and control the boundless desire that it called forth. [8]

John D. Rockefeller, Jr. (Junior), tried to pass on this heritage and its relevant skills to his children Abby, John D. 3rd, Nelson, Laurance, Winthrop, and David. By that time, however, the family's political and economic situation changed so dramatically that the old traditions no longer fit quite as well.

> Many motifs of their father's upbringing were repeated to their own, but the austerity of the boyhood at the Old Forest Hill estate in Cleveland, where he shared one bicycle with his sisters, and wore their hand-me-downs, was not one of them. Although not surfeited with possessions, Junior's children had what they

wanted. Yet, like their father, they earned their spending money—by killing flies for pennies, shining shoes, hoeing the garden. Like Junior, they kept accounts, having been shown grandfather's Ledger A and allowed to study its yellowing, brittle pages and faded ink entries as if it were church incunabulum. "I was always so afraid that money would spoil my children," Junior later said, "and I wanted them to know its values and not waste it or throw it away on things that weren't worthwhile." Any child with an unaccounted for item in his ledger at the end of the week was fined five cents; those keeping accurate accounts received a five cent bonus. Junior was interested that John 3rd was most often rewarded and Winthrop almost always in the red. He had to think that this means of coming to terms with their past financial expectations was a success, and was delighted by one story (admittedly apocryphal) told about his boys: one of their friends, having seen the boys' comparatively small sailboat, asked, as they passed an elaborate yacht tied up nearby, "How come you guys don't have one like that?" only to be answered scornfully, "Who do you think we are, Vanderbilts?" [9]

Despite the intrusion of the wider culture, and despite the progressive weakening of some historic traditions, some of the "brothers" (as the five young men were referred to) attempted to maintain these early training habits in their own children. Consider:

The message had not changed much since Junior's youth, and neither had the prescribed technique for sedating the desires the money incited. It was the account book. Laurance and John had let this tradition slide altogether. Nelson had gone through the motions with his children. But David took it seriously. It was something his father had done and his father's father before him. He had done it himself. His children, therefore, would keep their generation's version of Ledger A.

With David, Jr., he was fairly successful; but his daughters rebelled against the idea and became masters of fabrication and deceit. Abby and Peggy both took advantage of the long train rides home from boarding school at vacation time to fictionalize several months' accounting of their weekly allowance. They filled the lined pages with expenditures of brassieres and Tampax, hoping to embarrass their father to the extent that he would fail to carry out the audit. [10]

These quotations chronicle one family's progressive attempt to maintain its own version of the proper cultural orientation by means of early socialization into economic roles. Since each family is an intimate system with a shared history, internal conflict during the early socialization process may be quite minimal, at least compared with other more heterogeneous socialization agencies. But considerable tension does arise over time as a result of adult control of this familial process, and from resultant child-adult disparities. As contact with others grows, and as plural alternatives are available to the child, conflicts develop at home. In particular, as the child is introduced to new social environments, such as the school and the broader community, the influence of other adults along with changing reference and peer groups are likely to reduce the range of parental control over behavior. A variety of "secondary group" relations and pressures must be coped with alongside the "primary group" relations learned and practiced in the family.

In more heavily industrialized societies the areas of technical knowledge required to support economic and political growth have increased enormously; necessary information can thus no longer be shared and passed on by individual families. The relative homogeneity and tranquility of the socialization process is disturbed further by the presses of other value systems, communicated by dramatic increases in the number and influences of contacts with people who are different. On both counts, we have begun to experience an accelerating, widespread relaxation—even rejection, among our most highly industrialized and heterogeneous cultures—of some of these age-old familial perogatives. Some evidence indicates that the responsibility of child socialization is being relinquished by an increasing number of families, and that the legal system is prepared to intervene to protect the "rights" of children.

From Family to School as Socializing Medium

The transition from less complex, homogeneous preindustrial societies to highly diverse, complicated social orders of industrial-technological societies suggests also that we shift our focus of attention to the formal educational institutions and to those social, political, and economic forces which influence their development and control their destiny. As noted by Floud and Halsey:

> In primitive societies, the educational problem is that of individual socialization in the interest of consensus and integration: and an anthropologist interested in education in these societies is concerned with relations between generations wherever they occur, but especially with the family, and with substructures such as age-sets and religious fraternities carrying socializing functions. The focus of attention for the sociologist working in industrial and technological societies, however, must be on formal and specialized educational institutions. His concern is with the social forces which create and mould pedagogical aims and educational policies and the institutions in which they are embodied; and also with these institutions themselves, and with their functions as, in some measure, independent parts of a wider and changing social structure. [11]

In societies ruled by gesellschaft norms and mechanisms, the family has increasingly been supplanted in its primary socialization functions by secondary institutions, chiefly schools and often church or the media. Roles that were once performed exclusively by the family have now become absorbed by the school. Adult intimates who were formerly in charge of the socialization process have been replaced by professionals, adults who are expert in the enculturation of large numbers of young people without the "biases" of intimate connections. Activities that once were carried out in relatively small groups now occur in larger and more complex social settings. Hence, schooling as a transition from family to society reflects the larger transition—from a simple to a more complex society.

The transition of "schooling" from family to society was accompanied by a series of important changes that directly affected the content of socialization activities formerly ascribed to the family. For example, the rapid industrialization of American society and the increased urbanization of the population provoked a number of changes in the social fabric, characterized by heightened mobility rates and fundamental changes in social interaction patterns. In particular, the shift from work at home or nearby fields to work in large organizations outside the home had a profound impact on the family's social activities and on its socialization of the next generation of workers. The locus of control over many of these activities shifted to the school, and the increased professionalization of teaching helped to undermine the authority base of the family as the socializer of the young.

The content of necessary socialization activities was technically rationalized into a curriculum—a formal ideology and a set of carefully prescribed practices. What parents could do by instinct, and with love, professionals must do with clear regulations and justifications. Such regulations bureaucratize trust and intimacy, and ideally protect child and teacher with rules for their proper interaction. Practical courses, such as cooking, sewing, and industrial arts, were introduced and justified on the basis that these skills were no longer learned in the family circle. Courses particularly characterized by attempts at moral and ideological instruction (family living, sex education, and social studies) were rationalized on the premise that the traditional family loci of these values had been rendered incapable of transmitting them effectively by the external forces of change. Social activities (termed extracurricular), rationalized as character-building pursuits, also were devised. The latent function of these activities is to segregate the adult world from that of the child, controlling the young and minimizing the inevitable generational conflict. The secondary relationships that prevail in the relatively impersonal school experience provide an opportunity for young persons to live and work in nonintimate yet challenging and effective social situations. Obviously, in a large and complex society, learning how to develop effective secondary relationships with peers and authorities is every bit as important as learning how to develop effective primary relationships with families and friends.

CULTURAL COMMONALITY AND DIFFERENTIATION

Any society's socialization processes are oriented toward the particular culture and social structure in which adults will work and play. Thus, it may be useful to identify some of the key elements in our cultural system, both in general and as they may be interpreted uniquely by different groups.

Any cultural system serves two simultaneous purposes: (1) to *sketch out a version of the ideal* (values), a statement of what people ought to do or be like, and what the society should do, and (2) to *explain the present situation* (beliefs) and thus to explain how people or institutions currently operate—and how that is acceptable and desirable or objectionable.

Exercise 1−1. **Examining Home-School Conflicts**

This exercise can be done by students sharing experiences in small groups.

Consider the following issues pertaining to the relationship between how things were done in your family and how they were done in your elementary school.

1. Was it permissible to "curse" or swear in your family? Was it permissible in school? If there were conflicts in this area, how were you taught what to do/not to do in school? What role did your family play in indicating appropriate behavior?

2. What were the differences in how you related to your female elementary school teachers, compared to your mother?

3. Was it permissible for you to cry with unhappiness, yell with anger, or jump with joy in your elementary classrooms? Was that behavior permissible/appropriate at home? How did you learn what was appropriate in which place?

4. How are the answers to questions 1, 2, and 3 relevant to principles of primary versus secondary relations in organizations?

These questions could be the basis for individual research papers, especially if people have trouble remembering their experience. Research could involve interviews with parents, siblings, friends and teachers.

Many different approaches can be taken to identify and/or describe our cultural values and beliefs, and different observers or students each have their preferred catalog or list. In the following pages we present one such list; it was developed in a landmark study prepared for the United States National

Commission for UNESCO. Gabriel attempted to identify the traditional values in American life which seem to have been acceptable to the great majority of Americans. In effect, these represent the core values of our civilization—those ideals and beliefs about which there exists an apparent consensus and without which unity, cohesiveness, and integration are not attainable. In order to understand the American culture, it might be useful to summarize Gabriel's findings in those areas that are most appropriate for our analysis [12].

Social Values and Beliefs. Historically, American social values and beliefs spring from the religious and humanistic strands of Western civilization. But the conditions of life in the New World from the very beginning of the English settlement on Indian land have shaped the American outlook and given a particular stamp to American values. Out of this historic struggle have emerged the social values of the American people:

1. The dignity and importance of the individual person. The individual person is a unique center of power and value. The state is an instrument to further the welfare of the persons who compose it.

2. Freedom of thought and action of the individual person. If a person is to have dignity and if life is to have significance, he or she must have a large measure of freedom. Nature sets some limitations to that freedom; the prime social limitation lies in the fact that the individual person must manage his or her behavior so as not to impair the freedom of his or her fellows.

3. Equal opportunity. Freedom suggests each individual should have the opportunity to make of his or her life what he or she can in accordance with his or her abilities. As a corollary, one expects a status in society that derives from personal achievements.

4. Regard for the group as a means to develop individual personality and enlarge the possibilities for collaborative action. As a result, people form voluntary associations in extraordinary number and for a wide range of purposes.

5. Regard for the family as the basic social institution. Within the family, emphasis is placed on the separate individualities of husband, wife, and children.

6. Regard for work leading to recognizable accomplishment. There is a tendency to look down upon idleness unless it is the result of infirmity or age. The accumulation of property is seen as a normal aspect of the good life.

An examination of these core values and beliefs helps us understand the origins of the American ethos and the emergence of such dominant cultural orientations as capitalism, protestantism, and rationalism. It is also possible to imagine how these orientations, and the core values and beliefs above, support or justify and explain ideologies of race and class discrimination and prejudice.

While there is widespread agreement on many of these values and beliefs, the pluralistic nature of American society suggests complete consensus is highly unlikely. We can anticipate wide disparities in beliefs and values, especially between groups whose experiences and social situations differ markedly. Thus, these core values and beliefs may be contested by other groups who hold different views, or different groups may interpret the means and meanings of the broad cultural values in different ways. For example, native Americans, Hispanic subcultures, and a sizeable percentage of blacks do not find such core values as liberty, freedom, and justice operable for them in this society. Many minority individuals have personally experienced and suffered through the disparities that exist between the rhetoric generally associated with these values and the actual behavior that is manifested. As a result, they and others may see racism rather than equal opportunity as a core element in the dominant culture. Moreover, they often have conflicting values, which, at the same time, tend to enrich the pluralistic nature of the total culture. Thus, cultural pluralism and conflict are as natural and endemic as are a set of culturally dominant values/ standards.

It is always difficult to see our own core ideologies clearly, since we are so embedded in them and the culture they reflect. Thus, we often are surprised by conflicts or differences that we did not expect to encounter, and often fail to legitimize alternatives because they seem to depart from deeply held positions. One good test is to examine what we take for granted, what looks or feels unassailable. That often is the signal that we are in touch with a core value or a basic ideological principle.

The conflict between cultural and subcultural groups, as well as those between traditional and emerging values, in the American society has serious implications for the management and governance of public schools, particularly at the secondary level. Often, this conflict pits one age-status group against another—administration versus students; older teachers versus younger teachers; the board of education versus the parents—and tends to polarize the entire educational community. One observer identified value conflicts in school and in society as being traceable to conflicts between individualism and conformity, freedom and control, equality and inequality, materialism and idealism, and agrarian and urban culture; another observer identified conformity and creativity, competition and cooperation, the practical and the ideal, democracy and authority, puritanism and hedonism, and chauvinism and internationalism as the major sources of conflict [13]. Still another has portrayed the genesis of American value conflicts as follows: [14]

Conflict of Values

"Traditional" Values	"Emergent" Values
1. *Puritan Morality* (Thrift, self-denial, sexual constraint.)	1. *Relativistic Moral Attitude* (No absolutes; morality is group defined.)
2. *Work, Success, Ethic* (Hard work, top of heap.)	2. *Sociability* (Like people, get along.)
3. *Individualism* (Sacred; sanctions both independence and originality—also expediency and disregard of rights.)	3. *Consideration for others* (Tolerance for others, regard for feelings—harmony of the group.)
4. *Achievement Orientation* (Goal oriented; success defined as progress.)	4. *Conformity to Groups* (Everything is relative to the group—ultimate goal is harmony of group—"peer group belonging.")
5. *"Future-Time" Orientation* (Time is valuable—present needs must be denied for future satisfaction.)	5. *Hedonistic, "Present-Time" Orientation* (Enjoy the present—can't foretell future.)

Although certainly not always the case, students, younger teachers, and parents are generally viewed as conversant with emergent values, whereas administrators, older teachers, and board members are seen as custodians of the more traditional values. The situation is further complicated when economic, class or racial dynamics enter the scene, and the decline of, or adherence to, a particular value orientation is linked or attributed to the influence of a racial or economic group.

In general, emerging values are particularly threatening to established centers of power, since they represent deviations from prior standards and a possible loss of established control. Merton refers to this state of affairs as *societal anomie*, a condition of widespread normlessness or normative confusion [15]. In these circumstances, individuals within the society begin to lose their own bearings, to experience confusion and dislocation in their own values and changes that are disruptive of their own traditional sense of right and wrong. Increases in various forms of deviance, including illegitimate behavior, socio-pathology, and even suicide or mental illness are to be expected. This analysis assumes that prior to anomic times there was a well-ordered cultural belief system, one that all or most of the society believed in and was committed to. An alternative perspective might stress that normative agreement or consensus was primarily an artifact of the power and commitment of elite groups who generated a dominant but not necessarily encompassing cultural ideology. Some people, especially members of subcultural groups, resist or are otherwise not loyal to these dominant values. However, consensus still appears to reign because: (1) people who do not have access to the dominant group still adhere to many of that group's values, thereby placing themselves under control of an alien cultural system; (2) since those who differ are principally poor or members of minorities, disloyalty appears as due to a lack of education or confusion rather than legitimate difference or resistance. But when moderately powerful groups challenge the ability of elite groups to maintain a cultural consensus and their own cultural dominance, large-scale normative conflict does occur. Then normlessness or confusion and anomie is obvious to all.

MANAGING CULTURAL DIFFERENCES

The relationship between the general culture and the values and beliefs of subcultural groups is important for any society, especially for a democratic and pluralistic society. Several structural forms may be utilized to establish regularity in minority-majority relations. These forms stem from different assumptions about the meaning and value of cultural differences. Chief among these, and all within the range of the American experience, include: Anglo-Saxon conformity, segregation, the melting pot, various forms of genocide, and cultural pluralism. We treat these in some detail here because they are generic forms for organizing cultural regularity and control in other intergroup arenas as well—those governing sexual, social class, ethnic, and other regionally based differences.

Anglo-Saxon Conformity

In the early eighteenth century, white Anglo-Saxon Protestants established the dominant cultural pattern in this country. They conquered American Indians and Spanish-speaking peoples of the Southwest. Over time, they also conquered several neighboring provinces and outlying islands. As immigration increased in the nineteenth century, Anglo-Americans became alarmed for fear that their manner of life would be disrupted by the impact of foreign cultural groups. They tried to use the schools to create conformity to their own pattern of life as the American way. "It became popular for Anglos to believe that non-Anglos transplanted inferior modes of living, perpetuated low-class folkways, and yielded easily to the corruptive influences of political machines"[16].

Many groups of Caucasians, especially southern and eastern Europeans and Catholics and Jews were treated as inferior beings. Among those "white ethnics" who were discriminated against in school and society were Poles, Slavs, Italians, and Irish.

It was not surprising therefore that when the Irish famines of 1847 sent thousands of Irishmen to American cities, the first duty of the schools was to protect society from the "moral cesspool" they created in the cities by simply containing the newcomers, keeping them under observation, and subjecting them to the habits and values of their betters. [17]

Exercise 1—2. *Monoculturalism and Pluralism in Home-School Interactions*

The answers to these questions can be shared in small group discussions. It would be especially valuable to separate students by economic class and/or race. The exercise could be preceded by students' conversations with their own parents and their retrieval of parental reports of their own experiences.

1. Did your parents ever visit your teachers at school? Under what conditions and on whose invitation did these visits occur?

2. Did your parents know any/many of your teachers as social peers/friends?

3. Were your parents comfortable or uncomfortable talking with school staff? Did they talk the same language, same jargon, and so on?

4. Did a teacher or counselor ever visit your home? If so, why?

5. Were major holidays celebrated at your home that were *not* celebrated in school? Or were some events celebrated very differently in your home and in school? Which ones? Why?

From the earliest days of extensive Irish immigration, urban teachers consistently classified the children of Irish immigrants as dull, unambitious, and of low intelligence. This anti-Irish sentiment persisted well into the 1920s, as reported by Kane in Greer:

> There may be some kind of lower middle or lower class orientation among them to education and occupation which tends to anchor Catholics in the lower socioeconomic groups and which limits those who do achieve higher education to certain fields which appear to offer more security, albeit less prestige and income. It may also be that leadership, even outside the purely religious field, is still considered a clerical prerogative, and the same seems that Catholics creep forward rather than stride forward in American society and the position of American Catholics in the midtwentieth century is better, but not so much better than it was a century ago. Neither is it as high as one might expect from such a sizeable minority with a large educational system and reputed equality of opportunity in a democracy. [18]

Similar beliefs were later held about the American black population who replaced the Irish and non-Protestant Europeans as the prime target for negative stereotypes.

Segregation

One outcome of this conformity-creating process was that nonconformers had little room for mobility, especially if they could not, or would not, pass as the majority. When these minorities failed to conform to majority cultural styles, the majority rejected and isolated them in specific areas such as ghettos and barrios. The majority had the power to segregate the minority, and as the minority lived within forced economic and geographic segregation, increasingly more limited contact between different groups ensued. Unlike experiences with voluntary segregation, the American variety maintained unequal advantage between majority and minority groups. Thus, segregation was never a voluntary adaptation on the part of various minorities but was rather a condition enforced by the superior power of the majority groups.

Some immigrant groups were able, over time, to overcome the barriers of segregation, and to achieve geographic mobility and dispersion. However, black, Hispanic, and American Indian groups still have not broken the fetters of segregation enforced by law, custom, and economic necessity. Since "neighborhood" schools draw their student population from local attendance areas, enforced housing segregation generally has resulted in racially segregated schools and school experiences as well.

Melting Pot

The third historical form of managing cultural differences deals with a fundamental process that has been active in the intermingling of many peoples who comprise the United States. The "melting pot" refers essentially to the process of social assimilation that goes beyond negotiated conformity. Different cultures were assumed to enter the same pot, and in a large "stewing process," differences were expected to melt into sameness. The history of intergroup rhetoric indicates that the melting pot ideology has been potent throughout a large portion of American history. However, its reality is decisively less dominant upon close examination of current social practices and policies. Some ethnic groups have cherished their distinctiveness, whereas others have emphasized broad cultural homogeneity. Overall, dominant Anglo groups have managed to control the content of the melting pot, while edges of Italian pizza, Polish sausages, and Chinese chop suey seem well mixed.

The constant struggle of eastern and southern Europeans to stem the tide of social assimilation and to retain a measure of their ethnic identity is poignantly portrayed by Novak in the following excerpt:

> At no little sacrifice, one had apologized for foods that smelled too strong for Anglo Saxon noses; moderated the wide swings of Slavic and Italian emotion; learned decorum; given oneself to education, American style; tried to learn tolerance and assimilation. Each generation criticized the earlier for its authoritarian and European and old-fashioned ways. "Up-to-date" was a moral level.

Whereas the Anglo-Saxon model appears to be a system of atomic individuals and high mobility, our model has tended to stress communities of our own, attachment to family and relatives, stability, and roots. Ethnics tend to have a fierce sense of attachment to their homes, having been homeowners for less than three generations: a home is almost fulfillment enough for one man's life. Some groups save arduously in a passion to *own*; others rent. We have most ambivalent feelings about suburban assimilation and mobility. The melting pot is a kind of homogenized soup, and its mores only partly appeal to ethnics: to some, yes, and to others, no. [19]

Exercise 1—3. *Family and Ethnic Socialization Regarding Pain and Illness*

This exercise can be a focus for discussion in small heterogeneous groups. Novak reports that people of different economic classes and ethnic groups have some very different ways of handling physical pain and illness.

Examples

How did people in your family handle pain and illness when you were growing up?

1. Did you ever break an arm or leg? How much attention or nurturance did you get? How were you treated when you had a bad headache? A toothache?

2. What illnesses were considered serious enough to let you stay home from school? On what occasions would your parent write a note to your school, excusing you from gym or other activities?

3. How did your mother deal with female children's physical discomfort during menstruation?

Again by Novak:

If you are a descendant of southern and eastern Europeans, everyone else *has* defined your existence. A pattern of "Americanization" is laid out. You are catechized, cajoled, and condescended to by guardians of good Anglo-Protestant attitudes. You are chided by Jewish libertarians. Has ever a culture been so moralistic?

The entire experience of becoming American is summarized in the experience of being made to feel guilty.

The *old* rule by which ethnics were to measure themselves was the WASP ethic. The *new* rule is getting "with it." The latter is based on new technologies and future shock. The latter could not have existed without the family life and social organization of the former. In the middle—once again—are southern and eastern Europeans. We are becoming almost Jewish in our anticipation of disaster. When anything goes wrong, or dirty work needs doing, we're *it*. [20]

Whereas such tenaciousness to maintain the cultural heritage and reject the melting pot has often been ascribed to Poles, Sicilians, and Hungarians, many others have succumbed to the forces of assimilation and (except for some "telling" last names) are not readily distinguishable from the more dominant cultural groups.

Exercise 1—4. *The Melting Pot and Conflict Between White Ethnic Groups*

What does Novak mean by the following phrases appearing in the excerpt?

1. "You are catechized, cajoled and condescended to by guardians of good Anglo-Protestant attitudes"?

2. "You are chided by Jewish libertarians"?

3. "We are becoming almost Jewish in our anticipation of disaster"?

The following two excerpts from the experience of poor Jewish immigrants reflect some of their dilemmas in coping with cultural control and dominance. These passages are taken from letters addressed to a public advice column of a New York Jewish-language (Yiddish) newspaper. Concerns about Anglo dominance and oppression as well as of assimilation and loss of identity clearly are evident in these letters. The first letter was written in 1909, the second in 1938. As the years go by, the issues become more subtle for this group, but the fundamental tensions clearly remain.

Dear Editor,

We, the unfortunates who are imprisoned on Ellis Island, beg you to have pity on us and print our letter in your worthy newspaper, so that our brothers in America may know how we suffer here.

The people here are from various countries, most of them are Russian Jews, many of whom can never return to Russia. These Jews are deserters from the Russian Army and political escapees, whom the Czar would like to have returned to Russia. Many of the families sold everything they owned to scrape together enough for passage to America. They haven't a cent but they figured that, with the help of their children, sisters, brothers and friends, they would find means of livelihood in America.

You know full well how much the Jewish immigrant suffers till he gets to America. First he has a hard enough time at the borders, then with the agents. After this he goes through a lot till they send him, like baggage, on the train to a port. There he lies around in the immigrant sheds till the ship finally leaves. Then follows the torment on the ship, where every sailor considers a steerage passenger a dog. And when, with God's help, he has endured all this, and he is at last in America, he is given for "dessert" an order that he must show that he possesses twenty-five dollars. [21]

Dear Editor,

I come to you with my family problem because I think you are the only one who can give me practical advice. I am a man in my fifties and I came to America when I was very young. I don't have to tell you how hard life was for a "greenhorn" in those times. I suffered plenty. But that didn't keep me from falling in love with a girl from my home town and marrying her.

I harnessed myself to the wagon of family life and pulled with all my strength. My wife was faithful and she gave me a hand in pulling the wagon. The years flew fast and before we looked around we were parents of four children who brightened and sweetened our lives.

The children were dear and smart and we gave them an education that was more than we could afford. They went to college, became professionals, and are well established.

Suddenly, I feel as if the floor has collapsed under my feet. I don't know how to express it, but the fact that my children are well educated and have outgrown me makes me feel bad. I can't talk to them about my problems and they can't talk to me about theirs. It's as if there were a deep abyss that divides us.

People envy me my good, fine, educated children but (I am ashamed to admit it) I often think it might be better for me if they were not so well educated, but ordinary workingmen, like me. Then we would have more in common. I have no education, because my parents were poor, and in the old country they couldn't give me the opportunities that I could give my children. Here, in America, I didn't have time and my mind wasn't on learning in the early years when I had to work hard. [22]

Genocide

Genocide, as a form, has many meanings within the history of intercultural relations and has taken on these same meanings within our own society. Some forms of genocide are directly physical in nature, and refer to the elimination of a race or culture in material terms—violent warfare or murder. This was the early settlers' posture toward native inhabitants of the new American territories—Indians. When direct warfare was seen as too brutal a form of genocidal treatment, our social policies reflected a more subtle program of gradual elimination by depriving people of access to food, shelter, and clothing, and then encouraging "nature" to take its course. The fact that Indian nations still exist in this country is a monumental tribute to their perspicacity and survival ability, rather than to any well-managed set of positive intercultural priorities. Incarceration of races or cultural groupings may represent another form of genocidal treatment. We have experienced these forms in our national attempt to place Indians on certain reservations, and the incarceration during World War II of Japanese-Americans, Asians who were American citizens. Attempts to eradicate the cultures of certain groups can be seen in our calculated ignorance of minority cultures and in their exclusion from the compendia of cultural heritages and works. Only recently have we seen the growth of prideful public presentation of varied minority cultures—and with them novelty shops that reexploit the native and minority cultures of America.

Cultural Pluralism

Advocates of pluralism believe that the era of the arbitrary domination of minorities must pass. In its place, they endorse a live-and-let-live policy—a policy that decrees that each ethnic and racial group should respect the other's rights and encourage the maximum freedom of all groups within the democratic value system. Payne portrayed the concept of cultural pluralism as follows:

No culture contains all favorable elements but each group that makes up the total American population has unique values; and the nation will be richer and finer in its cultural makeup if it conserves the best that each group has brought. . . . . Their natures, characters, and personalities are built out of cultures different from our own, and the method of effective cultural transmission requires that the fundamentals of their heritages be preserved for generations. [23]

Exercise 1—5. *Social Class and Ethnicity in Family Life*

This exercise can be done best if students are organized into small groups that are fairly homogeneous by economic class or location of students' families of origin. Experiences and ideas can be shared in small groups and can lead to total class sharing and/or individual student papers.

Consider the nature of your family when you were an early adolescent (eleven to fifteen years old);

1. What was the race and ethnic identification (religion, national ancestry) of your family? If your background is mixed, what was the mix and which part was dominant?

2. Who was considered part of your immediate family? How many parents, siblings, other relatives, and/or others lived in your home?

3. Who was the primary wage earner or breadwinner in your family? What job did he or she hold, or how was that money garnered? What images did the family have about the adequacy of the income, the appropriateness or value of that occupational role, and the talent/ability of the wage earner?

4. Who made family decisions about different family issues? Food and meals? Child rearing?

5. How did adults feel about their own and your education? How was your performance monitored, supported, or ignored?

6. How was conflict between adults in your family handled? How was conflict between adults and children handled? What forms of punishment or control were used with children?

7. Can you see ways in which your current views of (1) marital/family roles, (2) educational goals, and (3) future occupational choices and roles have been influenced by these earlier family patterns?

In the realm of abstract ideals, cultural pluralism sounds easy to accomplish. But cultural values and beliefs often are related to the material conditions of life, and patterns of segregation and stratification indicate the constraints that may be placed upon people who think and act "differently." Moreover, in our society some ideals and ideas are valued more than others, and this highlights the low level of pluralism throughout our society. In practice, the advocacy of cultural pluralism has often been used as a mask for subtle attempts by culturally dominant groups to enforce Anglo-conformity or the melting pot, without admitting it directly.

SCHOOLING AND SOCIETY: ALTERNATIVE MODELS

Although education is a universal feature of societies, educational systems vary widely in their organizational structures and pedagogical practices as well as in their philosophical and cultural orientations. This may be readily observed when one examines educational systems in a variety of cross-cultural settings, and even among the myriad of public, private, parochial, and alternative educational networks that are found in American society. "What is to be learned" as well as "How is learning to occur" is to a great extent a function of the culture in question. Thus, the substance or content of learning varies from one culture to another and fundamental differences in the organization of schooling are tuned to the nature of the social order.

Insofar as the institution of education is concerned, what has gone on before is important in attempting to predict what is likely to occur in the near future. Institutions, by their very nature, are highly resistant to change, particularly when the impending change is perceived to threaten the very moorings of the institutions. However, as has occurred in China, Cuba, and Tanzania (and more recently in Iran), shifting political and economic sands and cultural revitalization movements can bring about drastic changes in the social fabric. And frequently, institutions such as schools have either experienced radical overhauling or have been abandoned in favor of newly created ones. Out of that social and political ferment have emerged alternative systems of education. The variations in form and content of these systems are often unrecognizable to the Western mentality. In most instances, this may be attributable to the emphases that are placed on areas of knowledge and experience which are ordinarily ruled out of the curriculum of the American school.

How then do we account for these different modes of schooling? What are some of the determining factors or forces that distinguish one educational system from another? Some scholars would focus on historical forces as determinants; others would concentrate on the political-economic structure; and still others would stress the prevailing ideology of the society. From our vantage point, an understanding of the society's dominant value orientation, as seen through any focus, provides one clear lens for viewing the school enterprise.

For example, we would expect to find quite dissimilar modes of schooling in societies that differ markedly in their dominant cultures or value orientations— orientations that are reflected in their political and economic structures. Although all societies tend to be in a somewhat continual state of transition of one kind or another, it may prove instructive insofar as the development of educational systems is concerned to view these societies at certain critical junctures in their historic evolution. If we classify societies with respect to their dominant societal value orientations, we should be able to better comprehend the kind of schooling that is required and the functions that schools are likely to perform in the society. We suggest a tripartite classification that views the particular society as exhibiting one of the following value orientations: (1) a *revolutionary*, or visionary, orientation; (2) a *conservative* or ideological, orientation; and (3) a *reactionary* orientation [24]. No society fits wholly and neatly into one of these categories, but it is reasonable to identify the dominant cultural trend or orientation of the society at a given point in time.

Revolutionary societies are those in which a deliberate, organized, and conscious attempt is exerted to construct a more satisfying culture. In such societies, institutions often become the prime targets of change since they are presumed to bear the trademarks of the old order. China and Cuba are examples of politically inspired revolutionary societies, whereas Iran offers the classic example of a society that is religiously or divinely inspired. "The code of the (revitalization) movement defines the previous state of society as inadequate, perverse, even evil, and depicts a more or less utopian image of the better society as the cultural goal toward which the ad hoc and temporary social arrangements of the present transfer culture is carrying the society." [25]

Conservative societies are those that have undergone revolutionary or revitalization movements and have established successful, stable new cultures. In these societies, the task is to ensure efficient control and monitoring of the cultural machinery with periodic programmatic modifications required to still the voices of protest and reaction. Examples of conservative societies are the United States and Great Britain, both of which have earlier experienced revitalization movements. The Soviet Union represents a more recent example of a society that is undergoing transformation from that of a revolutionary status and is now rapidly accruing all the characteristics of a conservative society.

The reactionary society is one that regards as alien those ideas that challenge the elite's dominant values. Reactionary societies tend to expend a disproportionate amount of their energy and resources to ward off budding revitalization movements. Essentially, they may be referred to as postconservative societies. The Union of South Africa and some of the established theocratic states of the Middle East are examples of reactionary social orders.

Within the context of these three contrasting value orientations, any number of alternative systems of schooling are possible. Accordingly, the role expectations and functions of schools are likely to show wide variation. In a revolutionary society, there will be a need to revitalize the culture and to create cadres of dedicated, resourceful elites, in whom the responsibility for transformation of the culture will be vested. Emphases in the schools will be placed on morality, with special reference to the development of character and the learning of such traits as loyalty, commitment, and self-sacrifice. Intellectual training will also be emphasized but will be generally restricted to the ideological boundaries dictated by the revolution. The teaching of technical skills and trades are likely to be devalued, at least in the early stages, until such time as the revolution is secure and the transformation of the culture has gained momentum. China and Cuba are examples of revolutionary societies that have ascribed to their educational systems key roles in the transformation of their respective societies. The "politicization" of schooling, which is anathema to most American educators, is often a prime objective of many socialist nations as well as Third World countries which embrace "leftist" ideologies and are desirous of placing the common school in the forefront of cultural transformation and social change.

It is ironic that, as in the case of revolutionary societies, reactionary societies tend also to stress morality in their educational systems, but for quite different reasons. Generally, revitalization movements present serious threats to the traditional values of any society. But in the case of a reactionary society (such as South Africa), the impending changes are perceived as dismantling of the entire social structure, and hence, are aggressively and often violently opposed. Under such circumstances, the schools become the "guardians" of the traditional values and the bastions of reactionary thought. Reactionary societies are frequently linked to powerful religious ideologies, as in Brazil and the Middle Eastern Islamic states.

Conservative societies present a much different picture. Here, the social order is well established and generally stable and the dominant concern is with the maintenance and improvement of the society and how to cope with social change. In these societies education will concentrate on technical skills, on "how to do" certain things, such as driving, accounting, voting intelligently, and handling people efficiently" [26]. Obviously, neither morality nor intellect assumes as vital a role in a conservative society as each would assume in a visionary or reactionary society.

From the depiction of these three ideal types of societies and their likely educational imperatives, several images of schools immediately surface:

1. Images that portray schools as dynamic, active partners in social change and cultural transformation.

2. Images that depict schools as instruments of ideologically dominant political and economic groups, who are generally in harmony with the present state of the social order, but who recognize the need for modification and minor changes so as to reduce stress and tension on the system and satisfy dissident groups.

3. Images that paint schools as repositories of traditional values—as creatures of an eroding but dominant group clinging tenaciously to the past and threatened constantly by even mild stirrings of revitalization.

The images of humanity and learning that emerge from the values and orientations of revolutionary, conservative, and reactionary societies are reflected in the basic assumptions underlying their various educational systems—since these assumptions are presumed to be compatible with those embedded in the cultural orientations and structure of the social order. Otherwise, schools and society would be at loggerheads, a situation in which the schools could hardly expect to survive.

For example, differing assumptions are made as to the nature of human nature—whether it is assumed to be fixed by birth or malleable and, therefore, alterable by external manipulation. Varying assumptions are made as to the nature of man—whether man by nature is good or bad, or whether the culture defines that which is regarded as good or bad. Assumptions also vary as to the nature of the social order—whether the social order is considered to be perfectable, requiring only minor correction or whether it requires major surgery, even revolution, to effectively meet the needs of its inhabitants. Further assumptions relate to the concept of the child—whether all children are pretty much the same, or whether no two children are alike, the individual differences between them stemming from the outcome of collective, group, or community participation in learning activities. And finally, varying assumptions are centered about the relationship of one's schooling with respect to societal problems and community life—whether schooling is viewed as unrelated to community life or whether it is assumed to play an integral part in social action and community life.

These assumptions are inherent in the political and social ideology of a society. When they arise, the various forms they assume are crucial to the learning environment of its schools and the images of humanity that ultimately are projected.

In Tanzania°, a revolutionary visionary society, a major thrust of the educational system is directed toward molding a citizenry that is dedicated to "socialism" and "self-reliance." The president of Tanzania, Julius Nyerere, acknowledged that "we in Tanzania have to work our way out of poverty, and that we are all members of one society, depending on one another" [27]. In Tanzania, interdependence and collective activities are stressed in the schools; individualism, which is considered the legacy of colonialism, is devalued. A close proximity of vocational aspirations and social realities is encouraged. Classroom work and extracurricular activities are linked through teaching and learning methods that emphasize experimentation and experience. Children at all levels of schooling are afforded the opportunity to experience the society's critical problems and to gain the rewards of undertaking cooperative endeavors on behalf of the community.

In Tanzania, the image of the school that is projected is one in which learning activities are thoroughly integrated into village life; this orientation is vividly portrayed in the following excerpt:

1. The school farms must be created by the school community . . . They must be used with no more capital assistance than is available tb an ordinary, established cooperative farm. . . . By such means, the students can learn the advantages of cooperative endeavors . . . They will learn the meaning of living together and working together for the good of all . . . the nonschool community.

2. (School members should learn) that their living standards depend on the farm. . . . If they farm well they can eat well and have better facilities. . . . If they work badly, then they themselves will suffer. . . . Pupils should be encouraged to make many of the decisons necessary . . . only then can the participants

---

° Tanzania is the prime example in Africa of an independent nation that managed to cast off the shackles of British colonialism and create a truly African approach to education. Dominated by colonial powers since 975 A.D., the country has been known successively as German East Africa (from 1880—1920), Tanganyika Territory (from 1920—1947), and Tanganyika (from 1947—1961). After gaining independence in 1962, it was known as the Republic of Tanganyika; and with the union of Tanganyika and Zanzibar in 1964, its official name became the United Republic of Tanzania. Under the leadership of its dynamic president, Dr. Julius Nyerere, Tanzania has emerged as the model for many Third World nations with its emphasis on self-reliance and its creation of a truly indigenous educational system.

practice—and learn to value—direct democracy. (Although some guidance and discipline are necessary) this sort of planning can be part of the teaching of socialism.

3. Many . . . activities now undertaken for pupils . . . should be undertaken by the pupils themselves. . . . Even at university, medical school or other post-second-ary levels, there is no reason why students should continue to have their washing up and cleaning done for them. Nor is there any reason why students at such institutions should not be required as part of their degree or professional training, to spend at least part of their vacations contributing to the society in a manner related to their studies. In short, much can be done to counteract narrow elitism and intellectual arrogance.[27]

The Soviet society reflects a different political ideology that has spawned an educational system in which the images of humanity portrayed and the function of schooling stand in contrast to Western models. Some of these differences are played out on a much larger stage—that of the constant jockeying for power and influence between the United States and the Soviet Union in the global context.

Testing, on a large scale, is discouraged in the Soviet Union because the Soviets generally reject the concept of individual differences in the native abilities and aptitudes of children. Competition, in the highly individualistic sense, is frowned upon in the Soviet educational system because of the firm belief that the human personality achieves its full potential only in the collective environment. Hence, the term *collective* is used often in reference to classroom learning, youth groups, farms, and the like. The well-publicized experiment of attempting to produce the so-called "new Soviet man" was an expression of the Soviet belief in the malleability of human nature. The expected outcomes of schooling in the Soviet Union are clearly stated in official public documents. Parents are even provided manuals as guides to be followed in the proper raising of their children.

Soviet schools are the prime agents not only of socialization but also of the "Sovietization" of society. To accomplish this end, vast systems of reinforce-ment have been created in the Soviet Union to ensure compatibility between school and society.° The school is viewed as a political instrument of the government and is therefore a vital factor in the maintenance of social control.[29] The Soviet model has been emulated in several of the eastern European nations and in many of the rising Third World countries.

Depending upon historical antecedents and their political-economic struc-tures, the educational systems of other countries may reflect quite different images of humanity and learning. China's massive educational system has

---

° Prominent among these reinforcement systems are networks of youth organizations that function as parallel systems of schooling. Notable among these are the Pioneer Palaces which accomodate youngsters of between nine and fourteen years.

boldly attacked the "rationing of privilege," which, prior to the Chinese revolution, had been characteristic of its schools and universities for centuries. Cuba has decided to obliterate illiteracy, and has launched one of the most successful literacy campaigns in recent history. Iran, on the other hand, is attempting to eradicate what its leaders view as the negative virtues of modernization and to create a truly Islamic state based on the precepts of the Muslim religion. In most Islamic states, the "moral man" is the predominant image.

As the noted Brazilian educator, Paulo Freire, observed: "Every educational practice implies a concept of man and the world"[30]. The concepts or images of man and his work are rooted in the culture itself. Schools play a key role in transmitting these cultural values and beliefs, and revolutionary, conservative, and reactionary societies create different kinds of schools to accomplish these purposes. The content of dominant cultural themes and the procedures for their transmission must be closely related to one another. Thus, the educational practice and the cultural concepts of man and his world are reflections of one another.

This discussion of alternative models of schooling should demonstrate that the cultural and educational options are broad, both throughout the world's cultures and within our own society.

Educational and Cultural Values in Our Society

As we have indicated, not only the content but also the characteristic modes of socialization and education are themselves culturally prescribed. The process of role learning and role taking is not just general and whole; we also learn specialized roles, one or several out of an entire range of possible roles. The actual roles we learn are consistent with our assumptions about the culture in which we live and our experiences with the social structure we encounter. What is learned is usually what is required for the individual to assume the status of adulthood in a given culture, and youngsters of different backgrounds are prepared for different adult statuses largely on the basis of race, economic class, and sex. The instructional or transmission processes stress Anglo conformity and assimilation. Clearly, schools are selective and are committed to an ideological and operational base that is both tolerant of the prevailing culture and reinforcing of the political-economic structure. Friedenberg likens the school's performance in the value domain to that of a Darwinian function.

> The school endorses and supports the values and patterns of behavior of certain segments of the population, providing their members with the credentials and shibboleths needed for the next stages of their journey, while instilling in others a sense of inferiority and warning the rest of society against them as troublesome and untrustworthy. [31]

In this manner, the school contributes to the broader social process of differentiating people into various roles, statuses and strata. Partly a function of family experiences, and partly a function of school experiences, young people complete the socialization process by learning their appropriate place in a nexus of political and economic roles and statuses.

In an earlier section of this chapter (page 16) Gabriel's conception of core aspects of the American culture were identified. In the evolution of our society and school system, these values and beliefs have taken particular shape in our educational system, forming the cultural base and rationale for our educational apparatus. According to Gabriel, our core educational values and beliefs include the following:

1. That effective self-government requires that a significant proportion of the electorate have sufficient education to be able to inform themselves of issues and to consider them rationally.

2. That equality of educational opportunity for all citizens is the just and desirable foundation for a democratic society.

3. That the state has an obligation not only to provide educational opportunities from kindergarten through the university but also to require children to attend school.

4. That advanced education, by training specialists to work in a society that emphasizes specialization, increases the opportunities of the individual person to find for himself or herself a useful place in the community and to achieve an income that is commensurate with his or her abilities.

5. That schools exist to train students as social beings as well as for the intellectual and cultural enrichment of the individual.

6. That education should be a lifelong process and that opportunities for postschool training should be available to adults. [32]

These educational values help determine the shape of our educational institutions and the ways they operate to educate the young.

Different formal institutions may emphasize varied and often opposing cultural values, but public schools presumably extract the core norms of the entire society for transmission to the young. In practice, however, the values represented in the school reflect a rather narrow band of the cultural spectrum. Moreover, the school, as the culture itself, is fraught with disparities between cherished ideals and operative values or behaviors. Inconsistencies often exist between values of equality and race/class injustice, of individualism and of conformity, of human enrichment and bureaucratic efficiency. For the most part, these inconsistencies or conflicts are resolved by schools in ways that reflect the nature of external control over the school. The ideological perspective of the school is limited to that which is acceptable to the more influential segments in society—one that in effect supports the values of the dominant economic and political structures. As noted before, part of the purpose of culture and of institutions that pass on the culture is to legitimize dominant values. The adherence of the schools to cultural values of *capitalism*, the *Protestant ethic, rationalism*, and *racism* represents the power of the dominant social structures over the institution of public education.

The competitive norms and values of the American society developed from an ideology of capitalism and achievement-oriented Protestantism. These values are reflected in our schools in a clear emphasis upon academic achievement and performance. Peer collaboration in academic tasks obviously is curtailed in favor of an individualistic approach to knowledge. Learning is seen as a form of work, and its rewards are hoarded. Good social relations are not seen as matters of personal enjoyment, but a criteria of good adjustment, and an effective standard for future role success. Social relations can even be competitively graded.

The ideology of efficiently rationalized bureaucracy, already evident in the corporate economic form, is further standardized in the professional organization of the school. Mass instruction, by means of the arrangements of one teacher supervising twenty-five to thirty students, is done in the name of efficiency. An ideology of professionalism promotes trust in the power of expertise and a commitment to technical information and skill. Such loyalty to expertise not only promotes good order in school but it also is effective socialization for respect and obedience to authoritative expertise in adult life.

The dominance of certain cultural prescriptions is strengthened by the development of educational systems whose classroom patterns reflect the segregated and stratified character of society. This is particularly critical in schools whose geographic location reflects large demographic shifts and transitory populations. Demographic movements in the society at large triggered off a mass migration of rural southern blacks to urban areas in the North. This was followed by a steady exodus of more affluent whites and some blacks to the surburbs, and served to strengthen the white and middle-class culture of their schools. The exodus to the suburbs not only reinforced the physical segregation patterns of society but sustained cultural segregation in the sense of homogeneity, exclusiveness, and isolation from the values and beliefs of others.

The current reflection of cultural racism is also clear in the content and organization of our schools. The curriculum reflects a white view of American history and social studies, and the major symbols and school artifacts similarly deny the existence of pluralism. Educators partake of an embracing ideology that explains the school failures of black, Chicano, and native-American students in terms of their inadequacies—usually created elsewhere. The various forms of this ideology have been clearly visible in special programs that have attempted to socialize America's minorities into conformity with values they often do not share, the acceptance of which would seriously impair their cultural integrity.

Many of the concepts used to describe the programs and their clientele—"culturally deprived," "disadvantaged"—served as rhetoric to clothe an ideology that deprecated poor people and minorities. We were led to believe that "The poor aren't motivated to learn; the blacks are incapable." "Slum families are disorganized, ridden by social pathology." "Inner-city neighborhoods reflect the worst in American urban life." Thus, ideologies of racism and class differentiation have been combined with the value bases of individualism so that individuals, rather than cultural and social structures, are seen as responsible for their own status. These ideological frameworks, aided and abetted by the professional mythology of expertise and service, have thus been used to avoid blaming the schools' failure on the schools. Rather, failure is seen as a fault of the individual or culture being served. Ryan has referred to this interpretive framework as a new liberal scientific ideology called "blaming the victim" [33].

Surprisingly, in the face of historic affluent and white cultural dominance in the public school, America's poor and racial minorities still cling to their faith in the institution of education as the avenue for equality and social justice. Perhaps this is because the poor and minorities have no other recourse in a society that so highly values these technical credentials.

In order for one to fathom the American education scene, one must be conversant with the historical background of American education and its cultural content. But it does not suffice for one to be merely knowledgeable with respect to the historical and cultural backgrounds of American education; one must also be aware of the forces that govern education in this country and the mechanisms that control it. The subtleties involved in transmitting a culture and orienting one to a social structure may be partially explained by the reluctance of those in control to admit that schools are not impartial, that they are not prone to examine and express all cultural values, and that, in fact, they do socialize different students in different ways. There does exist a central core of values and a set of norms taught by the schools. Moreover, cultural values and beliefs support and promote certain behaviors rather than others, and persons internalizing dominant beliefs are more likely to find and take advantage of political and economic opportunities.

2

THE POLITICAL-ECONOMIC
CONTEXT OF SCHOOLING

Schools exist within the political and economic environment that characterizes any large society. These political and economic structures interact with
cultural systems, and together have a great deal of influence on schooling. In
this chapter we review some of the major outlines of the American political-
economic system, and the ways in which these aspects of our society may affect
the schools.

First we discuss some of the cultural values and ideologies that underlie and
support our political and economic system. These values and norms help
interpret institutional workings, and legitimize our economic and political
system as just and good. Then we examine how our political and economic
system works, and how it solves basic operational problems and organizes land,
resources, labor, and capital in meaningful and productive ways. Finally, we
discuss ways in which this economic and political apparatus interacts with
schools and schooling. As a powerful set of institutional forces, this apparatus
often controls many aspects of education at the federal, state, and local levels.
As a primary utilizer of the "products" of education, political and economic
institutions are the recipients of students who have been socialized and/or
educated in ways relevant for entry into these worlds of work and play.

THE CULTURAL BASE OF OUR
POLITICAL-ECONOMIC SYSTEM

In Chapter 1 we indicated some of the major cultural value and beliefs of the
American society. From some of these same works by Gabriel we can indicate
key cultural values that relate to and underlie our economic system [1].

1. Work on the part of the individual person has been valued since the theology of the seventeenth-century Puritans sanctified it. A job, no matter how humble it may be, gives honorable status to an individual.

2. The economic well-being of the individual person is valued as the cornerstone of a sound economy and is the essential foundation for a full and rounded individual life. It is frequently defined in very simple material terms.

3. The sanctity of contract and respect for property are valued as the foundation for orderly and dependable economic relations.

4. Production of goods is valued as a prerequisite to economic well-being. The drive toward more efficient and increasing production is very important.

5. Private enterprise is valued because it gives opportunity for the creative potentialities of the entrepreneur or of corporate management. It gives entrepreneurs the largest measure of freedom in working out their work destinies, because the opportunities of sharing in the profits provides the best stimulus for individual effort.

6. The profit system is valued because only where profits are made can private enterprise long continue. The profit system is modified or limited by the entry of government into the economy through laws and regulations.

Thus, economic values in the United States center around personal and natural rights to life and property, hard work and its just rewards, and the pursuit of dignity, wealth, and happiness. In the views of some groups these "natural rights" are God-given, but they are given to all people as a basic condition of existence as humans. This ideology is a departure from earlier views that provided these rights to a select few who had received the grace of God or had derived them from divinely inspired kings and monarchs.

The notion of private and personal rights is essential to our current political and economic forms. For instance, these rights are the cornerstone of beliefs in individual liberty and freedom. They also are the basis of beliefs in rights of personal property and of the liberty to pursue and accumulate material wealth. Our own cultural values and beliefs sometimes seem so natural that we fail to be aware that private and personal rights are not universally valued. In some cultures, personal rights do not exist, and only the tribe or collectivity has rights. The concept of private property does not exist in all societies. In some cultures everything belongs to everybody, or to God, or to nature, and the idea that someone could "own" God's handiwork or pieces of nature is totally alien. For instance, when the first European explorers "bought" Manhattan Island from the "Indians," they thought they were getting a grand bargain for $24 and trinkets. The native people who "sold" Manhattan to the settlers also must have chuckled at the bargain, for they did not feel they owned this property in the first place. The natural environment was seen by native peoples (as indeed it is to this day by many native-American groups) as something that man tried to integrate with and live with and work with; not as something to be tamed, controlled, owned, and hoarded or exploited. Another important example of conflict in values, within our own cultural history, is the concept of human beings as property. Early European and North American slavers bought and sold black and brown people as property, and the slave system supported private ownership of these human resources—people. Some people and cultures could not conceive or allow of people owning people, and denied the relevance of private property rights in this regard. Or, they denied the humanity of the slaves themselves, thereby permitting private ownership of these "non-human" sources of labor.

Some early Protestants saw earthly material wealth as a measure of one's ability to glorify God and an indication of dedication to hard work and thrift. The avoidance of waste and sloth in economic enterprise was likened to rigor and vigor in one's personal discipline, both to the greater glory of God. For others, the commitment to hard personal labor and the accumulation of wealth represented evidence that God smiled on them and had announced them as the elect of the Lord. Max Weber made an extended study of the way in which Puritan morality and ethics supported these values, and aided the development of rational capitalist economies in Europe [2]. Thus, our society has a religious background of cultural values and beliefs that sustains notions of private property, achievement motivation and hard work, and the private accumulation of wealth.

The commitment to individual rights and liberties also is a key component of our political system. The belief that certain natural rights to freedom and liberty were rooted in the inherent nature of mankind meant that individuals had rights to elect their own destinies, and to govern their common lives. Thus, the basis of political revolutions in Europe during the eighteenth and nineteenth centuries, and our own revolution as well, was an opposition to the concept of the divine rights of kings and an attempt to create some measure of popular control over national life. In the United States, with less of a monarchical heritage, the democratic adventure became possible, if not absolutely necessary. A representative system of government emerged, to be ruled by coalitions of diverse political persuasion and not by any person or group's divine right.

Since these cultural attributes of the political and economic system in the United States clearly affect the character of our educational system, it is worthwhile to try to identify some of the more contemporary and concrete manifestations of these core values and beliefs. One predominant framework is an ideology of *capitalism*, a belief system that supports and justifies certain political and economic structures and operations. Our forms of political-economic organization stress private property holdings and try to use capital, or money, as a key means to taking profitable advantage of processes of production. The stress on maximal profit motivations has led to larger organizational forms in all sectors of our economy, and the attempt to take advantage of various economies of scale. The maximization of profit requires greater efficiency in the use of resources, and thus an attempt to reduce waste and unprofitable activities. The commitment to capitalist economic organization also creates an acceptance of divisions among the populace, since some people are private owners of productive enterprises and others are privately hired employees working within these systems.

The resultant stratification of people into owners and employees, and into groups of employees with different shares of resources and rewards is seen as the outgrowth of hard work and achievement. Therefore, economic inequality is valued as consistent with basic norms and ideologies. Beliefs in the private sphere of family life, and of the private disposition of wealth, also support maintaining one's accumulated status for one's children, thus preserving and maintaining economic divisions across generations. The potential rigidity and injustice of this tradition is muted by our cultural commitment to the Horatio Alger myth, that "anyone can make it," if one works hard, and especially if one is lucky. Thus, not only does individual achievement counter the divinely structured status systems of feudal history but also suggests people can change the status into which they were born.

Successful capitalist activity requires each person and company to achieve a greater concentration of resources in order to take and hold an advantageous position with regard to competitors. This results in the accumulation of larger amounts of economic resources in the hands of a relatively small number of firms and owners. Moreover, the owners accrue a parallel amount of political power, partly because the money and status derived from successful enterprise puts one in a position to influence policy, either in a formally elected or an informally influential role. This concentration of political power is not only seen as permissible, but often preferable, because of the belief that economic power and success reflect competence in general. Moreover, it often is thought that our entire society depends upon successful private enterprise for its health and that the welfare of the poor is served by the welfare of the rich and powerful. This view once led a former chief executive of a corporation, serving as a cabinet officer in the political system, to say: "What's good for General Motors is good for the country." Although others may agree or not, this view reflects acceptance of the concentration of private economic and political power as good for us all.

Rationalism as an intellectual attribute and rationality as an economic attribute stress the role of reliable techniques and intellectual discipline as organizing principles of our political and economic system. We assume that people will behave thoughtfully and reasonably, with some clarity about what is expected of them and what they should do. As a result, scientific knowledge has become an important guide for action and for planning future economic and political decisions. When combined with the stress on efficiency, these values about knowledge and reason promote reliance on proper prior planning, advanced industrial technologies, and continual technical innovation in politics as well as in economics. In addition, the technical expert, the professional, has become a most highly valued societal and organizational role.

The original Protestant stress on *independent and self-reliant* individual action has given way to an emphasis on interdependence and cooperation with others. Restraint of one's natural or unique needs or impulses, and a commitment to follow reasonable compromises and guides helps support the development of groups of people who can work together—as a team. As guidelines for cooperative or interdependent action are formalized into organizational rules and regulations, and as larger and larger groups of people work together, we have formed vast bureaucracies. Enormous economic enterprises and immense governmental agencies reflect the ideal of bureaucracy in operation. Although some have begun to articulate the many inefficiencies and inadequacies of such large-scale organizations in the public political sphere, many Americans continue to extoll the virtues of large economic bureaucracies.

Equality of opportunity is another cherished value in the American system. The assumption of a natural equality of creation does not guarantee what people will do with their talent, but our political and economic values stress the position that equality of opportunity and outcome exists if people elect to work hard. This cultural ideology places responsibility for unequal outcomes (or success or failure) squarely in individual hands, further stressing the previously identified themes of individualism and hard work.

Alongside our commitment to equality, the American society is also characterized by political and economic values that reflect and justify *racial injustice* and oppression. From our beginning as a society, blacks, Chicanos, native-Americans, and other non-Anglo minority groups were systematically denied access to major social opportunities and rewards. An elaborate self-justifying ideology of racism explains why it is acceptable for these patterns to ensue. Whether couched in biogenetic determinism or sociocultural deficit, the white American culture has many explanations for why minorities are unable or unworthy of full membership in the society. Our existing political structures and the distribution of political and economic power further determine the kinds of racial contacts and opportunities for advancement that exist at any moment in history. This combination of a belief in equality and beliefs that at least covertly support the racial superiority of whites has been called by Gunnar Myrdal *The American Dilemma* [3]. The dilemma obscures our ability to act clearly one way or the other on matters of race and racial equality, and often obscures racial issues in American politics and economics.

The belief in the North American *frontier* represents an additional element in our national value system. Until fairly recently, one could always "go west," and discover a new land and a new life. The taming of nature has been central to our growth as a nation and reflects our way of exploiting natural resources.

The notion of a new start elsewhere is an antidote to feelings of oppression in a current job or community. No situation is hopeless if a new start is possible, and no excuse for failure is appropriate if one can improve one's position over the next hill.

Some observers believe that these (and other) values help shape our political and economic institutions. Others argue that it is the other way around, that our economic and political systems help create acceptable value systems. Whichever is the dominant force, it is clear that these values and structures are related. We now turn to a brief outline of the nature of our political-economic system.

OUTLINES OF THE AMERICAN POLITICAL-ECONOMIC SYSTEM

The American form of capitalism is not pure. The role of the government and the political system in our economic enterprise suggests that we have a welfare-oriented or state-supported form of capitalism. Moreover, this state capitalism is not cast in the laissez-faire image of early economic thinkers. According to laissez-faire economic theorists, individual economic actions could operate independently of one another, and the state (or political system) should let them alone. An invisible hand of the marketplace would help regulate and integrate the actions of these separate economic entities and would prevent sheer chaos or economic anarchy from occurring. Now, and certainly in our system, economic action is highly organized into vast corporate forms that concentrate power and wealth, political and economic resources. Separate firms and the state all are concerned with the problem of regulation and interdependence, and with deliberately planning ways of avoiding anarchy and/or chaos. Our particular form of capitalism creates some pervasive or continuing dilemmas, and our way of coping with or resolving ongoing economic and political problems shapes the major structures of national life.

Core Dilemmas or Problems

Every social system has some underlying problems or dilemmas that are difficult to resolve. These problems are usually the focus of debate and controversy. One core dilemma in the North American political-economic system involves questions about the appropriate priority and mix of the *public and private spheres* of activity. How much of the allegedly private enterprise system should be subsidized, regularized, controlled, or made to work to the benefit of the general public? Stated in reverse, how much of government operations ought to be responsible to, or controlled or affected by, concentrations of private economic wealth?

A second major dilemma concerns the wisdom of *large concentrations of economic and political power*. As the size and stability of public and private organizations grow, many people are concerned about potential losses of efficiency that may accompany great size. Moreover, great concentrations of private wealth may defy notions of open economic opportunity; great concentrations of public power may defy notions of political democracy. People who want to have political influence must have a lot of wealth to get a lot of power—is that opportunity or limitation? At what point does concentration cease meaning freedom to acquire wealth and power and begin to mean restraint of the freedoms of others? At what point does the large size of operations involved in concentrated economic or political enterprise cease to create efficiency and start to be inefficient?

A third major dilemma concerns the balance between *free competition and regulation*. Most observers agree that stability and rationality are essential for the smooth operation of any organization, and are certainly important for a large society. But movement and change are also essential if organizations are to be adventurous or innovative, and if the society is to flourish. What is the proper trade-off between spontaneity in finding new resources and productive activities and planned stability in the operations of a total input-output market system, or between spontaneous movements for change and the stable operations of a two-party political system? One of the issues in this vein is how much public regulation and planning ought to occur. However, a more important issue is highlighted by the ways in which private industry may regulate itself. Combinations or associations in restraint of trade, conferences sharing new ideas among top competitors, and well-organized political parties who control enormous resources all work to decrease extreme and/or innovative forms of political and economic competition and to substitute collaboration and perhaps restraint of opportunity.

The fourth dilemma concerns the location of operative *control in the economy and polity*. Owner-run economic firms have given way to manager-operated entities, and considerable argument and debate ensues as to whether owners or managers are the major controllers and/or major beneficiaries of our economic operations. Little serious argument so far has focused on whether lower level employees should exercize control or be among the prime beneficiaries of economic enterprise. Considerable argument and debate also occur regarding the primacy of the executive, legislative, and judicial branches of government, or whether any of these public political arenas can withstand the power of private economic wealth. These are important questions because they speak to the location of actual ruling power in our economic and political system, and to the legitimacy of those managers or representatives who appear to be running major economic or political organizations [4].

A final dilemma in capitalist systems arises in considering *who benefits* most from this way of organizing the political life of the nation. Some observers argue that when capitalism operates well it works for the benefit of all the people. Capitalism creates jobs, investment opportunities, taxes to support public services, opportunities for advancement and adventure, and a reward for freedom and creativity. Others argue that capitalism provides many benefits to a select few highly placed managers and owners, but does not work for the benefit of most people. For the majority of people, according to this position, capitalism creates large pools of unemployed or underemployed people; taxes the public system with the need to support privately used roads, utilities, and educational systems; and creates highly stratified and unjust opportunities for advancement, and a highly competitive ethos and life-style.

Organizing the Means of Production

A brief introduction to some basic principles of political-economics as they relate to the means of production is critical for the subsequent treatment of schools and their local as well as national environments. The reader interested in more technical and precise discussions of these matters should consult more detailed popular sources.

The means of production are those mechanisms or procedures by which raw materials are converted into useful purchases. For instance, in the chain of production one important component is the *raw materials* required as basic resources to be transformed by the workings of economic organization. Raw materials can include energy, in the form of coal and gas and oil, as well as iron and steel or aluminum. For other industries, timber, grain, and water are the key natural resources. For almost all industrial purposes, land is an essential resource: it is the location of other resources as well as a place to build a plant or factory.

A second important element of the means of production is the *machines and labor* required to transform these raw materials into useful, or at least sensible, products. Machines can vary in their technological complexity, from simple hoes to more complex tractors to much more complex and vast rolling mills for steel, as well as integrated assembly lines for automobiles. Human labor varies as well, ranging from direct manual work, such as hand farming and mining, to secretarial and service work, to human and machine interactions on assembly lines. In addition, human labor is used to direct machines, as in computerized production, and in the management and direction of other humans, as in secretarial supervision, executive roles, and the like. Machines and human labor usually are organized into patterns that regularize work and the interrelations among numbers of individuals. In terms of an individual's relation to capitalist principles of organization, labor can be surplus (unemployed), hired (workers at an hourly or yearly wage/salary), hired and provided with considerable power (managers), or owning and operating in control of the system (owners).

The third potent component of the means of production is *capital*, the funds required to make these resources work together. The increasing potency of this element in the developing industrial revolution is what marks the use of the term *capitalism* to describe the entire econ˅mic system. For instance, manufacturing operations must gather raw materials, utilize machines and human labor to transform these materials into products, and develop a marketing apparatus long before they actually receive funds from sales. Without up-front funds, none of the other means of production can be mobilized. In the beginnings of capitalist production, during the early stages of the industrial revolution, enterprising individuals brought together several craftsmen and large amounts of raw materials in a common place. It took some extra money to attempt such centralization, and people with that money, or with the vision and risk to establish such ventures, thought that they deserved the extra profits generated thereby. But to work effectively on the large scale that is now required for profitable enterprise requires a great deal of money. Therefore, a manufacturing firm must borrow money in order to set these other means into operation long before it can generate sales than mean capital input. Moreover, as time goes on, so much capital becomes tied up in plant and materials that a firm wishing to expand also must generate capital first. Thus, our system includes various institutions that are capital-intensive and that make their capital resources available to other firms as a means for their production. Capital-intensive industries include banks, first and foremost, but also insurance companies and major investment firms. All three of these industries gather large amounts of monies from the public at large and pay the public for the privilege of using these funds to generate a profit for themselves and to sustain industrial growth and expansion for the rest of the economy.

The fourth major component of the means of production is a *marketing system*, and an apparatus that facilitates the actual transmission and sale of finished products to consumers. Sometimes these systems are relatively simple, as in having an open house at the furniture warehouse, next door to the manufacturing plant. In other cases they are very complex, as in developing a fleet of tanker trucks to transport oil to outlying service stations so that consumers can buy gasoline from the local marketer of a major national company involved in energy development.

THE ROLE OF THE POLITICAL SYSTEM IN DEVELOPING/MONITORING THE MEANS OF PRODUCTION

Different observers of American history have offered alternative interpretations of the role of the government or political system vis-à-vis economic enterprise. Indirectly, their commentary helps elucidate alternative notions of the relation between our political system and our economic system. In general, most observers agree that a basic requirement for the economic functioning of our society is a stable and orderly environment. That orderliness is important in the society at large, and in how the society goes about its business. Obviously, a stable economy requires a stable political system as well.

For some, government has played the role that was originally indicated by Hobbes, that of a fair-minded regulator of special interests. Hobbes conceived the natural social order as one in which various groups competed vigorously against one another in a war of all against all. Groups seeking economic or political advantage over others would use any means, force or fraud, to achieve this advantage. His notion of government, then, was that it should step in to mediate these disputes and maintain civil order.° For instance, it has been argued that government has stepped in occasionally to limit and regulate the excesses of rapacious forms of capitalism, especially when one major economic enterprise appears able to exert unilateral power (a monopoly) over other firms or over other important sectors of the society. We can point to the activity of Theodore Roosevelt's administration in "trust busting," in acting to limit the size and power of interlocked companies that began to operate as virtual monopolies at the turn of the century. Moreover, we could look to the efforts pioneered during Franklin Roosevelt's administration to establish programs to care for those who were thrown out of work and left out of the system by private enterprise. Various welfare programs were created to ensure that unemployed people could still survive and perhaps get the help and training to make them more employable. During the Great Depression, many people needed this governmental assistance.

It also has been argued that the major role of government has been to protect industrial advantage, and to use governmental powers and wealth to give private industry greater advantage in its operations. Adherents of this view identify the governmental policies that frustrate labor unions from organizing and prevent secondary boycotts which would increase national labor's clout vis-à-vis national industrial powers. Regressive taxation measures, and only minimally progressive income tax programs, are other examples of what might be called a tax on the poor and the public in order to gather resources that could otherwise be gathered from the richer. Other observers point to the government's role in permitting logging from public lands, in permitting tax depreciation on oil and energy sources and technology, in building highways, and in subsidizing railroads as examples of political activity designed to pay part of the cost of developing the means of production of private industry. The government is a source of capital to much of North American industry with its massive defense appropriations; substantial purchases of weapons, buildings, and building materials for offices; and the services of various kinds that it provides. Some critics have also pointed out that public tax funds have been used to help

---

° Since the only thing that could keep warring groups in order was superior power or force, Hobbes foresaw government ultimately becoming a Leviathan, a totalitarian superpower that ruled all social life.

create a welfare system that functions to pick up the slack in the economy. They argue that private industries created the slack in the first place and should be taxed to pay a larger portion of the costs for this by-product of our economic system.

One of the basic necessities of capitalism is a large pool of educated labor, men and women who are vocationally trained to run machines, who are skilled at managing and supervising other human laborers, or who are technically skilled in directing large corporate firms. But private firms do not have to pay for the full cost of generating the needed labor for these human tasks . . . a public educational system, including elementary and secondary schools, as well as many public colleges and universities, develops this trained talent for them. Although governmental support for schools aids the poor by providing low-cost education, and thus increases their economic opportunities, it also may be viewed as another subsidy to private industrial enterprise. If government funds were not available, private industry would have to pay for the education of these forms of human labor and capital. One likely outcome, and the main argument for public funds in this regard, is that industry would siphon talent from among the more affluent classes, the sons and daughters of already well-trained operatives, and thus increase the already existing inequality of wealth and opportunity.

Regarding the need for capitalistic enterprise to maintain large pools of vocationally trained men and women, it has been argued that the increase in the number of years spent in schooling is directly attributable to the growing complexity of industrial jobs, which, in turn, created a need for high school graduates who had more technical skills and training. A number of critical theorists, however, insist that this is not accurate—that it is a myth. They argue that people were led to believe that the increased complexity of many jobs required more education, although it had been demonstrated that job complexity had not really increased that much, or that if it did, more training for students did not necessarily provide students greater access to these jobs. Rather, the ideology of capitalism made it seem that way, and therefore justified expanding schooling. According to this view, the screening activities of the schools ensured that white-collar students got access to those more complex and higher paying jobs and working-class students stayed where they were. Expanded schooling gave the school more opportunity to train people for relatively obedient conformity to new industrial situations and to the authority that was located therein.

We can see on these dimensions some of the interaction between our political system (our government) and our economic system. The various forms of political intervention and support detailed here have led some to call our economic system a unique variant of capitalism, a welfare-oriented or state-supported capitalism, one with all the private advantages of private capital industry, plus significant public financial and other support to cut private losses and risks.

HOW IS OUR POLITICAL-ECONOMIC SYSTEM INTEGRATED?

Our political and economic institutions form a vast and complex enterprise. They are articulated and interdependent with one another in ways that permit the entire system to work effectively. How does this occur?

Various mechanisms function to establish regularity and order throughout our society. Distinct from a completely laissez-faire capitalism, with all the potential chaos and untrammeled competition of independent industry operating with no "guiding hand," our major capitalist institutions interact with one another in fairly regular manner. The interactions of these institutions with one another, and with the natural and human environment, is continually regularized and stabilized, in order to decrease the possibility of chaos and to increase predictability and control. Obviously, the more a person, a firm, or a system can predict and control its internal and external environment, the more it can enjoy, profit from, and satisfy its needs and goals. This dominant trend toward regularity or rationality in social life is aided by several specific patterns or forms of political-economic activity that tie our system together.

One major trend promoting industrial interdependence and rationality is evident in the increased degree of *economic concentration*. One of the priorities of major industry, indeed of any process of transforming natural resources into finished products, is to increase the efficiency of doing it. This requires greater control over all the means of production, greater regularity in access to raw materials and supplies, technology and labor availability, capital resources, and markets. Regular access and control go hand in hand; in a competitive system in which many firms are competing for low-cost resources (or labor), how can one be sure of maintaining continuing access to these vital means of production? Ultimately, continuing access can be guaranteed only by control over these resources. In order to gain such regularity and control, industry has steadily centralized authority and increased operations of scale. That is, the general size of major firms has increased, further concentrating authority for multiplant and multicompany operations in the hands of a small governing group. As industrial firms grow larger, they are increasingly able to command access to larger amounts of raw materials, partly by purchasing them wholesale or by purchasing the firms that own these resources. Moreover, the large industrial firms can employ highly efficient, yet costly, forms of technology, since they are able to allocate the cost of technologic improvements over a large number of finished products. The same is true of labor and capital supplies.

Over the past several decades the United States has seen a gradual movement away from small or single-owner forms of enterprise, to more complex corporate bureaucracies, and finally to national and multinational conglomerates. For instance, in 1950, the 100 largest domestic corporations held 40 per cent of the nation's total manufacturing assets: by 1970 the largest 100 corporations held 50 per cent of assets. In 1945, the United States had six million producing farms, averaging 167 acres each: by 1971 the number of farms had dropped to three million, with an average acreage of 389. Thus, large agribusiness units have been developing out of a prior history of small farms. In general, the larger the asset size of an industrial corporation the greater is their rate of profit, a finding that stresses the role of economies of scale and the power of economic concentration.

Within given industries, the same pattern of concentration often is clear. One example from a fairly highly concentrated industry will illustrate this phenomenon. In 1911 the federal government ordered the dissolution of the American Tobacco Trust, a holding company operating many other companies in the area of tobacco production and sales. The American Tobacco Trust was split into several large firms, including household names in the current tobacco industry: British-American Tobacco, American Snuff Company, United Cigar Stores, P. J. Lorillard, and R. J. Reynolds. R. J. Reynolds alone now accounts for one-third of all cigarette sales, producing Winston, Salem, Camel, Vantage, Doral, and More brands. In addition, its Prince Albert is the country's leading smoking tobacco, and Days Work is the leading chewing tobacco. If R. J. Reynolds itself dominates the tobacco industry in this way, imagine the degree of dominance the American Tobacco Trust might have had if it had continued to exist.

The second major industrial pattern promoting interdependence throughout our society is *economic diversification*. The growth of corporate mergers and conglomerates means that many different organizations, perhaps producing very different goods, can be brought under one corporate roof. The advantages of integrating companies from widely varying industries are several: (1) if business is seasonally or temporarily bad in one industrial area, loss can be compensated by higher activity levels in another (such as buying a fuel oil company to compensate for business losses in the sales of an air-conditioner company in the winter); (2) if a company wishes to enter a new arena, it can gain a good foothold by selling products well under the competitive price, and taking a temporary loss, if it has other profitable activities to pick up the slack for a while . . . until other competitors are driven out and prices can rise once again; (3) reciprocal arrangements can be made with other companies or with dealers to buy each others' products. Parenthetically, each of these competitive advantages has been investigated as a potential source of illegal restraint of trade, or unfair competitive practice, by the Federal Trade Commission.

Between 1950 and 1960, 20 per cent of the largest 100 domestic firms merged. Obviously these largest 100 companies were not unhealthy or sick firms; generally, they were among the most effective and profitable North American enterprises. The merger process usually replaces large healthy firms with even larger healthier ones.

Conglomerates differ from other immense corporations in that they bring together firms from several different industries, often with no particular logic regarding the use of similar resources or technology, labor pools, and the like.

Examples of such corporate conglomerates include I.T.T., Ling-Temco-Vought, and Textron. Textron, for instance, was founded and composed of ten companies, all within the textile industry, in the early 1940s. At that point Textron was concentrating, but not diversifying. By 1964, Textron had become a giant conglomerate composed of over 60 companies, in industries as varied as plywood manufacturing, machine tools, underwater exploration, electronic equipment, agribusiness, aircraft and parts, and optical instruments. It no longer held any of the original textile companies.

The third major industrial pattern creating interdependence throughout our society is *access to and control of financial resources*. One of the means of production central to our form of economy, and to large-scale enterprise especially, is capital. Major capital-intensive institutions, such as banks, insurance companies, and investment firms are active in loaning monies to needy firms. In return for such loans, these banks and other capital-intensive firms receive interest payments, and thus money makes money.

Exercise 2−1. *Identifying Corporate Concentration in an Industry*

Beatrice Foods and Hershey are two of our largest parent companies in the field of candy manufacturing. To better understand their role, go into a local candy store and "randomly" select 10 candy bars. Identify the parent company, as well as the manufacturer of the name brand, on the following list.

Brand Name	*Manufacturer*	*Parent Company*
		Beatrice Foods Corp.
		Hershey Food Corp.
		Other

The relationship between capital-intensive firms and companies requiring capital is solidified further when companies offer the lending institutions a measure of control, and also seek their expertise and talent, by inviting the officers of these concerns to sit on corporate boards of directors. For instance, officers of the Morgan Guarantee and Trust Company have sat on the boards of directors of General Motors, Ford, and Chrysler in the automobile industry; Merck Sharp and Dohme, Mead Johnson, and Smith Kline & French within the pharmaceutical industry; Boeing and General Dynamics within the aerospace industry; and Harcourt Brace Jovanovich and John Wiley and Sons within the publishing industry. These directorship linkages reflect Morgan's continuing interest in being tied to firms that utilize its capital as well as that obtained from other banks. However, this also raises questions about the character of competition possible within these industries if such directorship networks do exist. What does it mean for competition in the automobile industry if Morgan officers sit on the boards of all three major automobile manufacturers? If Morgan has loaned money to all three companies and oversees the uses of these loans from their directors' chairs, doesn't Morgan then have an interest in ensuring that all three profit, and that none causes another to lose money, go bankrupt, or default on its loans? Plans of one firm can be shared with others, as can joint efforts to stabilize and control common markets. This situation has also led to investigations about compacts in potential restraint of open competition.

Capital-generating firms also "own" a great deal of the stock of major North American corporations, and not only through the use of their own funds. These firms are the investors and controllers, or agents, of other peoples' monies—their investors', clients', and so on. Such "institutional investors" can loan or invest large amounts of money, and thus generate their own economies of scale, follow up investments with previously noted patterns of supervision, and by their position exert influence on policy, in addition to just receiving profits. Although a company may issue millions of shares of stock, and several hundred thousand people may own shares of the company's stock, a few large institutional investors may own a dominant or controlling portion of these shares.

Federal investigating commissions have raised questions about these concentrated forms of stock ownership, and have suggested that they may lead to certain excesses of control and interdependence, such as

Exaggerated impact on public prices of securities by virtue of the actions of a few large investors.

Excessive pressures for conversion of fixed assets to liquid forms to pay back capital investors who have power and presence in company policy making.

Self-dealings and conflicts of interest as a function of insider information

and increased loans to companies in which firms already have directorship membership.

Concentration of available capital in these firms, to the exclusion of new
risk ventures.

A presumption of control when stock ownership reaches the level of 10 per
cent, and certainly 20 per cent, because an institutional investor can
marshall all of its voting stocks, quickly, whereas 3 million individual
investors are hard to mobilize and organize.

Our diverse economic enterprise is also regulated by the power of *interlocking directorates and corporate interconnections*, even beyond the role of
capital-intensive firms. One of the reasons for having a diverse board of directors is to extend responsibility and accountability beyond those persons holding formal managerial roles to involve "outsiders." However, it is illegal for
officers of two companies in competition with one another to sit on each others'
boards; that would be a possible combination in restraint of trade and create
conflict. Who actually does sit on a corporation's board of directors? First,
owners, especially to the extent that they may be large stockholders. Second,
most boards include representatives of financial institutions who are actively
engaged in loans with the company, as has been observed. Third, officers of
companies located in the same geographical area also sit on major corporate
boards. In part, this promotes regional coordination of various industrial
concerns in a given city or metropolitan region, thus ensuring environmental
control and coordination of common labor and market needs. Fourth, officers
of parent or subsidiary companies also may hold seats, facilitating intraorganizational or intraconglomerate control and coordination, as well as rapid exercise
of expertise. Fifth, directors may be sought who have substantial expertise in
some problems the firm is encountering, such as accounting or transportation.
And sixth, other representatives are friends and associates of owners or
managers. Many observers thus see these boards as facilitating communication
and exchange within the upper classes and among powerful groups or families
in general.

Some examples of the reciprocal and interlocking character of boards of
directors are found in data suggesting that of the largest 800 domestic
companies, 401 had "double locks," that is, two or more common members.
Consider the following examples of "double locks": A few years ago the chief
executive officer of Anaconda Copper sat on the boards of

Chemical Bank of New York
Celanese Corporation
Union Pacific Railroad
Lever Brothers
Metropolitan Life Insurance

And, on the Board of Anaconda Copper sat

> Chief executive officer of Celanese Corporation
> Partner in Brown Brothers Harriman (Investment)
> Executive vice president of the First National City Bank
> Chief of Union Pacific Railroad
> President of Mine Equipment Leasing Corporation
> (a subsidiary of Anaconda)

Even at first glance these examples of double locks illustrate the previously noted principles of representation from capital-intensive firms and from subsidiaries.

Figure 2–1 shows how a variety of these interconnections may work to link directors of various textile companies to one another. The link is never direct between two firms in the same industry, since this probably would be illegal. But officers are linked through common membership on the boards of many other firms, and representatives of other firms sit on several boards at once, making the link indirectly.

The coordinative power of *social networks* is another mechanism for communication among the upper classes and for the coordination of various economic and political enterprises and personnel. Several books document these connections in some detail, but it will suffice here to note that various

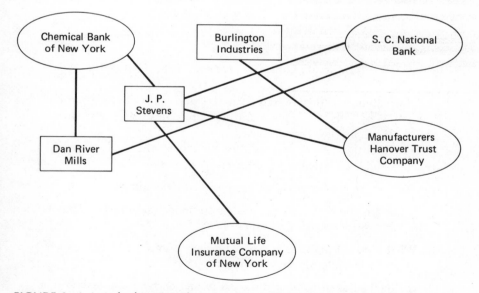

FIGURE 2–1. Interlocking textile companies. These data are taken from a larger chart indicating how several textile companies (those within rectangles) are interlocked through their relationships with financial institutions (those in circles). Each line represents one or more directors on the board of the other company [5].

social clubs and interest group organizations generate arenas in which leaders of North American industry and government can meet, talk, learn from each other, and generally increase the interdependence of their various economic activities. These clubs are important. In 1976, for instance, both presidential candidates Ford and Carter spoke to the Detroit Economic Club when they visited that city. And various cabinet officers regularly provide briefings to meetings of this organization. Other clubs such as Links and Bohemian Grove, have members from the top echelons of American industry.

What takes place at the meetings of these clubs? Certainly nothing sinister. Domhoff indicates that people meet, talk, and learn, just like the rest of us [6]. They also have the opportunity to promote interdependence and discuss industry- or region-wide problems requiring solutions they might well be able to act on together.

Certain other major institutions provide important resources in coordinating American industrial and governmental enterprise. One of these is the *information and educational systems* of the society. Every form of enterprise needs to develop and promulgate an ideology, a rationale, for its existence and for its continued good works. Thus, major social institutions whose purpose it is to create and transmit social information and belief systems, such as schools and universities, are constantly engaged in developing the ideas that push our economic and political systems forward, and that cohere public support for their activities.

Exercise 2—2. *Understanding Governance of the University*

Information for this exercise can be gathered from editions of "*Who's Who,*" the College or university business office, and library materials on corporate operations.

Who are the people who sit as the governing body (trustees, regents. and the like) of your college or university?

1. Are they elected or appointed (appointed by whom)?

2. What are the social characteristics (residence, ethnicity, religion, income, sex, occupation) of these people?

3. What kinds of political and social organizations are they members of, and what roles do they perform?

4. Do they sit as officers or directors of any corporation? Are any of these corporations linked to the university (as contributors, funders of research, investments in university portfolio, or the like)?

Governing bodies of public and private universities often are dominated by members of major corporate systems, and these firms often donate research dollars or just plain contributions to these universities. As universities have become capital-rich organizations, they often invest their monies, as do other investment firms, in the stocks of these companies. University officers also sometimes serve on corporate boards of directors, further solidifying the links of coordination between the private sector and the public sector, between manufacturing goods and materials and generating and transmitting ideas and belief systems.

One example of the investment linkage can be gained from the stock portfolio of the University of Michigan, a large public university with considerable amounts of investment capital, considerable as far as universities go—some $200 million. As of 1977, the University of Michigan had invested major amounts of money in stocks of energy and petroleum companies [7]:

$1.8 million in Exxon
$1.1 million in Mobil
$1.5 million in Standard Oil of Indiana
$1.0 million in Texaco

The university also had significant investments in major firms located in and around Michigan. These are not unusual patterns for a university investment portfolio. But in recent years many student and community groups have raised serious questions about these investment patterns. Of particular concern has been university investment relations with, and support for, companies heavily involved in the Union of South Africa. Public hearings and protests have focused on this particular aspect of the relationship between our economic system and our educational institutions.

Exercise 2—3. *Common Symbols among Corporations and Colleges*

How many colleges or universities can you think of that were named after the founder or leader of a major North American corporation?

On your campus, how many buildings were named after such people?

Why were they so named?

The final form of interdependence is the direct *linkage between political and economic elites*. Many of the members of economic ruling groups have similar social backgrounds and socialization experiences with members of governmental elites and political ruling groups. Typically, leaders of political and economic systems have been more highly educated than the rest of the population. Moreover, some studies have suggested that certain colleges and universities train more of these leaders than others. At the very least, our political and economic leaders often know each others' language and customs, attend similar social functions, and belong to the same social clubs.

There also is a constant flow of personnel from industry to government, and vice versa. For instance, a vice president of Union Oil of California became Secretary of Transportation during the last years of the Nixon-Ford administration. At that time the Secretary was involved in negotiations concerning the approval of the Alaskan pipeline. After the Carter victory in 1976, this official left the government to return to an executive position with Union Oil, one of the companies that had an investment in the Alaskan pipeline. As another example, during the 1970s, two secretaries of Agriculture came from executive ranks of the Ralston-Purina Company, a major agribusiness firm. We do not suggest that these activities constitute a conspiracy or inappropriate behavior. Rather, the frequency and appropriateness of these interchanges reinforce our sense of the integration of private and public spheres, and of our economic and political systems.

The political priorities of the federal government often aid economic stability and growth through various purchasing programs. For instance, between 1947 and 1962, 18 corporations broke into the group of the largest 100 domestic American corporations. Five of these additions were in the defense and aerospace industries (Boeing, Lockheed, North American Aviation, General Dynamics, and Martin-Marietta), industries heavily subsidized by governmental expenditures in research and development and the production of military hardware. Two more were in aluminum (Kaiser and Reynolds), which were greatly facilitated by the federally mandated breakup of ALCOA's monopoly on its patents, and the need for postwar construction of housing.

We have previously noted the presence of federal regulatory commissions that inquire into the effect of these forms of interdependence upon free trade and fair economic activity. Agencies such as the Federal Trade Commission, the Securities and Exchange Commission, the Federal Power Commission, the Interstate Commerce Commission, and the Civil Aeronautics Board regulate industrial activity in their respective arenas. However, a recent study indicates that of all the people who left these agencies for other employment between 1971-1975, 48 per cent went to work for companies operating within the industry they were regulating (or they went to work for a law firm representing one of these industries) [8]. Sooner or later such exchange must raise questions about the possibility of conflict of interest that could impair fair regulation and the protection of the public's interest.

Finally, we now have to contend with opportunities and problems of *worldwide integration of the means of production*. Raw materials and capital, in particular, are increasingly being found more cheaply outside the United

States. The same is true for labor: in underdeveloped or dependent nations nonunionized labor will work more cheaply than union labor in the United States. Moreover, many more market opportunities exist outside the United States for certain goods. For all of these reasons, which involve almost all the means of production, the North American economy increasingly functions on a multinational scale, involving many political systems.

Throughout the world, all economic enterprise shares an interest in a politically stable and affluent society. Without such stability economic enterprise could not depend on regular access to the means of production. And without some measure of affluence, the enterprise could not find buyers and profit from its manufactured goods. The political system can help create such stability by developing a climate of well-being and satisfaction throughout the society, and by keeping a tight rein on potential challenges and disturbances. The political system can help develop affluence by permitting people to accumulate and multiply their wealth, and by subsidizing economic enterprises with massive purchases of their products. In turn, the economic enterprises support the political system in general, and certain figures in particular. Affluence and apparent economic well-being are prime requisites for any domestic or foreign officeholder.

THE CONTROL OF EDUCATION BY THE POLITICAL-ECONOMIC SYSTEM

From the middle of the nineteenth century, when universal compulsory education won general acceptance, the American school system has attempted to serve the needs and interests of various groups in the society. As an agency influenced and controlled by the economic and political system, education has served especially the special interests of groups with power in these systems. The culture and organizational forms of capitalism lead to certain kinds of preferred outcomes and goals for public schooling. For instance, schools traditionally have treated the children of the affluent differently than children of the poor, and have mirrored the stratification of economic life in the internal apparatus of the school. Moreover, the schools have inculcated in all children a generally benevolent view of the capitalist political and economic system, and of the ways that system appears to work to the benefit of all or most people.

This is indirect service or control, and the political-economic system has influenced or controlled the educational system in a variety of other ways. For instance, interconnections between the public school and the local business community are of long standing. Not only do local firms "use" or employ public school graduates but the origins of concern for educational efficiency, "business methods" of management and accounting, and vocational/skill training, are all linked to ideological principles underlying capitalist economic organizations [9].

The business and industrial communities, together with their organizations

and associations,° also constitute major sources of political support for education. Although federal and state governments comprise the official implementation arm, local and national economic groups are also active in molding
public opinion, supporting certain educational agendas, establishing joint
industry-school programs and employing graduates. One of the most overt
forms of political-economic control stems from the close relationship that
schools have with the state. As revisionist historians such as Greer, Katz, and
Carnoy have continually emphasized, the genesis of the mass public education
system in the United States has resulted in a state-directed monopoly of
education and great federal influence over both public and private institutions
[10]. Educational institutions thus derive their political legitimation and
economic sustenance from the power and authority of the state. Private capital
plays a minimal role in elementary and secondary school districts (although it
can be a potent force at the college or university level). Therefore, private
economic interests must work through the public apparatus of the state, since
whoever controls the state controls the educational system that the state
approves, manages, and funds.

The structure of formal political control of education is depicted in Figure 2—
2. Citizens of the nation, and of each state or local community, elect representatives in general, and often elect special representatives to govern school
systems. National and state policymaking agencies, and their advisory and staff
offices, make constant input to local school boards and staffs. Local superintendents manage an administrative staff that progressively delegates power and
professional guidance to administrators and teachers working directly with
students and/or parents.

The legislative and executive arms of the federal government began to be
felt most strongly in local educational matters in 1958, with the passage of the
National Defense Education Act. Spurred by the threat of "Sputnik," and
concern about the Soviets outstripping the United States in technical education
and scientific developments, funds were provided to boost programs in these
areas at universities and colleges, and in academically oriented secondary
schools. In 1965, Congress passed the Elementary and Secondary Education
Act, and attempted to directly influence local school districts' efforts to improve
the quality of education for children of poor families and racial minorities. A
separate Office of Education was established within the Department of Health,
Education and Welfare, and in 1979 Congress and the President decided to
establish a separate cabinet post for a Department of Education. Throughout
these efforts, as the federal government has become more involved in providing
funds and suggesting policy directions for local school systems, vigorous debates
have ensued regarding the proper balance of initiative and control between
federal and local educational and policymaking agencies.

°Examples of these at the *national* and *state* level include Chambers of Commerce, National
Manufacturing Association, and oil and utilities' lobbies. At the *local level* these include Junior
Chambers of Commerce, Kiwanis Clubs, and Rotary Clubs.

FIGURE 2-2. The educational pyramid [10].

Similar issues were raised when the Supreme Court in 1954 ordered the alteration of schools so as to create desegregated patterns of education. Subsequent to the 1954 order, both the Supreme Court itself and the rest of the federal judiciary only sporadically and cautiously moved ahead on the desegregation agenda through the 1960s and 1970s. The judiciary, the national legislature and the federal executive machinery could have mobilized many aspects of the national political system to this end: they do and can affect local schooling quite directly. Although many positive efforts were made, not all those resources were mobilized effectively; or, if they were, the tradition and power of local and state agencies have managed to frustrate their efforts. Several times during those two decades the federal executive's (Department of Justice, Department of Health, Education and Welfare) threat to withhold funds from southern segregated school systems was used as a substantial stick: corollary extra funds to support new programs necessitated by interracial education was also an enticing carrot. The national legislature has been much less supportive, and several times during the 1970s the House of Representatives and the Senate seriously considered riders to bills or constitutional amendments opposing busing of youth for desegregation purposes. The leadership of the economic community in general has supported desegregation as a national policy. It was in their interest to increase the numbers of well-educated and assimilated workers, both minority and majority. Moreover, desegregation often seemed essential as a strategy to maintain peace and to advance economic opportunity in rural southern and urban northern ghettos. Peace, or orderliness in community life, is a necessary ingredient for the environmental stability and regularity that were previously described as vital to economic gain.

The relevance of state and local governments, and their political systems for influencing the economics of schooling, is shown in Table 2−1 (pp. 62−63). It clearly reflects wide disparities and variations in per-pupil expenditures among state school districts; it also demonstrates enormous differences among states in levels of economic health and wealth, as indicated in the average assessed valuation per pupil. Partly as a function of such economic bases, but partly on the basis of political choices and priorities, different districts within states have very different expenditures for schooling. The extremely high maximum district expenditures per pupil in Wyoming and Texas ($14,554 and $11,096) obviously stand out, as do the lowest district maximums in Alabama, South Carolina ($580 and $610), and other Deep South states. But it is especially interesting to consider districts within those states with a fairly common average assessed valuation per pupil, such as Arkansas, Florida, Maine, Oklahoma, and South Carolina (all between $22,000 and $23,000). Local district expenditures vary considerably even within this narrow statewide average valuation range, from district per pupil lows of $215 in Maine to $582 in Florida, and highs of $610 in South Carolina to $2,565 in Oklahoma.

Another way in which the state and local government or political system influences education is through the establishment of elaborate credentializing criteria and certification agencies that serve to organize and direct the schooling enterprise. Thus, employers can hire students and colleges can admit students who have a high school degree with some assurance that these students have gained specified skills, attitudes, and so on. In this effort, the government is aided by the nation's colleges and universities that function as consumers of the public schools' best products and provide an invaluable service by recruiting and channeling students into higher-level credential and certification networks.

Exercise 2−4. *Understanding School Budgets*

This exercise requires the use of a library or field research in local communities and/or school system records.

Find copies of, and review, the budgets of two school systems: (1) the school system you attended (or one of them if you attended several) as a secondary student; (2) the school system of the city in or near which your college/university is located.

What are the major differences in these two budgets:

1. With respect to total size of budget.
2. With respect to sources of funds.
3. With respect to expenditure categories.
4. With respect to average salary levels.

Can you explain any of these differences in terms of:

1. Size of community served (number of students).
2. Racial composition of the community.
3. Comparative wealth of the community.
4. Different services provided to students.

At the level of higher education, the state helps to create the "myth" of professionalism, and suggests that there is a direct relationship between the acquisition of educational credentials and competence in a profession or field or specialization (such as law, medicine, social work, nursing, and teaching). Recent experience with these professions suggests that the educational credential does not always reflect competence in the profession; at best it indicates competence as a beginning student of that profession. Nevertheless, the political system establishes the criteria and sets the standards for professional attainment, whereas institutions of higher learning provide the training and legitimize the credentials. Such abstract definitions of professional skill are an especially potent factor in maintaining control by colleges over the education of our nation's teachers and school administrators. These teachers and administrators, in turn, use the same concept of the credential in justifying professional control of schools and educational programs for young people.

Still another means by which the political-economic system influences education is through the various roles that business leaders play in serving on federal commissions, state boards of education, citizen advisory groups, and local boards of education. In particular, representatives of "big business" tend to dominate educational policy-setting boards at the state level, whereas "small

Table 2—1. Disparities in the Distribution
of Educational Resources [12]

State	District Minimum per Pupil Expenditure	District Maximum per Pupil Expenditure	Average Assessed Valuation per Pupil
Alabama	$294	$ 580	$ 4,662
Alaska	480	1,810	36,486
Arizona	410	2,900	14,561
Arkansas	294	1,005	22,725
California	402	3,187	52,271
Colorado	444	2,801	8,166
Connecticut	499	1,311	21,281
Delaware	633	1,081	21,349
Florida	582	1,036	22,877
Georgia	364	735	23,588
Hawaii (1 school district)	489	489	—
Idaho	483	3,172	4,858
Illinois	390	2,295	19,196
Indiana	373	961	9,338
Iowa	591	1,166	36,521
Kansas	489	1,572	10,364
Kentucky	344	885	24,253
Louisiana	499	922	5,335
Maine	215	1,966	22,643
Maryland	634	1,036	19,101
Massachusetts	454	4,243	28,189
Michigan	409	1,275	14,880
Minnesota	373	1,492	28,920
Mississippi	321	825	3,936
Missouri	213	1,929	8,783
Montana	467	8,515	5,117
Nebraska	274	3,417	26,221
Nevada	746	1,678	13,728
New Hampshire	280	1,356	34,022
New Jersey	484	2,876	36,300
New Mexico	477	1,183	35,203
New York	633	7,241	25,770
North Carolina	467	732	23,050
North Dakota	327	1,842	3,676
Ohio	412	1,684	13,892
Oklahoma	309	2,565	22,711
Oregon	431	4,491	36,748

Table 2–1 (continued).

State	District Minimum per Pupil Expenditure	District Maximum per Pupil Expenditure	Average Assessed Valuation per Pupil
Pennsylvania	535	4,230	17,141
Rhode Island	531	1,206	21,428
South Carolina	397	610	22,936
South Dakota	175	6,012	24,802
Tennessee	315	774	28,303
Texas	197	11,096	17,213
Utah	533	1,514	29,081
Vermont	357	1,517	25,839
Virginia	441	1,159	24,119
Washington	433	3,993	32,394
West Virginia	502	721	14,517
Wisconsin	408	1,391	29,347
Wyoming	617	14,554	11,582

business" owners and managers dominate at the local level. Together with their professional counterparts (lawyers, engineers, and doctors), experienced businessmen are also conspicuous on the governing boards of major state universities and elite private ones. To a very real extent, economic leaders constitute an extragovernmental body that is not subject to the precise guidelines and regulations of formal political leaders and state and federal bodies, and is yet capable of making critical decisions on matters of public educational policy. In their roles, they also approve financial resources and make special monies available for educational programs. These leaders' expenditures generally are consonant with their immediate special interests, and with the long-range goals of the political-economic system.

Perhaps the most powerful link between the political-economic system and education may be seen in the latent reinforcement that education provides for society's social stratification systems. Since the school is a subsystem of the society, it follows that stratification of the sort found in the society at large would also be found in the educational systems of that society. Educational systems can be expected to reflect the political-economic order, and help to maintain and reinforce societal priorities and outcomes. Thus, educational systems function as essentially stabilizing influences in society.

The relationship between the political-economic order and society's social stratification systems merits close scrutiny and has important implications for understanding the nature of societal control over education. Whereas some of the control mechanisms discussed earlier are readily apparent and affect the cultural and formal organization of schooling, stratification processes can be quite subtle. One observer of the North American social scene summarized the social-psychological implications of social stratification systems as follows: [13]

1. Social stratification systems function to limit the possibility of discovery of the full range of talent available in a society. This results from the fact of unequal access to appropriate motivation, channels of recruitment and centers of training.

2. Social stratification systems function to distribute favorable self-images unequally throughout a population. To the extent that such favorable self-images are requisite to the development of the creative potential inherent in men, to that extent stratification systems function to limit the development of this creative potential.

3. To the extent that the sense of significant membership in a society depends on one's place on the prestige ladder of the society, social stratification systems function to distribute unequally the sense of significant membership in the population.

4. To the extent that participation and apathy depend upon the sense of significant membership in the society, social stratification systems function to distribute the motivation to participate unequally in a population.

The societal stratification system reinforces schooling systems and is, in turn, reinforced by schooling. The differences in available talent, self-esteem, sense of competent membership, and motivation help students of different status perform differently in school. The school reinforces these differences (sometimes consciously and deliberately, sometimes automatically and unintentionally) and helps create even more dramatic differences among young people of different status with regard to these and other variables. That stratification systems exist and have these implications is clear. The exact role of the school, and the degree to which it adds to the societal trend in these directions, is a matter of much debate. In several later chapters (especially Chapter 10) that debate is considered in greater detail, but we can consider at this point in the discussion some preliminary notions about *how* the school reproduces the society's political-economic stratification system across generations.

SCHOOL SOCIALIZATION MECHANISMS

Our discussion of the means by which the political-economic system controls and influences the educational system inevitably leads to an examination of the internal school mechanisms that sustain such control and influence. Or more explicitly: What are some of the school socialization mechanisms that produce outcomes which serve the political-economic elites? Clearly, many of these mechanisms, such as psychological testing and curriculum differentiation or "tracking," are matters of general knowledge and conjure up images of superiority-inferiority, ineptness-competence, adequacy-inadequacy, and brightness-dullness among students and parents. Other of these mechanisms, such as labeling and channeling, are more subtle in their impact but perhaps are equally as potent in their long-range consequences.

As Jencks points out, schools select, sort out, and distribute students into various roles and futures [14]. This selection process has the latent or un-acknowledged function of meeting a portion of the society's economic and political needs without seriously altering the stratification structure. In some cases, this political-economic filtering process helps realize the democratic ideology by providing opportunities for economic mobility by selecting and training the most able and industrious youth for higher-status positions. In other cases, the system maintains existing class distinctions and ensures that those who start life with advantages will advance further and achieve more than those who do not. Seekers of high-status occupations qualify for entry into college and professional schools. Those who cannot qualify, for whatever reason, tolerate the system and scale down their ambitions and expectations accordingly. In this context, Christopher Lasch makes the following observation:

> Those who had no aptitude for school, who could not afford it, or who merely hated it, tailored their expectations accordingly. In this way the school system came to serve the function . . . of limiting the number of aspirants to high-status jobs— jobs that are widely believed (not without reason, but with less reason than is commonly supposed) to depend on schooling. Educational credentials came to serve as "a legitimate device for rationing privilege" in a society "that wants people sorted and graded" but does not know precisely what standards it wants to use. [15]

Aptitude and motivation also are obvious outcomes of societal stratification, as the prior quotation from Tumin indicates. These outcomes are made possible, as well as legitimate, by means of the ingenious labeling and tracking system of the schools, and the effect of these experiences on youngsters' concepts of self and their appropriate roles. The school preserves the status quo by placing children of different social status in different tracks, thereby reinforcing existing social class differences in apparent "ability." To the extent that race and social class overlap, these operations also maintain the economic and political segregation and oppression of blacks, browns, native-Americans, and other Third World minorities. Given the related character of ethnicity and class in American economic life, the school also helps maintain less affluent whites in their place in society.

The result is that the external political and economic stratification system is "reproduced" in the school, thereby creating another generation that fits into the statuses of their predecesors. The professional testing, tracking, and teaching apparatus makes this process legitimate and acceptable by arguing that these outcomes are merited by individual peformance and sound pedagogical principles.° Thus, there is no revolution or public outcry regarding school differentation, or against the inevitability of failure for some and success for others. The populace has come to see this process as quite acceptable, and as an appropriate way of sorting and screening people on the apparently fair basis of talent and tests.

And indeed, what good would it do to challenge the national structure of schooling on these issues? If Michael Katz's thesis is valid, that "by about 1850 American education had acquired its fundamental structural characteristics, and that they have not altered since" [16], then we should not be surprised at the failure of subsequent change efforts. With rare exceptions, attempts at school change have been largely programmatic adaptations within an unaltered political and economic system. Efforts at school desegregation, new school curricula, lessening the reproduction of stratification, and so on have "tinkered" with the internal system of the school without focusing on the relation between the school and its political-economic support base. And in those cases in which serious attempts have been exerted, the efforts have generally faltered as a result of the lack of nourishment from powerful groups in these systems. Thus, an understanding of the political-economic system is fundamental, since the basic structural outlines of schools are linked to the continuing nature of our political-economic order.

° In Chapters 8, 9, and 10 we deal with the issue of *how* and *in what ways* tests, teachers, and tracks discriminate against minority and poor children.

3

THE CHANGING NORTH AMERICAN SOCIETY: IMPLICATIONS FOR SCHOOLS

We have previously suggested that the institutions of education are woven inextricably into the entire fabric of society. As such, these institutions are integral parts of the North American culture and political-economic structure, and their various elements reflect those larger contexts. American schools (public elementary and secondary schools, private schools, trade schools, community colleges, universities) can be viewed as extensions of the dominant ideology and values of the wider culture, as well as a series of adaptations to prevailing belief systems. They also reflect and implement the major expectations and needs of the political and economic order within which we live.

Although this depiction is not necessarily unique to the United States or to the Western world, its precise manifestations in our society are unique, and the implications of this for "schooling" are quite profound. The stress on local control of education in the United States means that schools are subject not only to the bevy of national economic, political, and cultural forces that impinge on all institutions but also to those forces operating at the local level, some of which may be at variance with the larger society. This tension is further compounded by the tempo and direction of social change throughout the American society and its local communities.

This chapter describes some of the more salient forces that seem instrumental in changing the nature and character of American society and in governing the tempo of local change. In particular, we focus on those arenas of change that appear to have the most profound implications for the educational process and the conduct of schooling.°

° We express our appreciation to Dr. Richard Schmuck of the University of Oregon for his assistance in preparing the ideas and data for an earlier version of this chapter.

The pace of social change in North America is so rapid that in some ways our society has changed more in the past thirty years than it did in the two hundred preceeding years. All predictions indicate an even more rapid series of societal changes for the next thirty years. Some of the outstanding arenas of social change during the past several decades have included the character and ecological distribution and migration patterns of the population; the nature of the economic system; the structure and operations of government, politics, and partisan activity; and cultural values and institutions concerned with moral and legal standards. No segment of daily existence or of the population has been left untouched by these far-reaching changes. Moreover, not all these changes are quantitative extensions of previous trends; some are qualitative departures from the past, creating a very different society, with different values and life opportunites. One of the things they create is different educational values and organizational forms, involving changing personnel, instructional procedures and patterns, and outcomes.

Major changes in the social structure and institutional patterns filter down to individuals through their connection with the larger society in their work, leisure, family, and community roles. In addition, parents and educators pass on their own views and experiences with the world and its demands through the ways in which they socialize their children. Changes in institutional structures and norms have placed great strain on various organizations and groups in the general population. Whereas some people easily adjust to social changes, others flounder in political, economic, or moral confusion. The personal implications of living in a profoundly changed and changing world are enormous.

THE CHANGES

Ecological and Population Patterns

Some of the major changes in the American society have occurred in the character of the national population. The total population of the United States more than doubled from 1900 to 1960, and it is predicted that it will double again by the year 2000. By and large, more people are living longer; medical advances, greater affluence, and other forces such as better public health practices, sanitation, and so on have increased the average life span. In 1900 the typical American life expectancy at birth was 48.2 years; in 1970 it was 70.9 years. A graphic illustration of life-expectancy changes over these seven decades for different portions of the population is shown in Figure 3−1.

One result of these increases in life expectancy is that an increasing percentage of our population is over sixty years of age. Since the 1940s a major increase has occurred in the number of young persons under the age of ten and in their early teens. The growing teenage and young adult population has become a source of particular concern for many Americans. The visible age

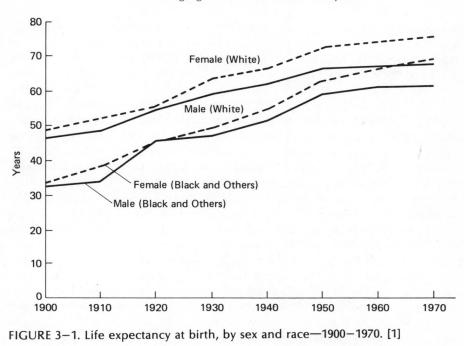

FIGURE 3—1. Life expectancy at birth, by sex and race—1900—1970. [1]

Exercise 3—1. *Understanding Different Life Expectancy Rates*

This exercise can be done by students individually or in small groups. Individuals or group reporters can share their ideas, and a class list of explanatory variables can be created.

Life expectancy among Americans has been increasing steadily since 1900. The average American can now expect to live beyond seventy. But these predictions are not equally valid for both white and black populations or for males and females. Examine Figure 3—1 and speculate about the reasons for different life expectations. What is there about the quality of life and/or inheritance or social structure that can create different life expectancies?

differences, buying power, and group behavior of the young often threaten established notions of dependent, obedient, and "seen but not heard" youth.

Since the turn of the century, and especially since the start of World War II, Americans have been on the move. Although some of this geographic mobility has been from one city to another, or from one suburb to another, one of the most dramatic shifts in the American population accompanied a movement off the farmlands. In 1920, 30 per cent of the American population was living on farms, and by 1940 the percentage had dropped to 23 per cent. However, that percentage represented a minimal numerical decrease in the actual farm population, which was 31,974,000 in 1920 and still 30,547,000 in 1940. For the most part these figures meant that the population was increasing faster in urban than in rural areas—not that a great movement necessarily was occurring. But from 1940 on, both the real numbers and percentages of farmers dropped rapidly. By 1960, only 8.7 per cent of the population was still living on the farms, and the number of farm persons had dropped to 15,635,000; by 1970 the per cent was 4.8 and the total number had dropped to 9,712,000. These dramatic shifts in the farm population are related to a number of societal factors that were precipitating changes throughout the fabric of American society. Perhaps among the more influential factors were the pace of industrialization in major urban centers, the unsettling impact of World War II, and the tremendous growth of agribusinesses, which forced many small, family farms out of the competitive agricultural market.

. As people left the farms, and especially southern rural areas, they moved to the burgeoning metropolitan centers. Recent population growth has been greatest in satellite areas and suburban communities surrounding large urban centers. One result of these population increases is that more Americans are coming into increasingly close physical contact with one another. The data in Table 3—1 summarize these patterns of mobility away from rural areas and into urban centers.

Not all Americans are participating to equal degrees in the major rural to urban to suburban shifts that are occurring. Table 3—2 shows that over the past two decades blacks moved out of rural areas and into central cities at an even higher rate than whites. But whereas the major increase in the movement of blacks has been into urban centers, the major white population increases have come in other areas defined as urban and semiurban; in satellite and suburban communities. Thus, black people start the journey even more often, but do not make that last leg of this trek as easily as do whites. The demands of urban. black groups to ameliorate segregated residential patterns are as familiar a feature of our times as are the housing and mobility patterns themselves.

One result of contemporary mobility and population trends has been the development of new centers of population. Especially noticeable has been the

Table 3—1. Percentage of the Population, By Urban-Rural Concentration [2]

	1900	1920	1940	1960	1970
Urban	39.7	51.2	56.5	69.9	73.5
Rural	60.3	48.8	43.5	30.1	26.5

Table 3−2. Percentage of the Population in Urban and Rural
Areas, By Race [3]

	1950	1960	1970
Urban center			
Black	40.6	51.4	58.2
White	31.2	29.9	27.9
Urban other			
Black	21.9	21.7	23.1
White	33.1	33.2	44.6
Rural			
Black	37.5	26.9	18.7
White	35.7	26.9	27.5

growth of communities close to new business establishments that are involved in defense and aero-space activities, and vacation and retirement areas suitable for the affluent and aging elements of the population. One example is the Southwest crescent, a chain of cities extending from Houston westward and northward to Los Angeles and San Francisco; a center for missile bases, the space industry, and retirement-vacation communities. Ten of the fifteen American cities in which the population grew by 75 per cent or more from 1950 to 1970 fall in that crescent. Four of the remaining five cities are major resort and retirement towns in Florida.° In general, the Pacific states, especially California and Washington, and the Southern Mountain states of Arizona and Nevada, and Texas and Florida continue to lead the pace from the 1940s on in receiving native immigrants. As large industrial firms establish plants in those areas, business executives follow, often moving from plant to plant as their job opportunities improve (or change). Former centers of industry in the North, East, and Midwest lose jobs and corporate taxes as a result.

Economic System

Chapter 2 discussed the major outlines of our political-economic system. We now turn our attention to some of the extensive changes in the economy during the past several decades. Perhaps the most outstanding feature of American economic life has been the increase in the Gross National Product (GNP). From

---

° In order of their rate of growth: Fort Lauderdale-Hollywood, Florida; Anaheim-Santa Ana-Garden Grove, California; Las Vegas, Nevada; Midland, Texas; Orlando, Florida; San Jose, California; Odessa, Texas; Phoenix, Arizona; West Palm Beach, Florida; Colorado Springs, Colorado; Miami, Florida; Tucson, Arizona; San Diego, California; Alberqueque, New Mexico; San Bernadino-Riverside-Ontario, California.

Exercise 3—2. *Personal History and Meaning of Population Shifts*

This exercise can be done by students working individually, reporting the results of their research in class or in a paper.

In Table 3—1 we noted that from 1900—1970 the percentage of the population concentrated in urban and rural areas was completely reversed. What do you feel to be the significance of such a change? Talk to your parents and/or grandparents about their own history of movement and migration? Does your family reflect the patterns found in the society at large? You might use the following chart as a guide for collecting information on your own family's migration:

	Birthplace	Residence As a Young Adult	Residence Now	Reason for Moving
Mother				
Mother's mother				
Mother's father				
Mother's sisters or brothers				
Father				
Father's mother				
Father's father				
Father's sisters or brothers				

a 1940 level of 100.6 billions, the GNP rose to 284.6 billions in 1950, and more than tripled to 982.4 billions in 1970. Such a rapid expansion in national wealth has been encouraged by a parallel growth in human material productivity. Real gross output per individual doubled between 1900 and 1940, and then almost doubled again by 1960. Partly a product of increased size and organization of machine and capital improvements, these trends highlight the tremendous increase in the capacity of the American domestic economic system. The possibility that both GNP and productivity rates are growing more slowly in

Exercise 3—3. *Understanding Black-White Differences in Current Migration Patterns*

This exercise can be done in small groups of students or as an open discussion in class.

1. Why do you think the black population has remained concentrated in central cities rather than move to suburban areas, as did many whites? Would the reasons that whites move to these areas also be relevant for blacks? Do you think that this nonmovement of blacks is the result of many "freely made" decisions by individual blacks, the result of deliberate exclusionary practices by white homeowners, the result of a discrimminatory real estate and home financing industry, the normal pressure of economics, or what?

2. Why do you think the white population has begun to move out of urban centers into suburban and outlying areas? Is the availability of jobs and easy transportation to them a factor? Is better schools a factor? What other reasons might be involved?

recent years is causing consternation among high-level political and economic planners and scholars.

Some marked changes also have occurred in the types of occupations and work roles that are available and demanded by economic operations. Consonant with great rural to urban migrations of the past forty years there has been a decline in the percentage of workers employed on farms and in farming roles. There has also been a marked increase in opportunities for employment in a variety of white-collar roles in clerical and sales positions, and in a wide variety of professional, technical, and managerial occupations. Table 3—3 demonstrates these trends.

Parallel to these shifts in occupational roles has been a shift in the nature of

TABLE 3—3. Percentage of Major Occupational Group of Economically Active Population [4]

	1900	1920	1940	1960	1970
White-collar	17.6	25.0	31.1	42.2	47.9
Manual	35.8	40.2	39.8	39.7	36.3
Service	9.1	7.9	11.7	11.8	12.7
Farm	37.5	26.9	17.4	6.3	3.1

the industries in which large portions of the population work. Manufacturing, mining, and transportation, for instance, employed well over one half of the total working population in 1920; by 1940 well under one half of the active population was employed in these industries; and by 1970 this number had declined to under 40 per cent. Personal service and retail trade industries, hospitals and schools, governmental organizations, and financial and insurance establishments all grew during this same period. Those industries that require and cater to a high degree of human interdependence in delivery of social services have shown the most growth. Professional and managerial roles, by their very nature, require the occupant of the role to attend to the management of human resources; thus there is a need for skill in relating with others in groups. Clerical and sales personnel, as well as service role performers, are engaged everyday in relating to others, typically in subordinate situations. For these people, there is a necessity to learn and practice effective skills in getting along with colleagues, superiors, and customers. Friendship, impersonal obedience, and interpersonal skills in adaptation have become matters of high priority in view of these contemporary changes and trends. It has become at least as important to get along with others as it is to achieve highly on one's own. Thus, the individual goals and achievement drives of an earlier generation are, in part, mitigated by the job security and interpersonal priorities of the present and future.

In addition to these changing occupational choices and demands, personal goals, and social skills, some major reorganizations have been made in the typical structure of economic enterprise. As noted in Chapter 2, business firms have grown in size, and concentration has led to larger firms having a greater share of the market and employing a greater percentage of the work force.

Men and women who are in constant and close contact, often in interdependent roles in large organizations, must place priority upon their ability to get along together, at least in the interest of economic survival if not interpersonal harmony. At the same time, employees have to learn how to cope with larger and more impersonal bureaucracies. Perhaps in larger firms, additional skills are needed to deal impersonally, but correctly, with others, whereas smaller firms might require a higher order of social skills in closer types of interpersonal relationships.

With the growth of economic concentration and diversification has come an increase in the number and importance of multiunit organizations. Such enterprises necessitate a higher proportion of managers who must be employed to oversee and coordinate more complex organizations. Several categories of hierarchical and parallel organizations must be managed by trained professionals. The growth of such bureaucracies is not limited to trade or service industries alone; it is characteristic of manufacturing as well.

At the turn of the century, approximately 70 per cent of all manufacturing employees were working in corporations. By 1929, that percentage had risen to 89 per cent, and by 1972 it had reached 93 per cent. Nonincorporated enterprises, such as single proprietorships and partnerships, now employ a small percentage of all workers, no longer contribute as great a share of the manufacturing value added, and no longer account for as large a proportion of the national wealth and income. Most North Americans employed by manufacturing organizations work in large, complex, corporate bureaucracies (multiunit as compared with single-unit), and this fact of one's working life must affect one's thinking, feeling, and behavior in other areas of life. No longer is economic work ruled by a single owner; more often, professional managers run most large organizations, wheareas the actual owners are far removed from the actual scene of events. This places greater emphasis on objective, rational, and impersonal forms of organizational authority. Workers are asked to owe allegiance to an organization, a permanent entity, rather than to a single personal authority. Rules rather than personal power govern work arrangements, and teams of workers collaborate for their own and the organization's welfare. Men and women who spend large portions of their lives in work groups learn to support and guard the welfare of their co-workers; even to forming organizations such as unions to protect their welfare, mobilize self-help opportunities, and advance their interests vis-à-vis management.

Problems encountered as a result of these changing styles of work and work relationships have been articulated in Riesman's discussion of "the organization man," and in Miller and Swanson's study linking America's changing economic structure to altered child-rearing practices [5]. Many observers now express a concern for the demise of the individually concerned person, who looks out for self, and whose behavior is not largely determined by the needs, demands, and concerns of others, especially groups of others.

On the one hand, highly specialized and differentiated occupations generate unique demands on people to be specialists in their own area of skill and competence. This characteristic of modern industry tends to keep persons separate and apart from one another, so different are their skills and productive acts. But on the other hand, such specialization of function requires other specialists to fulfill transitive and collaborative roles, to engineer social cooperation and interdependence. Thus, a new generation of specialists has grown up, specialists in bridging the gaps and ensuring communication between other specialists.

Change in the distribution of economic rewards over the past 20 years has resulted in a small increase in real income for the middle classes. The lowest 20 per cent of the population received 4 per cent of the national income in 1929 and 4.2 per cent in 1964. There has been a rise in the middle and upper middle groups' share of the total national income—from 32.1 per cent in 1929 to 39.6 per cent in 1964. During the same period, the share of the upper 20 per cent of the national income fell slightly—from 54.4 per cent to 45.5 per cent. Progressive income taxes, unionization, and the boomtime urban labor market of the war and postwar years help explain this slowly decreasing gap between income levels. However, it really is "slowly decreasing" and represents a minimal change for a society ostensibly committed to equality and economic mobility.

The inclusion of more formerly "poor" people into the middle classes has made the latter a broad category indeed. For those American families earning between $10,000 and $25,000 in 1971 (46%), income levels may no longer signify very different opportunities and life-styles. Family income, by race, sex, and age of family head are portrayed in Table 3—4 (we return to a discussion of race and sex issues later). Even though there are major areas of poverty throughout the nation, ours can largely be characterized as an "affluent" society. The majority of Americans, regardless of their income levels, are relatively comfortable economically. Even though the data clearly indicate rising economic and financial status indices, the "security" blanket one might expect to accompany such trends is being seriously eroded by rising inflation, which, according to Labor Department statistics, rose to at least 1 per cent/per month (April 1979). If unchecked, this would mean an annual inflation rate of 12 per cent/per annum. A rate of inflation of this magnitude would strike at the very heart of whatever resources the poor have been able to muster and would alter the life-style of America's middle class.

Many North Americans, particularly those of the upper middle classes, are able to spend substantial amounts of both time and money enjoying themselves, pursuing more hedonistic gratifications in eating, drinking, and leisure-time activities. Increased mobility and recreational travel is made possible by leisure time and participation in nonwork activities. The average American spent approximately four times as much money on recreational activities in 1960 as in 1940, and more than three times as much in 1970 as in 1960. A substantial

Table 3—4. Family Income, By Race, Sex, and Age of Family Head: 1971 [6]

Total Money Income	All Families	Race of Head		Sex of Head	
		White	Negro	Male	Female
Number of families (thous.)	53,296	47,641	5,157	47,105	6,191
Per cent	100.0	100.0	100.0	100.0	100.0
Less than $4,000	13.1	11.2	29.2	9.6	39.4
$4,000 to $6,999	16.6	15.8	24.8	15.4	26.4
$7,000 to $9,999	18.5	18.6	18.3	18.9	16.0
$10,000 to $11,999	12.5	13.0	8.8	13.3	6.7
$12,000 to $14,999	14.4	15.0	8.4	15.6	5.2
$15,000 to $24,999	19.5	20.6	9.5	21.4	5.4
$25,000 and over	5.3	5.8	1.1	5.9	.9

proportion of this expenditure went for hotel and motel accommodations. The number of motels and motor hotels, in particular, grew from 13,521 in 1939 to 40,584 in 1963. The most recent hotel and motel facilities tend to be larger and accommodate more guests.

One side effect of the changes in occupational demands for less manual labor and for more clerical and sales personnel, of the increasing need for more creative ways of spending leisure time, and of the middle- and lower-classes' needs for more than one income per family is reflected in the growing number of married women who are part of the economically active labor force. In 1920, 22 per cent of the female population over age fourteen was in the labor force; by 1940 this figure had increased to 27.4 per cent; and by 1970, it had increased to 32.6 per cent. Perhaps more important than these overall figures is the fact that most of the women in the labor force in the earlier years of this century were single, widowed, or divorced. Currently, a greater percentage of employed females are married women, some of whom are joining their husbands in working for familial affluence, not for personal survival or the necessities of life. Not all however! The data in Table 3—4 indicate that many working women are indeed working so they and their families can survive. Families headed by females have consistently lower incomes, and are more likely (65% to 25% of male-headed families) to be earning less than $7,000 per year. The entrance of large numbers of women into the active labor force is inconsistent with many traditional value positions and often leads to debates about the proper role of women and the sanctity or demise of the family. Cultural values about the "proper" role of women often support discriminatory treatment of women in the labor market. These treatments limit women's access to certain occupational roles, frustrate women's mobility to higher status occupations, and may provide unequal pay for women's work.

Throughout all of these new and changing economic patterns runs the theme of racial distinction and disadvantage. Disproportionate numbers of blacks, Hispanics, and other minority groups remain in laboring and operative categories; many more minorities than whites are in the lower 20 per cent of the population in income received; and in a variety of ways minorities participate only minimally in the society's increasing affluence. For instance, the data in Table 3—4 indicate that twice as many black families are clustered in income ranges below $7,000 than are whites (55% compared to 27%): conversely, black families are much less likely to be in higher income groupings. Equally dramatic data regarding racial disadvantage exists in the comparison of unemployment rates by age, sex, and race. In some of the large urban centers of the nation, the unemployment figures for 1978—79 reached as high as 60 per cent for blacks ranging from sixteen to nineteen years of age. These economic realities are being integrated into the long and varied demands by blacks and Hispanics for equal legal rights and treatment; it is a protest basis that is likely to be more disruptive to established interests and last longer than the demand for legal equality itself. One observer has estimated that at the current rate of

Exercise 3—4. *Advantages/Disadvantages of Racial and Sexual Status*

This exercise requires the class to be divided into at least four groups—minority males, minority females, white males, and white females. Each group should be divided into smaller units that can promote face-to-face sharing. Results can be shared in the total class and recorded for later connection to objective (demographic and other) data available elsewhere in this book and in other sources.

1. What are the advantages you gain as a member of your sexual status in this society?

2. What are the advantages you gain as a member of your racial status in this society?

3. What are the disadvantages you experience as a member of your sexual status in this society?

4. What are the disadvantages you experience as a member of your racial status in this society?

progress in the economic sphere, blacks would approach parity with whites by approximately the year 2000 [7]. This relatively unchanging aspect of the changing American economy is a major source of tension, conflict, and suffering in minority communities across the nation. The restlessness and pain of Harlem, Watts, Wounded Knee, and other ghettos, barrios, and reservations are a warning of new changes and of new pressures for economic changes yet to come.

Governmental Activity and the Political Process

Over the past several decades Americans have witnessed a rapid increase in governmental activities at all levels—federal, state, and local. Partly a result of experiments in public welfare that were initiated during the Depression which continue today, partly a result of the growing size of regulatory agencies dealing with private enterprise, and partly a result of a national ideology becoming increasingly comfortable with public activity to supplement gaps in the economy, government has grown larger and has undertaken a wider range of functions. Since 1950, employment in state and local government units has grown even faster than in the federal sector: these employment trends are reflected in Table 3—5.

Considerable amounts of public money and energy are currently being channeled into programs to aid the plight of the economically deprived and

Table 3—5.
Public Employees (Thousands) [8]

	Total	Federal	State	Local
1940	4,474	1,128	Not Available	Not Available
1950	6,402	2,117	1,057	3,228
1960	8,802	2,421	1,527	4,860
1970	13,028	2,881	2,775	7,392

oppressed. Public conscience was triggered by various social critics,° and public expenditures for welfare, urban renewal, youth corps, and other assistance and treatment programs have risen markedly in recent years. The greatest expansions have come in the social welfare areas of veterans' care, education, public assistance, medical care, and miscellaneous services such as children's school lunches. Social welfare expenditures as a function of the Gross National Product have risen from 4.1 per cent in 1929 to 9.1 per cent in 1940 to almost 12 per cent in 1965 and 15 per cent in 1970. Table 3—6 depicts the rise in such funding, and also corroborates the changing federal, state, and local relationship in these areas.

Increasing welfare and public aid disbursements represent a clear transition

Table 3—6.
Federal Grants to State and Local Governments
(in millions) [10]

Purpose	1930	1950	1970
Total	100	2212	23585
Social Welfare	23	1731	16546
Public Assistance	—	1123	7445
Health	—	123	1043
Education	22	82	3017
Miscellaneous	1	402	5041
Highways	76	429	4392
Other	1	53	2648

° Although many programs were initiated during The Great Depression of the 1930s, a new spate of programs were associated with the War on Poverty of the 1960s. Among the many social scientists involved in publicizing the need for such later efforts, the most effective was probably Michael Harrington, *The Other America* [9].

from the individualistic, self-responsible frontierism of the North American past. Individuals are no longer obligated to "make it" on their own, and society is formally committed to step in and help out in certain situations. Although many Americans still regard poverty, unemployment, and sorrow as individual and idiosyncratic problems of deviants, loafers, or parasites, we increasingly understand these aspects of society as reflections of weak links in the structure of the economy. As such, the total society has taken a formal responsibility for redress of at least some degree of such deprivation and oppression. Not all Americans could or can ever agree to these ideological propositions about the nature of economic advantage/disadvantage and the role of government; but it is a mark of our times that this philosophy does guide a vast series of public programs and a network of private and public organizations.°

One aim of social welfare and insurance programs is to break the link between steady gainful employment and livable material resources. These programs seek to provide or guarantee a livable income that is independent of employment status. These programs do not always succeed in this regard; the lack of adequate coverage, eligibility and benefit limitations, and problems in the administration of funds inhibit the attainment of these goals. For instance, administrative procedures and the bureaucratic lacunae of welfare agencies are legion and are a matter of serious controversy and concern. Many welfare programs are accused, by friends and foes alike, of serving to increase the recipients' apathy and despair rather than alleviating it. These programs carry the danger of creating dependency relations that foster apathy and tie poor people to public programs for their only sustenance.

In addition to the distribution of public monies, the federal government has become more active in intervening into other areas of national life. Federal officials who are concerned with inflation and the balance of power in the economy have entered into labor policies and industrial pricing and merging decisions. A concern for justice and equality in public services has led federal courts and the Departments of Justice and of Health, Education and Welfare to intervene in altering state and local policies and prerogatives in education, voting rights, and public accommodations. These activities further reflect a new national perspective on dilemmas of state intervention, public enterprise, and national responsibility. They further challenge the notion of a free enterprise capitalism and raise the possibilities of state capitalism, increased state power, and national control of local options. None of these extensions of federal activity has gone by without serious and sometimes severe debates over their constitutionality, moral appropriateness, and strategic wisdom.

° Recently, there has been a well-organized backlash against this philosophy. Witness the success of Proposition 13 in California. However, much of the rancor is directed toward the property tax as the major revenue-producing source at the local and state levels, although a general criticism of social welfare programs and big or wasteful government bureaucracies is involved as well.

One example of the Supreme Court's influence on local changes was felt by state legislatures, who came under pressure to redistrict voting units so as to more nearly equilibrate population concentrations and political representation. These redistricting procedures increased the political representation of densely populated urban areas at the expense of more sparsely populated rural areas. This trend politically corroborates the immense geographic shift of this century; consolidates urban dominance, particularly in the northern states; and places a premium on persons rather than land as a political power resource. Another result of court activity (as well as executive action) in the electoral arena is the increased registration to vote of large numbers of blacks in the Deep South. Table 3—7 indicates the existence of a new political force, and the need to cater to them has seriously altered many plans and programs of southern politicians. In some counties throughout the South and West, minorities have recently established numerical political dominance, and many southern states now have black state legislators and local officials for the first time since the days of Reconstruction. The passage of national civil rights legislation, occasionally vigorous enforcement action by the Justice Department, and review by the courts have greatly facilitated this process. Without years of mobilization and courageous challenge by local and national civil rights groups (NAACP, SCLC, SNCC, CORE), it is doubtful whether these governmental agencies would ever have acted—but they did.

Since 1932, all branches of the government have been part of a growing political hegemony of the Democratic party. On the brief occasions when Republicans have broken through to establish their own political dominance in legislative or executive chambers, they have done so only for short times and generally with moderate or liberal standard-bearers. During the Eisenhower presidency, for instance, the Democratic majority in the Senate was whittled back somewhat, but regained dominance when Kennedy was elected and increased it during the Johnson years. Table 3—8 suggests the degree of the

Table 3—7.
Per Cent of Voters Registered in the South, By Race [11]

	South*		Deep South†	
	White	Nonwhite	White	Nonwhite
1960	61%	29%	63.6%	18.6%
1970	69	62	75.6	61.5

*South: Alabama, Arkansas, Florida, Georgia, Louisiana, Mississippi, North Carolina, South Carolina, Tennessee, Texas, Virginia.

†Deep South: Alabama, Georgia, Louisiana, Mississippi, South Carolina.

Table 3—8. Congressmen, By Party
(averaged throughout several elections) [12]

| | Representatives | | Senators | |
	Democrat	Republican	Democrat	Republican
1921—1931	177	263	41	54
1931—1941	288	137	64	29
1941—1951	236	195	56	39
1951—1961	241	195	51	45
1961—1971	261	174	60	36

Exercise 3—5. *Understanding Democratic and Republican Party Politics*

This exercise can be done in a large group or by students sharing views in small groups.

Table 3—8 indicates that the general trend of national politics has moved from the Republicanism of the pre-Depression years to more support for Democratic party politics.

1. Is this trend reflected in your family's voting behavior? In yours?

2. Is this trend likely to continue? Why or why not?

3. Are the party labels Democrat and Republican meaningful indicators of a certain stance on political and economic issues? Give examples.

Democratic party's numerical dominance in the national legislature since the 1930s.

The consolidation and continuance of Democratic and moderate Republican political economic power at the national level forces an apparent consensus in two ways. First, it encourages everyone to join a winner, and to repress minor disagreements in the attempt to maintain party power. Second, the power at the disposal of apparently liberal forces of both parties makes dissent less possible, and forces dissenters to select more dramatic and extreme means of expressing their views. During the 1940s and 1950s, the only defense that the conservatives had against this liberal hegemony was the growth of a cross-party organization of conservatives. Thus was born the Dixiecrat bloc and the working collaboration of conservative southern Democrats and conservative northern

Republicans. When the Republicans supported the southern Democrats on racial issues that were critical to the latter, they could, in turn, count on such Democratic support against foreign aid measures and money bills, and for conservative labor legislation. Left-wing radicals, or liberals dissatisfied with the corporate liberalism or moderateness of Democratic party politics, also had to organize protests outside of regular party alignments.

Young people growing up under a Democratic or moderate political administration tend to adopt these public images of political life and policy as their own. These national trends can thus be expected to perpetuate themselves as youngsters who grew up during heavily Democratic or liberal Republican administrations come of age and vote in consonance with their earlier experiences and exposures.

The character of intragovernmental politics, itself, has been changed as the executive branch of the government has steadily taken more initiative in planning public policy. The need for centers of information gathering and processing, coupled with the increasing need for rapid executive action in the event of a national or international emergency, has resulted in executive dominance of the national legislature. Members of the national Congress, and particularly those of the minority party, can often be heard bemoaning this shift in power. They argue that Congress is becoming a rubber-stamp mechanism, that policy is often made before it comes to them for approval, and that they do not have the resources to deal with executive recommendations and suggestions. Great debates are fostered on the wisdom and meaning of this power balance. Clearly, the shift of power to the executive branch is a less direct form of representative democracy than in those times when the legislature was an effective check on executive power. According to a number of observers, we are beginning to see a shift back, a move to reassert the power of Congress over the executive branch.

Finally, the interdependence of our economy and polity is indicated by the fact that national politics have increasingly become a rich man's game. Campaigning and recampaigning are so expensive that most newcomers must be independently wealthy to aspire to a Senate or major congressional seat from a large district. Failing this, they usually align themselves with someone or some organization who is willing to guarantee them financial support. Each national presidential campaign during the 1950s cost the two major parties together over $12,000,000; more than twice the cost of presidential campaigns during the 1940s. In 1968 the cost of presidential campaigns rose to more than twice that, 37 million; in 1980 each presidential candidate could spend up to $19 million in the primaries alone. The net effect of these rising campaign and administrative costs is that it becomes less possible for poor people, or even persons of moderate means, to aspire to be the peoples' representatives. Moreover, it creates even greater psychological distance between the electorate and their representatives, and widens the gap between active politics and the daily life of the working people. Even though new legislation seeks to finance campaigns with public funds, it will not dramatically alter the ways in which private and personal wealth is an effective weapon in national politics.

The ultimate effect of rising campaign and administrative costs of congressional and presidential campaigns on voter participation is unknown. What is known, however, is that the members of minority groups, the unemployed, and the undereducated show significantly lower levels of participation in national elections. This is illustrated in Table 3—9, which provides participation figures on the 1972 national election by popular characteristics.

In still another arena, since 1940 the federal government has engaged in increased commitments and interdependent relations with many other national governments. Although it was common for earlier political leaders to warn of the danger of entangling alliances, current administrations have pursued such entanglements with an élan and vigor that often surprised even our allies. For example, the government has established various multinational alliances, of NATO, SEATO, and CENTRO nations, with the OAS, and with the United Nations. The United States also contributes a major portion of the financial base for the United Nations and its specialized agencies. These arrangements reflect the changing character of the international governmental system. Many nations, both new and old, are undergoing turbulent reorganizations, and new patterns of international interdependence are being created. Previous enemies are also drawn into collaborative and cooperative relations, as in our visits and treaties with the Soviet Union and The People's Republic of China. Despite a historical tradition of mutual belligerence and threat, these nations are becoming increasingly involved with us in joint ventures and exchanges. Most of these rapid and dramatic changes in the international attitude and role of the United

---

Exercise 3—6. *Interpreting Patterns of Voter Participation*

This exercise can be done by students in small groups or as a short paper assignment (see Table 3—9).

1. How could you explain higher voting percentages among the white population? Among people with a higher education?

2. What does the act of voting represent? A sense of control? Faith in the future? A sense of involvement? A sense of duty?

3. If voting is considered a specific example of general citizen participation in public affairs, what patterns of activity would you expect to see in a local parents' organization? Are there any conditions in which you might expect some of the trends in the table to be dramatically altered?

Table 3–9. Participation in the 1976 National Election
by Popular Characteristics [13]

	People of Voting Age (In thousands)	People Reporting Voted	Per Cent Voted	Per Cent Reporting Not Voted
Male	69	41.1	59.6	40.4
Female	77.6	45.6	58.8	41.2
Race—				
White	129.3	78.8	60.9	39.1
Black	14.9	7.3	48.7	51.3
Hispanic	6.6	2.1	31.8	68.2
Age—				
18–20	12.1	4.6	38.0	62.0
21–24	14.8	6.8	45.6	54.4
25–34	31.5	17.5	55.4	44.6
35–44	22.8	14.4	63.3	36.7
45–64	43.3	29.8	68.7	31.3
65+	22.0	13.7	62.2	37.8
Residence—				
Metropolitan	99.6	58.9	59.2	40.8
Nonmetropolitan	47.0	27.8	59.1	40.9
N. and W. Residence	99.4	60.8	61.2	38.8
S. Residence	47.1	25.9	54.9	45.1
Years of School—				
8	24.9	11.0	44.1	55.9
9–11	22.2	10.5	47.2	52.8
12 (H.S.)	55.7	33.1	59.4	40.6
12+	43.7	32.2	73.5	26.5
Employment—				
Employed	86.0	53.8	62.0	38.0
Unemployed	6.4	2.8	43.7	56.3
Not in Labor Force	54.1	30.6	56.5	43.5
Total	146.5	86.7	59.2	40.8

States occurred after World War II, and are markedly divergent from the nation's prewar positions of isolationism and neoisolationism. These changes can be traced to newer conceptions of the role of the United States as a first-rate world power, and the mutual interdependence of all nations. These changes may also be tied to the increasing power of multinational corporations. National governments may find their hands tied and their actions constrained by the multinational operations and power of certain corporations. If these are

North American-based corporations, their multinational character obviously reflects the commitments and priorities of our entire political-economic system. As such, our international governmental activities reflect concerns about the responsibility of the United States for international affairs and for the peace and security of other nations around the world, as well as for our own economic and political interests, security, and dominance.

Changing Cultural Values and Institutions

In addition to changes in the economic and political systems of our society, we can also see vast cultural changes. Some of these cultural changes occur in those institutions that are primarily responsible for teaching and enforcing cultural values (agencies of socialization and social control), and others appear to occur in our general ideology or beliefs and values as a people.

Churches. Among those institutions primarily responsible for moral and ethical training and elaboration, and for passing on a common cultural tradition, are the churches, which have also undergone major changes in the past several decades. More people are church members now than in the past, although that does not mean that church members now more often observe all the rituals or attend religious functions. The average membership size of churches, like other institutions, has increased. These trends are illustrated in Table 3—10.

As church memberships increase, the distance between members, lay leaders, and religious leaders increases. Similar to the growth of industrial and governmental institutions, the size and financial assets of churches and the managerial demands placed upon religious leaders by this growth have created a new and highly trained professional bureaucracy in the church. These religious managers are no longer of the same flock as their members. Instead, they have been especially trained not only to lead religious services but also to supervise and coordinate the many and varied functions of a business and service organization. One result of this trend is a lessening of the intimate sense of communion

Table 3—10. Church Membership, as a Percentage of the Total Population, and Members per Church [14]

	1906	1926	1950	1970
Number of church members (in thousands)	35,068	54,576	86,830	131,046
Per cent of population church members	41.0	47.2	57.0	63.0
Members per church	165	235	304	399

Exercise 3−7. *Growth and Meaning of Growth in Size of Institutions*

This exercise can be done by students individually, preferably as part of a paper or assignment.

1. If you and/or your family were active church attenders, talk to your local clergyperson about the data reported in Table 3−10. Has your local religious establishment grown in ways that reflect these national trends? Has it been affected by the advance of ecumenicalism? If no, why not? If yes, how have either trends affected the conduct of worship? Of voluntary social services to church members? Of external public services?

2. Select another local religious group or institution and conduct a similar inquiry.

---

between worshipers, leaders, and God. A depersonalization of the traditional religious experience leaves many older churchgoers dissatisfied.

Another major trend in churches and church organizations in our time is an increasing degree of ecumenicalism. For instance, Protestant ecumenicalism has created mergers among sects, and even between different sects. These mergers threaten to dilute the theological and organizational purity of separate sects and belief systems with new syntheses. Catholic liturgies and dogma have been liberalized, and masses previously said only in Latin have begun to be presented in English. Moreover, priests now involve worshipers more through responsive singing and by facing the congregation while partaking of communion. In addition to changes within each tradition, there now is increasing contact, collaboration, and religious cooperation among Catholics, Protestants, and Jews.

Some worshipers, especially youthful ones, appear to desire a tighter and more intimate religious community, perhaps one with a more direct and personal relation to God. As a culture provides meaning to our lives and the world around us, new cultures and new religious forms can give new meaning. This struggle is often reflected in the rapid growth of "religious cults," of religious groups formed around a charismatic leader or a charismatic tradition of worship. Although the search for intimacy and community in the religious context and the attraction of an appealing charismatic figurehead has positive outcomes for some, it can also lead to alienation and tragic outcomes for others.

As large bureaucratic churches have expanded their membership and resources, a professional class of religious leaders has become free to concentrate on the relation between the church and society. And as the problems of society intrude into every walk of human life, certain sects and organizations have become highly involved in partisan and controversial political and social activities. Many churches now seem less concerned with smoking, drinking, personal immorality, and sin, and more attentive to social issues such as poverty, race relations, and local forms of injustice and inequality. Attention to the church's social mission, or social gospel, necessarily creates new debates within local groups of worshipers. It is one thing to expect every worshiper to share a common view of God and the church, but to expect agreement on political and social controversy stretches the concept of the religious community.

These problems of internal strife are compounded by the controversial activities in political and social matters of the National Council of Churches. The resultant tendency is for church spokesmanship to be located further and further away from the local churches and their own members. Like a family, the local church is built upon the premise that people can share some intimacy in their relation to others; in the case of the church, to God. But this intimacy is hard to share publicly with others with whom one disagrees firmly on matters that are moral as well as political, social, and economic, and that are argued in an institution that is morally focused. Members are seriously threatened by their debates with one another and with the relation between their religious ideals and their social commitments.

Police. Another institution concerned with cultural preservation, and with enforcing standards of behavior consistent with our dominant cultural values, is the police. Increases in criminal and deviant behavior alarm the public and threaten both a sense of order in society and a sense of cultural integrity. Available data indicate that reported crime is on the increase, particularly in urban centers and their suburban surroundings. Between 1958 and 1976 crime rates per 100,000 increased fourfold.

Although crimes against people have increased, crimes against property have increased at least as fast. The effects of crime and its attendant publicity create an aura of instability in the society, and threaten the basic assumption of orderliness and the regularity upon which people base their daily activities and society maintains its cohesiveness. Whether in the affluent suburbs, in the smaller farming or college towns, or the centers of major cities, people are more aware and afraid of the potential for immorality, crime, and violence in their communities. People who are afraid to walk the streets, afraid to help victims of car accidents or crime itself, or afraid of what their own or others' sons and daughters might do, live in a dangerous world.

The increasing incidence and notoriety of apparently immoral and criminal behavior, particularly among young people, leads many Americans to the conclusion that our cultural standards are crumbling and that the moral basis of our society is under severe strain. Whether attributed to the glut of affluence and boredom, to the pangs of poverty and desperation, or to the oppression of a society that is very age conscious, it is clear that youth are especially affected by social problems. The proportion of persons under twenty years of age who are imprisoned in correctional institutions increased from 7.4 per cent in 1950 to 9.5 per cent in 1960. Similarly, the number of inmates in juvenile training schools increased more rapidly than corresponding numbers for older offenders. Illegitimate teenage births and forms of sexual behavior considered by many as immoral is openly discussed as epidemic in many forums and institutions.

Obviously not all of this immoral behavior is criminal; and not all of this behavior is seen as immoral by all people. But a concern to caution and/or control youth, the carriers of our culture to another generation, runs deep on these issues. Some adults explain youth's apparent immorality and occasional criminality as a cautious hedonism, a demand to have all of life's pleasures at once, and without paying for any of them. One outcome of this view of youth, and the reaction to youth's apparent instances of immorality, is a general mistrust and distrust of young people. Seldom before in our society has there been such a wide gap of misunderstanding, mistrust and conflict between the generations. Abdication of moral responsibility as a function of parental indulgence, the permissiveness of youth workers, and societal corruption are seen by some as the major causes for this gap between the generations. Youth's perception of this mistrust, their search for rapid adult status, their ability to penetrate adult hypocrisy, and their search for a new and active identity are seen by others as causes. Still others attribute the conflict to adult attempts to control and constrain a population that is struggling to assert its own rights and power.

Emotional Needs. The cultural conflicts in the United States and the moral and mental strains of our contemporary life-styles are not only reflected in speculations or data about immorality and crime. Fear, anxiety, and uncertainty wreak an internal price as well. The number of mental patients in hospitals, outpatient psychiatric clinics, or institutions for the retarded almost doubled between 1940 and 1960, from 595,000 to 1,003,000. In 1960, some 60,000 institutions, clinics, and service centers were dealing with the needs and problems of this portion of the population. These data reflect and report only those who are ill enough to seek out help or be sought out by helpers; innumerable other Americans are also ill but are not seeking treatment.

One explanation for these increases in the number of institutions devoted to the care of the mentally ill is that much more national attention is now being paid to the care and prevention of mental illness. Emotional health is no longer only the concern of the schools and parents. Many business concerns now require applicants to take psychological tests and write psychiatric treatment into health and insurance policies.

The most potent way that current cultural and societal trends, conflicts, and values are incorporated into the individual's daily life pattern is through mechanisms of socialization. Bronfenbrenner suggests that those persons or families that have greatest access to societal channels and sources of information will incorporate these changes more rapidly [15]. Thus, families in urban areas with higher education, and of middle- and upper middle-class backgrounds, are most likely to lead the way in adopting new cultural values and behavior

Exercise 3—8. *Interpreting "Immediate Gratification"*

   This exercise can be done in small groups, with students defining issues and identifying concrete behaviors.

   One of the more consistent criticisms of today's youth is their alleged inability to delay gratification—in other words, to expect and demand immediate gratification and satisfaction for their wants and needs. This alleged style seems to fly in the face of some of our most revered, traditional values of discipline, futurism, and pay-as-you-go.

1. What behaviors can you identify that reflect these alleged trends?

2. What behaviors reflect the opposite or a countertrend?

3. What are some of your own values and behaviors on these dimensions?

modes. Of the many examples of major shifts in North American values throughout this century, we explore just the few that seem outstanding and that shed light on the dynamics of contemporary schooling. Many of them challenge the traditional ideals identified by Gabriel in prior chapters, and many help sharpen Spindler's notion of the conflicts between traditional and emergent values (p. 18).

   One of the major changes in values seems to be the movement away from individual glorification and reward for individual effort, to a priority upon cooperative and collaborative work in teams. In many areas of life, at work and at leisure, people undertake their activities in groups more often than they did in the past. This trend has also been reflected in some of the institutional changes that were previously discussed; in the decrease of small and individually owned farms, in the growth of bureaucracies, and in the increasing demand for white-collar and service occupations. As a result of these value shifts, new members of the society are being prepared for adult roles in different ways. Children are being taught to "get along" very early, and in both the family and the school more time and energy is being focused upon socializing youngsters to behave well with peers. In Reisman's terms [16], aspects of the North American character have shifted from inner direction to a greater concern for the feelings, reactions, and desires of others.

   With regard to child rearing, it appears that parents express their own feelings of love and affection more freely than in prior generations, and more often try to attend to the child's needs and demands. As a result, the child learns the friendly and rewarding character of social life. As parents pay more attention to the child's social needs and demands, they reinforce expectations of a social response and provide a model for the child's attentions to others.

Child rearing in the past was more often scheduled to fit the parents' comfort or established notions of what's right for baby. As Bronfenbrenner reports, "Over the past quarter of a century, American mothers at all social class levels have become more flexible with respect to infant feeding and weaning" [17]. By flexible, he means more willing to adjust to what seems to be the child's comfort and capabilities. In much the same vein, Miller and Swanson document how greater flexibility and permissiveness in child rearing can be connected to new demands for performance and functioning by adults in our great modern welfare bureaucracies [18]. To be attentive to one's own feelings, and to have others be attentive to them too, is part of the flexibility around the mother-child relationship in permissive child rearing. Similarly, in the adult interpersonal relationship, bureaucratic and service roles demand and expect more attention to the nuances of feelings between people.

The increasing prominence of the Freudian and psychiatric traditions of thought during this century reflect another cultural shift. The potential existence of an unconscious, the psychological as well as moral concept of guilt, and the reality of mental illness are all important parts of our national culture and thinking. People are concerned about such issues, and employ these explanatory constructs to their own and others' behaviors. Emotional health or fulfillment has become a public and important value for many contemporary Americans. But these very human concerns also raise serious questions and debates about contemporary moral responsibility. To what extent is criminality or deviance, for example, a moral problem or a psychological problem? Or is it a political problem? Should people be "treated" for their illness, "punished" for their transgressions; or "tolerated and rewarded" for the responses to oppression? If all, what should be the mix? To define the problem clearly in one of these categories is to decide unequivocally upon the personal and societal response that is most appropriate. Our public ambiguity about the unsettled character of this problem creates a great deal of value-conflict in the treatment of the mentally ill, the deviant, and the criminal. The conflict itself is a recent reflection of the increasing prominence of psychiatric ideology.

Values. Another recent cultural theme is the concern for changing values of society, particularly as opposed to earlier concerns with achievement. Since Americans have achieved greater material success than any other people in history, and are more affluent themselves than ever before, the maintenance of that comfortable and sometimes privileged position is an important value for many. We have documented how bureaucratic enterprises and governmental programs seek to insure and guarantee at least a subsistence income for everyone, and how these efforts support and encourage a concern for security. But the trend may also be reflected in a diminution of adventurous and risk-taking behavior. If most middle-class persons are assured relative material comfort unless they slip up somewhere, why should anyone take a chance of slipping up? The values of playing it safe or "cool," or conforming to the expected, are instrumental for many Americans who want to remain secure about their assured futures. And in an uncertain economy, playing it safe and looking out for self is one and the same.

In general, the weight of traditions is being lessened, not only by new traditions but also by the increasing dependence of society upon new and scientific information of all kinds for all kinds of tasks. The knowledge explosion and the growth of scientific and intellectual pursuits lessens the weight of tradition and intuition as epistemological styles of life. From establishing foreign policy to repairing a new automobile, from deciding whether to develop and market a new product to hiring new personnel, special kinds of knowledge and specialists in the collection and organization of knowledge are needed and called upon. The expectation that we can derive viable and utilitarian knowledge from scientific and intellectual pursuits, and that these pursuits are essential for personal success and societal advance, leads to new values regarding science and knowledge. These new values often view science and technology as ends in themselves rather than as the means by which human problems are resolved. Humanistic values are increasingly called into question as technology assumes the stature of an ideology.

Particularly at the societal level, the American culture is experiencing a new prominence of the conflicting nature of public values regarding order and justice. The essentially Hobbesian dilemma has been brought into new focus by increasing public attention to national and regional problems of injustice and inequality. For the past several decades, and particularly in the mid-1930s and late 1960s, reactions to legal, and economic injustice and inequality have come to threaten the very existence of public order. Protest movements, strikes, riots, large-scale apathy, illness, and despair threaten the orderly consummation of public life. Much public attention and effort is currently going into seeking a redress of these injustices and inequalities, with the assumption that such redress would best preserve social order and individual conscience. At the same time, and perhaps even more seriously, we have fortified the legal and military power of the police and other institutions concerned with maintaining order, per se (even at the cost of maintaining injustice and inequality as well).

IMPLICATIONS FOR THE SCHOOLS

Although we would expect societal changes, in general, to have an impact on all social institutions, it does not follow that these changes will demonstrate an equal effect on all parts of the social order. We anticipate not only differential rates of social change in different geographic regions and economic sectors but also differential impact on different institutions. Hence, given the tempo, profundity, and wide-ranging consequences of social change in our society, what is the impact of this change on the nature and organization of the schools?

There is little question that demographic transitions that have characterized the post-World War II period dramatically altered the population profiles of the cities and their immediate environs. Rural areas and small towns declined and suburbia and its satellites experienced unparalleled growth. Large cities became increasingly black and suburbs remained mainly white, except for the occasional migration to these areas by minorities whose educational background and economic status permitted them to break institutional color and ethnic barriers. The social compositon of the school populations changed accordingly, and, despite sometimes vigorous attempts by the federal courts and local groups to intervene, segregation by race and social class has remained a reality in school.

In this complex technological society, changing economic and social conditions mean that new skills are constantly in demand. As new skills are required, new kinds of training and occupational preparation must be designed and eventually institutionalized in the public schools. Thus, public schools have been called upon to produce men and women who are trained in the social, intellectual, and technical skills that will permit and encourage them to fit into changing societal patterns. In order to be prepared for more technologically advanced and complex occupational roles, more young Americans are going to school and staying in school longer. Table 3-11 depicts the magnitude of this trend.

As youngsters stay in school longer, they also delay the time when they enter the outside world and make their own way as independent citizens. But as we argued previously, the occupational system they will enter is no longer attuned to independent activity. Although school constitutes a longer moratorium between adolescence and adulthood, it may be a fitting moratorium, an appropriate training ground for the secure bureaucratic system that many young adults are likely to enter when they leave the schools.

As advanced training becomes more important, the percentage of students entering institutions of higher education also increases. This increasing percentage, in addition to the rise in numbers of young adults in the population at

Table 3-11. Percentage of Students at Various Age Levels in School, By Year [19]

	1900	1920	1940	1960	1970
5-17-year-olds	78.3	83.2	94.2	95.0	97.8
5-6-year-olds			43.0	80.7	89.5
7-13-year-olds			95.0	99.5	99.2
14-17-year-olds			79.3	90.3	94.1
18-19-year-olds			28.9	38.4	47.7
20-24-year-olds			6.6	13.1	21.5
25-34-year-olds				3.6	6.0

large, has led to a tremendous increase in the number of students enrolled at colleges across the nation. College enrollments doubled from 1920 to 1940, doubled again from 1940 to 1960, and have more than doubled since then; more than 7,100,000 young adults were attending college in 1970. The faculties of four-year colleges have increased even more rapidly, doubling every two decades since 1900, with a 1970 total of over 550,000.

As a result of the limited capacity of large four-year colleges, many new colleges and educational systems sprang up during the 1970s. High school graduates who do not go to a regular four-year college had many more opportunities for further education than in the past. The number of students enrolled in various junior and community colleges increased approximately 120 per cent during the decade from 1960—1970 alone. Similarly, vocational and technical school enrollees increased from 2,290,741 in 1940 to 3,768,149 in 1960, dramatically jumped to over 8,700,000 in 1970, and leaped further to 13,566,000 by 1974. However, the period from 1975—1979 has shown a decided downswing in college enrollment, which is generally attributable to three factors: (1) the end of the post-World War II baby boom; (2) reductions in funding higher education resulting, in part, from unsettling economic conditions and changing societal priorities; and (3) a growing public perception that postsecondary educational experiences do not lead necessarily to better jobs. There is also a strong feeling among educators at the college level that the infatuation of the American public with higher education has peaked and may be on the decline.

For many Americans, education does not cease when they leave elementary or secondary school, or even college. Vast numbers of Americans are now involved and enrolled in part-time courses and are acquiring credits in a variety of fields. Adult-education courses, both those oriented to leisure-time skills and to industrial or administrative retraining, have increased enormously. Many industrial enterprises now have their own schools for on-the-job training. It is not uncommon for a college graduate to go to work with a large industrial firm and find himself or herself spending the first one to three years in a training program in that firm, learning aspects of the business and specific technical skills that are relevant to that particular enterprise.

The data in Table 3—11 also make it obvious that the "drop-out" problem so widely touted in the 1960s is not prominent simply because more students are leaving school early now than did a generation or two ago; rather, the reverse is true. The problem is prominent because of the different meaning of "dropping out." Since so many more youngsters graduate from high school, and since education is such an important credential for occupational opportunity now, a dropout's chance for economic success are endangered and restricted to a greater degree than was previously the case. Moreover, dropouts are more highly concentrated in certain sectors of the society, typically those sectors that are already disadvantaged and oppressed by economic and educational forces. Over the long term, length or amounts of education are related rather directly to future occupational location and income. Whether that is because of the effects of education itself, or to the prior influence of family background, or to other factors is a matter of substantial debate.°

In addition to the increasing numbers of students attending schools of various sorts, the schools themselves are changing. For instance, the average school year is longer than it was in the past, and schools are generally larger, reflecting the societal trend toward increased organizational size. School districts are also larger, reflecting the consolidation of many smaller districts into larger ones. Table 3–12 depicts some of these changes in the size and organization of schools and school systems.

Schools grew in size because residential density became greater, because more expensive plants and facilities were needed and could be maintained economically only with a large clientele, and because more attention was being paid to special training programs for different developmental levels and learning tasks. An increase in plant size permits greater variety in the kinds of programs and facilities than can be made available in single or small school buildings or systems. As a result of these organizational expansions, students must learn to deal with an ever-expanding peer and adult learning culture, and a more complex organizational system. Obviously this is good preparation for adult roles in large, complex, and impersonal bureaucracies. The expanding size of most schools may work either against or for greater learning, depending

Table 3–12. Selected Statistics on the Size of Elementary and Secondary Schools and Districts [20]

	1920	1930	1940	1950	1960	1970
Number of one-teacher schools	190,700	149,300	113,600	59,700	20,200	1,800
Number of school districts			117,100	83,700	40,520	17,995
Number of public elementary and secondary schools		262,200	228,500*	152,800	117,600	91,200
Number of students per public school		102.1	113.3	164.3	306.9	500.2
Number of teachers per public school		3.3	3.8	6.0	9.1	23.4

*1940 data are not available; figure represents an average of 1938 and 1942 data.

° In Chapters 9 and 10 we discuss this association and alternative explanations or views of causality in some detail.

on how the resources of this school culture are organized and transmitted to the students.

As schools have increased in size, they also can serve multiple community needs; some schools often are open late in the afternoons and evenings to provide community services to adults and youngsters of all ages and social and economic strata.

Some noteworthy changes in the character of the domestic economy and in the kinds of skills their employees require have been discussed previously. In response, schools have attempted to train youngsters in these skills. Greater attention is being paid to the social sciences and to social skills at all levels of schooling. Part of this change is reflected in the kinds of subjects in the curriculum. In 1900, 56.3 per cent of all students in the public schools took algebra; by 1920 the percentage had dropped to 40.2 per cent and by 1960 it had dropped even further to 26.8 per cent. Similar statistics are available for geometry and other advanced forms of mathematical training. In 1900, 50.6 per cent of all students studied Latin; in 1920 that percentage had dropped to 37.3 per cent. and by 1949 it was down to 7.8 per cent. The same pattern holds for other foreign languages, although none dropped as far as Latin, since French, German, and Spanish were not as popular as Latin at the turn of the century. Students study less botany and physiology now, although there is a growing emphasis on the alternatives of biology and the general science courses. In addition, 92.9 per cent of the students studied English in 1949, compared with 76.7 per cent in 1922, and 38.5 per cent in 1900. Various industrial subjects and homemaking courses also are being taken by more students, as well as physical education, music, and art.

Thus, the curriculum of the schools has changed in a direction that stresses the socially utilitarian and personally expressive courses. There is less emphasis on rigorous learning of content that may never have any practical utility, but that presumably taught one how to discipline oneself. Since a greater percentage of students are going on to college, the assumption is made that those students will get such courses later, and the others do not need it anyway. The flurry of concern over Sputnik in the late 1950s created a new emphasis upon mathematics and science in the schools, but even here the concerns were more utilitarian than academic in the traditional sense.

In addition to these changes in the school curriculum, teachers, administrators, and ancillary school personnel are placing greater emphasis upon the students' mental health and emotional growth. Many schools have instituted emotional, as well as vocational counseling services, parent-teacher conferences, community development and at-home field services, and the like. More teachers are trained in the psychological and social sciences, and they concentrate more upon issues of student self-esteem, peer-group relations, and general social skills than in the past. Students are more often encouraged to bring the entire range of their daily experience into the classroom and to express their feelings and reactions in class. These concerns, coupled with the increasing sophistication of professional social scientists, have given rise to the expanding utilization of psychological testing and counseling in the public schools. The simplistic concern with the three "R's" is a thing of the past, and current debates focus upon the appropriate division between these standard intellectual skills and newly demanded social skills [21].

More money is being spent for education now than at any time in our history. In 1920, federal, state, and local expenditures per pupil amounted to $53.32; in 1940 the figure amounted to $88.09; in 1960 it had risen to $375.17, and in 1970 it reached $816.00. As these costs of education have increased, greater portions of school revenue have been derived from state sources and from agencies further from the local school community. Table 3—13 documents these trends.

These data fail to indicate that the federal agencies are taking over financial support or control of the schools, since on the contrary, the federal contribution still amounts to only a fairly minimal percentage of public sources.

Table 3–13. Per Cent of Public School Revenue By Source [22]

	1920	1940	1950	1960	1970
Local	83.2	68.0	57.3	56.5	52.1
State	16.5	30.3	39.8	39.1	39.9
Federal	.3	1.8	2.9	4.4	8.0

SUMMARY

At the beginning of this chapter it was argued that educational institutions—reflections of the social order—change as the society's basic nature changes. In some ways these changes may be profound; in other ways the reality may be quite similar and constant. Ogburn has estimated that the cultural lag between the initial thrust of social change and its ultimate impact on social institutions is likely to be great—often as much as a quarter of a century [23]. Because of the peculiar mythology and mysticism that surrounds schooling in the United States and the unique place of education in American culture, the time interval for basic changes in educational practice and policy can be even greater.

Forces that are external to the school's existence, and over which schools have little or no control, are paramount in determining the behavior of schools and defining their limitations as social systems. This is not to imply that all schools are destined to behave as amoebas, responding only to stimuli from the outside world. Many educators are planning how to anticipate these pressures for change and how to alter the school deliberately. The range of the responses of these educators varies enormously, and schools have different experiences of failure or success in coping with change and meeting the diverse and newly emerging needs of their clients. A key factor in school response is its ability to identify and take advantage of those external forces that are capable of providing support for internal changes that are deemed necessary.

However, in attempting to bring about fundamental changes in the structure and behavior of schools consonant with the changes occurring in the larger society, change-oriented educators find themselves locked on the horns of a perplexing dilemma. People's perceptions of the tempo of change and their acceptance of change are remarkably congruent insofar as the technological domain is concerned. However, in the nontechnological domain—that of values, ideology, attitudes, and expectations—resistance to change is likely to be greater. Innovations in the technological realm are seldom granted the lengthy debate and community input regarding their desirability as are those proposed changes in the curriculum that are linked to strongly held beliefs and social values. Computer systems that promise more efficient fiscal and record accountability, technically constructed teaching modules that promise greater levels of achievement in reading and mathematical skills, and commercially based testing programs that promise precise assessment as to the attainments of students find a wide degree of community and professional acceptance. However, attempts to institute new curricula in such areas as family planning, sex education, and human relations, which promise to provide students with a greater awareness and understanding of the salient social problems of society, are wracked by incessant debate and community polarization. The former represents a significant investment of the communities' economic resources; the latter commands little economic investment but a great deal of commitment to possible changes in areas of high sensitivity for the school.

The lag between more broadly based social changes and institutional responses to such alterations is perhaps best exemplified in the societal expectations regarding the outcomes of schooling. In the midst of changing values, divergent ideologies, and the general decline of the Protestant ethic as a dominant force in the American consciousness, individual achievement remains as one of the most savored and legitimate outcomes of formal education. The very tempo of change in American society, together with its quantitative and qualitative manifestations, suggests a wide range of schooling outcomes that have previously been accorded little or no serious consideration. We turn to a more thorough discussion of the outcomes of schooling and their support systems in North American society at a later juncture. In the next several chapters we examine a variety of internal school phenomena, educational factors, and mechanisms that intervene between the broader society and the outcomes of schooling.

4

COMMUNITY GROUPS AND COMMUNITY SCHOOLS

In the preceding chapters we suggested that schools are affected by the nature of national political and economic issues regarding war and peace, industrial concentration and reform, urban and metropolitan affairs, racial and sex role relations, and the like. On all these matters different groups of people have different values and policy goals. The fact that education is a public institution means that varied interest groups contend for influence over school matters. Eventually "the people" control their schools, but "the people" is divisible into numerous interest groups, each having its own priorities and concerns for educational outcomes and procedures.

One of the most important "people" contending for school influence is the professional educational establishment itself and its many national, regional, state, and local components. School governance and decisional procedures provide a great deal of latitude for the professional staff to exercise authority at the local level. In fact, many school decisions tend to be implemented as professional-internal issues, and are often arrived at without external-citizen input, provided that a "low profile" is maintained.

The school is located in a local municipal context, as well as in a regional and national arena. As public institutions, schools are very vulnerable and responsive to the nature of the state and the local civic community. Not only do different states have different administrative systems for their schools but they also have different financial resources, curricular concerns, and sometimes value priorities. In the local community, many different groups of citizens, of different races, ages, and economic classes, are affected by schools and are concerned about school policies and programs. As in most other matters, affluent and powerful community groups generally have more impact on schools than do poor groups. For instance, knowing who the mayor is, and what the political priorities of local elites are, is very important in understanding local school governance and educational decision making. The economic character of the local urban or rural community and the way the community decides to allocate its economic resources have a tremendous impact on the financial status of local schools. These factors also affect the nature of the local job market and the employment opportunities available for graduates, which, in turn, affects the vocational orientation of the school curriculum.

In this chapter we review the nature and degree of influence that various community groups have in the conduct of local schooling.

COMMUNITY ELITES AND COMMUNITY SCHOOLS

All communities contain local leadership groups that exert considerable influence on many aspects of the municipal scene. In some cases these leadership groups, which we can call the "civic elite," have and use direct and official influence, as when they are elected or appointed officials—mayors, city councilpersons, judges, or heads of major corporations. In other cases, however, these individuals operate indirectly and unofficially, merely as private citizens. Even as unofficial citizens they have access to people with official decision-making power because of their associations in powerful families, important clubs or informal networks, major political parties, neighborhood associations, and the like. Some examples of other roles involved in this civic elite might include leaders of banking institutions, influential lawyers, directors of municipal agencies, respected doctors, newspaper editors and publishers, and leaders in the private cultural or social sectors. These people may be aided, on various issues, by subelites, people who are important but generally not as powerful, such as clergy, directors of volunteer social and service organizations, small businesspeople, union leaders, and maybe even the superintendent of schools and his or her assistants.

These elites are usually representatives of centers of historic and contemporary power in the community. Although they may sometimes act as individuals, they usually act in terms of the institutions of which they are a part. For instance, if the president of a major local corporation or bank retires or changes jobs, he or she may or may not still be an active community leader, but the new bank president will almost automatically become part of this leadership group. Thus, membership in the civic elite is usually a function of powerful institutional and community position, rather than personality.

Community leadership groups, by definition, are involved in leadership of the local community's political-economic structure. How do they get to these positions of ascendancy? Essentially no leadership group of any coherence and power springs unaided and spontaneously from a single issue or single neighborhood. Rather, members of community leadership groups generally have a record of leadership in public or private service and prior experiences of power and control in the community, or in key community institutions. Sometimes, civic elites are part of, or are spun off of, larger regionally or nationally based centers of power and fortune. For instance, the Ford family has long played a role in the civic elite of Detroit, the Mellon and Carnegie families have done the same in Pittsburgh, and the Rockefeller family (families, to be sure) have played a similar role in New York. But not all local elites are linked to these truly national histories; many are based in the history of community growth and the role that key families and institutions played in the local arena.

Generally, those people who have a record of political, economic, and social power in a community have amassed considerable wealth. That wealth may have been a result of land ownership (real estate development), natural resource discovery and development (minerals, food, energy), production of consumer goods (steel, automobiles), the management of finances and financial institutions (banks), or a high level of sustained salesmanship (retailing, insurance). Civic elites with such records of community leadership are doubtless invested in the maintenance of their images of the community, and in preserving their roles of community service and leadership. Just what this investment looks like and how elites maintain or exercise their power are open to debate and disagreement.

According to some theories of political influence, all members of these leadership groups are likely to be linked together, and are likely to act together as a unified power bloc to make and implement policy for the city. Such a unified power bloc would link direct and indirect, official and unofficial, and political and economic forms of influence. These theories assume that all members of the civic elite are likely to agree with one another with regard to major community issues, and, therefore, can operate in consensus with one another. Or, they assume that even if these community elites differ, they have a common stake in preserving the power that enables them to act together and to override any internal differences. *If* such a unified power system *were* operating in a city, it would not identify itself as such: rather, it would couch its decisions in language such as "serving the common good" or "advancing everyone's welfare."

Other theories of city politics suggest that these leadership groups seldom (except in a large-scale municipal crisis) act together in a unified manner. Although they may all be powerful, and more powerful than most other community members, these elites do not always agree with one another. Leaders of economic institutions often conflict with leaders of political groups; some leadership groups may advocate higher taxes as a solution to urban problems, whereas others may advocate cutting the social service budget. According to these theories, there are multiple centers of elite power, and on any given issue different combinations of civic elites might band together to constitute a majority that is powerful enough to make decisions for all. But that is not the same as their acting as a unified system.

Although it is impossible to determine the shape of these theoretical differences in any given city, the possible conflicts among civic elites often stand out. For instance, conflicts between wealthy people often center on whether their money is new or old, a product of many generations of wealth or the result of speculations of a more recent vintage. And industrial leaders and clergy or heads of volunteer organizations may differ on issues of balance between environmental and economic priorities. Most importantly for our purposes, various members of the civic elite may differ over school policies and programs.

One feature of elite conflict regarding the control of schools is the struggle between those local elites advocating more control of education at the national level and those advocating more control of schools at the local level. The underlying issue is one's definition of "community." If the community is the locale, it is clear that the local political structure governing schools is most often dominated by the property-owning classes, including the social and business elite of the community [1]. These local elites typically favor stability and the maintenance of their preferred interests in the operation of schools. However, if the community is defined not as a locale but as a set of people with common interests or goals, we can review the actions of leaders from political groups, business, and the university. These people occasionally meet with others on a national level to share concerns about society-wide issues that affect education. Their concerns are likely to be broader than the local community

---

Exercise 4−1. *Identifying the Civic Elite Active in Education*

Start with the school board. Go to a meeting and ask the board members to identify others who have influence in this community on educational matters. Once others have been identified, ask them to suggest other people who are influential in educational matters.

Keep doing this until the cycle is completed, and no new names are suggested. It will not take very long! Then take these data and create maps and tables that indicate the following:

1. Who is connected to whom by the process of nomination? Is there more than one relatively distinct network? If there are several networks, what distinguishes them from one another?

2. Which people are most often nominated as being influential?

3. Of these "most influentials," what are their values and beliefs on educational matters and what interests do they represent or reflect?

---

and its stability, and their actions may challenge local educational values and elite formations.

Some poor or minority interest groups also have a great deal of power as they organize on a translocal basis and form national organizations and national communities of interest. Thus, the "pooled power" of the national NAACP may be far greater than the influence a minority group could have if it only operated on the local level. Minority interest groups operating at the national level may even form coalitions with national business elites to advocate educational changes that are very different from the priorities of their local counterparts. For example, Coleman points out that much of the energy for school change, such as technical innovation, desegregation, uniformity of standards, and the like comes from the national level [2]. We often see local resistance to national or centralized agendas for change partly on the basis of resistance to outside control, regardless of the specific issue. Thus, the concern for local community control of schools is one indication of a wider national trend of dissatisfaction with highly centralized and bureaucratic organizations. Some analysts identify this dissatisfaction as a worldwide trend [3], and others see it as a relatively unique or extreme trend in the United States [4].

Since the conduct of local educational operations is an important part of the life of a city, local civic elites can be expected to be concerned about the shape of school and school-related issues. As the children of most members of the community attend public schools, are prepared there for adult roles in the economic community, and are oriented there to the citizenship loyalties and responsibilities of public life, what happens in school is important to the community. If the entire civic elite is not directly concerned about school life, then those portions that constitute the elite of the socialization community are concerned. Chapter 1 identified the socialization community's elite as usually including leaders of the educational system, churches, police agencies, youth recreational and cultural activities, youth-serving businesses, and the like. These agencies and their leadership personnel all are involved directly or indirectly in monitoring or planning the way a city responds to the needs of its young.

Crain suggests that schooling issues, and especially issues involving school desegregation, highlight many important issues that the civic elites care about. He sees the key issues of concern to elites as maintaining:

Peace . . . or social order and stability.

Prosperity . . . or the stabilization of economic order required for profitable enterprise, including workers who can and will work and consumers who can and will buy.

Charity . . . or concern for the welfare for others who are less fortunate, and making sure no one is so alienated as to cause major threats to peace.

Progressive reform . . . or concern for gradual and planned change to make the city better, at least in ways that the civic elite can approve of and direct. [5]

In this context one would expect civic leadership groups to be interested in playing key educational roles—sometimes in overt public ways, sometimes behind the scenes. And it seems that this leadership often has a positive effect, at least on desegregation. A report from the United States Commission on Civil Rights indicates:

Of 411 districts where superintendents reported no serious disruptions on the issue of school desegregation, superintendents said:
   Business leaders were supportive or neutral in 65 per cent
   Political leaders were supportive or neutral in 67 per cent
   Religious leaders were supportive or neutral in 87 per cent

Of 95 districts which reported serious disruptions:
   Business leaders were supportive or neutral in 27 per cent
   Political leaders were supportive or neutral in 27 per cent
   Religious leaders were supportive or neutral in 66 per cent [6]

Many things may be occurring to affect both community peace and elite support of desegregation at the same time. Whatever the causal chain, it seems likely that strong elite support affects both school change and community peace or stability.

The federal judiciary also may be considered part of the local elite, particularly inasmuch as federal district court judges are often drawn from powerful groups in the local legal or political scene. These authorities are often caught between the conflicting demands of local and national politics, or between local cultural values and national constitutional priorities. In a number of communities federal and state judges have intervened in the educational life of the community, especially on matters of equality in financial support for schools, due process, or civil liberties. These include the management of student or teacher dissent, educator conflict over employment contracts and potential strikes, and racial desegregation in student bodies and faculty composition. In some cases in which local school boards have objected to, or resisted, specific judicial findings, the courts have ordered schools to change.

Community leadership groups typically are in direct contact with local boards of education, those official and formal bodies designated to represent the community and exercise authoritative control over schools. Mayors who appoint school boards generally check their alternatives with community leaders, and people who run for election seek the economic and political support of these groups. But this relationship to formal school authority is only one mechanism of elite penetration into the school organization. Board of education members and education leaders often become members of subelites as a function of their new leadership roles; thus they are integrated into an informal sociopolitical network.

Other informal political and social networks in the community facilitate meetings and associations between local community leaders and those responsible for directing schooling. Community agencies may create special events to discuss and explore local school policy. For example, in many cities, local foundations have planned retreats, seminars, and other events that bring together leadership groups who are concerned about schools. The New Detroit Committee in Detroit, the Cleveland Foundation in Cleveland, the Mott Foundation in Flint, the Danforth Foundation in St. Louis, and the Kettering Foundation in Dayton are examples of foundations with such agendas and programs. These foundations are concerned with the future of schools in the urban community. Most of them act on this interest by funding innovative programs and by gathering together people who have the interest and the power to make a difference in the local schooling situation. These activities provide an arena for elites to gather information, exchange perspectives, manage internal conflicts if they occur, and set at least a context for school policy.

Community leadership groups also play a potent role in managing the boundary mechanisms of the local school organization. Whether at the level of the entire system, or at the local school level, they are the major employers of the young, and they can help suggest new programs for increasing employment opportunities for young people coming out of school.

School leaders sometimes seek out collaboration with these elites rather than the reverse. For instance, when schools seek special millages and bonding funds they often establish working relations with leaders in the political and economic arenas of the local community. These "friends of the school" lead such financial campaigns, contribute to their funding, and help convince others to mount public relations efforts in order to approve special funds. Frequently, when millage campaigns and bonding efforts fail, special interest groups will launch fund-raising drives of their own in order to revive anemic programs that were

---

Exercise 4—2. *Relating Community Politics to School Policies*

Attend several meetings of the city or village council. Identify the major issues discussed, or the major community conflicts that surface at these meetings.

1. How might these issues affect, or be reflected in, educational systems?

2. To what extent are any of these issues discussed at school board meetings?

3. Consider the reverse: does the council ever directly discuss school problems and issues?

Exercise 4—3. *Connecting Community Conflicts and School Problems*

Read several months' editions of a local newspaper and identify the major conflicts present in the community, as reported therein: observe several school board meetings and talk with several members about the major problems facing schools. Try to understand the following:

1. To what extent do the media and board members agree on the community's major problems? How are these problems related to underlying issues of racial, sexual, and economic injustice or inequality?

2. How do community conflicts seem to penetrate the school and/or be reflected in school issues and vice versa?

important to them. In the midst of repeated millage failures and severe reductions in the academic curriculum, business leaders and other subelites have rallied financial support for athletic teams and other extracurricular activities that have historically been a source of community entertainment and pride.

In some cases, the children of these community leaders do not attend the local public schools; but instead, attend private schools, which are far removed from direct confrontation with heated school problems and the problems of school change. This is particularly true in the major urban centers where changing neighborhoods and demographic shifts have altered the racial composition of the public schools. Many community elites, especially whites, view these changes with alarm and harbor fears of racial conflict and declining educational quality in the schools. Because of those trepidations, many parochial as well as private schools have enjoyed a significant rise in enrollment. Elite members of minority groups sometimes respond similarly: it is not at all unusual to find powerful minority group leaders sending their children to private or parochial schools as well.

THE PROBLEM OF LOCAL CONTROL: COMMUNITIES, BOARDS, AND ADMINISTRATORS

Control of schools by a local community may, in reality, mean different things to different groups. One issue is who in the community is in control: we have addressed this issue, in part, by discussing the role of community elites. But another issue is what does control mean: here a major distinction must be made between community control of major decisions and community participation in giving advice, solving problems, or exerting influence on decisions made by others.

Debates about experimental programs for community control and/or decentralization of urban school districts have highlighted this distinction. For instance, Fantini suggests that most plans for school decentralization generally stress an administrative process in which clients are permitted and/or encouraged to have a say in the operation of the schools [7]. This "say" may range from giving advice to having an equal vote. Administrative decentralization, which may involve community participation, seldom is instituted by a local school or neighborhood, but is usually generated from higher levels in the school bureaucracy. System administrators retain authority over fundamental educational and political decisions, whereas the local community and clientele share partial responsibility for school operations.

Political decentralization, on the other hand, is the key to real community control. Here authority for the actual governance of the school is shifted to a local school board or consumer/client group. In order for the community to be the primary governing agency, it (or its board) must operate independently of any central board or centralized educational authority. This design also is called self-management, and has its parallels in industrial organizations in movements for worker control [8].

The Detroit public schools represent an example of administrative decentralization that, at the same time, publicly displays the rhetoric of political decentralization. Mandated by the state of Michigan to decentralize its school system, the Detroit board of education proceeded to "regionalize" the system. The board carved out eight regions, each with its own elected board of education and regional administrative staff. In effect, these regions could be considered analogous to eight separate urban school systems. There is little doubt that considerable community involvement and participation in school operations takes place under these arrangements, and there is substantial evidence that some community groups managed to marshal their forces with sufficient intensity and pressure to bring about changes in the various regions. However, not much real change in community control of the schools has occurred, since the central administrative board and its staff still retain major control over fundamental political and educational decisions. The allocation of resources and the key administrative appointments remain in the custody of the "central" authority.

The differences between these two models of decentralization are also reflected (or implemented) in the kinds of school decisions a given community controls. Several observers indicate that local control of staff, curriculum, taxation, and budget allocation are essential for any decentralization program to be meaningful [9]. Moreover, Gittell argues that the methods of selection of local board members, as well as their constituency links, are other essential procedural elements of viable community control efforts [10]. These criteria clearly support programs of political decentralization, and suggest that administrative decentralization may be a sham, offering only the appearance of community control.

Some observers point out the dangers of political decentralization: for instance, Moore and Johnston warn that concerns about democratic participation can "subsume all other issues" in organizational decision making; it can be expected to "exacerbate(s) conflicts, long kept implicit, or at least 'managed,' in local political systems" [11]. The "politicization" of schooling is also raised as a warning; it, too, represents a concern that political conflicts usually settled in private (among elites) will have to be settled in public, accompanied by great debates, side taking, and escalated conflict. These fears about the possible exacerbation of conflict undoubtedly account for some of the resistance to political decentralization and to some forms of community participation or control. In fact, the basic conflict in the great majority of these cases is precisely over the issue of control itself. Community control debates were, and continue to be, classic power struggles between previously decisive civic elites and newly powerful community groups. As these struggles take shape, they often involve, at one point or another, many organized segments of the community. Local schools thus serve as the battleground for the real struggle over social control of education and other municipal services.

The concern for increased community participation, and even control, is especially strong among members of minority groups. These groups historically have been excluded from those civic elites that have meaningful influence in the schools, so it makes a great deal of sense for them to be most vigorous in their pursuit of new arrangements. Roughly the same concern has been expressed recently by representatives of poor or working-class whites. In a more critical vein, some see the desires of these groups for influence as a natural outcome of the ruling white elite's inability to deliver a high-quality educational program to urban poor people and minorities [12]. The argument often is made by community groups that professional educators and white community elites have failed to consider the true social and psychological needs of blacks and other minorities in the creation of an educational program.

Some analysts who have looked at the community control movement in education, as well as other areas of life, believe that community "self-management" under current political-economic conditions is unrealistic and, therefore, dangerous to its advocates. They maintain that untrained community groups often try to administer organizations without the necessary political and economic support from their mobilized constituencies and coalitions. As a result, they hold an empty organization, which is unable to control and hold accountable the actual decision makers. Many of the actual decision makers, those who determine the school or school system's policies and resources, are outside of, and invulnerable to, community attack and control [13]. As another example, James and Levin indicate that local boards will have a hard time financing the kinds of education they deem necessary in the context of severe municipal financial distress [14]. Even if the local boards did have taxing

Table 4—1. Arguments Raised over Community Control [15]

Arguments for, by the Proponents	Responses by the Critics
1. Community control will make teachers and administrators accountable to the people.	a. It will lead to vigilante groups (as in New York City and Detroit). b. It is questionable whether parents and community representatives can objectively assess the performance or the output of teachers and administrators, since the experts in the field of testing and evaluation find it difficult if not impossible to evaluate teachers and administrators with reliability and validity. c. Many community representatives have already reached the conclusion that the professional educators are the only ones responsible for students' failure; other influences such as the home, community, and students themselves must be taken into consideration.
2. Community control will lead to educational innovation.	a. The local school boards will concentrate their interest on politics and issues of self-interest and ideology. b. Innovation is based on pilot testing and evaluating programs; community control has not been sufficiently pilot-tested or evaluated.
3. Community control will lead to greater parental and public participation.	a. The majority of people, including parents, are indifferent to educational issues—or at least do not participate in school meetings or vote on educational issues. b. Politically oriented groups, ranging from black militants to white segregationists, will gain control of the schools for their own purposes (as in New York City and Detroit).
4. Community control will enable local school boards to hire qualified principals and superintendents (on the	a. This will lead to increased ethnic and racial favoritism in appointing and promoting administrators (a pat-

Table 4−1 (continued).

Arguments for, by the Proponents	Responses by the Critics
basis of their ability to relate to ghetto children and serve as models).	tern which is already evident in many city school systems).
5. Community control will enhance flexible hiring and promotional practices and will attract teachers and administrators with more initiative and imagination.	a. Flexibility connotes that competitive performance, experience, and objective tests can be replaced by patronage, nepotism, and pork barrels. b. Initiative and imagination are difficult to define; they mean different things to different people and, to some, euphemisms for reverse discrimination.
6. Community control will raise student achievement.	a. There is no proof that this will happen; we should pilot-test this assumption before we make massive changes. Achievement may remain the same or even decline with community control. b. There is no evidence that black teachers and administrators can do a better job in raising achievement among black students, as indicated by school systems in which there is a majority of black teachers and administrators (e.g., black schools in the South and in Washington, Philadelphia, St. Louis, Baltimore, Gary, and Newark).
7. Community control will promote self-government by blacks as well as by other minorities.	a.. This is a return to the myth of "separate but equal." b. This will foster white ethnicity and backlash. c. Inherent in this concept is the surrender of the suburbs to white domination while blacks obtain control of the ghetto—a ghetto depleted in finances and saddled with decay, drug addiction, violence, crime, traffic congestion, pollution, population density, etc.

Table 4–1 (continued).

Arguments for, by the Proponents	Responses by the Critics
8. Community control will lead to educational reform.	a. This thwarts future possibilities for school desegregation, which should be the immediate goal for educational reform. b. Despite the present shortcomings of the federal government, it is recognized as the only institution with the strength, expertise, and financial resources to reform schools and society. (In the past, virtually all major social reform—in education, welfare, housing, health services—has been initiated by the federal government.)

power, the questions remain of whether there are sufficient local resources to be taxed, and whether the community control movement would thus divert attention from other broad reforms in educational and municipal financing.

What happens as a community group tries to manage a school, factory, or mental health center? Often the group loses its direction and becomes absorbed in the same bureaucratic procedures its members objected to. Under present conditions, some observers argue that the realistic role of local community groups should be to monitor and evaluate the service-providing organization, and to confront the external political limitations imposed on the service organization with which it is dealing [16]. Thus, local groups would avoid the encumbrance of daily managment problems, but would still maintain major influence of policy making and evaluation activities—clear routes to holding the higher level elites accountable.

The School Board

The official governing body of local school systems is the board of education. In 90 per cent of the educational systems across the nation, the local school board is elected by the local community. In the remaining 10 per cent, school boards are appointed, usually by the local mayor or city council. Although the school board officially represents the entire community in setting and monitoring overall school policies and programs, it usually is composed of a fairly narrow range of individuals representing a selected portion of the total community.

The initial study of the social composition of American school boards was done by George S. Counts in 1927 [17]. The study was based on the assumption that occupation is central to the life of the ordinary citizen and is therefore instrumental in shaping one's values and beliefs. Collecting data on the occupations of board members is thus an indicator of the breadth and variety of interests and points of view represented on boards. Table 4—2 portrays the results of Count's classic research [18]. Note that with the exceptions of district and county boards which are understandably dominated by agricultural service occupations, business and professional people comprise 60 per cent of all boards. There are very few representatives of clerical and manual workers.

A more recent report by the National School Boards Association indicates just how skewed these representations still are [19]. In its study of the boards of America's fifty-one largest school systems, the association collected the data on board membership reflected in Table 4—3 [20].

The demographic characteristics of these boards are changing in the direction of greater alignment with the characteristics of local taxpayers and students: still, their degree of representation of the overall community remains an issue.

Table 4—2. Occupations of Male Members of Public Boards of Education in the United States (Facts Given in Percentages) [18]

Occupation	District Boards	County Boards	City Boards	State Boards	College and University Boards	All Boards
Proprietors	2	18	32	18	33	21
Professional service	1	22	30	53	41	29
Managerial service	*	5	14	2	5	5
Commercial service	*	3	6	*	1	2
Clerical service	*	2	6	1	*	2
Manual labor	1	4	8	*	0	3
Agricultural service	95	44	2	2	9	30
Ex officio	0	2	*	24	11	7
Unknown	1	0	2	0	0	1
Total	100	100	100	100	100	100
Number of members	2,545	299	2,943	252	351	6,390
Number of boards	974	58	509	39	42	1,622

*At least one member was reported for this occupation, but the representation is too small to show in this table.

Table 4—3. National School Board Membership, Fifty-One
Largest U.S. School Systems [20]

	1973—74 Per Cent	1964—65 Per Cent
Sex		
Male	69	78
Female	30	22
Race		
Caucasian	71	87
Black	22	13
Spanish surname	4	—
Other	2	—
Occupation		
Professional	9	8
Business and white collar	32	36
Lawyer	12	21
Housewife	18	16
College educator	16	3
Clergy	4	—
Union officer	1	0.9
Retired	5	2
Other	3	6

In 1974, for instance, well over 50 per cent of all the students in these urban school systems were racial minorities, whereas only 26 per cent of the board members were. The large numbers of working-class taxpayers and students are also not represented in any notable degree on these boards.

Even in areas of the United States where relatively large populations of ethnic and minority groups reside, state boards of education continue to reflect an unrepresentative membership. Table 4—4 [21] portrays this imbalance in the Southwestern corridor of the United States.

The social background characteristics and resultant attitudinal priorities of most school board members generally mark them as representatives of economic and political elites. As such, they can be expected to make policy that more nearly meets the needs and interests of the relatively advantaged or privileged groups than of the working-class and poorer groups or of racial minorities. There are times, however, when these same elites elect to champion the causes of the poor and the less fortunate. Some of these reversals in expected social policy may be attributed to purely altruistic motives. As often, the special interests and status of the elites are subtly at stake. Impending crisis, potential turmoil, racial disturbances in the community, and the like may pose a threat to

Table 4—4. Mexican American Representation on State
Boards of Education [21]

	Number of Mexican American Board Members	Total Number of Board Members	Percentage of Total Board Members that is Mexican American	Percentage of Total Student Population that is Mexican American
Arizona	0	9	0	19.5
California	1	10	10	16.5
Colorado	0	5	0	13.7
New Mexico	3	10	30	39.4
Texas	2	24	8.3	22.6

the peace and stability of the community and thus serve to alter the educational priorities of the elites.

School superintendents officially are appointed or selected by the school board, and are accountable to the board for managing the professional system of educators. As professional educators as well, most superintendents stand at the top of that professional educational group. They have loyalties to that group, to the board, and to their own values and beliefs regarding education, young people, and the like. Most superintendents establish their own linkages to various constituencies or interest groups in the community. Through this mechanism they build the multiple loyalties that permit effective work with the entire community, and that may permit them an extra measure of power and independence in dealing with the board.

The conflict of interests in the local community often is so intense that boards sometimes take the decision-making initiative away from all but the most active and outspoken superintendents. Superintendents who do not wish to get actively involved in mediating or advocating major school disputes often get out of the way and let the boards pick up the responsibility. The superintendent, then, can retreat to a more technical executive role, one offering wisdom about educational planning to implement the political decisions the board makes.

Crain indicates that most superintendents he studied initially resisted the efforts of civil rights groups and judicial litigants to act on a desegregation agenda [22]. The reasons for this posture rested partly in a universalist philosophy of human relations, a position that articulated color blindness as the appropriate racial stance. Other superintendents stressed the educational executive role noted previously, and tried to stay out of the thick of this political conflict. Some superintendents also adopted a defensive stance with regard to any criticisms of educational quality or the equality of service delivery for

Exercise 4—4. *Understanding Who Do School Boards Represent*

This research/inquiry project can be done by students individually or in groups, in one or several school districts.

Identify a local school board or the one in the community from which you came and discover who are the members. By observation, examination of records, and personal conversations with board members (and/or others), determine:

1. What is the racial, sexual, educational, and occupational characteristics, and residential locations of the board members? How does their distribution on these characteristics compare to overall community composition?

2. Who do the school board members appear to listen to (who influences them) in formulating policy and program decisions? What local associations, clubs, or neighborhood or friendship networks are they part of?

3. On matters affecting different interest groups (racial, professional educators, age, educationally "gifted," "disadvantaged"), what interests do the board members appear to favor?

---

which they were responsible. Any criticism related to issues of racism and preferred treatment may rouse feelings of insecurity and defensiveness, and thus retreat, on the part of superintendents. As a link to various and often conflicting interest groups, with few clear criteria for success, superintendents may not be willing to move visibly and vigorously on issues that do not fit familiar educational criteria and assessment paradigms.

The board may not be in a much better position, at least as the board members see the situation. Since the members of the board are elected to represent a variety of interest groups and community coalitions, they are responsible to conflicting groups in the community. As members of the local decision-making unit they are often the target of vigorous presentations by a wide variety of interest groups. As such, the board is constantly under attack and pressure from these external community groups, and also is frequently under considerable pressure from internal school groups, from teachers and teacher unions or associations, from bus driver and custodial unions, and from superintendents and their staffs.

When they had to act in desegregation controversies, superintendents and school boards sometimes responded in ways that escalated the possibilities of local controversy and discord. For instance, according to a report of the United States Commission on Civil Rights:

Exercise 4—5. *Understanding What Do School Boards Do?*

This research/inquiry project can be done by students individually or in small groups, in one or several school districts.

Attend several meetings of a local school board. After your first visit make up a list of things that go on that you can observe more systematically. For instance, you might observe the kinds of issues discussed, the degree to which board members seek to lead or follow public opinion, the ways in which people address one another, the degree to which the general public attends or participates in meetings, the major lines of disagreement within the board, and board-staff interaction.

Take notes and discuss your findings in class. Consider how your observations connect to the analysis of board operations presented in this chapter.

Ordered by the Federal district court to eliminate every form of racial segregation in the public schools of Boston, The Boston School Committee has pursued a deliberate policy of minimal compliance. The effect of the Boston School Committee's statements, policy and inaction was to foster within the community outright resistance to school desegregation. [23]

Moreover, in Pontiac, Michigan, community leaders identified some of the ways in which their board and superintendent contributed to strife and violence in that city's desegregation efforts:

The school board knew it was in the wrong, but refused to admit it, even after all court appeals had been exhausted; the board misled the public. The community would have been more cooperative if the superintendent had said, "we are desegregating because it is the right thing to do for the children." [24]

On the other hand, the relevance of positive action by leaders of the school system also has been acknowledged in various communities. The Community Relations Committee of Charlotte-Mecklenburg, noted, in 1972, that:

Our first and firmest attention should be turned away from discontent with courts . . . to our schools and the way in which they educate our children. The Committee believes that leadership from the Board of Education and from others—elected and private civic leaders alike—will cause this community's parents to reaffirm their belief in good education. [25]

One of the strong currents running through the executive and policymaking channels of education alludes to the feeling that boards of education are generally in "no-win" situations—that is, in the case of the many controversial and often critical decisions in which they are embroiled, they never seem to please anyone. The political nature of crucial educational issues implies a political response on the part of board members. Thus, they find themselves confronted by an imposing array of constituencies, many of whom are vigorously pursuing their own interests and concerns. When board members decide to take "moral" stands on selected issues or are compelled to make or comply with unpopular decisions, they are frequently subjected to harassment, public indignities, and even recall petitions. Issues such as sex education, finances, and "busing," to list only a few, are examples of the more volatile ones. Complete boards of education have occasionally been recalled because of vigorous stands they have taken on such issues.

PROFESSIONAL AUTONOMY AND REACTIONS TO THE COMMUNITY

The way educational leaders respond to issues of community participation and control has major implications for the structure of professional roles in the schools. Fantini points out that the nature of the American educational system involves the delegation of control to professionals who are expected to be accountable back to the public [26]. The failure of this accountability system between professionals and the public leads to community disaffection and demands for change. When educators and elite groups fail to be accountable to the minority and poor publics, new community control demands spring from the urban minorities. Thus, Gittell argues that community control involves a shift in the balance of power away from the educational professionals and toward the community [27]; it also shifts power away from elites to indigenous community groups.

One result of this challenge is the professionals' efforts to "blame" the victims, the community members and their progeny, for the failure to educate minority and poor youngsters. Miller suggests that this is a natural development, in that elites will try to turn the community-institutional conflict into one between different community groups or between community groups and low-level or front-line workers [28]. One result is the perception that community control is an attempt at "busting" teachers' unions. Grant indicates that in Detroit it took the efforts of State Senator (now mayor) Coleman Young, a black, to put together a pro-union, pro-community control package that passed the state legislature [29]. The failure of such municipal or high-level educational leadership in New York City helped maintain the focus of conflict between white teachers and Third World community groups.

As the chief local professional agent, the school principal is required to play a key role in preserving the professional integrity and security of the organization. Becker notes that the principal "is expected to provide a defense against parental interference and student revolt, by protecting the teacher whenever her authority is challenged" [30]. In this respect, teachers prefer their principals to have power, and to better serve the interests of school personnel by buffering them from the community.

As a result of these community-school dynamics, educators typically have felt isolated from, and vulnerable to, the parents of the students they teach. The professional status of educators often helps them believe that they can do their jobs without collaborating with parents. Parents are expected to "cooperate" with the school, but educators may not reciprocate. As parents become active, airing their discontent with teachers and schools, they pose a threat to some educators and a challenge to others.

In the normal course of school affairs, educators have very little contact with community members. Since many educators in urban schools live outside the school neighborhood, they have no sustained relation to the community they serve. The academic isolation of the curriculum also maintains walls of separateness that keep teachers and students in school, not in the community. The isolation of educators from parental and community views results in substantial distrust and often stereotypic views of the community. Table 4—5 reports on some examples of teachers' views of community interest in, and support of their work from seven schools in seven different communities° [31].

In schools A, C, and E the faculties are divided quite evenly, with substantial internal disagreement. Majority staff opinion is most clear in schools B and D, even though these opinions are in opposite directions. Teachers in the most affluent school (B) report the strongest feeling of both understanding and support from the community.

When these views of the community are combined with traditional professional perspectives and prerogatives, it becomes evident why substantial numbers of educators oppose giving communities more influence in running the schools. Aside from the threat to their own freedom and status, teachers suggest that such procedures would not better serve the needs of pupils. Rossi et al. report that 58 per cent of the white educators and 45 per cent of the black educators they interviewed expressed such negative views of community control programs [32].

Educators generally feel especially vulnerable to groups of black or Hispanic

---

° These data, and following data from Chesler, are from a national action-research project involving seven high schools experiencing conflict and tension. Data was collected from representative samples of approximately 800 students and 410 teachers altogether, as well as from the principals of these schools. In addition to research and data collection efforts, various intervention activities were conducted in these schools in order to alter the structure of student, staff and school-community relations. Numerous quotes taken from workshops, confrontation meetings, public events, and private interviews are presented throughout Chapters 4, 5, 6, and 7. Although these data were collected at times and in schools experiencing occasional disorder, they appear to effectively highlight fundamental problems and processes in schools. Later research by this team and by other investigators of American secondary schools, continue to confirm these outlines. Perhaps, indeed, the subtle outlines of these schools were thrown into bold relief by their experiences with challenge and disorder.

Table 4—5. Per Cent of Teachers' Viewing Community
Appreciation and Support of "Good Education" [31]

	A	B	C	D	E	F	G
				School			
Most of the people in this community understand and appreciate a good education.							
Agree	50	75	49	17	50	39	34
Disagree	49	22	47	77	50	53	45
This community is willing to support a good program of education.							
Agree	51	62	40	21	57	51	68
Disagree	45	34	59	68	43	41	32

parents and citizens who seek to create change through the application of direct pressure. Leaders within the minority community have pressed school administrators to include ethnic group history, better vocational programs, and improved basic skill education. Direct attempts to counter staff racism often have included demands to alter traditional teaching practices and to discipline or terminate educators who were guilty of overt racism. Some principals argue that members of the black-Hispanic community help students to organize protests and to support student dissent and confrontation. For instance, when community groups supported the rights of students to wear Afros in the early 1970s, it was difficult to see the issue as simply students versus adult authority—it became instead a political issue among adult groups of black parents and white educators. When community groups are rebuffed in their attempts to implement influence, students may take dramatic actions to make the authorities listen. The adults possess legitimacy; students are willing to possess and express disruptive power. When these twin sources of influence are tied together, they constitute a very potent force upon school administrators.

But it is not true that all blacks, Hispanic and other community groups support the demands of students. When there appears to be conflict among groups within the minority community, administrators tend to be especially confused and hesitant to take action. Many school administrators feel particularly unable to tell who is the "voice of the community."

The minority community is not the only client population for public schools, and educators historically have been much more concerned with the response of the white community to school policies and programs. Since the white community is more affluent, administrators fear this sector's ability to strike back at the schools through the rejection of tax levies and subsequent financial cutbacks. In several cities, the introduction of minority history programs has stirred white resentment, and efforts to hire more minority educators resulted in charges of favoritism or "reverse discrimination." Plans to build racially desegregated schools in white areas have raised previously dormant opposition, and negotiated settlements with protesting youngsters, white or black but especially black, have brought cries of "permissiveness" and "anarchy."

One of the forces complicating the responses of school administrators to change seems to be the character of some state educational codes and departmental policies. Some state codes and a number of colleges and accrediting agencies do not permit much local latitude in curriculum design. By giving high evaluations to programs that help prepare students for college, but low evaluations to programs which help students prepare for work, these agencies help make secondary school less relevant for substantial portions of the population.

One of the ways in which demands for community-school collaboration affect administrators is in the request for increased public access to educational leaders. The school superintendent must attend important community events, must demonstrate his or her concern for the community's welfare, and must constantly be on call to make immediate decisions. Some administrators believe that the demand for visibility is a burden which takes up too much of their time, and the effort to share some of these responsibilities results in widespread resistance and resentment at their absence. Pressure groups may resist meeting with subordinates because they do not believe that the subordinates have sufficient power to make decisions. As one administrator reported:

> One of the big complaints the students around the city had with me, with all the principals was, "You don't communicate." One of the problems I keep running into is, "I wanna see the head man." All of a sudden, "Where's the principal." Then the student council meetings; you go to the student council meeting today and your assistant goes next week; "The principal's hiding, he doesn't want to come to the student council meetings and face us." So you don't go to all the community meetings. "Where in the hell is the principal? He doesn't want to come out and meet the community."

Many administrators are just not trained for these roles in community leadership.

Administrators also report that actions of the news media pressure them severely. The media increase public awareness of issues and aid the mobilization of pressure groups by the pattern of general coverage and by taking direct stands on some issues. The degree to which administrators believe that this is a pressure for or against them varies considerably. Some administrators find the news media very useful because the media help to mobilize pressure for new programs that the administrators support. Others find the pressure nearly intolerable, especially when they believe that what was publicized was "inflammatory and false" information.

THE NONSCHOOL SOCIALIZATION COMMUNITY

As indicated previously, the school is not an isolated organization. It does not set its own goals; neither does it have the mandate to implement these goals independently of the community. The operational structure of the school is constantly besieged by external forces, all attempting to influence the cultural transmission process in their own ways. Accordingly, what occurs in the daily management of the school system is affected by the values and operations of other organizations with which it interacts; that is, families, community agencies, and the like. Moreover, although the school is an institution designated by society for the formal education and control of the young, it is not the only institution contributing to that mission.

As a mass and public system, the school is obligated to supplement the socialization process occurring in the family. The school is secular where the family may be sacred, assimilationist where the family may prefer separatism or legitimate difference. Sometimes the school and the family stress the same norms or goals and values; at other times they conflict. Given the nature of these differences and the power to make school decisions, the school and the family are most likely to be alike when the students are white and middle or upper middle class. In other cases we may expect conflict between the home and the school or between the school and the community or neighborhood. On occasion, the parties to the conflict may be students and the school, with the parents still in the background; on other occasions the parents may be in the forefront of the conflict.

The local community itself is a broad arena for the socialization of the young. Community values and beliefs are likely to be passed on to young people through a variety of agencies, including local media, entertainment and recreational opportunities, churches, police and courts, youth clubs, and YM-YWCA's and YM-YWHA's. All of these agencies seek to train youth to believe in, and to act in accordance with, the cultures of the local community. The business of these agencies is not instruction; they are not educational in any strict sense of the word. However, these agencies do engage in cultural training and socialization. They also help plan the politicization of the young in directions that are sanctioned by the local community. Figure 4−1 illustrates

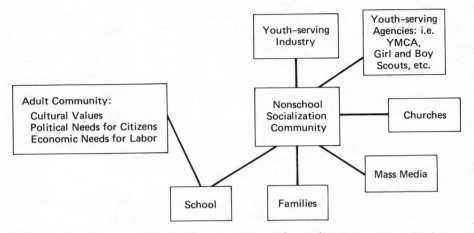

FIGURE 4—1. Diagram of school community and socialization community interface.

the constellation of these nonschool socializing systems, and their interaction
with other aspects of the adult community to impact on schools.

Some schools seem to be in a constant state of warfare with these community
socializers, primarily because of the nature of the lessons or values being taught.
In some instances, for example, youth agencies have so opened the eyes of
young people to alternative futures that the young have become disaffected
from the schools and taken their schools to task on the inadequacy of their
education. In other instances, outside groups have espoused particularistic sets
of values that run counter to those the school tries to maintain as the arbiter of
a general consensus.

THE SCHOOL AS A COMMUNITY
ORGANIZING CENTER

The school's inability to cope with particular cultural values and beliefs held
by community groups and to actively involve parents and youth in the
educational process is partly attributable to the narrow conception of the school
often shared by community groups and professionals alike. The tendency is not
to view the school as a potential important cultural and political force but
rather as an institution concerned primarily with educational instruction and its
own internal stability. The notion that schools are community organizations,
fraught with cultural conflict, seems anathema to most people. Thus schools are
relegated to passive political and cultural roles, and fail to broaden the cultural
base of community life or to engage in the political issues that make education
important for young people. As a consequence, the school often appears isolated

from community life, and its consumers also become detached from their most import laboratory for learning and cultural action.

Foremost among the educational ideas that have been advanced to prevent the isolation of the school from its local community is the community school concept. An idea that found receptive soil in the 1930s, the concept of the community school has proven particularly successful in rural communities and small towns. The adaptation of the community school to urban areas has been slow, but has achieved some successes. In particular, the Greater Cities Project in Detroit created networks of community schools throughout the city, and represented one of the first major urban efforts at adapting this concept to the inner city.

One of the classic descriptions of the community school concept is credited to Elsie Ripley Clapp, a pioneer in the community school movement in the United States:

> First of all, it meets as best it can, and with everyone's help, the urgent needs of the people, for it holds that everything that affects the welfare of the children and their families is its concern. Where does school end and life outside begin? There is no distinction between them. A community school is a used place, a place used freely and informally for all the needs of living and learning. It is, in effect, the place where learning and living converge. [33]

The idea of the school as an integrating force in community life was compelling to progressive minds. Thus, new approaches were hatched. For example, in Michigan grants from the W. K. Kellogg Foundation helped to establish the "Community School Service Program" and finance several experiments in "improving community living" through the services of the public school. The concept of the community school assumes that the local community is the educational starting point and that it should create some of the following outcomes:

1. Improve the quality of life in the community.

2. Use the community as a laboratory for learning.

3. Organize the curriculum around the fundamental processes and problems of living.

4. Include parents, students, and community representatives in program planning and policy making.

5. Make the school plant a community center for all age groups.

6. Assist in the coordination of community educational activities.

7. Encourage and develop networks of Adult Education programs throughout the Community.

8. Practice and promote democratic behavior in all human relationships.

9. Provide an educational forum for public participation in discussing and debating the salient political, social, and educational issues that transcend the local scene.

10. Establish an expansive political and economic base for the interpretation and support of public education. [34]

In order for these outcomes to be realized, the marshaling of all the community resources together with the strategic use of their respective networks is indispensable. This approach clearly suggests that a school can and should be more than a center for educational instruction; it can be a cultural and political organizing center for the community. The school building and its cultural role can be broadened as it becomes an institution that serves many of the local community's needs. Wilcox and Hamilton especially stress these aspects of the school in minority communities, including its uses as a recreational center, a site for meetings on local community governance, an adult education center, a day care center, and so on [35]. These uses can help schools overcome patterns of age segregation in educational agencies and patterns of separation between the school and its consumers.

The extension of the school's resources to the community provides educational opportunities and experiences to adult citizens as well as to youth. It also creates a new service relation and partnership with community members that often calls for increased citizen participation in educational decision making. The school board of a large district is far too removed from the local school or neighborhood to oversee a broadly based program aimed at many different age groups. Newer arrangements often take the form of citizens advisory councils, community councils, school councils, and, in some cases, politically active community organizations. It is important to note that in all instances, the process of citizen participation is enhanced.

Figure 4—2 is illustrative of the ethnic, racial, economic, and geographic representation that has comprised the makeup of some community school councils [36]. The purpose of a representative council is to provide access to the school for a full variety of local community groups. Moreover, these councils serve as vehicles to bring together many of the community's human and financial resources so as to improve the quality of education and living for everyone concerned. Unlike the officially elected (or appointed) school board, local councils lack formal authority to make public policy, but they can help to govern local educational innovations and new school-community programs. In addition, local councils can help design educational programs that address the needs of people who do not have to be in school, adults who are voluntarily attending educational efforts that truly speak to their individual and community needs.

FIGURE 4—2. Who should be on your council.

SUMMARY

This chapter addresses the problems that a public institution such as the school faces when varied interests and pressure groups contend for influence over its policies and programs. A particular focus is placed on the role of elites and the inordinate influence they wield over the conduct of local schooling. Social control over education is linked to the local community's political-economic structure, and this in turn helps to define membership in the "civic elite."

Examining the social composition of boards of education generally proves to be a fairly accurate barometer of the nature and extent of elite influence over the educational system. The historical record indicates that business and professional groups have dominated the membership of local school boards. Recent studies of the social composition of boards of education confirm the dominance of these two elite groups with respect to their influence in educational decision making. As noted, the extent of elite influence frequently goes beyond the local and state levels to the national scene. Local elites typically share common goals and concerns with other leaders from business, university, and government sources who represent powerful economic and political constituencies. Whereas there may be conflict among local elites as to the exact locus of control of education (national, local, and state), the need to maintain elite control is shared at all levels. Unless school issues arise that threaten the stability of community life, the maintenance of elite control is subtly managed without much public attention.

It is not unusual to discover that the civic elites are not directly concerned about school life. Disturbed over issues such as desegregation and by conflict and disruption in the schools, they find private and parochial schools more to their satisfaction. Whereas some community leaders may withdraw from active participation in school affairs, however, the elite of the socialization system—namely, church leaders, educational leaders, officers in police agencies, leaders of youth recreational and cultural activities, and the like—remain actively involved in seeing that their agencies and constituencies respond to the needs of school youth, or at least to their version of these needs.

One of the more pervasive issues in the local educational scene is the nearly universal concern over the patterns of control and centralized school authority. Citizen response to this trend has been to advocate more community control over the schools and decentralization of the educational decision-making process. A great variety of community control, community participation, and community advisory programs have developed as a response to these tensions and conflicts.

The nature of the home-school or community-school partnership is increasingly problemmatic, as more poor and minority parents and community groups feel estranged from their local schools. School administrators and teachers often fear parental involvement or community "interference" in school, and therefore wish to be buffered or protected against such intrusion. The dilemma of the public school in seeking to respect plural cultures or to promote the dominant culture is writ large in these conflicts. Some observers have suggested new visions for the local school that establish it as a community-serving institution. As such, the school tries to meet a variety of local educational needs, not just those of young students. Various community service programs, recreational projects and social welfare activities can be generated from the school's operation as a center of community political and cultural events.

5

ORGANIZATIONAL STRUCTURES OF SCHOOLS

Organizations regularize the work of people and the society, and provide an orderly process for the sometimes chaotic nature of social life. There are many kinds of organizations in a given society; families, clubs, political parties, and athletic teams are just a few. But the school, which is a *formal* organization, is formed of complex social units with set rules and roles, oriented to clearly announced goals, and supported by regular patterns of authority. Each of these characteristics is important by itself, and each gives special meaning to the study of the school as an organization.

The individual behavior and interactions of students, educators, parents, and others are arranged into patterns by means of their occurrence within this formal organizational framework. In this way the intensely personal acts of teaching and learning, the intimate responses that occur between two persons engaged in information exchange, are regulated and systematized. As a result, efforts by larger groups of educators and students can occur at the same time. The formal organization also provides a stable arena within which these events can occur and on which external social groups can focus.

The school is not simply an aggregate of individuals: it is composed of complex social units, roles and rules that people are expected to follow. Classrooms and grade levels, learning teams, student and/or teacher peer groups, are among the smaller units that are fit together into this more complex unit called a *school*. Individuals fit themselves into set rules and roles that govern their behavior. Although there are many informal rules and expectations in schools, no unwritten and obscure code could establish so many units doing so many similar things across the country. Attendance at school is mandatory until the child reaches a certain age, and this is a legal requirement, as is the certification of teachers. Classes have formal curricula, and everyone within the school operates according to a set of prescribed rules. Nearly everyone, or at least everyone who operates succcessfully in this setting, understands the difference between the role of the teacher and the role of the student. Moreover, youngsters who wish to be successful in school must learn the difference between the teacher's role as an adult authority and the role of their adult family members.

The school is also oriented to clearly announced and prescribed goals. We may disagree as to the levels of rhetoric and reality in school goals, but all observers agree that the school is a value-centered organization. It has goals, tries to achieve them, and directs its operations toward the accomplishment of these specific purposes. As in all social institutions, the need for survival and maintenance of its own personnel and accustomed ways of proceeding is also important to the school. Sometimes, attempts to achieve goals of survival and self-maintenance may well conflict with the "altruistic" or service goals of the organization. One of the distinguishing characteristics of schools is that they do have an altruistic purpose, one of rendering service to their least powerful members. The idea of more powerful people rendering service to the less powerful, rather than the other way around, is generally an anomaly. Thus, this particular aspect of the goals of the schools generates considerable inspection and room for doubt.

All operations in this formal organization, as in others, are governed and implemented by patterns of authority. No mere consensus of members directs action; previously established and certified authorities are responsible for the effective governance and administration of the school. Just as teachers are the established authority in the classroom, principals are the established authority in the building, and superintendents and school boards govern on behalf of the community in a school system. In some organizations authority is unclear and is to be settled by means of personal charisma or contest (political clubs, athletic teams); but in formal organizations such as schools the patterns are established by impersonal rules and positions in the system.

In this chapter we review alternative perspectives on the nature of the school as a formal organization, and on several important issues in the organization of life in a school building. We take as the focus of our analysis the local school building: an observable complex unit of the larger school system. First, we examine some competing perspectives that have been offered as ways of analyzing the organization of schooling. Then we consider the special roles of organizational leaders, the school principals. In the interactions among different administrators, between administrators and teachers, and between administrators and students, we should see the organizational features of school writ large.

ALTERNATIVE PERSPECTIVES ON THE
SCHOOL ORGANIZATION

Two different theoretical traditions generally have provided most of the thrust for the study of schools as organizations. One has its roots in bureaucratic theories, such as those orientations to social organizations generated by Max Weber. Currently, this tradition has taken form in scholars generalizing to schools from studies of the industrial bureaucracy [1]. The bureaucratic model of school stresses those variables that are considered as essential elements of bureaucracies in all areas of social life—efficiency, legitimate hierarchy of office and authority, formal rules and roles, morale of workers and consumers, cost accounting and input/output ratios, and the production of finished goods, for example, skilled wage earners and citizens.

A second theoretical tradition, rich with implications for schools, perceives the school as a professional-collegial system. This view is derived from social welfare theories of the service mission of schools, and of the professionalism of workers in the educational setting [2]. The professional-collegial model of school stresses another important, yet limited, set of variables in organizational life—specialized expertise, professional autonomy, facilitative management, techniques of shaping client performance, and reliance on the authority of experts.

Scholars operating within either of these perspectives readily admit that these models do not fit precisely, and that there is room for better-fitting paradigms or models. At the same time, little attention has been paid to the promise of a primarily political analysis of the school organization.° Those political analyses that have been applied to the school typically have considered either the historic roles of the school in the American political-economy and culture [3], or the local community as the political context, and its interactions with its schools [4]. Baldridge does focus upon decision-making processes in schools, but to date such efforts have been limited to higher educational institutions [5]. In primary and secondary education, organizational studies of schools that explicitly start with a political model would force attention to such internal variables as power, trust, efficiacy, conflict among groups with differentiated goals and resources, and legitimate and illegitimate authority. Crises and conflicts around professional/adult/white controls and cultures have been the operational foci around which political analyses of the school as an organization are just beginning to appear [6]. Generally, Americans have not wanted to see their schools as political and partisan institutions, but rather they have wished to imagine the schools operating outside of political functions and

---

° Primarily political, because all models admit that political interaction and influence do take place, just as all admit to the presence of a bureaucracy and the existence of professional colleagues.

structures. And, generally speaking, scholarship on schools has been conducted within this framework of values and beliefs.

The various models that have been explicitly or implicitly used in the scholarly study of schools each make certain assumptions about client needs and relations, and each model generates prescribed measures of the outcomes of schooling. The demonstration of marketable economic skills, compliant citizen behavior, acceptable social interaction skills, societal commitment, mastery of academic tasks, and intellectual performance all have been used as measures of outcomes in a variety of studies. These measures all are tuned to the expectation that the school can and should nurture, shape, or mold students so as to inculcate or produce in them certain prescribed attitudes and skills.

In each model, organizational goals and conflict processes are seen to operate in different ways. In the bureaucratic and professional-collegial models, organizational goals are not seen as problematic, and assumptions are made about goal consensus rather than conflict. In fact, conflict generally is seen as illegitimate or unfortunate, and primarily a product of school-community misunderstanding or extraschool forces. In the political model, organizational role and status groups (teachers, students, principals) or demographic and cultural groups (on the basis of race, sex, and economic class) are seen as natural sources of continuing conflict within and without the school. The most potent intraorganizational focus of such value and status divisions would occur between professionals (adults) and students (youth) of varying races and sexes and classes.

Control is seen as being rooted in conceptions of legitimate authority for the bureaucratic model, and in professional expertise for the professional-collegial model. Implementations of administrative decisions, rather than processes of partisan decision making themselves, are stressed by these two traditions. Students generally are viewed as "throughput," material to be processed, rather than as organizational members. In contrast, community or client representation in decision making is essential from the political point of view. Students and/or parents would have to be seen as legitimate organizational members, defined in terms of their lower power status, rather than as nonmembers or raw material of a professional system. Variants of a political model may differ in the degree to which they are concerned primarily with the maintenance of power and control in the hands of elite and/or professional managers, or in the hands of clients and consumers. The former variant is indeed highly political, but it may just as well be categorized as bureaucratic or professional, because it supports the professional bureaucracy's legitimate role as exerciser of political power in schools. The focus of the political model on its client-serving or consumer-serving aspects is where new scholarship and new school-community practice may break with more traditional service or research models.

The Katz and Kahn categorization of human service systems as "people processing" organizations is indicative of the interface between the two traditional models, i.e., the professional-collegial modification of bureaucratic systems built for material production [7]. They argue that "people processing" is different than material "product processing," and suggest the need for more individualized and humane forms of organization and management for people-processing systems. However, the locus of legitimate authority to define organizational goals and to provide, control, and evaluate that service clearly still lies in the professional managers and processors. According to the "people-processing" view of human service systems, people in authority (by virtue of expertise and credentials rather than ownership or seniority) still "do" things to or for others—they "process" them—with or without direct and informed client consent. Thus, a review of the politics of such organizations may clarify their fundamental nature as vehicles of adult (usually white and male and affluent) control rather than as altruistic servers of needy youth (and perhaps other low-power groups).

Another way to compare these different perspectives is to examine some of the critical factors that provide integration in complex and diverse social organizations, such as power and trust. Gamson has developed a theory of organizational governance and citizen protest that suggests that these two factors may covary systematically in organizational operations [8]. Some social systems can be held together on the basis of an informal social contract wherein members trust one another. This trust may be based on a network of social relations and expectations embedded in personal friendships and goodwill. Or, especially in the case of human service organizations, this trust may be based on assumptions of the competence and ability of professionals to perform the task for which they are in business. In this case, the trust is more functional or instrumental than friendly or consummatory. In schools we see both these forms of trusting relationships at work [9]. Some groups of students and faculty work (teach and learn) well together because they are, or feel they are, close to and caring about one another as persons. In other cases, trust may exist without such closeness, but with the students' belief that the faculty do fulfill their functions of providing a good education, teaching well, or helping them get jobs or into college. In many schools, and for some clients and professionals, a lack of trust may exist on both these dimensions. The recent history of school failure would suggest that more parents and students believe that they do not receive very effective payoffs from their high school experience; nor do they find school a pleasant place in which to work and play. On both counts, therefore, trust may be eroding rapidly as a workable means of integrating students in some schools.

Social systems also can be held together on the basis of a decision-making system that legitimizes leaders in terms of their real or alleged ability to satisfy the interests of varied system members. Some of these forms of power or control sound very much like our usage of trust—especially "referent" or "expert" power [10]. These forms usually are accompanied by, or all too often supplanted by, institutionalized threats or the actual exercise of coercive power. It matters little at some levels whether this power is seen as legitimate or not; its very enforceability may be enough. For instance, the operation of partisan and coercive power in schools may be seen in the mandatory character of school attendance [11], in adult and white control of instructional content and process [12], in the use of corporal and humiliating punishment [13], and in unilateral professional evaluation of students.

The political rebellions occurring within many human service systems suggest the need for serious study and potential reorganization around the status and rights of recipients [14]. Recent studies of the politics of social welfare agencies, schools, and the like, stress the importance of evaluating these organizations in terms of the quality of services they provide to clients, rather than in their traditional roles as shapers and changers of people. More explicitly, we now can and should begin to sketch an outline of client-serving systems wherein the focus of attention is on providing accountable services to clients, rather than on processing them according to managers' or professionals' definitions of needed services and resources, and clients' self-assessments of the adequacy of service delivery.

In a political system that serves the welfare of clients, the appropriate output of organizational operations is programs and policies that clients or constituencies can utilize for their own benefit. The perceptions of the members or recipients of the benefit or satisfaction they derive from the organization are likely to be one of the most important measures of organizational outcomes—at least as far as the clients are concerned. The locus of controls would be located with the clients or their representatives; services would be delivered in ways that the clients, not the professionals, would find and determine to be useful; staffing competence would rely less on abstract credentialization than on performance in terms agreeable to the service recipients. The use of a political and client-serving paradigm also highlights the plural political functions of such institutions, and the ways in which power and control, which often are utilized to meet the needs of professionals and managers, can be used to meet the needs of the clients themselves.° Clearly, this orientation requires different decision-making mechanisms, service delivery procedures, staffing roles, and feedback and accountability systems than the bureaucratic or professional-collegial modes.

This discussion is summarized in Table 5–1, which compares aspects of the three organizational models of schools and schooling. It is too early yet to know

---

° According to this model there may be a congruence of interests between clients and professionals or managers, but it is more likely that they will be in conflict. Not only do conflicts occur between clients and professionals serving them, but between the different latent roles of sex, race, economic class, and education and age normally associated with professional status (white, male, affluent, educated, adult) and client status (minority, half female, poor, less educated, and often young). Those conflicts must be negotiated and resolved on terms satisfactory to everyone, but still primarily client-serving.

Exercise 5—1. *Comparing Three Alternative Views of the School Organization*

This exercise can be done by students individually or in small groups.

Consider the three alternative views of the school organization presented—bureaucratic, collegial, and political. Compare them in turns of their probable analysis of:

1. Expected divisions and tensions (if any) among the professional and nonprofessional staff.

2. Teacher unions and/or associations.

3. Inequality in treatment or outcomes of students.

4. Role of the teacher in the classroom.

5. Relation of the school organization to the school board and city council.

---

with certainty what models, or mix of models, will be best for the general purpose of explaining contemporary school dynamics, but it is clear that we must move beyond the limits of the two traditional research and service approaches.

THE ROLES OF SCHOOL ADMINISTRATORS: POLITICAL LEADERSHIP IN A PROFESSIONAL BUREAUCRACY

School administrators are in prominent positions to exercise authority and expertise in the management and leadership of school affairs. At the local school the principal represents the system administration. The principal's leadership style may help establish a school climate and conditions that contain high levels of staff and student-staff trust. Or, the principal may act in ways that generate or escalate staff and student distrust and disrespect. Either way, the principal's role is potent!

Although they are part of a larger and more complex system, individual principals generally have considerable operational latitude to make decisions and mobilize resources if they are so inclined. The professional status of principals provides them with substantial subunit autonomy and influence. As a result, various scholars stress the crucial role played by principals in most

Table 5–1. Comparison of Three Models of Schools and Schooling

	Bureaucratic	Professional-Collegial	Political Client-Serving
Goals	Profit to society Productive efficiency of schooling	Change in clients' lifestyles, skills, goals, attitudes	Service to clients
Goal assessment—outcome measures	Productive attributes of students as wage earners and citizens	Client achievement—learning	Client satisfaction of needs by means of institutional policy and program
Base of control	Legitimate office and pyramidical delegation Proven ability to perform	Expertise Credentials alleging competence and certified by state	Representation of service recipients (clients/constituents) Client satisfaction with service Negotiated
Source of institutional conflicts	Divison of labor Authority too tight Unwilling or unmotivated "workers/students"	Societal strains and latent roles Community-institution Bureaucracy-profession Professional-client or adult-student	Latent roles/statuses of race, sex, economic class Institutional power allocations among age/status groups

134

Table 5–1 (continued)

	Bureaucratic	Professional-Collegial	Political Client-Serving
Role of educators	Agents of larger political-economic structure Control agents	Altruistic deliverers of service Agents of the public Creator and interpretor of client needs	Responder to clients' needs and goals "Enablers"
Educator accountability chain	To larger social order	To peers	To clients
Internal "glue"	Legitimate division of labor well integrated by authority	Client trust in altruism and skill of professionals who are loyal to each other	Power concentrated in client authority
Group Relations: Administrator—Administrator	Collaboration Implement supervisor's plans	Sharing of ideas	Struggle for power
Administrator—Staff	Provide supervision Integrate diversity	Aid sharing Support autonomy Provide resources Buffer versus intrusion	Negotiate priorities
Administrator—Student	Control deviance Make decisions	Gain trust Deliver services	Respond to challenge Satisfy consumers

schools in determining what organizational variations do exist, and in contributing to differing levels of teacher and learner satisfaction.

As do most supervisors, principals can utilize a range of behaviors in order to carry out their functions and respond to the needs and concerns of the professional staff. Principals can be mainly concerned with classroom performance, or with the feelings of their teachers, or with some combination of these dimensions. The traditional dichotomization of leadership roles in task or socioemotional areas has been investigated in the school setting by several scholars. Halpin discusses the distinction between task-initiating and personal-consideration roles of the principal, whereas Getzels and Guba use the terms nomothetic and idiographic to describe essentially the same functions [15]. Getzels also suggests another style, that of the "transactional" leader, who achieves a balance between these divergent polarities [16]. Getzels argues that the principal who is seen by the staff as being transactionally inclined seems to generate the greatest staff confidence and effectiveness. Bidwell also records the desires of teachers to define the principal as an informal colleague rather than as a formal and distant administrative manager [17]. This is an example of the different, and often contending, themes found in the professional-collegial and bureaucratic perspectives on school life.

But there are additional concrete aspects of the supervisor's role in his or her relations to professionals in the school. The principal may or may not be concerned with teachers' professional activity and growth; and may or may not be concerned about a tight organizational administration. The principal can choose to meet with parents and community leaders a great deal or not at all, and can choose to be, or try to be, warm and friendly, or cold and impersonal. The principal's formal and structured or relaxed and informal behavior may be an essential element in the acceptance by the teachers of leadership role behavior.

The political perspective would stress the importance of another issue; that principals can choose to share decision-making power with their staff or keep it to themselves. Tannenbaum and others report that workers feel more satisfied when they feel that they can have some influence on management officials [18]. Similarly, teachers who feel that they are participating in policymaking roles, and have a say in what goes on in the school, may be more satisfied with their work. To the extent that teachers feel involved in important professional decisions, they are likely to be more interested and involved in other professionally creative activities, such as innovative teaching. However, as Tannenbaum warns, some individuals will be less satisfied by involvement and participation in the decision-making process [19]. We may expect that the general rule that involvement leads to greater satisfaction will hold in most cases, with the reverse being true for teachers with certain personality characteristics and in schools with certain principals and certain histories.

The Gross and Herriot studies suggest that effective principals are likely to be committed to the professional growth and development of their staff [20]. A personal commitment is only one factor, however, and principals must behave in public in ways that emphasize this concern if they wish to influence teachers to adopt new professional activities. Extrapolations from many leadership studies also suggest that principals may operate as role models for teachers. For instance, if principals demonstrate an interest in professional growth and innovative teaching, their enthusiasm could well be passed on to the staff. The perception of the interest and potential support of their principal helps establish firm and visible organizational norms for teachers to follow in the classroom.

All efforts at creative professional leadership must confront the ongoing inertia created by the daily demands of school management. Goodlad points out that administrative priorities run to maintenance of the bureaucratic form, as opposed to change-oriented leadership [21]. The power of the bureaucratic model of school organization and of school leadership undoubtedly is reflected in these priorities and in these limits to new visions. The result is a corresponding limitation in the mechanisms by which principals are rewarded—for running an efficient and trouble-free "tight ship." In addition, Goodlad notes that "principals and supervisors tend to be recruited from among teachers who demonstrate these orderly qualities" [22]. The consequent difficulty in performing creative staff-oriented leadership roles is very frustrating. In the words of one principal:°

> Most of us view the job of a school principal as being primarily one of instructional leadership. In the last several years instructional leadership has been virtually at a standstill. There is hardly any progress on that in any school because there are so many demands made. I think we all feel a certain level of frustration because we can't do what we believe we ought to be doing. We are doing many things for which we are untrained.

The oppressive and uncreative nature of the principal's job is aptly described by many high school administrators. In reviewing their daily duties, principals often note that in addition to internal problems, there is an excessive number of requests for reports from bureaucratic headquarters. Often there is a checklist to help keep track of the completion of these reports. Many principals believe that the time they spend on such daily administrative responsibilities leaves them with little energy to provide leadership to their colleagues, or to meet with students. In addition to problems of time, principals stress their lack of training for many of the responsibilities with which they are faced. In sum, many principals feel that they have neither the time, resources, nor power with which to acquire necessary training.

Staff Autonomy and Relations with the Principal

Some research suggests that the principal's style of supervision cannot be effective if the teachers believe that it encroaches on their professional

---

° This quote, and later samples of administrator, teacher, and student dialogue, are taken from files of workshops conducted by the Educational Change Team, University of Michigan.

autonomy. In particular, close bureaucratic supervision of supposedly autonomous professionals may be very dysfunctional and may trigger substantial
hostility and resentment from these colleagues. Gross and Herriot highlight this
issue, as they point out that some efforts by administrators to help teachers
"might be construed as betraying a lack of confidence in them and as out of
bounds. Or, if administrators urge their subordinates to try a new practice, it
may be viewed as an encroachment of their rights as professionals" [23]. In
over 55 per cent of the schools studied by Gross and Herriot, the teachers
wanted principals to exert less control over their professional activities; in the
remaining 45 per cent the teachers wanted more exercise of principal controls.
According to Gross and Herriott, "The principal of the school may, for example,
be expected by some teachers to visit them regularly to give constructive help,
and by others to trust them as professional personnel not in need of such
supervision" [24]. So an effective role for the principal vis-a-vis his or her
professional subordinates must combine the exercise of control with the
provision of autonomy. These priorities are central to the professional-collegial
model of school organization and they suggest the need to modify traditional
leadership patterns. One way principals can support staff autonomy is to buffer
or mediate external parental and community pressures. This can be done best,
when they have actual influence on community leaders and higher level
administrators.

It also is apparent that effective educational managers must be in touch with
the different standards and relationships of staff members. Teachers must feel
that they have all the necessary information in a situation, and that there is
two-way access to and from principals. This pattern of shared communication
can be expected to minimize staff alienation and to increase the potential for
collaboration. To the extent that principals have accurate information about
the character and organization of collegial relations, we can expect that they
would know what to do if they wanted to exert influence.

Biddle et. al. discuss the unique form of role conflict that occurs when
individuals face a situation wherein different parties have different norms and
expectations for their role performance [25]. For instance, high school students
and faculty, or faculty and administrators, may disagree strongly on the kinds
of behavior that are appropriate for them in various situations. In some sense
this is one of the most elusive forms of conflict imaginable, since these different
groups generally do not have access to each other's minds, and seldom are able
to appreciate the other group's reasons for determining the appropriateness of
their behaviors. Thus, some principals are confused by student or faculty
rejection of behaviors that they themselves felt were appropriate.

In these respects it is not enough to know what principals report about
themselves. It is perhaps even more critical to know how teachers perceive and
interpret their behavior. For here, as elsewhere, the teachers' phenomenological
views of the social system are among the most important determinants of their
behavior. In the several high schools studied by Chesler et. al., it was clear that

different principals were viewed and evaluated differently by their respective staffs [26].

The seven schools described in Table 5–2 differed in the degree to which the teachers believed their principal was or was not an outstanding leader. School D is especially negative because it began the school year with a new principal who resigned within two months; an acting principal served for the next four months until a permanent replacement was found. Teachers in schools A and D, which had the next most negative evaluations of their principals, also reported the greatest amount of conflict between teachers and administrators. School G is noteworthy in its staff's extraordinarily positive evaluation of its principal's performance, although the staffs in schools C and E were very positive as well.

Some more teachers' perceptions of their principals' stance are illustrated by data from the same seven high schools shown in Table 5–3 [27]. In all the schools the principal was seen as providing considerable collegial or professional help in coping with classroom problems by less than 50 per cent of the teachers. In several other areas that are quite critical for effective staff relations, the behavior of some principals was not seen as particularly helpful.

The kinds of help that teachers desire vary considerably. Some teachers want a great deal of support from the principal and colleagues; others cherish the autonomy of their own classroom. But these two concepts are by no means contradictory or exclusive. As Edgar and Warren point out, teachers often desire greater autonomy in decisions about curriculum content and teaching method [28]. On the other hand, they desire more help with administrative and clerical tasks and discipline problems. An able administrator must know how to walk this tightrope with different teachers.

Staff cohesion and collaboration are essential components of an effective educational program. If principals are unable to provide the skills and energy to encourage these patterns, they may develop without or even against them. But the waste of resources in this instance is great. One example of such waste

Table 5–2. Teachers' Assessments of the Performance of Their Principal Compared with Other Principals [26]

Principal Performance	School (Per Cent of Teachers)						
	A	B	C	D	E	F	G
Far above average	30	64	72	9	79	49	91
Above average	35	10	13	15	10	35	6
Below average	10	8	11	17	3	8	3
Far below average	24	12	2	51	5	0	0
No answer	1	6	2	8	3	8	0

Table 5–3. Per Cent of Teachers Indicating That Their Principal, to a "Considerable" or "Great Extent," Does Certain Things [27]

Behavior	School (Per Cent of Teachers)						
	A	B	C	D	E	F	G
The principal helps teachers deal with their classroom problems	11	24	42	6	46	16	33
The principal demonstrates a warm personal interest in the staff members	35	62	74	15	84	33	71
Teachers feel that it is all right to ask for the principal's help	21	38	70	13	82	43	67
The principal encourages continued professional training	41	68	51	6	59	20	27
The principal has ample time for conversation with teachers	14	18	25	19	25	8	16

can be found in most staff meetings: although they could be an effective vehicle for creative organization of the staff, they seldom focus on such issues. Most of the time is taken up by administrative announcements and trivia, a vehicle for the principal's communication, not staff collaboration. As one teacher indicated:

> We have too few faculty meetings in which faculty can air their gripes. And I would hope that we will have more faculty meetings—make them short—get things off their chest. Sometimes the administration is the last to know what's real—they may be doing something that's really irritating teachers and we may not tell them. And I think there must be that communication back and forth, a chance for us to speak when all our cohorts are around so we don't feel left alone and say what they think.

In such circumstances the teaching staff is left on its own to develop effective peer support systems—alone in the face of institutional pressures for autonomy and noncooperation.

Staff Power Relations—Influence and Control

One of the key issues in relations with peers and supervisors in school is the nature of their politics, one piece of which is evident in the character and distribution of influence among educators. The fact that this is also one of the key issues in the content and tone of student and parent concerns highlights teachers' concerns and undoubtedly influences their response to a variety of student and parent demands. Chesler's studies of seven conflict-ridden schools posed a number of questions regarding teachers' perceptions of the distribution of influence in school. The teachers' answers to the most general of these questions are reported in Table 5–4 [29]. The data indicate that few teachers see themselves as a group as having considerable influence; only 10–31 per cent. Teachers in some schools believe that their group has more influence than students or parents, and in other schools they believe that they have less. In all but one school (D), teachers reported that they have less influence than their principal. It should be recalled that school D had three different principals in the period of one year.

One way to dramatize these data is to present them in the form of a graph or curve of perceived and desired distribution of power and influence. Teachers' views of the current power structure of the local school then would be expressed in the manner of Figure 5–1. Of the seven curves, there are only three major patterns that are visible. School G (representing schools A and F as well) shows teachers perceiving the principal as having much more influence than any other party, with students also having more than teachers—the low group in the local system. School E (representing schools B and C as well) also shows the teachers perceiving the principal as having much more influence than any other party; but here the teachers themselves are perceived as having more influence than the students. It is especially interesting to contrast schools E and F, wherein teachers assign the same influence to principal and students (57 per cent and 18 per cent), but differ considerably on teacher influence (school E—

Table 5–4. Per Cent of Teachers Reporting What Groups "Have" or "Should Have" "Considerable" or "A Great Deal" of Influence on School Policy [29]

Group	\multicolumn{7}{c}{Have Influence}						
	A	B	C	D	E	F	G
Principal	47	69	41	15	57	57	65
Teacher	13	26	28	28	31	14	10
Students	27	15	22	30	18	18	18
Parents	25	26	24	17	13	16	21
	\multicolumn{7}{c}{Should Have Influence}						
Principal	58	78	64	60	80	58	82
Teacher	64	78	74	66	82	53	65
Students	23	18	22	28	18	29	22
Parents	17	19	18	26	30	29	30

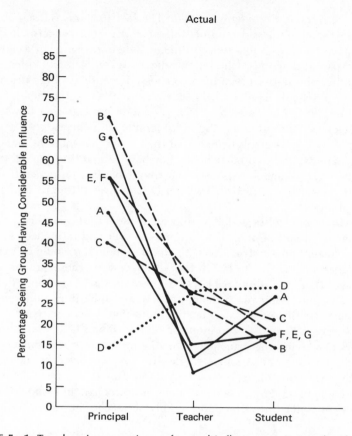

FIGURE 5—1. Teachers' perceptions of actual influence among school groups.

31 per cent and school F—14 per cent). In school D, which represents a markedly unique pattern, the teachers perceive the students as having the most influence, with teachers next and the principal the low party.

We can also graph the desires or preferences of teachers for the ideal internal influence structure (see Figure 5—2). Several features of this second figure are immediately noticeable. First, in every school, the teachers wish that the principals' influence were greater than it is in Figure 5—1: this mean across all schools increases from 50.3 per cent to 68.3 per cent. (If we omit the unique case of school D, the means increase only slightly: from 56.0 per cent to 59.2 per cent). Second, in every school the desires of teachers for their own influence increases considerably: the means across all schools increase from 21.4 per cent to 68.9 per cent. Third, the teachers' preferences for students' influence is quite close to the current status of student influence: it goes up a bit in some schools and down a bit in others, but the means across all of the schools only change from 21.1 per cent to 22.9 per cent.

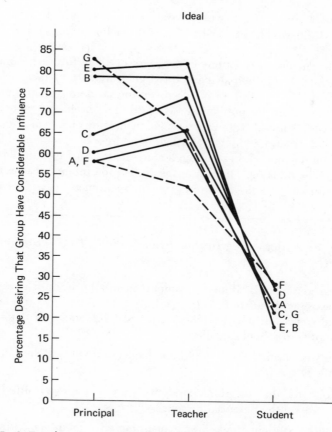

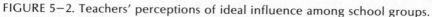

FIGURE 5–2. Teachers' perceptions of ideal influence among school groups.

Only two distinct patterns can be discerned from this graph. School C (representative of schools A, B, D, and E) prefers teachers to have the most influence. Teachers in schools B and E of this group prefer principals to have almost equal influence with teachers. School G (also representative of school F) is hierarchical by status—teachers preferring principals to have the most status, followed by teachers and then students far behind.

We can see that the desires by teachers to reform current allocations of power are strikingly uniform in all schools. They desire universally to (1) increase the influence of principals; (2) increase markedly the influence of teachers; and (3) maintain approximately the current influence of students. Such changes in the political process of schools might decentralize and diffuse decision-making power from central offices into the hands of local principals, engage major teacher resources in helping to establish policy, and greatly improve staff commitment to their organization. Teacher-training programs, curricular changes, or other bureaucratic and professional reforms that seek to engage teacher support for changes will have to take account of these political preferences within which teacher-teacher and teacher-administrator exchange take place.

Despite the current perceptions of teachers or their future aspirations for greater influence, the principal maintains final authority in most schools. As Clark points out, the "notion of a self-governing academic community . . . is only weekly voiced in the public schools" [30]. The problems rooted in such collective powerlessness also are well detailed in an issue of *School Management* [31]. A forum of superintendents was asked to address the problem of how they would handle a teacher who encouraged students to campaign in the community on a school bond issue. The consensus of the superintendents was that they would reprimand this teacher, defining such innovation as too dangerous to get involved in.

Exercise 5—2. *Reflecting on the Organization of the Professional Staff*

This exercise can be done by students in small groups or in a total open classroom discussion.

When you were a high school student, did you ever attend a meeting of your school's faculty?

1. Were you permitted to? Could you have attended (watched) if you wanted?

2. If no, why do you think students were not so permitted . . . speculate on the potential reasons?

As college student, have you ever attended a faculty meeting of your school or of the academic unit or department in which you are enrolled?

1. Are you permitted to attend? Can you attend if you want to? Can you watch? Speak? Vote? Under what conditions?

2. If not, why do you think there are barriers or limits to student attendance or participation at such meetings? Speculate on the potential reasons. Ask a faculty member or administrator (usually a dean or department chairperson) what the reasons might be.

3. Attend a unit or department faculty meeting, if you can. What kinds of things do they discuss? What procedures do they use to discuss and decide matters? What seem to be their views or general stances on students and student issues? Does attendance at this meeting provide you with any insight into the general limitations on student attendance?

Other Staff Groups

Other relevant staff groups in school include a number of human service staff members who are not classroom teachers. These professionals include counselors, psychologists, class advisors, social workers, and career planning advisors. Obviously this staff group is important because of their skill and responsibility in assisting students with critical decisions and in dealing with life problems.

Such human service workers often are expected to be friends and helpers of youth. However, as they operate within the organizational structure of the school, counselors also are expected to be the key agents in maintaining organizational values and rules. Thus, counselors are often the official source of labeling, intervention,' and record-keeping systems that identify the causes of problems as lying within students and then try to alter the students' behavior. Questions always arise regarding the role boundaries for counselors, and how to provide mutual clarity of expectations between counselors and students. Counselors are pressed to make decisions and take committed stands on controversies that tend to focus on drugs, sexuality, student rights, and teacher violations. For many counselors, such interactions with youth are strange, risky, and unexplored territory. They are caught, once again, between adults (the official organization) and youth (consumers and clients).

A typical problem in the nature of counselors' working conditions is the number of students assigned to an individual counselor. In high schools, it is not unusual for a single counselor to be responsible for four to five hundred students. As a related issue, counselors are frequently involved in an extraordinary number of activities—work study programs, school award programs, and student service programs such as medical, hospital, accident, and life insurance. In the local economy, for instance, the counselor can reach out to concerned business people and union representatives to discuss youth unemployment, programs of public service employment, job training targeted at minorities, public and private affirmative action programs, and projects employing labor intensive services and technology. Under such conditions of overload, the attention of counselors is often narrowed to individual crises rather than ongoing programming. As a result, they are unable to play important roles in altering the organization of the school.

Many other people on the staff of schools are excluded from the traditional category of "professional educators." Yet these excluded people play essential roles in the operation of the professional educational system. They interact with students and often fulfill their social and psychological needs, represent the school in the community, and perform important tasks that are essential to the efficient running of the school. Such "nonacademic personnel" refer to custodians, secretaries, cafeteria workers, bus drivers, bus assistants, clerks, security guards, maintenance employees, and crossing guards. Staff in nonacademic roles still have considerable impact on students and educators. Most often the organizational impact of these people is positive, particularly when they meet the unfulfilled needs of students by informally providing psychological support, by providing services that meet material needs (e.g., transportation, heat), and by sharing important information with teachers, students, the school, or the community.

Nonacademic personnel can also have negative impacts by their wholesale resistance to innovative educational practices and policies, or by their refusal to provide adequate services (e.g., late transportaton, cold food, or dirty facilities). A specific example would be a teacher needing his or her room arranged in a new way to support the creation of a new classroom structure and climate. Such an innovation requires change in the custodian's pattern of doing things and a great deal of work in initially rearranging the furniture. Unless the teacher can gain the custodian's cooperation, this attempt at educational innovation can be stymied.

The areas of responsibility of many nonacademic personnel are very visible to community members. Parents sometimes come into more contact with bus drivers and secretaries, for instance, than with teachers or administrators. And sometimes the community has unreal expectations about the actual competencies or responsibilities of many nonacademic personnel. Thus, it is difficult for the community to provide adequate salary support and esteem. The two following newspaper editorials illustrate typical community attitudes:

> The figures on the relative salaries of teacher and school custodians make strange reading. In Bay City a teacher, even if he has a doctor's degree, can only earn $6,600, while a senior custodian receives $7,151. It is explained that teachers work only nine months of the year and custodians work all twelve. . . . That explanation will satisfy some; it would be more convincing if the custodian system provided a round-the-clock watch which made successful vandalism impossible.

> The fight for non-academic pay raise promises to be a real donnybrook. . . . Leading the pack to cut up the extra $5 million (allocated over last year's school budget by the School Board) are the school janitors, who are now just about the highest paid broom pushers in the city [32].

Nonacademic personnel are in situations in which they must relate to a dual authority structure in the organization. The custodian is impacted by the school principal and at the same time is accountable to the head custodian. In addition, teachers expect these personnel to respond to their needs in certain helpful ways. Such multiple-service and accountability arrangements are not unusual in large bureaucratic organizations, but give rise to problems for such organizational role occupants. Often these staff people are not involved in the decision-making process and miss valuable information. They also are sometimes held responsible for conditions or situations over which they have little or no control. Moreover, the professional staff often lacks both an awareness of and a sensitivity to the responsibilities, skills, and need for training of the nonacademic staff, to say nothing of their distrust of the expertise of the nonacademic staff in dealing with children. Similar disrespect is sometimes shown the nonacademic staff by students, particularly at the senior high school level.

PRINCIPAL RELATIONS WITH STUDENTS

The final major structural relation to be discussed in the internal organization of the school is that between the local administrator and the students. Interestingly, one of the most distinctive characteristics of student-administrator relations is the sheer distance between them. Typically, there is little direct contact between these parties in school and the contact that occurs usually is focused on adult control of the deviant behaviors of students. This distance contributes to students' feelings of alienation from key educators and adults in school. Many students feel that the principal isn't on "their side," and thus can not be counted upon as a political and educational ally. Part of the reason for this situation undoubtedly lies in the complex demands that principals must face daily. For instance, when asked by students how he viewed his role, one principal responded in terms of his desperation.

> Let me describe the administrative role, because that's my bag. I feel that I am overwhelmed with personnel and students. There are over 200 adults for which I am mostly responsible, and 3,400 students, 27 acres of land, and a five million dollar building. I can do nothing at the present time in terms of educational leadership. My primary job is to keep that place open and running. That's all I can see.

Clearly such views leave little room for educational leadership, for close relations with the faculty, or for responses to anything but emergencies in student relations.

To a certain extent, the principal symbolizes the school for the students. If the principal is seen as competent, friendly, open, and positively concerned, that matters a great deal in building and maintaining a role model for teachers, and in generating student trust. If the principal is seen as incompetent, brutal, disrespectful, racist, and distant, the school is also seen in these terms. One result of students' loss of trust in, and respect for, their educators is that new types of students' challenges to administrative authority are occurring. Students who do not believe that the school will have positive payoff for them are no longer prepared to trust completely in the principal as leader and reflector of their interests. This functional distrust then proceeds to take on intergroup proportions, as stated by one black student,

> You need trust. It's gotten to the point don't nobody trust nobody. And that's all the student body's got to look up to. You know, if you've got a problem, you're supposed to take it to the administration. If you feel that your counselor couldn't handle it, you know, you go to the administration. And when you can't do that, what can you do?

One of the key problems in institutions that no longer are held together with trust is that low-status groups must develop new means to control their own future. In this context student pressures for more power and influence in school policy are one of the most common confrontations between students and administrators. In the study by Chesler referred to earlier, approximately 800 students from grades 10 to 12 were sampled in seven secondary schools undergoing serious crisis and disruption [33]. The percentage of students in each school reporting on what groups have or should have "considerable" or "a great deal" of influence on school policy is shown in Table 5—5.

The students' answers indicate that in all but one school they see the principal as having the greatest influence on school policy; in all but one school they see the students and the teachers as having the least influence. (The data also indicate substantial variation among these schools.) School D, in which students saw the principal as relatively lacking in power, had several principals in one year and was without a principal at the time of the survey. In all schools the students think that their collective influence and that of teachers should be substantially increased. Moreover, in all but one school the students think that they should have more influence than the teachers. Students generally do not wish to increase student influence at the cost of reducing seriously the principal's influence on school affairs. But they often do insist on limiting the arenas of such adult power and influence. For instance, students do wish to limit arbitrary authority and educators' intrusion into "private" or "personal" areas of dress, fashion, and political expression. Student concerns about due process and civil liberties mark the end of their automatic obedience and conformity to the unilateral exercise of administrative authority.

Table 5—5. Per Cent of Students Reporting What Groups
"Have" or "Should Have" "Considerable" or "A Great Deal"
of Influence on School Policy [33]

| Group | Have Influence | | | | | | |
	A	B	C	D	E	F	G
Principal	49	45	68	19	53	43	62
Teacher	24	20	28	23	24	26	31
Students	31	25	18	21	31	29	34
Parents	28	39	35	21	43	30	52

| Group | Should Have Influence | | | | | | |
	A	B	C	D	E	F	G
Principal	50	60	68	43	62	37	57
Teacher	46	51	43	42	36	30	41
Students	62	61	44	38	42	39	57
Parents	38	23	28	38	54	32	53

An informal survey of school principals demonstrated that many of them indicate a desire and willingness to reallocate greater amounts of influence on policymaking to students [34]. In some cases they are prepared to advocate greater change than would be acceptable to their faculties. The degree of trust that principals have in young people, in their sincerity, responsibility and/or competence, is a crucial determinant of school responses to the desires of students for involvement and influence. One principal, for instance, publicly cautioned his teachers at a staff meeting not to trust protesting students, noting that "they're not much for work." Some teachers argued that students are and will be responsible if given the opportunity and support, and the superintendent of this system suggested that administrators "recognize that students will be inventive, responsible members of the school community." Considerable conflict in views of students' capacity for collaboration in school affairs exists in many school systems. One result is that it is hard to create a consensus among educators on these matters.

Power and trust are hard to exercise or share in the abstract, and must be tied to the making and implementing of important specific decisions. One specific circumstance illustrating the problems of priorities was reflected in the following dialogue between a principal and several visiting students:

(*Principal*): We have one teacher, who is a fine teacher and well-liked by everybody. But he just won't have a long-haired boy in his class. If anyone comes to his class with long hair, he says either you get it cut or you don't come into the class.

(*Student*): Do you think it's fair for a teacher to do that just because his personal taste makes him get up-tight about a guy with long hair? Do you think he has the right to do that?

(*Principal*): Do you want a personal or official opinion?

(*Student*): Both. Do your personal and professional opinions differ? I think when a person has a prejudice against someone with long hair that's the same as saying you can't come into my class because you're black and I don't like black people.

(*Principal*): I don't like him to take that position. I don't think he should have that authority. But what do I tell this guy? Should I prohibit him from doing it?

(*Student*): Yes. Tell him if that boy has been assigned to his class, he has no right to kick him out because he doesn't like his face or because of the way his hair grows.

(*Principal*): This is going to ruin a fine relationship, a personal friendship, and it's going to do a lot of harm, a lot of damage.

(*Student*): But what about the kid?

Another principal argued that although he disagreed with this teacher's position, maintaining a good relationship with the teacher was more important than allowing students the right to decide for themselves how they would like to dress. This principal was questioned regarding the value of "a good relationship with the teacher" if the relationship could not bear criticism of this sort. He was also questioned concerning his priorities of good relations with the faculty over students' rights.

Although many principals profess sympathy with students desiring changes, few openly advocate the interests of the students or join forces with them. Even those principals who agree with student grievances often do not believe that they have the power to change things. Since students generally attribute great power to principals, the principals' perceptions of their low power set the stage for major conflicts in perception and expectation. There is no way for principals who feel trapped and impotent to behave in ways that are consonant with the students' expectations of their potency. Principals must thus be continual failures in the eyes of their students. Even moderate principals, who eschew control but profess communication and concern for all students, shy away from working closely or providing legitimacy to student grievances. As Janowitz notes, "School authorities seldom if ever seek to cooperate with the most hostile and coercive student leaders. . . . School authorities seek to resist such leaders or to export them out of their jurisdiction" [35].

Many of these issues are thrown into bold relief in the consideration of racial problems. Given the prominence of racial concerns in student demands, it is clear that principals must respond to such concerns by setting a good racial climate. Many school principals, black or white, feel they are caught between conflicting pressures from black and white students in their schools. The demands of black students generally include instructional programs that are responsive to their needs as a group and themselves as individuals, and action by school authorities to curtail discrimination against them by teachers. Many problems facing principals in this area become clear when the principals have to respond to specific events. For instance, one principal suggested that many school disorders at the time of the assassination of Dr. Martin Luther King

> . . . are traceable to a certain insensitivity on the part of school officials . . . (for instance) the failure of a school to close in honor of Dr. King . . . the refusal of school authorities to allow a group of students to leave a high school and conduct a memorial march for Dr. King . . . the failure to lower a flag at a local high school.

Wiser, more sensitive, or less racist school administrators helped observe this tragic event by closing schools or adopting other forms of official mourning.

Years later, some principals still felt they were in a difficult position in making policy regarding the commemoration of this event. For instance, in one school system, groups of black students recently approached their principals and asked that something be done to honor Dr. King's life and death. The principals felt, however, that if some event was held there was a very real possibility of backlash by white students and parents. As stated by one

Exercise 5—3. *Examining Status Interaction in School Organization*

This exercise can be done in two ways; (1) students can reflect on their images of their recent secondary school experiences, individually or in groups; (2) students can visit a school and conduct systematic or casual observations. In the latter case, the students' own elementary school, or a portion of the college or university may be selected as a site for observation.

1. Observe the way in which teachers of different ages, races, sexes, or status relate to one another. Who starts or stops a conversation? Who talks with whom? Who uses a first name address and who uses the more formal Mr., Mrs., Ms., and Dr.?

2. Observe the way in which teachers and administrators (principal, department heads) relate to one another. Who calls whom by their first name?

3. Observe the ways in which teachers relate to students. Who initiates the conversation? Who calls whom by their first name? Who touches whom?

4. If various members of the class have observed these patterns in different schools or different kinds of schools, discuss any comparisons. Do status interactions appear different in elementary schools than in secondary schools or in colleges?

administrator: "I have a concern that I am about ready for a white backlash. I have the makings of one. I pull another one of these big deals (like the assembly for Black History Week) and I'm afraid that I'll get what I almost got the last time." In this school, groups of white students had already protested a mandatory assembly for Black History week, and it seemed possible that these students could gain support for a protest or a walkout of an assembly in honor of Dr. King. The principal felt he had already made several concessions to blacks—he said he was afraid of doing anything further that might increase overt racial tension.

> We've got some very antagonistic white kids. They came to us and said, 'We don't want to go to the Black History assembly. We'll sit here in the office.' I'm talking about a small group of kids, but if we push this thing we could get into another situation. We have a lot of kids in that vast middle somewhere who could be rallied in this direction. That's what worries me—what we've built all year could go down the drain in ten minutes.

Exercise 5—4. *Designing a Nonracist School*

This activity can be done by students working together in small groups, potentially dividing up the general task and testing the fit of various parts.

Create some of the major organizational features or components of a nonracist school. For instance, what might this school look like in terms of its:

1. Social studies curriculum.

2. Staff composition and relations.

3. Classroom pedagogies.

4. Rules for governing the administration of student discipline.

5. Parent participation in school.

Feel free to explore other aspects as well.

Thus, each principal feels forced to take into consideration a number of political factors in planning any action that is relevant to racial relations. A principal's educational values and commitments often are overruled by his or her awareness of external pressures that could be exerted by various groups in the community and the school. White principals seem especially concerned about white backlash, and are more prone to respond on the basis of presumed community reactions than on the basis of educational values and priorities.

The stability of the principals' careers depends upon their ability to please the majority of the community, and it is neither unreal nor unwise to be sensitive to such pressures. When such pressures come from the white community that influences or controls most of school policy, including school board and millage elections, their potential responses to the principals' actions demand attention. Many principals now feel they cannot risk advocating any more racial programs that are unpopular or controversial to white students and educators. Thus, the principals collude with the white community and racist traditions to continue patterns of white domination and black exclusion.

OTHER ADMINISTRATIVE RELATIONS

Although the discussion has thus far focused primarily on relationships within a local school, it is obvious that no school exists in isolation, and that what affects one school affects others. Similarly, the total educational climate in a city or a school system inevitably affects what any single principal or local school can accomplish. A common problem for many administrators is the way some principals resent the changes that other principals make in their own schools. More specifically, it appears that the manner in which one principal responds to his or her staff or students may put pressure on others to respond similarly. Clearly, this pressure occurs because of the administrative staff's failure to come to common agreement about these matters, or their failure even to share concerns often enough for each principal to be aware of where the others stand. Even where a formal mechanism is available for sharing concerns, difficulties can occur in reaching agreement in areas that are usually protected with norms of great autonomy. Excerpts from comments by two principals in different cities are illustrative:

> This seems to be a situation where when one person says they are going to do something, the others of us are committed. There is communication among the students. The day of Dr. King's assassination many kids rushed into my office and said, 'We want to fly the flag at half-mast; the other school is flying it at half-mast.' If you do something, I don't think I have much choice not to.

> I've always tried to immediately establish communication with kids, with the organized and unorganized factions within the school. One of my students was so pleased and carried away with this that on his own he tried to start calling up some of his friends at different high schools and saying, "Why don't you have a student advisory council like we do, and we're going to have a meeting." And he started sending out letters to various schools. "Please send a representative and alternate, and we're going to have a meeting." And the principals started calling me; "What are you trying to do?" At first I didn't know what they were talking about, but it finally got through to me.

Many principals express a sense of constant frustration about their impotence to encourage local educational innovations. But part of the sense of impotence of most principals also stems from their inability to exert influence on upper-level administrators. For instance, principals often believe that they are restricted from putting new programs into effect because they do not have the required funds. Central office administrators generally decide how available funds will be allocated among schools. Principals often are not involved in making major decisions affecting their schools; most decisions are imposed from above. Feelings of personal impotence often result for principals who do not know how to fight central administrative policies.

Even in the midst of such collective impotence, many principals do not see the possibility or necessity of working together as a group in order to get what they need for their own schools. Consider, for instance, this dialogue among several principals in one urban system.

> I don't think we have to act as a group on an issue. I think I have the power in myself and I don't think I have to go with you guys to ask for something for my school. If I have a good enough case, I can get it on my own. I'm irritated at this notion of mass pressure. I don't think it is necessary.

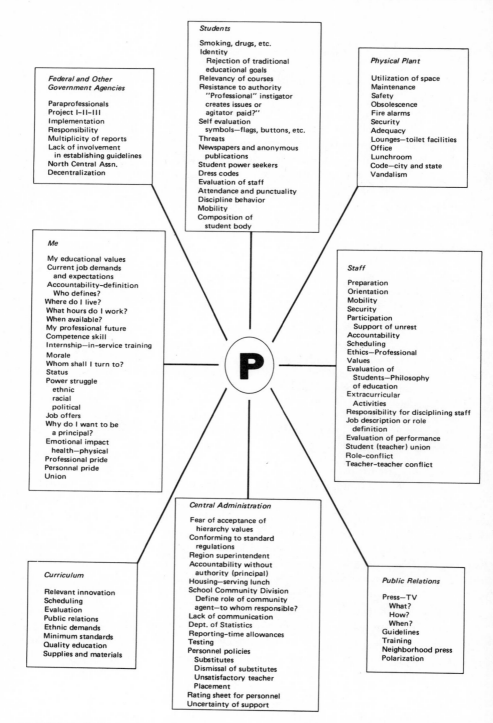

Students

Smoking, drugs, etc.
Identity
    Rejection of traditional
    educational goals
Relevancy of courses
Resistance to authority
    "Professional" instigator
    creates issues or
    agitator paid?"
Self evaluation
    symbols—flags, buttons, etc.
Threats
Newspapers and anonymous
    publications
Student power seekers
Dress codes
Evaluation of staff
Attendance and punctuality
Discipline behavior
Mobility
Composition of
    student body

**Federal and Other
Government Agencies**

Paraprofessionals
Project I–II–III
Implementation
Responsibility
Multiplicity of reports
Lack of involvement
    in establishing guidelines
North Central Assn.
Decentralization

Physical Plant

Utilization of space
Maintenance
Safety
Obsolescence
Fire alarms
Security
Adequacy
Lounges—toilet facilities
Office
Lunchroom
Code—city and state
Vandalism

Me

My educational values
Current job demands
    and expectations
Accountability–definition
    Who defines?
Where do I live?
What hours do I work?
When available?
My professional future
Competence skill
Internship—in-service training
Morale
Whom shall I turn to?
Status
Power struggle
    ethnic
    racial
    political
Job offers
Why do I want to be
    a principal?
Emotional impact
    health—physical
Professional pride
Personnal pride
Union

Staff

Preparation
Orientation
Mobility
Security
Participation
    Support of unrest
Accountability
Scheduling
Ethics—Professional
Values
Evaluation of
    Students—Philosophy
    of education
Extracurricular
    Activities
Responsibility for disciplining staff
Job description or role
    definition
Evaluation of performance
Student (teacher) union
Role-conflict
Teacher-teacher conflict

Central Administration

Fear of acceptance of
    hierarchy values
Conforming to standard
    regulations
Region superintendent
Accountability without
    authority (principal)
Housing—serving lunch
School Community Division
    Define role of community
    agent—to whom responsible?
Lack of communication
Dept. of Statistics
Reporting-time allowances
Testing
Personnel policies
    Substitutes
    Dismissal of substitutes
    Unsatisfactory teacher
    Placement
Rating sheet for personnel
Uncertainty of support

Curriculum

Relevant innovation
Scheduling
Evaluation
Public relations
Ethnic demands
Minimum standards
Quality education
Supplies and materials

Public Relations

Press—TV
    What?
    How?
    When?
Guidelines
Training
Neighborhood press
Polarization

FIGURE 5–3. Secondary school principals' perceptions of the forces/pressures operating upon them.

Exercise 5—5. *Understanding Multiple-Role Pressures on Professional Staff Members*

Consider Figure 5—3 in which secondary school principals described the multiple and often conflicting organizational pressures, demands, and interest groups impacting on them:

1. Reflect on the multiple demands and institutional pressures that operate on you in your everyday life as a college student.

2. Construct a chart similar to Figure 5—3, which reflects your perceptions of these various forces and pressures in your life.

The reason I'm not so sure that we can go this independent route, as much as I'd love to, is that as soon as I get one more administrator than anyone else, you guys are going to say, "What in the hell is that?" There has to be some accord. When I go in to talk about that kind of plan, he'll say, "What about the other schools? You want two more administrators. What's the other principals going to say?" Well, you're going to scream; we all know that. And I'm going to scream if somebody gets more than I have. We always find ourselves right back in that same box. We've got to work together.

As these principals discussed the problems of making changes in their own schools, it became obvious that positive autonomy and creativity for themselves in their own schools depended upon exerting common pressure on the central office. A negative autonomy expressed in the form of peer isolation and noncollaboration resulted from facing the central administration alone. The lesson of interest group organization is apparent to teachers and to students, who also have organized and exerted pressure for school change. Since most school principals do not work together with teachers and students to exert group pressure on those in higher authority, it is not clear what these groups could accomplish together. As members of the "administrative family," principals find it both occupationally and psychologically disloyal to consider joining others in advocate roles vis-à-vis higher level administrators.

The need for an administrative superstructure to guide a complex educational apparatus is obvious and paramount. At the same time, the special expertise and roles developed in these staff offices often set up hidden pockets of power that by their own weight establish policy. As one urban principal noted:

Even though no one means for it to happen, the principal ends up on the sideline because the central staff is the group that can find the time to make educational recommendations, develop programs, and write applications for federal funds. Thus, the principal finds himself administering a program that he had little or nothing to do with, and knows very little about the goals and objectives.

Thus, the cycle of low skill or trained impotence, and a lack of educational leadership is complete, including bureaucratic barriers to action and divergent pressure groups competing for control.

SUMMARY

This discussion of the multiple demands and opportunities for organizational leadership has stressed the extent to which the principal must manage, or help

---

Exercise 5—6. *Assigning Terms to Models*

This discussion of the multifaceted nature of local school leadership has stressed several different themes, which are more or less relevant to the alternative models of the school as an organization. The following terms are used in the preceding section: assign them to the model they most nearly fit.

task-initiating	check on teachers
collegial support	help teachers
professional development	cope with alienation
tight organization	teacher rights
worker influence	autonomy
role model	consult on decisions
reports for headquarters	mediate external pressure
manager	role conflict
instructional leadership	involve in decisions
student rights	standards for student behavior

Bureaucratic   *Collegial*   *Political*

---

manage, a complex social system. The series of tasks or pressures faced by principals include some from (1) their own roles and personal values and skills (or lack thereof); (2) their relationship with professional colleagues in the school system, supervisors, peers, and subordinates; (3) their relations to various clients or consumers, parents, students, and the community at large. Figure 5–3 illustrates some of these conflicting pressures and tasks as diagrammed by several high school principals [36].

6

THE BACKGROUND AND PROFESSIONAL SOCIALIZATION OF TEACHERS

Considerable attention has been devoted in the sociological literature to studies of the social origins of teachers and their progress through the professional socialization process. Studies of the social class background of teachers have implied that because their backgrounds were predominantly those of the middle- and lower-middle class, and their values thereby a reflection of that class stratum, teachers' entry into the profession was relatively free of conflict. However, some scholars have referred to this interpretation as a myth, pointing out that the available evidence indicates that *heterogeneity* rather than *homogeneity* characterizes the social class backgrounds of teachers—that their origins represent all strata of the social class continuum, and that the major socializing force is the profession itself [1].

In this chapter, we examine both the social backgrounds of teachers and the nature of the professional socialization process with respect to training, peer group and interest group relations, professional and extraprofessional experiences, and patterns of interaction with parents and students.

THE SOCIAL ORIGINS OF TEACHERS

Early studies of the social origins of teachers indicated that, for the most part, teachers were recruited from middle-class urban families and from rural backgrounds of the upper-middle and lower-middle class. Historically, teaching commanded respectability and status in the community, and relative to the general population in the early part of the twentieth century, those entering the teaching profession had substantially larger amounts of formal schooling [2]. At that time, teaching served as a respectable haven for well-educated women, and an avenue of social mobility for many young people of lower-status levels. Generally, teachers could be described as homogeneous—largely white, female, and middle class in cultural outlook and deportment. The social composition of the teaching profession thus reflected values and beliefs that were fairly congruent with those held by both urban and rural populations alike. This congruency was later to be shattered, however, by the impending social changes associated with rapid industrialization, urbanization, and the "mushrooming" of the educational system. As wholesale changes occurred in the society at large, so did changes occur in the schools and in the social composition of the teaching profession.

Clearly the evidence seems incontrovertible that many such changes have already occurred. Heterogeneity has replaced homogeneity, with the most pronounced changes being a decline in teachers of rural backgrounds and an increase in the number of those coming from urban working-class backgrounds. Perhaps reports from a few studies of this phenomenon may serve as illustrations of these changes.

Havighurst and Neugarten cite the following:

> As early as 1927, in a study of students attending midwestern teachers' colleges, it was found that over half came from working-class and farm backgrounds (Whitney, 1927). By 1939, Elsbree, in his book *The American Teacher*, was describing teachers as being predominantly lower-middle class in origin (Elsbree, 1939). In 1941, Greenhoe's study of over 9,000 public-school teachers, selected as a national sample, showed 38 per cent whose father were farmers, 26 per cent whose fathers were engaged in small businesses, 18 per cent whose fathers were day-laborers, and only 4 per cent whose fathers were professional men (Greenhoe, 1941). In 1948, a study of seniors in education at the University of Michigan showed a bare majority coming from white-collar families (Best, 1948). In 1950, studies of students in teachers' college in Chicago showed a majority coming from lower-middle-class families (Valentine, 1950; Wagenschein, 1950). [3]

The widely held supposition that teachers were primarily middle class in social origin was further challenged by Carlson's demonstraton that variation rather than uniformity best characterized the social background of teachers. Carlson's study indicated that:

1. Teachers have origins from all levels of the social class continuum.

2. Teachers overrepresent the top half and underrepresent the bottom half of the social class continuum.

3. Approximately 36 per cent of the teachers in the sample do not have origins in the middle class.

4. Various categories of teachers differ in their social class composition. As a category, male secondary teachers are lowest in social class origin, with about 48 per cent originating in the lower classes. Female elementary teachers are highest

in social origin, with about 23 per cent originating in the lower class, about 74 per cent in the middle class, and about 4 per cent in the upper class. [4]

National studies of the social class backgrounds of teachers also confirm Carlson's 1951 findings. Table 6−1 shows a substantial number of teachers in recent years have tended to come from various socioeconomic backgrounds [5].

Further documentation of this shift in the social origins of teachers may be seen in a study conducted by Wattenberg [6], in Detroit, which compared the father's occupation of a sample of younger teachers (under forty) to that of a sample of older teachers (over forty). The study disclosed a much greater range of occupational backgrounds among the younger teachers. Wattenberg's study also reflected a growing trend in the large urban school systems of the nation— that is, the presence of increasing numbers of public school teachers from labor backgrounds, differentially attracted to various grade levels and subject-matter fields.

In general summary of all the data, it would seem that within recent years in Detroit teachers have tended to come from a wider segment of the population. As contrasted with previous studies, this one has shown a comparatively large block of teachers with a labor background. This labor group is flowing most heavily toward

Table 6−1. Teachers' Family Origin (Occupational Background) [5]

Head of Household	Per Cent	
	1961	1971
Farmer	26.5	19.3
Unskilled	6.5	8.4
Skilled-Semiskilled	23.4	25.7
Clerical or Sales	7.1	5.5
Managerial-Self-employed	22.0	22.1
Professional-Semiprofessional	14.5	18.9

Exercise 6−1. *Assessing Sexual Composition of School Staffs*

What was the sexual composition of the teaching staff in your elementary school and secondary school? Was it any different in these two settings?

How do you explain this sexual composition pattern?

What impact, if any, does the staff's sexual composition have on students' experiences?

physical education, industrial education, home economics, and social studies. It is also leaving a distinct imprint upon the academic high school subjects. It is least felt in the kindergarten and elementary school grades. Thus, if teachers reflect their backgrounds, the elementary school would be most middle-class in their atmosphere, whereas in the secondary schools there would be large segments of the program in which youngsters of labor background would meet teachers who knew their problems from first-hand experience. [7]

A recent analysis of the social composition of Detroit public school teaching and administrative staffs relects an even more dramatic shift. Table 6–2 demonstrates the transition in Detroit from a predominately white staff in 1963 (73.7 per cent) to that of an increasing minority—group staff in 1977 (53.5 per cent) [8]. Table 6–3 demonstrates the results of a similar shift in the racial distributions of the central and region office personnel as of 1977 [9]. Although minority teachers comprise over half the teaching population in this city, they occupy only 40 per cent of the administrative roles. More white males than white females are represented in administrative roles in these regional and central offices, but black females predominate over black males.

Table 6–2. Numbers and Per Centage of White and Minority-Group Educational/Professional Personnel in the Schools, 1961–1977 [8]

| | White Personnel | | Minority-Group Personnel | | | | |
| | | | Black | | Other | | |
Year	Number	Per Cent	Number	Per Cent	Number	Per Cent	Total
1963	7,669	73.7	2,700	26.0	33	0.3	10,402
1964	7,757	72.2	2,961	27.5	32	0.3	10,750
1965	7,828	70.2	3,292	29.5	37	0.3	11,157
1966	7,792	68.0	3,628	31.7	39	0.3	11,459
1967	7,747	65.0	4,125	34.6	47	0.4	11,919
1968	7,733	62.9	4,490	36.5	71	0.6	12,294
1969	7,373	59.8	4,879	39.6	69	0.6	12,321
1970	7,189	58.0	5,106	41.2	93	0.8	12,388
1971	6,893	56.4	5,248	42.9	88	0.7	12,229
1972	6,366	53.7	5,380	45.4	102	0.9	11,848
1973	6,478	52.2	5,797	46.8	121	1.0	12,396
1974	5,704	49.6	5,676	49.4	119	1.0	11,499
1975	5,470	48.0	5,790	50.9	126	1.1	11,386
1976	4,929	46.8	5,485	52.1	116	1.1	10,530
1977	4,784	45.4	5,647	53.5	117	1.1	10,548

Table 6–3. Race and Sex Distributions of Regional and Central Office Personnel [9]

	White		Black		Other	
	Male	Female	Male	Female	Male	Female
Central Office						
Administrative	149	76	99	166	2	2
Nonadministrative	498	281	462	828	16	12
Regional Offices						
Administrative	76	41	46	94	0	6
Nonadministrative	39	94	19	186	0	9

It is also significant to note that the offices of general superintendent and executive deputy superintendent are both held by members of minority groups. As of 1979, the office of state superintendent of public instruction in Michigan was also held by a black male. These trends are also seen in several other of the more populous, heavily-urbanized states, the most notable of which is California. Despite increasing numbers of minority teachers and administrators, however, they do not equal the proportions of minority students in urban schools.

When one views the plethora of studies on the social origins of teachers, two factors emerge that are significant in understanding the professional socialization process. First, there is a rather constant shift in the social composition of the teaching profession that appears to be related to a host of political and economic forces. For example, the demographic transitions that many large urban centers are currently undergoing have attracted increasingly large numbers of minorities to the helping professions, notably teaching and social work. On the other hand, the unpredictable state of the economy has produced a "freezing" of many jobs in these employment areas and, in some cases, even mass layoffs. Such states of uncertainty create vigorous competition for relatively few openings, adding to the general scarcity of opportunities for the young and educated throughout the society. It is entirely possible that, given the limited alternatives confronting them, many more young people from higher socioeconomic levels and social class backgrounds will vie for the few professional positions made available in education. There is limited evidence that such a shift is already occurring. Ironically, qualified whites are competitive in applying for jobs in the cities, whereas qualified minorities do not enjoy a similar luxury in the suburbs.

Second, the increasing heterogeneity of teachers' social backgrounds would seem to bode a less than smooth transition into the profession. Teachers reflecting diverse social origins and conflicting value orientations are likely to be initially at odds with many of the values and practices that were considered appropriate to the profession. Moreover, innovative approaches to teacher-training programs increasingly are being adopted by many colleges and universities. Both trends make it less likely that prospective teachers come from middle-class origins, are socialized in teacher-training institutions harboring middle-class values, and enter teaching with minimal conflict with established white and middle-class beliefs and values. If teachers are not effectively presocialized to their roles, this implies that the major socializing forces will lie within the contours of the teacher profession—in the classroom experience, the peer system, the teacher organizations, other professional relationships, and daily interactions with students, parents, and community. We now examine these forces in the context of the professional socialization process.

THE PROFESSIONAL SOCIALIZATION
OF TEACHERS

Professional Training

Most teachers are trained in university settings; most are then retrained informally by colleagues and by the rules and role structures of the schools they enter.

The college and university instructors of teachers are likely to be former educators themselves, individuals with previous experience in the public or parochial schools. As representatives of an earlier generation of educators, their own background and professional socialization was likely to be more homogeneous and circumscribed than the students they are teaching. It is no secret that schools of education typically require students to take courses that are seen by many students as neither intellectually stimulating nor practically useful. Moreover, it would appear that the process of instruction in these schools is uniquely lecture oriented, seldom presenting students with a wide repertoire of instructional designs. Veterans of this preservice socialization are ill prepared for the reality of their roles in school, let alone for creative forms of instructional interaction with their students.

The common assumptions supporting teacher certification through college training include the faith that a thorough knowledge of a discipline guarantees the effective transmission of that knowledge. Common sense evidence tends to discourage this belief, however. Clearly it is not enough to know a subject well in order to teach it well.

On the Job

A new teacher generally lacks the experience and training that would permit him or her to diagnose the local school situation, or the seniority to command favorable working conditions. A substantial amount of anecdotal information suggests that the new and young teacher often gets the most "difficult" classes and the most onerous extra duties. In addition, the new teacher's anxiety and nervousness about the "first class" makes these duties even more difficult.

Willower's case studies of a junior high school indicate some ways in which teachers' beliefs about students are shaped and organized by professional peer relations [10]. Much of the real socialization of teachers occurred through the stress by older teachers on the need for control over students, and the establishment of strict rules and punitive behavior toward students. Problems in the control of pupils also apparently conditioned teacher-teacher, teacher-counselor, and teacher-administrator relations. Teachers who were viewed as weak on control and discipline of their students had "marginal" status among their colleagues. Newer teachers reported that one of their main problems with older teachers was convincing them that although they were less experienced they were not "soft" in the classroom. As Marker and Mehlinger point out, "The quickest way to be criticized by colleagues and administrators is to lose control of the class" [11]. In more public situations such as halls and assemblies, teachers made special attempts to ensure that their own students were orderly, often talking to their students with more than usual toughness. Faculty lounge conversation was dominated by boasts about the rigorous handling of discipline problems and by gossip about rebellious students. Punishments are neither the sole nor major weapon the teacher has at his or her disposal in such a system. Rather, subtle bribery often is used to maintain adult control; students who egregiously violate the rules and teachers' expectations are carefully excluded from special programs, job or college recommendations, and important extra-curricular activities.

Some aspects of this emphasis on control of students create uncomfortable feelings for teachers as well. Zeigler notes that, "The maintenance of the superior-subordinate relationship leads to personal rigidity, and the teacher's dominant need, based on fear of loss of authority, is for security" [12]. Such feelings of threat or insecurity may be uncomfortable, but in the absence of alternatives they reinforce the teacher's need for control over students who now have become threats to one's personal comfort. Teachers who wish to experiment in relating to students in new ways must not only battle their peers but students as well. Many students know no middle ground and respond negatively to classroom freedom because of their history of control and conformity in class.

Teacher pressures for strict and even punitive control of students are bound to clash with their values for an educational relationship that fosters affection, motivation, curiosity, and personal achievement. Bidwell articulates the contra-dictions between the nurturant role values of educators and their organizational role prescriptions: on the one hand, teachers feel obligated to maintain organizational authority and control over the students in their classroom; on the other hand, they wish to engage in meaningful and helpful educational relationships with students [13]. Walberg also points out that prospective teachers often have a genuine need to identify with, and associate with, the elementary and secondary students they are to teach. However, their personal needs to establish rapport with children "often conflict with the bureaucratic institutional role of the teacher" [14]. This conflict often results in lower satisfaction and effectiveness for the teacher in the classroom. Moreover, it may also produce loss of self-esteem and movement to even more depersonalized and institutionalized forms of instruction. To the extent that teachers cannot realize themselves or gain satisfaction from the teaching style they must adopt, they may progressively distance themselves from their role and occupation, and become even more impersonal and unreachable in the teacher-student transaction. It is also possible, although apparently less likely in practice, that they could try different teaching styles which strive for more personal and less controlling relations with their students.

PROFESSIONALS AS AN INTEREST GROUP: OCCUPATIONAL AND ORGANIZATIONAL ISSUES

Unlike other socializing systems, the school is based on the premise that in order for students to learn they must be deliberately taught by people who are experts in teaching. In families, on the playgrounds and streets, at parties and peer gatherings, and in front of the television set we assume that learning occurs without formal teaching or teachers.

Teaching in schools is done by professionals, specially trained persons who are assumed to be willing and able to help others. Shepard defines a professional

---

Exercise 6-2. *Assessing The Training of Teachers*

This exercise can be done by students individually.
What if you wanted to be a public school teacher?

1. How ready are you to teach now?
   Do you have fears or anxieties?

2. What substantive knowledge (mathematics, social studies) or procedural skills (in teaching) would you want?

3. What else would you want to know about the nature of young people, of schools, of budgets and policies, and the like?

4. Where would you go to get those things you need? Can you get them at a local school or department of education? Can you get them on the job?

as a person who can provide altruistic service out of a base of specialized knowledge and a high standard of conduct [15], reinforced by a code of ethics and controlled somewhat democratically by colleagues and professional peers. There is lingering doubt as to whether education should be accorded professional status alongside the more established professions, such as medicine and engineering; more often, teaching is viewed as a marginal profession. Some of this apprehensiveness is attributed to the public character of education, the fact that it receives its sustenance from public sources and is subject to the whims and fancies of taxpayers. Other, more substantive critiques relate to the lack of rigor in teacher-training programs, the relative ease of admission into professional schools, the absence of standards of excellence in both achievement and performance, and the general lack of accountability for the teacher's professional actions by either his or her colleagues or some external criterion. Nevertheless, educators do see themselves and are seen by their student-clients as possessing professional expertise and status.

The special competence of educational professionals allegedly revolves around their knowing what is good for their clients and being able to make impersonal decisions about experiences or treatments that are in their clients' best interests. In fact, some teachers who feel that they are experts in taking care of children resent interference from students or parents who are not experts. Further, teachers feel that parents are not able to treat their offspring with the objectivity that is necessary to really meet their interests fully. Since it is assumed that professionals can best serve ·clients' interests, a consensus between the needs and desires of the professional—to help—and those of the clients—to be helped—is also assumed. As a result, professionals are accorded a measure of political and social autonomy and power through which they are able to exercise this expertise in the service of the needs of others.

One of the characteristics of professionals is that in their interactions with clients, the latter are not normally invested with the power and privileges befitting citizens in a political system. Since it is assumed that the professionals can and will make judgments on behalf of their clients, the clients do not need power to protect themselves. Thus, the political power normally exercised by members of a democratic social system is not allocated to clients of most professionally oriented organizations. Other institutions invested with caring for the welfare of a client group are similarly organized; prisons, public welfare agencies, hospitals, and mental hospitals are examples.

Contemporary events in secondary schools, especially, indicate a breakdown in the traditional operation of professional systems. According to Haug and Sussman, "Students, the poor, and the black community no longer accept uncritically the service offerings of the establishment" [16]. They call this phenomenon the "revolt of the client." Whereas in the past, clients have accepted whatever services the professionals have provided, they now are beginning to raise criticisms and questions. There are three general bases for the current conflict between professionals and clients in the schools. First, many students and parents have argued recently that educational professionals are not necessarily competent, that some of them lack the technical skill to make decisions in the interest of others. Thus, it is pointed out that despite credentialization by the state, many teachers are simply not competent facilitators of students' growth, and many administrators are not well prepared for the complex job of educational management. Even if they had such skills at one time, new demands by more advanced and diverse clients seriously strain professional expertise [17].

In a second and more value-laden context, some clients disagree with the professionals' definition of the clients' interests. Since professionals and clients sometimes come from different cultural backgrounds, they may have different perspectives and goals. Thus, when professionals of a certain race or economic class serve students of a different race or class, this issue is likely to be most potent. The historic content of a curriculum may be in conflict with some students' and parents' current preferences and needs. When the professional defends and implements the historic plan, he or she may be in conflict with clients' notions of their self-interest. As Bennis points out:

> Questions of legitimacy arise whenever 'expert power' becomes ineffective. Thus black militants, drug users, draft resistors, student protestors and liberated women all deny the legitimacy of those authorities who are not black, drug experienced, pacifists, students or women. [18]

Moreover, the roles of teachers may provide another basis of conflict in values and beliefs—as exemplified by conflicts between students and teachers over the definition of effective order or discipline in class. To the extent that professionals retain the power to make decisions for others they are vulnerable to the challenge of conflict over values. Thus, as a profession develops and encourages special knowledge and roles of any kind, it may conflict with community perspectives in general. Furthermore, as a profession tries to cut across communities and serve city, region, or nationwide needs, it may conflict with the specific culture and needs of a given community.

A third base of contention derives from experience with the gradual accretion of privilege by professionals that now must be defended against violation or intrusion. The economic and political self-interests of a class of professionals establish new bases of interest group conflicts. For instance, teachers who have gained power over clients generally are not willing to relinquish that aspect of their role. Thus, Becker argues that teachers are most concerned with resisting any attempt to curtail or undermine their professional authority [19]. The professional structure of peer accountability also protects the educator from client evaluation and interference. This protection may or may not be in the best interest of the client, but it surely adds to the comfort and power of the profession, and illustrates potential conflicts between professional and client or community groups.

Teacher Unions and Associations

The actions of teachers as a professional interest group are reflected and crystallized in the operations of formal unions and/or professional associations. These groups have been publically active in defending and advancing teachers' interests that are threatened by the actions of administrators or local school boards. The history of school desegregation efforts provides us with some examples. For instance, in several southern school districts, boards of education tried to forestall the dismantling of dual school systems by threatening to lay off large numbers of black teachers and principals if they were forced to create a unitary system and staff. In fact, large numbers of black educators were terminated throughout the south as districts amalgamated black and white staffs, and the professional associations vigorously protested these actions to civil rights agencies and federal offices [20]. In a number of other school systems educational leaders have tried to limit teachers' roles in influencing school operations, and in deciding upon aspects of their own working conditions. Unions and associations often have been forceful in insuring teachers a voice over curriculum, class size, assignment policies and other important matters. Finally, numerous confrontations between teacher groups and school boards have centered upon wage and salary settlements, even to the point of strikes and lockout tactics similar to those prevalent in the industrial sector of our economy. Throughout the operations of these unions and associations, there has been a constant attempt to regularize and systematize the relationship between teacher groups and the official decision makers of the local school system. One mechanism for providing such regularity, and for resolving interest group conflicts that naturally arise, is collective bargaining.

Collective Bargaining

One of the newer themes in the organized role of professional educators has been the use of collective bargaining as a way to advance their particular interests and general educational concerns. Kalish and Goldner point out that bargaining has been advocated by teachers and other public employees who have experienced the failure of the consensual model of organizational harmony [21]. Many teachers believe that professional managers of schools and other public employee systems have not made decisions in the welfare of their employees. The loss of trust in benevolent paternalism has required professional employees to see the natural conflicts that are present in the public employer system. And, in the special case of educators, teachers can see themselves left out of the contest for resources among communities, principals, and boards. Thus, they themselves organized to obtain their share of the decision-making process and to press their own self-interests in this conflict scene.

Several causes of the rapid growth in teacher collective bargaining have been identified:

a. post-World War II increase in working-class males in teaching;

b. new teachers have accepted bargaining as an instrument to achieve their share
    of decision making, to raise salaries in order to eliminate "teacher moonlight-
    ing," and to remedy the loss of status and job satisfaction particularly in urban
    areas;

c. rivalry between the National Education Association and the American Federa-
    tion of Teachers;

d. passage of public employee and/or teacher bargaining legislation;

e. the 1960s as a period of rapid upsurge in participation in organizational decision
    making by previously excluded groups [22].

These conditions may generate and support greater teacher participation in
pursuing their concerns, but not necessarily lead to collective bargaining itself.
For instance, Metzler suggests an alternative to collective bargaining that he
feels can accomplish similar purposes:

> the only means by which educational issues can be wholly removed from the arena
> of conflict (which occurs) in negotiations is by enforcing the concept that the
> teacher, as a professional, must have an active voice in determining educational
> questions [23].

Although we do not object to this approach, several assumptions that Metzler
makes need to be clarified. He seems to assume that the conflict between
teachers and administrators is generated by the negotiating process rather than
surfaced there and created by other lasting group differences and commitments.
Metzler also seems to assume that conflict would not reoccur at newer levels of
collective decision making. We think they would, unless the acceptance of
teachers' representatives into managerial roles coopts them from loyalty to their
separate interests. Metzler's use of the term *professional* suggests that although
teachers should have an "active voice" he would not extend this principle to
include other parties who are not professionals but who also might engage in
bargaining or sharing power . . . students, parents, service personnel, and the
like.

The specific issues that are at stake in public employee bargaining, and
especially in teacher negotiations, may vary considerably in each situation. As
noted, there are three general areas: welfare issues, such as money and benefits;
input into managerial decision making about educational policies; and the
rights of parties, including the control of working conditions, agency shops, and
the like. Working conditions often overlap educational policies, especially in
areas such as class size, staff transfer regulations, student discipline, and the
like.

In private economic institutions, money and the rights of the parties are the most probable issues of conflict for owners/managers and employees. More input into managerial decision making is usually demanded by the more professionalized employee. In a system that has little control over its own funds, and thus minimal leeway in financial bargaining, the managers often may compromise on issues of institutional power and control in return for lowered economic demands. Gittell and Doherty both have noted the narrow conception of material self-interest that teacher groups have adopted in the past [24]. More recently, however, it appears that the priority on salaries and benefits is being challenged by greater concerns for input on policies and decisions about working conditions. Thus, a key issue in educational bargaining is disagreement or conflict over the appropriate scope of bargaining.

Additional complexities are encountered in collective bargaining in schools over the issue of who should be involved in bargaining [25]. Since the schools are public institutions, more than two parties are involved: more than managers and employees are affected by teachers' salaries and working conditions and a potential strike. The public at large has interests directly at stake in school negotiations: they have to foot the bill, they are the basic consumers of educational systems, and they may be maximally inconvenienced by work stoppages. Moreover, it often is unclear how the public's interests are represented in school negotiations, since educators and the board members who are apparently negotiating on behalf of the public "are frequently not accountable to the public" [26].

The Bay Area Radical Teachers Organizing Committee (BARTOC) has proposed that teacher groups consider advocating a wide range of issues, and have objected to the narrow focus of teacher bargaining for welfare issues and workplace self-interest. They note that a narrow-interest organization was a source of strength in the traditional employer-employee relation, but that:

> for teachers, and for other public employees, who work both for and with a client group, that perspective will mean growing isolation and alienation from the communities we serve. Our struggle for power will pit us against them [27].

Rather, BARTOC suggests that teacher organizations advocate antiracism and students rights' programs, as well as community controlled schools. In this way teachers and oppressed clients can join together and mobilize against school managers and against communitywide ruling elites. This is one of the few articles that connects organizational and latent interest group roles, and it does so in a radical way. Other articles link these roles by indicating teachers' location in white and middle-class statuses, and thus explain their being pitted appropriately against poor people, minorities, and the young, and in so doing fronting for even more powerful and distant elites.

The outcomes of the bargaining process are determined by the relative power of the parties. And, in the end, the power of the employees or the union is determined by whether or not they have the right to strike, to withhold services and interrupt or terminate the operation of the public service system. Limits on the public employees' right to strike vary in different states, and enforcement procedures, injunctions against a legal or illegal strike, vary from state to state. The general issue seems to be that strikes by public employees are more likely to be illegal (and to be enjoined) to the extent that they (1) fail to develop from clear precedent conditions of breaches of reasonable and good faith negotiations, and (2) present a clear and present danger to the public welfare [28].

At just what point a school strike presents a clear and present danger to the order and safety of a community is hard to determine. But it is clear, for instance, that strikes by policemen or garbagemen can be tolerated less well by the public than strikes by teachers. The meaning of the phrase "creates a clear and present danger or threat to the health, safety or welfare of the public" is clarified by Sagot and Jennings [29]: "In practical application, however, this limitation has meant that a lawful work stoppage of four days (or less) in duration can be instantly converted into an illegal strike . . ." One of the reasons that teacher strikes are not tolerated is the general public's commitment to their youngsters being in school, and to the continued operation of public schools. Other issues involved include

a. Potential loss of school state subsidy.

b. Loss of schooling seen as being very detrimental especially to/by poor and minority children.

c. Likelihood of gang violence.

d. Need for parents to care for out-of-school youngsters may mean loss of income.

e. Cost of police overtime.

One of the possible outcomes of teachers becoming more closely involved in the pursuit of their own material and professional interests through strikes, negotiations, and other forms of organizational pressure is the potential effect that these activities are likely to have on the public with respect to teachers and the teaching profession. There is some evidence that both the teachers' status in the community and their relationship with community interest groups is affected negatively by strikes, particularly if the strikes are prolonged.

Just as a strike is the ultimate weapon in teachers' power confrontation with educational managers, it is also the ultimate expression of teachers' interests that may be separable and in conflict with those of the community. This is especially the case when a strike is seen as a teacher action against the community, as opposed to a teacher action with the community against a different target, such as against distant ruling elites.

TEACHERS RELATIONS WITH OTHER INTEREST GROUPS: PEERS/PARENTS/ STUDENTS

Relations with Professional Colleagues and Administrators

A teacher's relations with his or her peers contributes crucially to the teacher's professional socialization and performance. Several studies from various fields stress the importance of informal peer relations on personal and group behavior. In some cases, peers develop expectations and informal rules that are strong enough to challenge supervisory regulations and other institutional constraints [30]. Peer group cohesion and loyalty apparently decrease interpersonal alienation and increase a sense of well-being among industrial workers. Although there are many dissimilarities between industrial and educational bureaucracies, it is not surprising that some of the same peer dynamics prevail among teachers. Inasmuch as any individual understands himself or herself through the reactions of others to him or her, teachers also discover their own professional competence and sources of personal enjoyments and satisfaction in their relations with their peers.

Studies of instructional innovation show that teachers who are integrated into the fabric of peer social relations are more likely to share new teaching practices with colleagues [31]. The support of one's colleagues appears to encourage teachers to try new ideas and to risk discussing these ideas in public. Teachers who feel liked by their peers, who feel that staff relations are personal and warm, and who engage in informal association with peers are more likely to share ideas. Teachers who serve on committees together or who travel to school together are more likely to know and support each others' innovations than teachers who do not have these kinds of associations with their fellow workers. Although members of a car pool, for instance, do not necessarily come up with more ideas and procedures than they would if they rode alone, being together gives individuals a chance to test out their ideas and, perhaps, win support for them. The job of teaching a classroom full of students is so complex that no teacher can do it well without ideas and help from peers.

At the same time, the education profession itself establishes barriers to such collaboration by promulgating the need for great autonomy and freedom. As Janowitz has asserted: "Rather than speak of overprofessionalization as the pathology of the classroom teacher, it is more accurate to highlight the excessive professional isolation of the classroom teacher. . . ." [32]. This isolation is so pervasive because each teacher is assumed to be a fully competent professional and often is shut off in his or her autonomous classroom. Review by peers is often received as an intrusive threat to one's own competence. Since the teacher who asks for help may be perceived as incompetent, it is understandable why wariness and isolation often characterize staff relations.

A study of several high schools in Dayton, Ohio, asked teachers to identify the issues that prevented them from sharing problems and solutions in desegregated education with their colleagues [33]. The following question was asked:

There are probably a great number of problems or barriers that discourage or prevent teachers from adequately discussing their ideas and working on the problems of race relations in their schools. The following list of barriers includes ones reported by teachers in other schools and communities. Please check *all* those items which you think are significant barriers, in *your* experience, to working on and discussing such problems in *your* school.

_____My feeling that it's not necessary to deal with racial problems.

_____My lack of knowledge or background about minorities and this community.

_____My high standards for classroom performance and the expectation that minorities won't meet these.

_____My lack of empathy with students.

_____My fear of criticism from my colleagues, friends, or from students' parents.

_____I am a young teacher reluctant to tell older teachers what to do.

_____My lack of confidence about what I am doing in class.

_____My desire to keep to myself and not take risks.

_____I resent the extra energy required to come to planning meetings, long staff meetings with colleagues, etc.

_____My colleagues criticize my leadership.

_____Colleagues don't recognize the problems.

_____Colleagues want to be left alone—the proper role of a professionally trained teacher is to act independently.

_____Colleagues' prejudices.

_____Colleagues resent extra time required.

_____Colleagues express resistance in ways I do not know how to handle.

_____Colleagues lack real concern for minority students' welfare.

_____School policy about racial relations isn't clear.

_____Lack of strong system support for working on racial problems.

_____Lack of direction for us in what to do and how to do it.

_____Lack of principal support for teacher initiative in the classroom or with colleagues.

——Lack of money for our extra time, school meetings, etc.

——Great gap between the school and most of the community with regard to standards for education, values about racial relations, etc.

——White parents resist classroom work on racial relations.

——Minority parents resist classroom work on racial relations.

——Social class differences between neighborhood groups.

——Parents harass teachers who try anything that increases interracial activities.

These are formidable barriers indeed. Some of these barriers lie within the personal style of the individual teacher (my own lack of initiative, I resent the extra energy), and some lie with the problems discussed in Chapter 4 regarding school community relations (minority parents resist, white parents resist, great gap, parents harass teachers). But the two most potent categories involve the organizational system of the school, both with regard to the kinds of leadership the principal provides (lack of direction, lack of principal support, lack of system support), and to collegial sharing relationships (colleagues lack concern, colleagues want to be left alone, colleagues resent extra time).

Especially when communities and schools are experiencing conflict, teachers' feelings of support from colleagues could be an important source of strength to prevent further deterioration. A great deal of conflict in the classroom or hallways, or even in faculty meetings, undoubtedly saps a teacher's strength and reserves. Antagonistic or strained staff relations further drain support from the harassed teacher. Moreover, in several schools fraught with tension the causal chain has appeared quite obvious; difficult collegial relations have

---

Exercise 6–3. *Assessing The Lifespace of a Schoolteacher*

This exercise can be done by students individually. Go back and visit the elementary or secondary school from which you graduated. Spend some time talking with a teacher, and try to find out:

1. How satisfied is this person with his/her career? Does she/he wish to continue in this role?

2. How does this person feel about the competence and motivation of current student groups?

3. Does this teacher experience support from staff, colleagues, and administrators?

4. Does this teacher experience conflict between the demands of family life and school? If yes, how does he/she cope with or resolve those conflicts?

initiated or spurred conflict among educators or between educators and students. In one suburban Michigan school, for instance, 49 per cent of the teachers belonged to the AFT affiliate and 51 per cent belonged to the NEA local. This division resulted in very heated debate and politicking within the staff, and exacerbated tensions in a school already troubled by interracial conflict.

In one city a group of young teachers tried to evade such negative peer pressures by forming a citywide teachers cooperative to provide intellectual and emotional support for innovative teachers. The youth-oriented character of this group caused older teachers to castigate it as a "Communist group." Some teachers engaged in trying to change their colleagues remarked on these problems.

> Some teachers think we're very radical, something to fear, young teachers. They don't understand how things really are. "Just cool it down and it will go away." There's no hope that they'll ever change.

> I try to make the fact that I was part of a change program unknown, because I was afraid of the others saying—"those kooks."

The fear of, and experience of, ostracism is an important barrier against efforts at peer organization and change in schools.

Teachers' perceptions of other staff members' expectations on key issues may help illustrate this perspective. In five of the seven secondary schools studied by Chesler and his colleagues, teachers were asked to indicate the extent to which there were strong expectations regarding certain staff behaviors. Their responses are summarized in Table 6—4 [34].

Teachers are clearly most unified in their perceptions of expectations to maintain order and quiet. In the one school that appears different, C, the principal urged a low priority for this concern compared with the learning benefits that are potentially freed by student interaction and, perhaps, even noisy exchange. There is also some agreement in all the schools studied regarding a priority on encouraging interracial communication and, although varying by school, experimentation in instructional strategies. However, little staff support seems to exist for commitments to aid colleagues' work and growth. These data strongly support the image of the isolated and autonomous teacher who generally operates without emotional and professional support and stimulation from colleagues.

Relations with Parents and Students

Teachers traditionally have been isolated from parents and the local community. Whereas one of the original purposes of this pattern may have been to free teachers from the personal pressures of friends and neighbors, it has resulted in a distance that sometimes works to the disadvantage of the teaching

Table 6−4. Per Cent of Teachers Indicating That Their Staff Is "Greatly" or "Very Greatly" Expected To Do Certain Things [34]

Norm	School				
	A	B	C	D	E
To help other teachers with their classroom problems	22	12	5	2	10
To talk informally with students after class	16	32	26	11	13
To encourage interracial communications between students	36	45	47	28	34
To maintain order and quiet in the classroom	78	72	24	62	57
To experiment with new teaching techniques	23	42	55	13	44

process. This is especially problematic in poor or minority communities where the school itself may not be in touch with the culture and needs of the local residents. White and middle-class teachers may then be especially isolated from poor and minority parents and students, and vice versa. In such cases, parents often feel that teachers do not care about them and their children, and teachers, in turn, often feel that parents do not care about the educational process.

The classroom teacher in a large high school is required to contribute to the learning of many students in spite of a minimal degree of contact with these students. Given most departmental arrangements a teacher may see as many as 150 different students for one hour a day, five days a week. Bearing responsibility for the management of so many varied human learning processes is difficult for even the most experienced teacher. As preoccupied functionaries in a complex bureaucracy, few teachers are able to take advantage of their job security to innovate with flexible and satisfying forms of teaching. This inertia of tradition determines most teaching processes and what occurs in most classes.

It is now clear that the organizational roles of dominance and submission are witness to, and perhaps the creator of, many of the problems people face in schools. Surely these roles help set groups of students and teachers against one another in forms of institutional conflict. In a survey of high schools experiencing a great deal of overt conflict teachers were asked about intra- and inter-role group conflict. The results are summarized in Table 6−5 [35]. Fewer teachers in schools C, E and G indicate constant conflict among most of these groups than in the other schools. An emphasis on conflict within student groups is suggested most strongly by teachers in schools A, D, and F, and more teachers in these schools also perceive teacher−administrative conflict. It is possible that

Table 6−5. Per Cent of Teachers Reporting Conflict *Often* or *Always* Occurs Between These Groups in Their Schools [35]

Conflicts	A	B	C	D	E	F	G
A. Student−student	58.7	28.4	9.4	72.3	22.9	55.1	19.1
B. Student−teacher	39.6	24.4	18.9	48.9	41.0	63.3	34.9
C. Teacher−teacher	25.4	13.5	24.5	23.4	9.8	47.0	14.3
D. Teacher−administrator	61.9	24.3	22.7	59.6	9.8	40.9	7.9

one reason for the teacher−administration conflict is that administrators in these schools do not deal with disruptive students in the way that faculty members would like them to. Many teachers in most schools report considerable student−teacher conflict as well. Thus, in almost all these schools, all parties or interest groups are seen to experience substantial conflict with one another.

Exercise 6−4. *Examining Social Relations Between Teachers and Students*

This exercise can be done by students individually or in groups. If the latter, it might be fruitful to divide the class into like-race and like-sex groups.

Do you have any out-of-class relationships with your college instructors?

1. How comfortable do you feel visiting a faculty member's office? Does it differ according to the rank or age or sex of the faculty member?

2. Do you ever discuss personal matters—other than classroom matters? Are your conversations with faculty members out of class mutual, or one way?

3. Have you ever met a faculty member's family? Have any faculty members met your family?

4. Do male students seem to have different experiences in these regards than female students? Do white students seem to have different experiences than black, Hispanic, Asian-American or American Indian students?

5. What seem to be some of the organizational barriers to personal relationships among college instructors and their students?

Teacher Roles in the Classroom

Most of the teachers' time and energy, as well as their interaction with students, takes place inside the formal classroom. In the exercise of classroom leadership, teachers have several different pedagogical roles or options available. Each carries different instructional and interactional values.

The most common instructional approach may be to transmit academic material. The direct transmission of facts, theories, and learning procedures from teachers or teaching materials to students has been the most traditional instructional method used. In this style of instruction, the teacher lectures, prescribes exercises, plans activities, and otherwise helps students absorb the curriculum content. The prearranged curriculum is the major, and sometimes exclusive, focus of school and classroom work. Students often feel that this instructional role is dry and unstimulating. Since this is the only way in which most teachers have been trained, the transmission technique is sometimes used even when students could learn more effectively in other ways and when teachers could use styles that are better suited to their special talents and skills.

At times, the teacher may consider and present himself or herself as a model of social behavior. Using the teacher as an image, students may identify with what it would be like to be a competent learner or a practitioner in a field. The teacher also serves as a social model in setting the tone of a classroom; students often take their cues from the teacher in deciding how they must treat each other. The teacher's actions and stated values must be consistent if they are to have credibility with students and be modeled by them. If students perceive that a teacher behaves one way, while expecting different or even contradictory behavior from them, they are unlikely to recognize or believe that teacher's example.

The teacher may also define his or her role as helping students discover their own learning needs and values. A heterogeneous class is often a place of confusion and conflict regarding cultural values—the teacher can help students explore their beliefs and values and to see the relations between these values and behavior. Transmission assumes teacher initiative; in contrast, discovery processes require students to take initiatives to which the teacher responds. The essential goals of the teacher's role in discovery learning involve the creation of appropriate situations that spark student's interest and help them review what and how they learn. The teacher is not a passive but an active guide for student inquiries. Discovery is a new process for most students in school, although it is a natural part of all learning. In all teaching efforts the teacher attempts to link the material to be learned with the discoveries that learners wish to make.

In the teaching of values, teachers traditionally have utilized the contrasting strategies of denial and imposition. While appearing to take a neutral position on moral issues, the technique of denial promotes a "laissez-faire" attitude and fails to guide youngsters to their own explorations. As a result school often seems to students to be a valueless world. Other teachers who deal with cultural and moral issues intend to teach the "right" positions on dress, behavior, sexuality, politics, drugs, and the like. Intentionally or unintentionally, these teachers impose and reinforce traditional community values by not allowing other opinions to be discussed or by defining alternatives as illegitimate.

Researchers also have indicated that teachers tend to reinforce community traditions by their adoption of community values around discussion and public expression in the classroom. Jennings and Zeigler, viewing the teaching occupation as embodying cultural expectations, examined the ideology of teachers in regard to their role in teaching political issues. [36]. They asked a national sample of social studies teachers whether they would feel free to engage in a list of eleven activities, ranging from speaking in class favorably about the U.N., the civil rights movement, or socialism, to running for political office, going on strike, or allowing distribution of political literature. Teachers more often felt free to engage politically in the community than in the classroom. Interestingly, it was also discovered that teachers who endorsed more political expressiveness in the classroom were also more likely to partici-pate in community political affairs; such teachers also subscribed less than others to the traditional goals of civic education, such as the teaching of good citizens. Whether because of selection or socialization, teachers with more seniority were less expressive on political questions in the classroom.

Jennings and Zeigler concluded that since teachers have very little regional mobility they reflect—in some cases exaggerate—the culture and political values of their local environment. Furthermore, the size and complexity of the community were also found to make a difference. The big city teacher, working in a heterogeneous setting, is more politically expressive; the small town teacher is more reticent, more likely to be expressive only when the issue appears to maintain the status quo.

As a teaching style, effective exploration of values requires the teacher to be open to students and nonpartisan with students' own self-discoveries. Yet the teacher must express his or her own values at times, or the entire process becomes unreal. Withholding appropriate value comments creates the impres-sion that the teacher fears confrontation or is confused. This may create more confusion, since students do not know whether to respond to the teacher as a person having individual views, or as a final authority on such matters. Withholding comments on values may also suggest a teacher's fear that any expression of adult values would be so influential as to damage students' autonomy. The teacher who is sensitive to these issues does not have to worry excessively. Students do not consider value statements as undue pressure if a genuine atmosphere has been established to explore, rather than to agree with or conform to, certain convictions. Strangely, some teachers who enunciate a concern about value imposition also complain about students' rejection of teachers. This is a heady and paralytic ambivalence.

On other occasions the teacher may be the organizer of a social climate of supportive interpersonal and group relations that can be consciously used in assisting academic learning and social growth. A teacher can facilitate positive peer relations between students by attempting to create a cohesive classroom group that develops its own rules as well as academic and social leadership patterns. Every class has in it the seeds of such student cohesion, but many teachers frustrate its develoment because of their control style. These teachers may fear their own inability to lead or influence a class that can provide leadership for itself. Other teachers fail to encourage meaningful student involvement because they fear an inhibiting rather than a liberating influence on academic growth. There are some grounds for such concern; student standards may result in a stifling conformity unless issues are squarely faced.

Recent research studies demonstrate that one way the teacher can impact upon classroom social relations is to organize the class into smaller working groups in which students cooperate to accomplish learning tasks. By stressing smaller working groups, teachers help counter the anonymity and impersonality of the large classroom setting. By stressing cooperative tasks, teachers help students learn to work together, rather than to compete with one another for the highest grades, most attention, and the like. These classroom options appear to be especially useful in interracial situations, where they provide the possibility of student equal-status contact and cooperation across racial lines [37].

On some occasions a teacher may try to organize community resources to overcome the unnatural division between classroom activities and community pressures and events. Strained divisions in young people's lives are ameliorated when classroom training is applied to the community in direct, relevant ways. To bring this about, the teacher may create models of the community and community pressures in class. Role playing and simulation programs may be very helpful in this regard. Students can learn about, and work directly in, community institutions and invite community leaders or parents into the classroom to observe and participate in activities and discussions. This style has many difficulties associated with it, especially for the teacher trained only in intraclassroom techniques. Moreover, those school personnel who live outside the community and who lack knowledge of its personalities and problems will not be able to create or deal with realistic programs.

Finally, the teacher can adopt the posture of a co-learner in a shared program of student-teacher inquiry. Many teachers look foward to teaching because they expect to learn from it. Unfortunately, few students know that they are, and can be, agents of their teacher's growth. Teachers can share teaching responsibilities with students and each can articulate what and how they may learn from one another. The reciprocal nature of teaching and learning is exemplified in such an approach. The teacher may give class time to a student or students who want to "teach" or share their learning experiences with the class and may meet with them prior to class to discuss teaching strategies. This approach may help students understand why the class is the way it is and how to use it more effectively as a learning environment. Redefining the roles of students and teachers as discussed previously may help them overcome the status barriers that prevent collaboration in the educative process. Admitting to the role of learner in no way diminishes a teacher's professionalism. In fact, admission and acceptance may enhance one's ability to be both teacher and learner. This technique helps distribute responsibility for teaching to all members of the class, making everyone aware of the possibility of learning together.

Each teacher may sometimes make different and equally valid choices among these alternatives or else mix these alternatives. Teachers who cannot imagine alternatives that work well, or who are uncomfortable with their own styles, may feel "in a rut" and unsure of their own ability to help youngsters. Then they often retreat from innovating in class, to the sanctuary of professional insulation and punitive control of the young.

Teacher Control Ideology and Student Behavior

A great deal of the technical training of teachers focuses upon learning various methods of instruction. However, actual behavior in the classroom is

---

Exercise 6–5. *Examining Interaction Patterns in Classroom Groups*

This exercise can be done by appointing one or two students to be observers or participant-observers of this classroom, or of a similar classroom engaged in group discussion. The results of these observations can be shared with the class.

Observe the workings of the classroom in terms of some of the following issues or phenomena.

1. How does the seating pattern in the class affect who can *see* whom?

2. Generally, who talks with whom? How much of the conversation flow is from teacher to students, students to teacher, students to students?

3. Do people in the classroom appear to know each other personally? Are first names used in conversation?

4. How would you describe the energy level of the class? Are people alert and active, passively listening, nodding out?

5. Are there any evident arguments, disagreements, or conflicts? What happens to them? How do people behave toward those with whom they are in conflict?

6. When people leave the class, do they stay together, say goodbye, or just disappear?

---

based on more than rational planning and design. In all of a teacher's relationships with students, his or her values, attitudes, perceptions, and assumptions about students influence his or her behavior. In discussing the very low percentages of youngsters who actually report participation in such "delinquent" activities as "stirring up trouble," and "drinking or smoking together," Coleman remarks on the large numbers of teachers who report these behaviors and reflects on the stereotypes and suspicions by which adults judge youngsters [38]. Many informal reports, which are based on observation of schools and teachers, document ways in which these educational agents

---

Exercise 6-6. *Designing Interdependent Learning Tasks*

Suppose you wanted to teach a group of five secondary school students about the diverse political, religious, and economic forces producing the first American Revolution. How could you design a set of individual and joint activities that required these students to learn from one another, and that did not permit them to complete the task (including being rewarded for it) unless they used each others' resources?

1. Pay attention to issues of differential student skill and interest.

2. Pay attention to the question of how individual work fits into a whole.

3. Pay attention to how students who are used to working alone can learn to listen to and work with one another.

4. Pay attention to the question of your continued supervision and input during their work.

5. Pay attention to the kinds of rewards available, and to the conditions under which rewards are provided to individuals or groups of students.

Some other topics that might also lend themselves to this task include:

1. Try to create an interdependent learning task that focuses on the topic of learning about future jobs and employment opportunities for adolescents.

2. Try to create an interdependent learning task that focuses on learning about the geography, politics, and economics of Eastern Europe.

3. Try to create an interdependent learning task that focuses on learning about the poetry of Robert Frost.

---

communicate to students that youngsters are evil or rebellious, or that certain students are bound to fail. Some educators communicate a negative trust and judgment of adolescents by the rules and regulations that eliminate student self-expression and try to regulate so many parts of their students' lives.

Milton Mayer voiced the unstated and, perhaps unconscious, positions of many educators when he admitted that:

> The young terrify me. They terrify me because I have mine, which I got by the exercise of the good precepts I got from my parents plus being white and landing on my feet every time I fell on my face. The young do not terrify me with their popguns; I have ten machine guns for every one of their popguns. They terrify me because they show some small sign of social maturity, of civic responsibility and human concern. [39]

Some adults are fearful of the popguns of youth, but more often this fear masks the more underlying threat to established values that some youth styles and activities represent.

The general proposition that students are to be distrusted and thus generally controlled plays a central part in the organizational life of public schools, and particularly in teachers' treatment of young people. The very character of educational organizations—service units that do not select their clients, yet whose clients cannot refuse to participate—establishes a strong control orientation. In one of the early empirical studies of this factor, Becker concluded that public school teachers in Chicago were primarily involved in maintaining their authority over students in the classroom and in resisting inroads on their authority in the school from administrators and parents [40].

Willower's research on the pupil control ideology of teachers illuminates many of the attitudinal patterns underlying contemporary classroom practice [41]. His efforts to divide teachers' ideologies into categories of custodial and humanistic are perhaps summarized in the statements that were used in efforts to validate their scales:

Custodial (Type C)

Traditional teachers who prefer to work in the formal atmosphere of a traditional school are typical of Type C. The primary concern of these teachers is that of maintaining order among the pupils. These teachers think of pupils in terms of stereotypes based upon appearance, behavior, and parents' social status. They look upon pupils as irresponsible, and undisciplined; therefore, they believe punishment is a necessary form of control. These teachers do not attempt to understand pupils' behavior, but instead view misbehavior in moralistic terms or as a personal affront. Teachers holding this viewpoint tend to treat pupils impersonally, to mistrust them, and to be generally pessimistic. These teachers prefer an autocratic school organization where teacher-pupil status is rigidly enforced and pupils accept communications and orders without question. Teachers and pupils alike feel responsible for their actions only to the extent that orders are carried out to the letter.

Humanistic (Type H)

Permissive teachers who prefer to work in an informal atmosphere are typical of Type H. These teachers view the behavior of the pupils in psychological and sociological rather than moralistic terms. Engagement in worthwhile activities is viewed as more important to the pupils' learning than is the absorption of facts. The withdrawing pupil is seen as a problem equal to that of the overactive one. These teachers are optimistic that, through close personal relationships with pupils and the positive aspects of friendship and respect, the pupils will learn to disciple themselves. Such teachers desire a democratic school organization with flexibility in rules, increased pupil self-determination, and two-way communication between the pupils and teachers. The difference between the teachers' status in school and that of pupils is minimized. Teachers and pupils alike are willing to act upon their own volition and to accept responsibility for their actions. [42]

Custodial and humanistic teachers are regarded as "ideal types" at opposite ends of the continuum, rather than as pure types that exist in reality. Throughout much of Willower's work he speaks of the dilemmas, adaptations, and inner tensions of the humanistic teacher in a custodial or control-oriented environment. Thus, even teachers who can affect humanistic classrooms must deal with the larger context of the school's organizational focus on control.

Nordstrom, et al. use the concept *resentiment* in analyzing the nature of some teachers' unconscious and negative orientations to students and the constraining atmosphere of the school [43]. This approach links some aspects of teachers' attitudes and values with the tendency to disparage and discourage students, perhaps even especially good students who tend to come up with unique and individualistic responses to school. The basic concept is that certain teachers, who are often blocked from their own personal-professional growth, who have systematically repressed certain emotions in themselves, and who are perhaps hampered by institutional arrangements, take out their feelings of frustration on their students, especially those students who resist repression. The effect on students is to dispel enthusiasm, stifle originality, and undermine intellectual courage.

An example of teachers' feelings of frustration and anger, stimulated by apparent student defiance, is provided by one teacher in an urban school.

Too often students just get away with something. It seems like a little thing—a boy walking through the hall with his hat on. So I reminded him that he's a boy and must remember to take his hat off. He said, "Oh, I will, sometime," and he didn't even look at me, he just kept on walking. I was a little apprehensive myself, so I didn't try to stop him physically; if I had, he might have said, "Take your hands off me." But the fact that he was able just to walk past me gave him the feeling, "Well, look how great I am, I showed her." Well, this is a mis-education.

The use of rigorous means of control, then, is partly an effort to maintain "law and order" to prevent students "from getting away with it" or "taking advantage of you."

Exercise 6—7. *Analyzing Staff Caring/Concern for Students*

This exercise can be done by students in groups or as a total class.
Consider your experience in prior schooling. How could you tell if
your teachers cared about you and your welfare?

1. What behaviors indicated caring?

2. How did that caring feel to you? Did it make a difference in your
   attitude or reaction to your teacher? In your work?

3. Was the kind of caring you experienced in secondary school
   different than in elementary school?

4. Is the kind of caring you receive different in college? Do you
   experience caring at all? On a different basis?

5. Did everyone receive similar caring, or did some student groups
   receive different kinds and different amounts of caring?

As a result of these and other factors, many teachers have difficulty being
effective with their students in the classroom. Subsequent feelings of impotence, incompetence, fear, and/or hostility eventually may be translated into
student-teacher tensions and warfare. In a study of secondary schools experiencing overt conflict teachers were asked to specify the classroom problems with
which they desired some help [44]. These data, which are summarized in Table
6—6 suggest that more than a third of the teachers sampled were pressed by a
need to improve in an area in which they are supposed to be most competent—
academic progress of students. How threatening, then, for teachers lacking
confidence in this central skill, that they are also faced by so many other tasks
for which they have even less preparation. The teachers' responses to the other
items suggest goals for fairly specific skill-development programs. The ability
to teach a class composed of heterogeneous groups of students is a prime
requisite in any pluralistic educational system. Attempts to cope with this
difficult task by segregating ability groups in school or class have led to serious
enclaves of frustration and/or failure. The teacher's inability to work with, or
teach about, differences in backgrounds, interests, or styles invariably pushes
some students out of the educative process. Teachers' insecurities about dealing
effectively with student defiance may lead to fear and hesitation, or to
resentment or righteousness, and to overreactions that escalate minor conflicts
into major eruptions. Problems in maintaining students' interest, or in getting
them to do assigned tasks, may well reflect differing social and intellectual
priorities between the curriculum and style that teachers use and the goals that
students seek. An irrelevant or obsolete curriculum that does not tap students'

Table 6-6. Per Cent of Teachers Stating They Desired Help
with a Variety of Classroom Problems [44]

Problems	Per Cent of Teachers Asking for Help (N = 410)
A. Teaching youngsters whose abilities are very different from one another	20.0
B. Racial or ethnic hostilities among students	11.5
C. Getting students to do assignments	19.3
D. Dealing with defiance	17.1
E. Trying to help students with their problems	10.5
F. Raising academic achievement of students	36.8
G. Maintaining interest of students	17.1

interests or encourage teacher creativity cannot be expected to contribute to the process of "motivating" students.

The problems that many teachers encounter when they attempt to use innovative instructional methods have been previously discussed. Few people in the system—students, peer, or supervisors—expect, are prepared for, or support such creative but deviant behavior. The following dialogue dramatically illustrates some of these issues:

(*Female teacher*): You know, I've been thinking about the workshop Saturday, and a lot of the ideas were pretty good. I really would like to try something with my kids. But you know, I looked at my students today and I thought, I can't try those with my students.

(*Male teacher*): Yeah, me either. All that's fine to talk about, but I don't know how we can get it done here in this school.

(*Female teacher*): You know, once I tried letting them have a discussion group.

(*Male teacher*): A discussion group?

(*Female teacher*): Oh, the kids got so excited, they made all this noise, and I got a note from the central office telling me to cut down the noise.

Professional Orientations in Interracial Situations

The crucial importance of teachers' skills, needs, and assumptions regarding their students is especially relevant in cross-racial or interracial situations.

Indeed, recent research suggests that some teachers may fail to be helpful to black or brown students precisely because of their own attitudes toward students. Niemeyer, for instance, argues that "the chief cause of the low achievement of the children of alienated groups is the fact that too many teachers and principals honestly believe that these children are educable only to an extremely limited extent [45]." Some scholars have argued that this belief is transmitted to students, affecting the students' own beliefs and expectations regarding their performance and thereby creating a self-fulfilling prophecy of minority failure [46]. This process can be reversed, as when teachers privately and publicly believe and profess an optimism about the capacities of minority youth and a faith in their ability to educate them.

The importance of positive staff attitudes toward minority students is especially critical in newly desegregated situations, in which students often experience staff rejection, discrimination, favoritism, or subtle disconfirmation [47]. In other cases, students may simply encounter disinterest or distance, and the teacher may just not invest energy teaching in ways that meet the needs of minority students. Gerard and Miller, for instance, note that teachers' attitudes toward minority youth had an impact on whether these youngsters felt they were welcome in interracial learning environments [48]. Moreover, they report, teachers with more positive attitudes toward minority students were more likely to try new teaching practices and curriculum innovations that were related to interracial problems in class.

In addition to these reports of teacher evaluation of the achievement potentials of blacks, some researchers note teachers behaving differently toward white and black children in class [49]. In their own social behavior, in their limits on peer activity, and in their use of authority, many white teachers consciously or unconsciously single out black youngsters in more negative or disapproving ways. Such differential behavior usually does not remain hidden from the students in the classroom. Some comments from black southern high school students in the early days of desegregation illustrate these messages.

My history teacher doesn't seem to know how to pronounce the word Negro.

The children would tease me and she would get up and go out to let them carry on.

Our history teacher, in class, she would never call on Negroes, she would give us our assignment last. [50]

Other examples are provided by the following comments of northern white elementary school children.

They just chew gum and candy and the teacher tells them to spit it out and they don't even spit it out. And she doesn't do nothing; she just lets them have it.

The Negro kids fall asleep at their desk and our teacher won't bother them. She just lets them sleep. If we were asleep, the teacher would get all hairy; she'd probably chop off our heads.

Sometimes the teacher looks down on Negroes in my room. It's because she's white, and she does look down on the whites too, but more on the Negroes. [51]

When students have these and similar perceptions of their teachers, they are less likely to make positive overtures and to create friendships or effective working relationships across racial lines.

Several scholars concerned with the quality of racial interaction in the desegregated classroom have indicated some of the issues and alternatives that teachers must confront in these situations. For instance, positive interracial attitudes are most likely to develop when students have positive interracial experiences, and deliberate attention must be paid to the creation of such experiences in the classroom. This probably requires the creation of tasks (such as learning math or reading or geography) in which every student's information or expertise is required for a group of students to achieve a solution [52]. In this way, students experience collaboration on a common task. Moreover, it is also useful for there to be "payoff" or rewards for these acts of collaboration, and thus some observers suggest that classroom rewards, such as grades and praise, be distributed on a group basis, to all members, thereby decreasing the intense individual competition that prevails in most classrooms [53]. Thus, the creation of interracial task groups that must work together for common success, and that are rewarded on a common basis, represents the best hope for creating equal status relationships that teach new and more positive forms of racial interaction and attitudes. In this same context, it is clear that students are no better prepared to work in such groupings than are teachers, and that students need special preparation to work in equal status relations. If some students are already educationally disadvantaged by their prior inadequate education, they may need special training to increase their skills so that they can cooperate on an equal basis and increase their expectations of their own and others' performance. All students need training in how to work together in independent and interdependent task groups [54].

The teacher who can neither model nor manipulate effective interracial relations, either because of his or her own attitudes or skill deficiencies, cannot provide leadership for students who are similarly resistant or unskilled. In this regard it is clear how some teachers' reactions, and their expression in classroom behavior, may help shape the racist quality of peer relationships.

Those teachers who are openly resistant to minority students or to interracial education may deliberately contribute to a negative experience in interpersonal and intergroup relations in the classroom. Those teachers who are inhibited or paralyzed by their own fears also may contribute to a negative student experience by ignoring or suppressing vital issues in the classroom or by managing these issues ineffectively. In a study of the responses by some southern teachers to school desegregation, Chesler and Segal reported that most white teachers indicated they were quite nervous on the first day of desegregated classes [55]. For some, this anxiety was a function of their own inexperience with blacks and was also connected to teachers' concerns about any major incidents erupting in their classrooms. For other teachers, it was ambivalence and confusion as to whether they should pay any special attention to the new students or to the new facts of racial mixture. When teachers suffer from such resistance, confusion, or hesitancy, students must perceive these cues of racism from the classroom behavior of these teachers. As a result, white students themselves are likely to become more tense, cautious, and distrustful of black students.

Further insight into teachers' professional orientations toward black or lower-class students comes from the works of Kvaraceus and his colleagues and Herriot and St. John [56]. Kvaraceus reflects some of the concerns voiced earlier by Willower and Nordstrom, as he points out:

> Many teachers today seem to be fearful, anxious, and angry. This is especially manifest in the teacher's relationship with the reluctant or recalcitrant learners in the big cities. The frequent cry heard for sterner and harder measures in dealing with these pupils and for their removal from the regular classroom or exclusion from school would indicate that too many educators are now more concerned with the academic reputation of their school than with the welfare and well-being of the non-achieving and non-conforming students [57].

Herriot and St. John validate Becker's finding that teachers in lower-class schools more often seek to transfer to other teaching opportunities and that teachers in lower status schools are more dissatisfied [58]. Whereas pupil performance was found to be the most significant item relating to teachers' job satisfaction, teachers working in poorer schools were less satisfied with adequacy of supplies, attitude of students toward faculty, school methods for reaching decisions on discipline, levels of competence of most teachers, educational philosophy of the school, and ways in which teachers and the administrative staff work together. Teachers in schools serving less affluent students also had lower morale. The city confirmed Becker's hypothesis that teachers in big-city systems tend to begin their careers in slum schools and then move on. A higher percentage of teachers in these schools had a greater desire for mobility, either horizontal (to "better" schools) or vertical (to administrative roles). Despite the overwhelming confirmation of this trend, staff composition in schools in minority areas remains distortedly white, a reflection not of teacher postures so much as the racist history and policy of teacher training and hiring. In New York City, where more than 50 per cent of students are black or Puerto Rican, 90 to 95 per cent of 57,000 teachers are white. Conversely, most black teachers live in cities, whereas mostly white suburbs may hire very few black teachers in an entire school system. This pattern is pervasive nationally.

Some white teachers in largely black or Hispanic schools feel they are on "missionary" duty; many feel that they are isolated from interaction with their colleagues. The reverse is often true as well; a typical staff procedure in a largely white faculty is to identify a minority teacher as expert in liaison for minority students, and to limit his or her role to that extent. The consequences of this attitude, as one black teacher pointed out, is that black teachers who do identify their own special commitment to black youngsters can get no supporting services for their efforts. They cannot get coordination from white colleagues, and eventually they become extremely pessimistic about their own capacity to affect the lives of black students. One result of these pressures is that teachers may identify with the assumptions and styles of the dominant white community and no one may be able to empathize with poor or minority youth [60]. Since principals and administrators are not necessarily trained or competent to deal with such issues in interracial staffs, hidden conflicts and tensions often bubble over, becoming overt and painful. When a staff cannot agree to work together, it is unlikely to offer effective models for student behavior. Faculties that have no time and energy to prepare for, or reflect upon, their own growth and mutual support, cannot possibly respond innovatively to student concerns.

SUMMARY

In this chapter we have discussed a number of issues related to the attitudes and actions of teachers in schools. Each of these issues is complex in and of itself, and together they contribute to an explanation of the patterned and consistent ways in which teachers behave in the school setting.

We first reviewed material relevant to an understanding of the social origins and backgrounds of public school teachers. All of us are substantially affected by our prior experiences—our families, our status as young children, and the kinds of schools we went to. These experiences all affect who we become as adults, and what attitudes and beliefs we have and what relationships we prefer. The same is true for teachers. Historically, teachers have come from middle-class backgrounds, and historically the teaching profession has been dominated by whites, by women at the elementary level and men at the secondary level. These patterns are beginning to change, and more people from lower economic class backgrounds are entering the profession. A higher percentage of teachers in the larger cities now come from the minority communities, although this trend still has not caught up to the preponderance of minority youth who are students and consumers of the urban schools. The sex barriers to the employment of teachers at the elementary and secondary levels has also been changing, and elementary and secondary staffs throughout the nation are increasingly more evenly distributed between men and women. This heterogeneity must mean that students begin to see people of all races and sexes as agents of education for them, and perhaps even as models for their own futures.

The background characteristics of teachers are modified (and often enhanced) by the preparation they go through in order to enter the profession of teaching. Their preparation includes college, and usually a special college curriculum in educational studies. In some cases, prospective teachers have a field or practicum experience in the classroom, but this typically is a very different experience from actually teaching. A teacher's preparation does not stop when one takes a job, and on-the-job socialization is usually a vital part of the young teacher's education. Here one learns that what one has previously learned in his or her studies to become a teacher is not necessarily what teaching is about—here the real internship begins. The beginning teacher is often shocked to discover that he or she must not only contend with demands from students but with pressures from other teachers, from colleagues on the staff. These staff pressures, representing the accumulated weight of tradition, or educational wisdom, or whatever, have their own impact on teachers' classroom operations, as well as on teachers' working conditions and interpersonal relations throughout the school. As in any other work organization, the staff must learn to get along together and, it is hoped, to provide mutual support and help.

The fact that teachers are organized in ways that produce clear expectations, socialize new teachers, conform to regularized ways of thinking about and behaving toward students, and systematize relationships among a staff, all point to the existence of teachers as an interest group—as a group of people located in a common status in an organization and/or community, who have fairly common values in their work. We have tried to begin an analysis of teachers as an interest group in the school, and to help the reader understand the implications that this way of seeing the facts has for students, teachers, parents, and other members of the school-community enterprise. Teachers, as an interest group, have some desires and demands that are different from those of other groups. In fact, some of the goals and needs of teachers may place them in conflict with other groups who want to compete for a share of the school's total financial or energy resources, or who want to pursue different versions and visions of education. In pursuit of their own demands and needs, and in order to protect their status from competitive pressures, teachers often have formed mutual benefit groups, such as unions and/or professional associations. Some of these groups stress further teacher learning and the improvement of the profession; others stress career and economic needs; and others stress safety and/or control of work-place (school) decisions. Whatever the plurality of goals, professional and union organizations crystallize the interest group format and conflicts that are usually under the surface in educational systems. Thus, teacher groups are often united "against" administrator groups or community groups.

We also indicated some of the options that teachers have in their working relations with students in their roles as classroom leaders. The evidence is that a greater variety of potential roles exist than is utilized by any or most teachers. The prior discussions of social origins, professional and job socialization, interest group demands, and the pressures of relating with so many other groups should help explain why this is the case.

In a final part of this chapter we reviewed teachers' relations with other parties to the educational endeavor. Extrapolating from the interest group model of schooling, we postulated the existence of other interest groups besides teachers, other relevant interested parties who care about what happens in school and who must be dealt with. Teachers, individually and collectively, must deal with administrators, with colleagues, with students, and with parents. Each of these sets of relations is formalized in the ongoing structure and operating patterns of schools, and research on each set of relations helps identify the particular nature of the teacher's roles and options. Since a major consideration of this book is the effect of economic class, sexual, and racial issues in schooling, we have drawn special attention to the ways in which teachers typically relate to racial issues in school.

Throughout the chapter we have stressed the potency of organizational roles as a way of understanding what happens to teachers and what happens in their relations with other people in school. Only in this way can we understand the uniquely interesting actions of teachers who break out of these patterns and who play key roles in creating organizational change in the school or individual change in the hearts and minds and skills of youngsters in class.

Many people are highly critical of teachers, accusing them of incompetence, bureaucratization, conformity, and the like. We hope our perspective has helped the reader to see these issues a bit differently, and to understand the nexus of forces that catches teachers, as all of us, in a web of conflicting demands, values, and loyalties.

7

YOUTH IN SCHOOLS: CLIENTS, CONSUMERS, AND VICTIMS?

Most scholars who have investigated youth and schools have treated students as more or less passive entities, whose lives are determined by cultural influences and family or peer pressures. Few studies have considered even older youth, such as adolescents, as willing or independent actors able to create their own fates.

We are concerned with the active roles available to youth in this society, and in this society's schools. These roles are rooted in the structure and culture of the larger society, and in the institutional frameworks of school organizations, which have been outlined in previous chapters. But these roles also are affected by the nature of youth, by the orientations, predispositions, and reactions of young people located in age-specific networks of social interaction. With an understanding of these societally relevant roles and reactions, we can begin to understand the particular nature of youth's situation in schools, and the schools' situation in dealing with, responding to, and educating our young.

This chapter begins with a discussion of the cluster of roles that mark American youth as a special class of people, a class with special privileges and opportunities, as well as special constraints and restrictions. Some of the more specifically school-related issues encountered in the interaction between youth and adult educators are then discussed. Rather than see these issues as the outgrowth of youth alone, we set these matters of grave public concern in the larger context of youth-school interactions.

THE SPECIAL STATUS OF YOUTH

Students as a Special Interest Group in the Society

Several authors argue that youth is more than a residual category in the society, and that young people are not simply older people waiting to grow up.

The status of youth is firmly fixed; there are definite privileges and opportunities, statuses and roles, and exclusions and limitations placed on people who are below a certain age. Thus, students and young people are a separable group who have their unique material self-interests and can be expected to have symbolic concerns and cultural values and beliefs associated with their status.

Ironically, part of the problem that youth faces is that their status, although fixed as separate from older groups, is constantly changing as they age. Not only do youth have to continually adapt to new stages or levels of development, but society is often ambivalent as to the expectations of youth at each stage of their lives. Adolescents represent a classic example of the "marginal man;" and, when youth are students, and thus excluded from the working classes, this status is even more slippery.

Rowntree and Rowntree suggest further that youth play a critical role in the maintenance of the overall stability of the American economic and political order: they believe that

> Domestic economic viability is being maintained by the rapid growth of the defense and educational industries, industries that focus their exploitation on young people. [1]

According to Rowntree and Rowntree, the United States faces a growing surplus of labor, and that surplus is identified in, and magnified by, the growing numbers of young people in the society. In order to absorb that labor, to keep it off the unemployment rolls and out of revolutionary forms of discontent, the twin industries of defense and education have expanded to take on larger numbers of the young. For instance, young people finishing high school in a society with few available jobs have four major alternatives: (1) employment, as scarce as it may be, in low-paying, menial jobs at the bottom of the blue-collar scale; (2) unemployment; (3) further education in trade schools, community colleges, colleges, or universities; and (4) voluntary enlistment in the military services. The choices are most limited for economically or culturally marginal (poor or minority) youth, who are not absorbed readily into educational or employment markets and who also happen to have a high rejection rate by the armed services.

The exploitation of the young, in this analysis, is severalfold: they are shunted primarily into nonpaying (or low-paying) roles as students or as members of the unemployed or underemployed classes; or they are paid but made to do the society's soldiering in the armed forces. The extension of this argument concludes that the "conflict between the generations" is not primarily a generational conflict, but rather a political-economic conflict. In other words, it is not the fact of "generationness" that creates conflict between the old and the young; rather it is the different economic and political statuses of the young and the old that creates the conflict. This is a good example of the class conflict that exists in several other sectors in the society. Race, sex, economic class, and now age or age-status, can be considered as basic societal divisions.

Dissenting views on these questions can be found among those scholars who see the conflict as primarily due to generational factors [2], and who understand the "problems" of youth as a function of growing up, perhaps even as a function of growing up in a stressful society. The focus of analysis and treatment, then, primarily is upon the personal and relational difficulties that youth experience, not their location in the social structure or the economic and political roles and resources available to them.

How would one further support the analysis that youth is a separate class?° One could look at the common legal definitions of youth, with regard to drinking, voting, driving, judicial treatment, and sexual freedom, and see that people of given ages are treated as a common category. One could look at their economic status, and see that all below a certain age are either nonemployable and/or economically dependent upon either the state or their parents. One could look at their educational experience and see that all below a certain age are required to be in a certain place—school—doing a certain thing. The evidence is clear; objectively speaking youth is a special class which constitutes a social group or category that commonly experiences certain social realities.

The youth class has been seen, imprecisely by some, as a youth culture. This is close to the same analysis as that of class but is somewhat different. The notion of a "youth culture" suggests that young people experience very different values and beliefs than the rest of us. Moreover, it suggests that youth are the creators of their symbols, values, and behavior patterns. Youth do have many cultural attributes in common, primarily as a reflection of their common economic and political situations. But the problem of a class is not solely that of values and beliefs: it extends beyond the cultural aspects of social relations to material and legal privileges and opportunities as well.

Another part of the argument for seeing youth as a class instead of a culture is that class carries the notion of oppression and control. Not only does the society lump youth together for common treatment, it solidifies this situation by distracting youth from a full realization and concern for their class membership, and from their oppression, in several ways. First, we remind them of their membership in other latent role systems of race, sex, and economic status. This may work especially for those in semiprivileged categories, such as white and affluent youth who identify with the benefits of the race and wealth rather than with their disadvantages of age. Second, we remind them that their status is only temporary, and that as they age they will leave their oppressed status and become unoppressed as an adult. Third, we absorb their energy in

---

° "Class" is used here in its broadest sense of a category or social group of people who experience a common social location and reality and not in the narrow sense of a group at a certain economic level.

various aspects of a "youth serving culture" such as athletics, intense sexuality, music, and the like. In this sense it is important to distinguish between aspects of a youth culture that is youth generated and potentially liberating, and that which is run for and on youth by adults and simply maintains their oppression. Compare, for example, the music of the young that speaks of liberation with that music which simply distracts, and the double level of meaning that much of the music of the young entails.

Students—A Special Interest Group Within the School

In addition to the roles associated with age that mark youth as a distinct class in the society, youth also constitute a unique class within the school. Teachers, students, and principals (other managers and service personnel as well for that matter) have distinctly different roles in the organization of schooling. Derivatively, they each have separable tasks, privileges, characteristic patterns of social organization, and systematic ways of relating to institutional authority. Various staff roles were explored in Chapters 5 and 6. We now turn to the roles of students.

The general view is that students are in school to learn; thus they are not expected to teach or to add to their fellows' learning activities. Students are not paid for this work; it is often assumed that learning itself is enough of a reward. If learning does not prove to be immediately rewarding, it is because future earnings that will be gained as a result of schooling are the delayed payoff. Students are required to follow the orders of various educational authorities in the school, and it is assumed that this authority is exercised in their best interest. Students lack certain privileges that are available to most adults in school: for instance, the opportunity to go to the bathroom without formal permission. They are expected to follow certain rules regarding social interaction with others of their class: not to congregate inappropriately, to congregate when asked to by adults, not to associate freely during instructional periods, and the like. They are excluded as a class from the management of the school. They are expected not to fraternize on a cross-class basis with teachers and other educational authorities, and the reverse is true as well. By all these tokens it is clear that youth is a separable and identifiable class in the organization of the school.

The patterns of power and privilege in school clearly indicate not just that youth is a class but that, by and large, they are an underclass or an oppressed class within the organization. When the professional apparatus of public education recognizes these objective realities, it is usually argued that youth need to remain as a captive class because they are ignorant, incompetent, and/ or irresponsible.

Educational institutions have a history of failure to acknowledge and redress the grievances of younger members within that institution. This institutional failure is not merely a case of bureaucratic malfunctioning, or lack of professional concern; rather it is a political result of views that students have no protected rights and no need to pursue their grievances against the school. It is a natural outcome of the assumption of professionals' rights to manage the lives of clients in the best interests of the clients. Thus, what often are a citizen's constitutional rights are denied to students because of their particular status.

Students' Rights in School

Many educators are offended by the proposition that civil rights of students exist or that they should be protected by political or legal constraints on educators' autonomy. The good intentions of professionals in charge of their clients is supposedly sufficient for the protection of their clients. Some scholars object to the entrance of the court or community in areas where other public servants are entrusted with the authority to make professional decisions. For instance, Haskell distinguishes between what he feels are serious matters, such as free speech and reasoned debate, and "minor" issues such as regulations about hair and fashion styles and political symbols. In the latter area Haskell suggests that:

> The courts allow experts in other fields such as public school administration considerable elbow room in their work even if it results in some mistakes, particularly where the student interest involved does not seem to be one of great importance.

> . . . matters of this nature are better handled by local authorities who are knowledgeable in school administration and in the peculiar problems which may exist in the schools for which they are responsible . . . it stands to reason that the school authorities know more about maintaining order in the corridors and concentration in the classroom than judges do. [3]

What is "minor" for an adult expert, legal or educational, is, however, not necessarily minor for students. Minor rules and regulations permeate life in school and add up to major constraints on students' freedom and initiative. As Friedenberg points out, the underlying purpose of many minor regulations "is to convince youth that he has no rights at all that anyone is obligated to respect, even trivial ones [4]."

The ways in which students are treated in school often requires some groups to advocate for their protection, and for the advance of their legal and/or political rights. In some cases, this defense is led by students themselves, in more or less organized forms of protest against their oppressed situation. In other cases community and/or parent groups have formed advocacy organizations designed to support individual or collective cases of discrimination or mistreatment of the young. And in some cases legal action has led to judicial entry into these issues, and judicial hearings on the rights of students in schools.

The hierarchical control orientation of the school often blinds educators to the assumptions they make about students and their rights.° Under such circumstances, it becomes both an educational and political necessity for communities and courts to protect the constitutional rights of students. Those who object to judicial intrusion in the educational apparatus, and those who decry the "politicization" of student concerns and status must deal first with the failure of the school to conduct itself on educationally and politically respectable terms. They must deal with the historic "politicization" of the educational process by people arrogating and abusing power entrusted to them for the care of others.

A landmark article by Glasser seeks to understand the constitutional rights of students in schools in the context of three general categories of violations [5]. The first of these is procedural rights, or the guarantee of due process in administering school life and adjudicating disciplinary cases. In the second category are those rights of free speech, assembly, the press, and dissent that are provided to all citizens by the First Amendment of the Constitution. The third set of rights discussed by Glasser involves the more informal effort on the part of the school to regulate vast areas of the private life of students, including dress and fashion regulations and the like.

School experience is rife with unilateral acts by which administrators judge students, rule on their infractions, and administer minor punishments or expel students from school. These acts are unilateral in the sense that they are often taken by administrators without the necessary consent or opportunity for response by those who are affected by these acts. The potential arbitrariness of these acts is increased when action is taken with little concern for, or attention to, the procedural rights of students and their opportunity to defend themselves. The case of *Dixon* v. *State Board of Education of Alabama* established the precedent that college students who are to be expelled or suspended must be notified of the charges against them and provided with a hearing [6]. This precedent can be expanded to include the secondary school as well, especially when secondary school attendance is legally compulsory.

Informally constructed guidance hearings are a good example of the way in which a professional concern for health and welfare may be used by administrators to conduct judicial as well as administrative activities. There is now substantial pressure for more formal guidance and disciplinary interviews in which students may have at their disposal some form of legal aid or counsel.

° For instance, the principal of one midwestern school asked one of us (Chesler) to give him the names of any SDS members or Black Panthers we identified while conducting research within "his" student body. He was told that this would be deceitful and unethical since we had told the students that their interviews were private. The principal was not impressed with this reasoning, and no discussion could convince him that he did not have the right to go to any length in preserving what he saw as a politically safe environment. For him, and for many but not all school administrators, constitutional or contractual rights are luxuries they have the authority to dispense; in this context, rights are converted into privileges, and those who are privileged dole out rights as they wish.

For instance, in a New York State case a senior high school student was held to have the right of counsel to face charges of cheating where the consequences would have been the denial of a diploma and scholarship. Apparently, the severity of the infraction and potential punishment makes a difference in a court's position on the rights of a student to counsel, to call witnesses, and the like.

Most high schools, in most civics and history courses, teach students about the grand history of first amendment rights as cornerstones of a free and democratic society. However, these rights and liberties are denied to students systematically by the normal operating procedures of most schools. It has been quite common for the school administration and teachers to deny students the right to express dissenting opinions in public forums, and for student government, clubs, and newspapers to be formally or informally censored from commenting on local educational or community issues. Westin points out that:

> These practices represent the traditional view that high school students are essentially immature adolescents who have neither the intellectual nor the emotional readiness to share responsibility.

> (they receive democratic) . . . messages in their classes but experience autocratic treatment in the decisions that shape their lives. The clear message of our era is that such treatment will not go unchallenged for long. [7]

Courts are increasingly expressing their concern for the preservation of this democratic heritage and for protection against the stultifying effects that school conventions can have upon students' intellect and political interest. The fundamental defense that the schools have utilized in the effort to curtail or prevent the expression of First Amendment rights by students has been that such curtailment is required to protect students' safety, school property, or order and the peaceful conduct of the educational process. The educative process without free speech, assembly, and dissent would seem to be a mockery of an effective climate for learning. But in the context of the school's preeminent concern for order and authority, it is not hard to understand these priorities. Berkman provides one interpretation of the historic views of both the educational and judicial systems in this regard.

> Intellection as an end in itself was secondary to the political goals of public education. Proponents of public education were more concerned with training citizens than with increasing scholarship. Many saw education as a means of taming and civilizing the anarchic instincts of the populace. Hence schools were expected to teach discipline and respect for authority.

> The educational purposes perceived by the courts originated in the overriding political, rather than intellectual, aim of American education. The view that discipline and respect for authority were major goals of public education was frequently enunciated by the courts. The court treated the disciplinary measures

not merely as neutral devices for maintaining an orderly learning environment but as normative principles themselves part of the content of education. [8]

In 1966, a federal court (in the case of *Burnside* v. *Byars*) decided that students could wear buttons and other symbols of political activity to school [9]. The political issues were especially intense in this case since the buttons said "Freedom Now," and the school system was in the state of Mississippi. *Tinker* v. *Des Moines' Independent Community School District* represented another such case; arm bands were seen by the court to be an appropriate expression of free speech in protest against national military policies [10]. In both cases, the schools had argued that the infringement on rights of free speech of students were appropriate given the possibility that disorder in the school might result. In the Tinker case, the Court of Appeals for the Eighth Circuit supported the school system's regulation on the grounds that school officials had "an obligation to prohibit anything that might be disruptive of such an atmosphere" of order and decorum in the school [11]. The United States Supreme Court, on the other hand, argued that the school system would have had to demonstrate far more than a concern about the disruption of educational order but, in fact, its material and substantial occurrence. In the Tinker case there was no indication that the armbands created, or were likely to immediately create, classroom and school disruption. Thus, the students were permitted to reenter school and the armbands were permitted as a form of free expression. The burden of proof of what constitutes actual distraction or disruption must fall on the school officials who are enforcing the rules, rather than on the litigants suing for their abatement. Ironically, these cases illustrate the school's penchant for reducing tension and stress in impending crisis situations by preventing the expression of concern.

It seems evident from these and other court decisions that where political protest has created, or even where there are lucid grounds to suspect that it will create, a threat to public order, a school will be upheld in its attempt to regulate such expression. Abbott points to a history of litigation in which objectionable signs and broadcasts, obscenities, the blockage of faculty or other student access to school buildings, and criminal damage to property were not tolerated by the court and did constitute grounds for the exercise of administrative authority [12]. The courts certainly have not advocated anarchy in the school at the service of political dissent.

ISSUES CONFRONTING YOUTH IN SCHOOLS

The class issues that mark youth as a special interest group in the school and the society also give rise to specific concerns that generate and reflect conflict between students and the school. The range of possible issues that youth experience in school is endless and takes different forms in different communities and schools. But some issues seem fairly general and appear to affect all students. In this chapter we discuss five general issues: (1) school authority and youth rebellion; (2) rules and rule enforcement; (3) students' relations with staff members; (4) racism in school; and (5) youth alienation.

Authority and Rebellion

The traditional role of the school as socializer of the young and as the agent of *in loco parentis* has caused it to exercise authority over many aspects of student behavior. Thus, schools enter into instruction, rules and coercion about personal and moral areas of choice that are quite distant from traditional academic concerns. The *in loco parentis* tradition also has permitted schools to exercise wide latitude in affairs that normally would be solely the concern of individuals. In the past this general power has resulted in the courts' upholding school sanctions on students for the following noneducational behavior.

1. Writing poems satirizing school regulations.

2. Joining a school fraternity.

3. Becoming intoxicated.

4. Getting married.

5. Becoming pregnant.

6. Engaging in "illicit" sexual conduct.

Attempts to regulate aspects of the personal life of students are wide reaching— they include both personal and locker searches in pursuit of drugs, weapons, and the like. In some cases schools are dealing with crimes and damage to persons and property. But in other cases this is not so, and student deviance primarily represents a threat to adults' feelings of authority and control in the school.

Tuma and Livson report that girls at all socioeconomic levels increasingly conform to authority at home and in school from age 14 to 16 [13]. Boys increase their conformity to authority at home at this age but conform less at school. When the authority issue is examined with respect to economic and geographic factors, the picture becomes more complex. Douvan and Adelson found that adolescents living in large cities are more often rebellious toward adult authority than are youngsters from the suburbs or small towns [14]. Both urban and suburban youngsters showed a heightened eagerness for adult status, preferred being with older youth, and wanted primarily adult social activities in their clubs. Middle-class boys reported more disagreements with their parents than did lower-class boys. Geographic-mobility factors differentiated economic groups even further; middle-class youngsters whose families had moved more often were less tied to their peers, were encouraged by their parents to be more autonomous, and more often asserted that they relied on their own judgment in making decisions. Urban schools, with their mix of middle- and lower-class youth, and suburban schools, with their preponderantly middle-class and mobile student populations, may thus be seen as having populations that, for a variety of reasons, are likely to be more rebellious against adult controls.

The response of youth to authority figures in school may contrast markedly with their orientations in the family context. For teen-agers, school authority often is linked to impersonal and bureaucratic controls and feelings of power-lessness and regimentation. Students are sometimes very aware of these issues, and sometimes they are not. The function of the public school in maintaining and reinforcing the American social-status system helps explain why power and authority can be exercised in these ways. As Wasserman and Reimann point out, the compulsory attendance law sanctions the school's power over students by giving the school the role of gatekeeper to positions of knowledge and power in the society [15]. Only those students who learn how to behave appropriately, both with respect to acquiring knowledge and relating to authority, will be passed on.

Many studies indicate that for most youth the school is a large part of their total world, and that it is often a world whose structure facilitates the roles and comfort of adults as the keepers of law and order, rather than of students, per se. As a result, teachers and administrators are perceived as caretakers rather than educators, and student resistance to them in both managerial and instructional roles is increased. Erik Erikson has noted the many socialization contexts that contribute to the rising role-consciousness of youth [16], and to their resistance to distant and untrammeled authority. In truth, he asks, how many youngsters have an opportunity to know nonparent adults in settings that are *not* control situations, where interaction is not dictated by the obligation of the adult to control youth? The school is a universal, visible, and potent example of just such youth-controlling systems.

Students' rebellion against the authority and control mechanisms of the school evidently can assume several different forms. Stinchcombe defines rebellious behavior in school by three components: truancy, difficulty in noncollege-preparatory courses, and being sent out of class [17]. These compo-nents are essentially negative reactions to existing academic and classroom practices. Furthermore, Stinchcombe also alludes to student rebellion and alienation as "responsive, non-ideological, unorganized, and impulsive" [18]. Although the protests and rebellions occurring in schools may occasionally be impulsive and responsive, they appear almost as often to be organized and ideologically based. That is, they seem to be collective phenomena not reducible to psychological terms by examination of individuals' delinquent records or pathologies. Moreover, their school components are often more than classroom-related, focusing as well upon aspects of the organizational structure and dynamics of the school. Stinchcombe's portrayal of rebellion places

Exercise 7—1. *Assessing Student-Parent Communication*

This exercise can be done by students individually or in groups.
Consider the state of communication between adolescent students and their parents. With particular respect to your own self and your parents, try to answer the following questions.

	A Lot	Some	A Little
1. How much information do your parents have with regard to your school activities?	___	___	___
2. How much information do your parents have regarding your dating, and/or sexual activities?	___	___	___
3. How much information do your parents have regarding your smoking, drinking and drug habits?	___	___	___
4. How much information do you have about your parents' occupational satisfaction, goals, and the like?	___	___	___
5. How much information do you have regarding your parents' marital satisfaction?	___	___	___
6. How much information do you have regarding your parents' educational history?	___	___	___

students' reactions to school authority and organizational characteristics in a limited political context.

It is a cliché that those who define the nature of the phenomenon can set the terms for its treatment [19]. To define rebellion consistently as evidence of personal pathology and impulse focuses on characteristics of the rebel, potentially protecting the system that may be the target of rebellion from investigation of its own complicity. Some examinations of the role of organizational factors in rebellion stem from educational and industrial systems which stress the importance of the distribution of influence among various parties. Wittes' application of these concepts to secondary schools indicates that students' perceptions of personal power to influence school policy have important implications for many of their feelings and behaviors in school [20]. For instance, when students feel that they are in a peer group that has access to power, when they believe that they can control their own educational lives, they are more likely to have motivation for academic success. Participation in school policy-making, then, may be meaningful for educational as well as political purposes.

Weinberg has reviewed recent literature on desegregation and reports several studies in which "the importance of student involvement and responsibility for the school's program was found to be vital" in producing positive racial interactions [21]. And Coulson et al. report that secondary students' "views of their control over their environment, as measured by the 'locus of control' scale, was positively associated with reading and math outcomes" [22]. These authors suggest that students be given more control over aspects of the school curriculum and instructional materials.

When an organizational structure does not permit students to participate in decision making, one of the results may be political rebellion. Some of the issues that lead to such rebellion are evident in the following dialogue of students:

> The administration invited us to this meeting, and said how they wanted us to make a new dress code and how it'd be real nice . . . and then they said that the only problem is that the Board of Education won't permit the different schools to have different dress codes. That's not true. There's high schools all over—two in one district—that have different dress codes. I don't know why they said that. Guess they just really don't want us to have a new dress code.

> The principal was supposed to bring it to the Board. He went to the Board meeting and he didn't bring it up. He just talked to them a couple of seconds before the meeting. And they said, "Well, don't bring it up now, we've got too much to do." And then he later told the student council advisor that students shouldn't come to the Board meeting any more because they might mess something up.

> Last time all the kids went to the Board meeting for something, and all they did was kick 'em out of school.

These comments indicate a certain confusion on the part of students about their appropriate participatory roles, a confusion exacerbated by administrative evasion and rhetoric. Students have a great deal of pluralistic ignorance about a system whose real operations are invisible to them. The system is more visible to teachers who already participate to some degree in decisions, or who at least are acquainted with the vagaries and nuances of school decision making. Likewise students who are active in school affairs and go to meetings are likely to have greater sophistication (and often cynicism) about what is happening. Others, who are uninvolved and ignorant about these processes, react blankly when asked about them and are certainly not informed followers. They are, in effect, noncitizens of the most important political organization in their lives.

Regardless of their economic, sexual, or racial backgrounds, or their places in the school status hierarchy, most students are engaged in a search for some control over their school lives. Despite verbalized values of democracy, community, national solidarity, and such, there is little real sharing of decision-making power across school roles. The disparity between power and rhetoric is particularly acute when youngsters actively attempt to influence their school lives. One urban teenager asserted:

Seems everything you try to do in this school . . . administration's always saying they want students' participation . . . it seems to me that all they wanted was to say, lookit, there's kids that are participating, there's kids that want to do something . . . but they don't really want us to get what we're asking . . . they just said why don't you wait until next week? Talk to some more people. Pretty soon everybody quit. Got tired out.

Many students seek now to control their own lives and to influence others in order to make their needs known and their demands implemented. These issues may surface most dramatically in school protests, where it may be argued that students have learned that power is not conceded but must be wrested or taken. They are learning that they often must pose a credible threat or engage in disruption before they are responded to by those in positions of authority.

A national study of high schools reported that 58 per cent of all students surveyed (rural, suburban, and urban) want a bigger role in deciding school policy [23]. Of the total group, 66 per cent want to participate in determining school rules and curriculum, and 48 per cent think that they should have a hand in determining disciplinary measures and the way classes are run. Although various progressive educators have similarly advocated greater student participation in school governance, what is most common in practice is nondemocratic student government, where students participate only by permission of duly constituted authorities. In a study of Michigan student councils, Weaver found that less than 25 per cent "assisted in policy formation," "supervised student elections," or "participated in adult community projects" [24]. "Sandbox" student government often produces misunderstanding, cynicism, distrust, and apathy. Certainly, the desires for participation reported here have not been and probably cannot be assuaged by the kind of student government found in most schools.

Rules and Rule Enforcement

The character of school rules and regulations is one arena in which issues of school authority and student needs for autonomy and self-control may come together; it is thus a prime arena for conflict. Forehand, Ragosta, and Rock indicate that students' academic achievement is significantly related to their perception of the school as a fair place [25]. Fairness is reflected for students in a principal who appears to care about them and who reaches out to various groups. It also is apparent in rules and regulations that represent a plural set of concerns—relevant to the needs of various cultural groups—and that are administered fairly across situations and interest groups.

According to some observers, school rules and regulations reflect commonly agreed upon ways in which people should relate to one another. They represent the traditions of the community and its notions of appropriate and decent behavior. Disciplinary codes and regulations are seen to regularize justice, to ensure fair play, and to provide an orderly basis for the conduct of education. Part of the reason for codifying rules is so that everyone can see them and they can be administered evenly, and not arbitrarily. There may be accidents: even under the best circumstances there are times when rules do not work out fairly.

From another point of view, disciplinary rules and regulations reflect the values of ruling groups and their attempts to socialize other people into dominant cultural patterns. They are not reflections of common values; in fact, the greater the number and specificity of rules and punishments, the clearer it is that organizational trust is failing and that coercion may reign. Thus, rules and regulations are seen to represent the arbitrary exercise of power that seeks to keep some people in positions of privilege and other people in positions of disadvantage. Rather than provide an orderly basis for education, rules are part of the technology of social control. Such control is implemented further in schools through surveillance, nonpublic conferences and conversations about students, and informal informer networks.

Students' concerns about disciplinary policies and procedures have been important issues provoking protest and disturbance. Control that has no apparent purpose other than to run a "tight ship," or that is inconsistent and unfair, is often the center of the outcry. Consistent with the prior discussion of the unique situation and class-related interests of students, youth and adult groups often differ with regard to their views of discipline and its enforcement.

Table 7—1 shows the result of one poll on how to handle unruly students

---

Exercise 7—2. *The Examination of The Place of Youth in College Dorms*

Do you live, or know of people who live, in college dormitories?
If yes, are there rules governing students' behavior?

1. Do any of these rules seem unfair or inappropriate?
   Do any of them prevent you from doing things that seem acceptable to you?

2. Do any of these rules seem really useful and helpful to dorm living?

3. To what extent are students involved in making these rules?

4. To what extent are these rules followed or broken?

Table 7—1. How to Handle Unruly Students [26]

	Students	Parents	Teachers	Administrators
Crack down on them	37%	63%	50%	41%
Try to understand them	56	35	46	54
Leave them alone	5	1	0	0
Not Sure	2	1	4	5

[26]. It is not surprising that students stress understanding most and propose cracking down least. What is surprising, perhaps, is that administrators profess opinions that are quite close to those of the youth themselves. Parents outstrip all other groups in their insistence on the prompt enforcement of "discipline." The perception of educators of this community pressure may help account for their vigorous actions.

Some students are concerned primarily with problems arising from the lack of clear and consistent purposes to school rules, whereas others are concerned primarily with fairness and respect in their enforcement. Differential administrative behavior toward black and white youngsters may reflect both these issues, and is a constant source of tension. As one black student stated,

> The discipline problems are wrong. They'll punish the Negroes greatly and let the white man get away with everything. And that's not right. You can disagree with it but you'll get your turn later on. Now, a Negro will come into class, and he comes late, he gets an after-school appointment, which is right because he has no business coming late. And when the white boy comes into class and don't get one, then that's not right . . .

A study of fifteen secondary schools throughout New York State indicates the degree to which such views are held by larger groups of students [27]. Table 7—2 presents these data, indicating that black and Puerto Rican students, more often than white students, see school rules as very strict, leading to perceptions that they are often punished without reason and that rules are enforced inconsistently. It often matters little whether such inconsistency is in the direction of greater leniency or greater brutality. Both communicate a message of invidious differentiation, whether out of pity or fear, anger or bigotry.

The issues of "fairness" in disciplinary enforcement is highlighted by data in Table 7—3 on suspensions from junior high schools in a small midwestern city [28]. We can see that different schools have quite different suspension rates, irrespective of the racial issues. For instance, compare junior high schools L and M; with the same proportion of black and white students, these two schools have different overall suspension rates and quite different black/white comparisons in suspension rates. Is it possible that the students at these two schools

Table 7—2. Students' Perceptions of School Rules, by Race [27]

	White (N = 1536)	Black (N = 228)	Puerto Rican (N = 117)	Total (N = 1881)
Rules are very strict	30.9%	50.0%	41.1%	34.0%
Often punished without reason	22.3	35.9	35.8	24.3
Rules are very inconsistently enforced	33.1	32.4	40.2	33.5

Table 7—3. Suspensions in a Small Midwestern City, 1976—77 [28]

Junior High Schools	Per Cent Students Suspended	Per Cent White Students Suspended	Per Cent Black Students Suspended	Per Cent Students Black
L	4.0	1.9	14.4	14.8
M	.9	.9	.9	14.8
N	28.6	23.4	47.4	23.7
O	5.7	2.9	27.6	11.7
P	1.2	.7	7.9	7.0

behave very differently? Or that policy is administered differently by educators in these schools? Overall, as is the case across the nation, suspension rates for blacks are several times greater than those for whites: only one of the five junior high schools deviates from this trend. Why?

A reaction that cuts across racial lines is student resentment of humiliating enforcement of disciplinary rules. Paddling by the principal or physical education instructor is fairly common and is likely to occur more often to poor students than to rich students, and more often to black students than to white students. Male teachers sometimes administer paddlings to female students; overt implications of sexual interest are avoided in some schools by having female teachers take on this job. One principal reported that it was unusual for him to go a week without "having" to paddle a student, and he regarded such a time period as a major improvement in student behavior in the school. Another principal noted that he usually called in twelve or fifteen other students when he was about to administer a paddling; these witnesses made the humiliation he was about to apply much clearer and thus a more effective disciplinary weapon. Machine shop and woodworking instructors often require their classes to make paddles, which are sometimes designed with airholes to speed the rate at which the paddle travels through the air.

This accepted pattern of physical and psychological violence has been noted by many observers; yet educators seem to ignore it when they take extreme umbrage at youth's retaliation. Commenting on New York City schools, Wasserman and Reimann note, "Almost all student assaults on teachers—at least by teenagers—are in response to hostile verbal or physical acts committed by the teachers against the students, or a series of such acts." [29] These acts by educators include rough handling, knocking students down, and various other expressions of thinly disguised hostility, contempt, or despair.

In one midwestern school, a hidden issue in adult-youth relations was vividly reported by several black girls. They noted that when they were "in trouble" in school they would find the male vice-principal. When asked why, they reported that this man was usually willing to forego administering punishment if the girl would engage in sexual intercourse with him. This report was confirmed by six other girls. It is an extreme example of the exploitation of power and position, but it also reflects the sexism that is rampant in our society and its schools. Such practices can continue without public notice even though the information was generally known among the students in that school.

Corporal punishment is not the only regulatory or disciplinary form that humiliates youngsters. Friedenberg describes many efforts at the application of rules as veritable "ceremonies of humiliation" [30]. The object is to make the rule breakers feel terribly guilty and apologetic on the theory that docile humility will keep them out of further trouble. For instance, it is not an uncommon experience for younger students who wish to go to the bathroom during class to be required to raise their hands and announce their need to their teacher in front of their peers. Sometimes the teachers asks; "Do you really need to go? Are you sure?" This reinforces the youngster's embarrassment, and for some teachers this is a conscious attempt to embarrass the student and gain humorous attention at the student's expense. Part of the reason for this procedure may be a history of attempts by the student to test or provoke the teacher. But the student's need to leave the classroom, obviously, may be real.

A similar practice is the requirement that girls who wish to be excused from swimming or other physical education classes because of their menstrual period must bring a doctor's note (sometimes a parent's note will suffice) to explain their excuse. An important by-product of this situation is that the girl student must keep checking with her doctor or announcing the facts of her private life to her parents in order to be relieved of certain school activities every month. This is another example of adult mistrust of students becoming formalized in a set of petty, impersonal regulations. The enforcement of these procedures often creates personally embarrassing, privacy-destroying circumstances for students.

Order is a meaningful issue in schools, as it is in any social institution. But the elaboration and escalation of this concern into an endless number of petty details must appear an absurd response to the fear of loss of control. According to one source,

> A typical high school schedule puts a straight-jacket upon a student who seeks to learn more. The typical high school schedule is the same, day after day, with no allowance for the student either to pursue individual interests or take extra courses or do independent study that he might want to do. All of these things are conducive to furthering one's education, but most present-day schedules hamstring the student from doing these things, thus inducing in him the feeling that he is doing only what the authorities will let him do and not what he may need. He, under this system, eventually loses all individual incentive and becomes an automaton. Thus rigidity produces boredom, resentment, and depression.

The degree to which the school attempts to regulate matters that are of trivial significance for academic performance, but which are crucial to the students' life-style choices, is a prime factor in the current school experience of many students.

Students and Instructional Personnel

> That teacher is only worried about "respect"—she might as well not have been here at this conference with us kids for five days! She didn't learn a thing.

This student's remark, made during a "retreat," reflects what many see as the preoccupation of educators with formal relations and social distance. Teachers, adults with whom students have the most contact, are the frequent targets of such criticism. In the previous discussion of the nature of professionalism and staff roles, several reasons why teachers often maintained distance from their students were discussed. In times of stress and tension, when conflicts between students and teachers are evident, the tendencies for adult protection and control are even greater. But the price of such distant role relations are clear: they create a mistrust between these groups who are essential partners in the teaching-learning enterprise.

A good deal of student concern is reflected in judgments of the teaching competence or academic performance of teachers. One poll found that some 81 per cent of students rated their teachers good to excellent [31]. Chesler's study of students in schools that had been severely disrupted indicated much less student satisfaction. Students were asked to compare the performance of teachers in their school with that of teachers in other schools, with the results presented in Table 7—4 [32].

Between 8 and 21 per cent of the students in these seven schools saw their teachers as "far below average" and 27 to 42 per cent felt their teachers were at best "below average." Notwithstanding a tendency of adolescents to indulge in hypercriticism of others, particularly adults, these findings point to the centrality of student disrespect of teachers. The spread of student responses in these

Table 7—4. Student Assessments of Relative Teacher
Performance [32]

	School						
Performance	A	B	C	D	E	F	G
Far above average	38%	30%	28%	23%	35%	16%	33%
Above average	23	29	41	27	31	32	23
Below average	20	18	19	21	28	19	15
Far below average	14	18	8	21	14	20	18
No answer	5	5	4	8	2	13	11

schools further indicates their ability to make distinctions among staff members. These are not arbitrary reactions: whatever the specific quality of their teachers, the students' comments must be seen as indications of a significant lack of intergenerational rapport and respect.

The well-liked teacher is most often liked in global terms. Students almost unfailingly refer to examples of caring gestures and the teacher's ability to understand and accept, to "talk like us."

> In college, they call you by Mr. or Miss. Here, you're just It or she. . . . My music teachers calls us Miss or Mr. He's real nice.

> See, like the young teachers, they talk like you. They know what you're thinking, cause they're pretty close to your age. Like this one teacher. He knows the kids, and he kind of, like, acts like them. Like he knows how to talk with them.

The disliked teacher is roundly denounced, starting with illustrations of his or her disrespectful treatment of the student. Strict control and tough work requirements are rarely cited as the only reasons for the student's hostile evaluation. A teacher's failings in competence or respect for students—even other students' accounts or rumors of these failings—are quickly picked up and add to the load of student disrespect, increasing their suspiciousness of the teacher.

Students' perceptions of educator disrespect for them is not universal, but neither is it limited to a few poor schools. This perception helps to explain the low impact of teachers on the values and beliefs of youth other than those relating to academic achievement. Brim's study of the influence of peer and adult roles on adolescent values indicates that teachers generally are excluded from having influence, and therefore students are outside the teacher's sphere of influence [33]. This certainly is one effective way for students to cope with the experience of disrespect or disconfirmation: to distance themselves from their disconfirmers and thereby negate their impact. But other students may not be so successful at this psychological defense and may internalize the message of disrespect and disconfirmation, leading to feelings of confusion, perhaps incompetence, and eventually behaviors that confirm these negative messages. It appears likely that the more such students do not conform to school regulations and expectations, the more they deviate, and the more the school sends them messages of disconfirmation, punishes them, and tries to further negate their own sense of respect.

A number of protests have been organized against the personally discriminatory behavior visited upon nonconforming youngsters by certain teachers, counselors, and principals. These protests seem to highlight the preferential treatment given to conforming, upwardly mobile students, those who are evolving in their educators' image. For instance, consider the following exchange:

Interview: How do teachers look at students? What do they think about them?

(*White student*): Well, the way that we felt, and I got the same impression from other kids, that the teachers and the administration here look down on us. We are supposed to give them respect because they are a teacher. But they don't give us respect as students. Now, like I'm a greaser, I dress with a leather coat, pointed shoes and knit shirts; and his skin, he's black. So they have prejudice against us. The greaser has a reputation as being a dummy, hanging on the corner with a cigarette hanging out of his mouth, and in nine out of ten cases, this isn't true at all.

(*Black student*): A Negro is just not accepted here. The faculty looks down on us. The climbers wear tight levis, sweat socks, loafers. They are, you know, all the brains. This is what the faculty takes as brains, you know. And these people they treat the teachers as though the teacher is a king or something. "You really look nice today, teacher" and all this. Greasers and Negroes just don't do it, and since we won't do what they want, what most people term is "grippin em" or something like this, they won't do it, so the teachers don't like it.

These comments reflect the feeling that there is a lack of open, honest exchange between many of the participants in the educational process. Students often request more opportunity for personal contact; they stress their concern for the quality of such human relationships. Many teachers in urban areas say that the most disturbing factor of their work is constant student defiance. Help in dealing with "defiant or openly aggressive youngsters" was requested by approximately 50 per cent of the teachers in three urban high schools in Ohio [34], and reported in Chapter 6 (Table 6−6) as a common problem by teachers from other schools. In the Ohio study, the only problem cited more often by teachers in these schools was that of "motivating youngsters." These two concerns can be seen as opposite sides of the same coin: failure to attend to the roots of students' motivation to learn often results in defiant interactions.

Similarly, many students report that what disturbs them most is their teacher's lack of courtesy and respect for them as individuals. Coleman reported just such a reverberating phenomenon in his study of high school cultures. One school in his particular study had both the highest proportion of teachers with negative views of students *and* the highest percentage of students who reported that teachers were "not interested" [35].

A set of guidelines created by students in a conflict-prone urban high school speaks clearly to these issues [36].

Suggestions From Student Groups

1. *Teachers should first overcome all fear.* They should not fear the student, what they think about you and how they feel about you being there to teach. The teacher also should not have fear of staff, heads of staff, administrators, etc. A teacher who is afraid cannot teach effectively.

2. Tell, show, or do both, but let the class know what you expect of that class. *Never say anything you don't mean* or won't prove as far as challenging a student goes. Don't do anything in anger. Leave the room to cool off. Think before you act.

3. *Teach your own way,* a way in which you will feel comfortable. You have control over the student, and you must use it wisely. Try to make the subject as interesting as possible, without being childish.

4. Teachers should teach or know how to *teach the student what is going on in the world.*

These suggestions make it clear that students are not naive about their teachers' real skills and anxieties. The students understand these adult fears and would like their teachers to be free, both for themselves and their clients.

Cross-race Relations

Our stress upon the existence of a youth class does not mean that we conceptualize youth roles and actions from a monolithic perspective. All youth in this class are not alike. American society is managed in ways that create other social groups based upon economic, racial and sexual categorizations. Moreover, our culture has reinforced these divisions to stress race, sex and class as major categories even more potently than age status itself. Therefore, any analysis of youth must attend to differentiation according to race, sex, and economic class. Black and other minority youth are in different situations from white youth; young women from young men; and poor youth from middle-class youth from truly affluent youth. The realities of racial oppression often have meant that black and minority youth are not as alienated from black adults as are white youth from white adults, for instance, (the common oppression of race appears sometimes to lessen feelings of generational oppression).

Major aspects of the school system reflect and maintain the institutional racism of American society. The term *racism* refers to institutional policies or practices that result in injustice or disadvantage to blacks, Hispanics, and members of other racial minorities. It does not necessarily involve conscious intent on the part of the actors. In other words, even if white teachers and administrators were to undergo major mind-change, the institutional fabric of the school would nevertheless perpetuate racism in terms of the advantages of the whites in the schools.

White children who have grown up in a segregated society naturally develop fantasies and stereotyped images of themselves and others. Citron elaborates the effects of such "white ghettoization," the process by which white youngsters unconsciously assume dominance and superiority over others [37]. Sometimes this feeling is directly related to minorities and to aspects of minority cultures; at other times the racism lies in the whites' conceptions of their ownership of the North American culture, of their historic right to establish the standards for goodness and rightness in school and society. These perspectives force blacks and other minorities to meet white cultural standards and often do not recognize the integrity of different values and beliefs.

Some examples of educational racism include insufficient hiring of black or Hispanic educators, predominantly Anglo curricula with few options, no provision for Hispanic students to enter bilingual programs, tracking systems that cluster black students in lower tracks, white-oriented clubs and activity programs, and higher dropout or failure rates or suspension rates for minority students. Bailey points out that under these conditions, which do prevail in the United States, racially mixed schools are likely to become scenes of unrest and disruption [38]. The issue that generates overt conflict is not racial mixing per se, but the educational system's support of racial advantages for whites.

Adults often accommodate to the fact that different groups of young people are treated differently and that they come to view the social system differently. Robert Coles quotes a white school teacher's observations of black children in Barbour County, Alabama, schools:

> I'm no great fan of the colored: I don't have anything against them, either. I do my work, teaching the colored, and I like the children I teach, because they don't put on airs with you, the way some of our own children do—if their daddy is big and important. The uppity niggers—well, they leave this state. We won't put up with them. The good colored people, they're fine. I grew up with them. I know their children, and I try to teach them as best I can. I understand how they feel; I believe I do. I have a very bright boy, James; he told me that he didn't want to draw a picture of the American flag. I asked him why not. He said that he just

wasn't interested. It's hard for them—they don't feel completely part of this country.

I have a girl once, she was quite fresh; she told me that she didn't believe a word of that salute to the flag, and she didn't believe a word of what I read to them about our history. I sent her to the principal. I was ready to have her expelled, for good. The principal said she was going to be a civil rights type one day, but by then I'd simmered down. "To tell the truth," I said, "I don't believe most of the colored children think any different than her." [39]

Thus, desegregation has brought new groups of people into contact with one another in school. But by itself desegregation has not improved educational experience or the quality of race relations in schools and the community. Research conducted in elementary and secondary schools supports the idea that merely placing black or Hispanic students in classroom contact with whites is not the best way to overcome historic racism and to improve student performance [40]. Many intraschool and classroom factors have to be considered. Katzenmeyer's early studies, for example, suggested that a black student's class performance depends upon a "commonality of experience with white pupils, the adequacy of his performance having increased as the degree of social interaction increased" [41]. The emotional impact of an interracial situation on newly transferred students is considerable; it is probable that the initial requirement to deal with white peers and authority figures is threatening. Katz's studies also demonstrated the likelihood that the threat inherent in the newly interracial situation will affect the academic performance of students. [42].

A number of studies document the important effects of classroom peer relations on a student's self-esteem, attitudes toward school, and utilization of his or her academic potential. Pupils who perceive that their peers reject them, and their attitudes differ from peers' attitudes, seem to utilize their potential less effectively in class [43]. The fear of peer rejection may even discourage some students from expressing themselves in class. Where social interaction is so fraught with danger that students cannot support one another's learning efforts, everyone in the class may be deprived of some key educational resources.

Some of these problems of interracial trust were explored with several hundred black high school students who desegregated previously all-white schools in the Deep South [44]. Almost half the group reported that they encountered considerable resentment and hostility from their white peers when they entered the white schools, ranging from general unfriendliness and teasing to name calling and physical violence. Another third of the desegregators experienced both positive and negative reactions, along with relatively neutral behavior, such as indifference and avoidance. Only 15 per cent of the desegregators felt that they were met by peer reactions of welcome, friendship, or courteous concern. Some of the reactions reported were as follows:

One girl was real nice the first two weeks of showing us around and playing with us, but after two weeks she stopped speaking. . . . I spoke to her in town when she was with her mother and she turned her around. On the next day she didn't speak.

There were stares and they treated us like dirt. They called us names. Some days they would hit you and run by sneaking up on you. You never know who did it. They would spit on us. That was mostly when we were going to our classes. They avoided us in the lunchroom. The only time they sat next to us is when the teacher made them. They didn't recognize us as their classmates [45].

It is easy to understand how prolonged social interaction in such an environment would fail to improve the quality of relationships between white and black students. After a year of attendance at a desegregated school, 30 per cent of these black students stated that their ideas about white people changed as a result; as many black students became less trusting of whites as became more trusting. Moreover, over 60 per cent of the black students, most of whom entered with a distrustful attitude, did not change in either direction.

These studies emphasize that the relation between majority and minority students is dependent upon the racial environment in which they learn. Gottlieb and Ten Houten further document that when there are few blacks in a largely white school, the blacks hold back and do not participate heavily in school activities. In schools with a sizable percentage of black students, "two separate systems will emerge . . . which result in both racial groups maintaining their own forms of social segregation [46]." When black students do become an active majority, white students may leave the field to the blacks and selectively pull out of social and athletic activities. At times, whites even cease attending school functions; they may not join basketball teams because other white students don't come to watch.

Racial solidarity and separateness in school organizations are very troubling to students who are trying to reach out to associate and to cooperate with each other. Black or Hispanic solidarity is especially visible and frightening for whites and is a source of threat and confusion to young white liberals who feel little solidarity of their own. Of course, these whites seldom see how unified they look to a group of minority youngsters.

Students often feel that educators add to the difficulties of racial interaction by failing, in direct or in more subtle ways, to encourage or facilitate new forms of social behavior. Students have reported that their principals will physically intervene if a black and white couple are holding hands or standing with comradely arms around shoulders, whereas uniracial pairs are not similarly bothered. Some administrations have gone so far as to record incidents in which white and black students date each other and report them to parents. For the school to see this behavior as within its jurisdiction clearly indentifies the school as implementing the racially separate standards for social behavior found elsewhere in the society.

The classroom also fails to provide new models of interracial cooperation. Chapter 6 discussed some of the new patterns of classroom instruction and organization that are critical if interracial interaction is to be positive and is to lead to positive and antiracist outcomes for all students. Some of these same principles, captured in the "contact" hypothesis of racial relations, are relevant throughout the school building [47]. Although some observers suggest that all that is needed to produce positive interracial relations is sufficient contact between students of different races, other, more careful scholars and practitioners have discovered that what is critical is the creation of positive forms of contact. Thus, contact within a setting or environment that is fraught with the racism of the larger society, or contact within tense and anxious conditions, or competitive contact where some win and some lose, cannot be expected to have a positive impact [48]. Contact that occurs in pleasant, peaceful surroundings, that permits students to relate together around common, not competitive goals, that puts students into equal status relationships with one another, and that leads to positive outcome tasks, is more likely to have lasting positive impact on youth [49]. Whether action is taken to create classrooms in this image, or whether complementary steps are taken to create lunchrooms, hallway assignments, and other student environments and responsibilities in this image will tell us a great deal about the school's commitment to racial change.

Some of these same principles apply to the different conditions of males and females in school. School policies and practices often reflect sexism in staff hiring and assignment, in curriculum offerings to boys and girls, in different behavioral standards for boys and girls, in negative or limiting images of women's roles and futures in textbooks, and the like. People who grow up in a male-dominated society often have difficulty achieving parity in the relationships between the sexes in school.

Youth Values and Ideologies . . . Cultural Alienation

Beyond student responses to issues of social power, rules, and intergroup relationships lies a conflict of values that causes many youth to question—and some to rebel against—the practices of schools and other institutions.

Flacks identifies the "overproduction" of highly educated middle-class youth who increasingly "find [their] fundamental values, aspirations, and character structure in sharp conflict with the values and practices which prevail in the larger society" [50]. What prevails in the larger society eventually prevails in the schools; youth act out their disaffiliation from social values in the arena of the socializing institutions.

In addition to greater knowledge about foreign and domestic injustices, students now ask questions about the school itself: What is the point of studying at all, knowing what they do about the world of the present and the future? What have the Bill of Rights and the Constitution to do with the way they are treated in school? Why should they trust adults who show them no respect? Why should they obey representatives of a culture that destroys its environment, and that accepts poverty and racism? As a result of these value conflicts,

Exercise 7—3. *Patterns of Sexism That Parallel Issues in Cross-Racial Relations*

In the preceding pages we have discussed some of the ways in which the organization of student and staff relations supports institutional racism. The same is true for sexism as well. Review the issues and situations discussed and see if you can articulate patterns of sexism and barriers to equal and effective cross-sex role relations that parallel these issues in cross-racial relations.

Issues in cross-racial relations	Parallel (?) issues in cross-sex relations

Institutional racism
  staff
  curriculum
  social events	

Prior role socialization	
Stereotypes of other races ghettoization	

Teacher behavior
  locking in stereotypes
  structuring positive situations	

Student performance
  expectations
  anxiety	

Student interaction patterns
  solidarity
  contact	

many students are alienated from school and much of the prevalent adult culture.

Within the school, the reasons for alienation vary for different groups of students. More radically oriented and affluent students often are protesting against the broader culture as it is reflected in their school curriculum. Many of these youngsters do not question their ability to "make it" in the system; rather, they question the system. Some of them want to disrupt those functions of the school that they perceive as reflections and extensions of societal values and beliefs with which they disagree. The affluent young often are in revolt against technocracy itself, against the lack of human sensitivity and value concerns that are typical of a system in which science, rationality, and efficiency define reality. Their view is captured by Roszak, who writes that technocracy subverts "the life of the mind" or "the pursuit of the truth" to "a matter of machine-tooling the young to the needs of our various Baroque bureaucracies: corporate, governmental, military, trade union, educational" [51].

Many of these students call for an education that examines life from a much broader perspective, dealing with such questions as: "What kind of human being am I—and what kind do I want to become?" For some of these students, a relevant education includes the affective as well as the cognitive domain and explores cultural and interpersonal values and choices.

Although students with such social values scorn the rewards of "making it" in the established business and professional structure, another group seeks to gain these very rewards. For working-class students—and typically for minority students, members of a white ethnic minority, or white "greasers"—relevant educational goals include being equipped for well-paying, middle class jobs. They perceive that their vocational education programs not only are inadequate but permanently bar them from access to the economic and social world for which their college-bound peers are being prepared.

Many minority students focus their alienation on racist policies in schools and on channeling processes that exclude them from the labor market or that consign them to low-status roles. Over the years, black and minority students have endorsed a curriculum to elevate their status, speak to their ethnic consciousness, and equip them to become free and equal in the society. They have demanded black history courses, Hispanic bicultural programs, the right to wear African-inspired dress and hair styles and to speak Spanish, and the academic instruction that will gain them college entrance. For some of these students, the image of the society of the future, the one to which they desperately seek entry, is the current Establishment version. For others, it is a better, more humane society, much like that envisioned by some white activists.

Most students are "straights" or "climbers." These are the youngsters who are, and like to be, in the mainstream of society, who are "making it" in the school. Many of these students appear to be without distinct values of their own; they pragmatically mirror the dominant adult values. Yet they, too, often feel impotent in the face of bureaucratic prohibitions. Hall passes, attendance slips, dress and hair codes, and other control mechanisms are a constant reminder of their powerlessness within the school. More and more "straights" are being recruited into activist groups.

Noyes and McAndrew asked dozens of youngsters across the country what they thought school was for [52]. Although fewer than half of these youths planned to enter college themselves, the majority felt that school was "to get a diploma so you can go to college." Beliefs like the following were common:

It's a system, you have to understand that. I guess it's because there are so many kids and they all have to be in school so many days a year, for so many hours. Or maybe it's because the people who run schools finally get to the point where they don't like kids and don't want to have too much to do with them. Anyway, it's a system. It's like a machine. One person, a person like me, say, can't beat it. [53]

The frequency of the words "system" and "machine" in students' descriptions suggests how far from their needs youth perceive school to be.

In his perceptive study of students in two leading urban high schools, Rhea found that the relatively affluent youngsters were highly tolerant of school requirements and limitations; they also denied they were powerless and that they desired more independence than they had [54]. However, their involvement in school stemmed neither from an intrinsic interest in learning nor from enjoyment of the school experience, but rather from their intense motivation to get good grades so as to realize their college aspirations. This need supported their belief that everything in the school, including repressive teachers, was benevolently intended for the furthering of their aspirations. One major implication of Rhea's findings is that student adaptation to benevolent paternalism is the price paid for maintaining order in these schools. What will these students do as adults? Another implication is that students who do not experience such intense motivation for success, or who perceive that the school presents an obstacle to their goals, are less predisposed toward faith in the benevolence of the institution. They may, in fact, rebel against it.

There are several natural consequences of these patterns of economic class alienation, both those that are derived from the latent roles of youth in the society outside of the school, and those that are manifest within the organization of schooling itself. One set of consequences concerns the reactions of adults in the roles of parents, teachers, educators, or other authorities vested by the state with the control and guidance of the young. As indicated in prior chapters these personnel may gradually lose sight of their humane and liberating goals, and often are trapped in a rut themselves; translating themselves into objects ruling other objects. The power relation of these adults to their charges become paramount as they become increasingly paranoid about the failure of traditional control patterns and more defensive and wary about any indication that the controls are slipping. Further distance is obtained by romanticizing about the roles of youth. As whites gain greater distance from blacks by romanticizing about the sexual behavior of blacks, as men gain distance from women by romanticizing about womens' roles, and as affluent people romanticize about the lazy or expressive lower classes, so do adults generate fantasies about the drug-related and sex-related carefreeness of youth. This flight into fantasy also

---

Exercise 7—4. *Reflecting on Ways of Coping with Youth Alienation*

Merton has suggested several different kinds of common responses people make to conditions they find alienating [55]. Consider your own and others' experience in response to school rules and regulations. Can you think of occasions when you:

Overconformed to minor aspects of almost all rules?

Discreetly deviated from rules?

Openly challenged or rebelled against rules?

---

stimulates vicarious expectations of revolution and danger, and the constant expectation that youth—unsocialized and rebellious by nature—will rise and overturn the stable social order as we know it: thus the need for vigilance and heavy controls.

As grades, the rewards of competition, and access to future roles are allocated by the controllers of school, youth orient their studying and learning—the school-related work—to the needs of adults who will reward them, whether or not this learning satisfies the needs of the learners. As youth are alienated from the content of their work in school, so, too, are there indications that they are alienated from the process of work, and from the work place itself. Resistance to rules, passive obedience to all rules, dropping out, and withdrawal are all classic examples of alienation. Walkouts, riots, trashing, and other manifestations of organized political rebellion are further examples of this alienation catalyzed into political reactions against exploiting and oppressing institutions and institutional roles.

SUMMARY

This chapter focused upon young people, and on the nature of their roles and experiences in schools. Strangely enough, this is an often overlooked group in books about schools, probably because books written for adults and by adults generally want young people to be "seen and not heard," an American aphorism that treats youngsters as a passive part of the school's operations.

No one can capture the realities of all schools, and certainly not of all students in schools. In our search for general patterns, we have elected to treat youngsters much as we have other groups, as an interest group in the school. This means that we have searched for those things that contribute to the common realities and experiences which youth encounter in schools. Youth do appear to us to be an identifiable interest group in the American society, a group with its own membership composition, social and economic status, political rights and privileges, and the like. There are youth of many races and classes, and each of these may be considered as subinterest groups, but there are many common aspects in the roles and access to resources and rewards of youth vis-a-vis adults in school. Youth also appear to be an identifiable interest group within the school, with special and limited sets of perquisites and opportunities.

The interest group approach to youth is illustrated by the concern with issues of student rights. But it is not just the attempt to "advance" student rights that makes this concern clear. The "opposition" to students rights also makes it evident that collective issues of power and control are at stake—that other interest groups also have concerns with these issues. Educational professionals want to run the school on their own terms, although in the name of service to youth. This requires the professionals to have control of the school, and they often oppose student power or student rights programs and policies that might

Exercise 7—5. *Observing Classroom Group Dynamics*

This exercise can be done by small groups of students who report back to the entire class.

Spend a day in an elementary school classroom. Some people should observe open or informal classrooms, others should observe more traditional ones. As the day progresses, students will be engaged in a number of different types of activities. For each activity look for the following things:

1. Size of group—(whole class; one group with teacher, the rest on their own; small groups; individual tasks).

2. Is everyone doing the same thing at the same time and at the same level? (Are some doing math, while others are doing spelling? Is everyone working on the same page?)

3. How much control do students have over:
      What they do (academically)
      When they do it
      Movement and interaction in the classroom
      Getting their own supplies
      Where they sit
      Going to the bathroom

4. To what extent are students' performance and evaluation of that performance public and highly visible to the rest of the class?

5. To what extent are students able to compare their performance and evaluations with others?

---

challenge, disrupt, or weaken their control. We do not think that there is anything malicious about this scenario; it is part of the nature of the ways we have organized schools. We have made a contest out of the potentially collaborative relations that might exist between educators and students. We have not done it willingly, but we have done it. As a result, the interest group analysis seems to fit. Some may resist this notion because they feel it does not fit the reality of youth, or of life in American schools. Americans are used to thinking of each other as individuals, not as members of more or less organized political groupings, particularly when it comes to young people.

Student encounters with the adult world of the school take many forms, and we have organized these encounters into issues that are often studied by social scientists and educators. For instance, the problem of authority seems to us crucial, as it is important in all social organizations in which one group does things to another group, even if the "doing to" is seen as "doing for." So then are the rules and regulations that guide behavior important to study, for where written guidelines for behavior are made and obeyed, individuals do not have to struggle quite so hard to control others by the use of naked force. The fact that students generally are excluded from rule making and rule enforcing, or, if included, are offered only token roles, makes these rules suspect as instruments of adult control, rather than freely made and internalized outlines of a democratic learning community. The nature of student-staff relations is reviewed as well, here from a viewpoint different from that taken in the prior chapter.

Major differences do exist within the broad group of youth, and we drew special attention to the role of race and sex and cultural values as differentiations that all people must learn to make. The ways in which youngsters of different races learn to relate to one another in school promises the shape of the next generation of race relations in our society—a critical issue for any analysis of schooling or society. The same can be said of sex and economic class relations. And the cultural commitments and/or alienation that youth carry with them as they leave school bespeaks much for the ways in which these young people view the future of our society and our world. They also tell us much about what we really have been teaching—intentionally or not.

8

THE OUTCOMES OF SCHOOLING

Chapters 1 and 2 discussed some of the educational values supported by our cultural and political-economic values and belief systems. These values are organized by formal educational institutions into goals, and as such they are reflected or realized in the outcomes of schooling.

Although a wide variety of educational outcomes or goals are discussed in the early chapters, not all of these are readily specifiable or observable, and not all those that can be specified can be measured well and easily. Educators seem to be preoccupied with cognitive development and with outcomes that readily lend themselves to quantitative measurement. This concern is reflected in a narrow range of preferred outcomes of schooling.

> We are creating a race of children whose value and progress is judged primarily by their capacity to do well on IQ tests, reading readiness or school achievement tests. We have an obsession with cognitive development and test scores. We rank and rate children, and we reward and stigmatize them according to their ability to do well in the narrow tasks that schools and/or psychologists believe can be measured quantitatively. [1]

Scholars conduct research and policy studies based on implicit or explicit assumptions about ways of assessing, measuring, or indicating the outcomes of the schooling process. Educators and citizens make policy and organize school life based upon explicit or implicit assumptions about the preferred outcomes of schooling. Thus, it is important to consider the definition of school outcomes carefully. Alternative ways of conceptualizing and measuring these outcomes are explored in this chapter.

WHAT ARE THE OUTCOMES OF SCHOOLING?

The outcomes of schooling can be divided initially into at least four categories. First, certain kinds of schooling outcomes can be specified for *individuals*. Individual students stay in school for different lengths of time— tenure—and when they leave school they have certain technical and academic skills, social attitudes, learned behaviors, and other orientations to their community and society. All of these can be conceptualized as outcomes. Teachers, principals, and other administrators also receive and experience various outcomes from the schooling process. These individuals may or may not learn new skills and attitudes as a function of schooling, but they certainly make a living, receive various rewards, and attain a status that places them in a preferred position in the community.

Second, outcomes can be specified for *schools as organizations*, as well as for individual students. Schools are expected to nurture, shape, or mold students in ways that ensure the attainment of certain prescribed attitudes and skills. Thus, creating academic mastery, teaching social interaction skills, helping students develop societal commitment and loyalty, and demonstrating marketable economic skills are examples of organizational goals that schools reasonably might be expected to attain. The organizational structure of schools provides the channels and creates the environment within which such outcomes are attainable. In many communities, citizen groups have adopted this view as they attempt to review the activities of their schools with their children, and therefore to evaluate the worth of the school organization.

Third, there are schooling outcomes for the local *community* and for the different elements of a given community. Since schools are instrumentalities of the state, it is reasonable to expect them to produce outcomes that benefit the local economic and political order. For instance, the local economic system in a community often utilizes those people leaving the elementary or high school educational system as workers. Students completing a college education often are utilized as line or staff executives. Thus, in the broadest sense, the local economy depends on schools to produce outcomes that conveniently and effectively mesh into the work force and the larger economic apparatus. Outcomes of effective economic preparation thus involve basic literacy, some transferable work skills, positive attitudes toward work and our economic system, comfort with bureaucratic authority and peer relations, and a beginning understanding or identification with a career.

The local political system also benefits from the schooling process. Since the political system is dependent upon the more or less orderly participation of young people as citizens, schools are expected to create outcomes that serve the community's priorities. Outcomes of effective citizenship training thus involve information about politics and political systems, positive attitudes toward the government, and acceptance of traditional styles of political behavior and action. The local community also is likely to be concerned with students' learning broad societal norms, adapting to local modifications or elaborations, and knowing something of the state and local history and culture.

Outcomes of the schooling process are also relevant for the larger *society*. The common socialization of young people throughout the nation, through a relatively common public educational apparatus, means that we can rely upon schooling to produce young people who are prepared to live comfortably in all geographic areas. The broader society also relies upon schools to produce outcomes that can effectively be channeled into a variety of political/economic opportunities and social statuses. In order to maintain and justify the orderly process of social stratification, schools must produce groups of students with inequality in educational outcomes. If schools actually produced outcome equality, the maintenance of differential levels of power and privilege would be made much more difficult. In effect, after the schools had completed their jobs, society would be forced to re-create a legitimate and respectable status hierarchy, and the effort to channel people into different status systems and roles could result in utter chaos. As the system works now, patterns of outcome inequality which are created or maintained in school fit neatly with the inequalities that exist throughout the society. No dramatic discontinuity or disjuncture exists, so that no major conflicts exist in this regard between school and society.

The outcomes of schooling, therefore, can be conceptualized in other than individual terms, and any effective study of the sociology of education must consider the outcomes of schooling in terms of the needs of the organization, the local community, and the larger society. Schooling is a societal process that serves not only individual consumers but a bevy of other public and private interests throughout the society.

The consideration of multiple levels of assessing outcomes makes it difficult to decide whether any specific outcome measure, such as achievement test scores, ought to be seen as an attribute of individual students or as a collective attribute of a given school organization or community process. This is a critical choice. If we believe that the critical variable in learning is individual talent and ability, then the responsibility for schooling outcomes lies in those genetic or familial situations that determine talent. If we believe that the critical variable in learning is hard work and motivation, then responsibility lies with individual students and their will to work/learn. If we believe that the critical variable is the quality of curriculum and instruction, then responsibility lies with the school organization. If we believe that the critical variable in learning is the kind of local support and resources that are available for schooling, or with future opportunities for rewards and success, then responsibility lies with the local community.

In another vein, if schooling is seen as providing all people with a fair and open opportunity to learn marketable skills, it would make sense to consider students as having individual responsibility for taking advantage of these opportunities for learning and performing. On the other hand, if schooling is seen as channelling students in one direction or another, perhaps even through unfair or closed learning opportunities, it makes little sense to hold students responsible for learning in these environs. Under these conditions, it makes more sense for schools to bear the lion's share of the responsibility for the structure they establish, and for students' performance in that structure. In any situation, citizens could hold schools and school personnel accountable for what they teach to the young people of the community. But professional educators are very reluctant to use outcome measures as indicators of quality of schooling delivered, rather than the quality of student performance. The reluctance is partly because such measures might be used to hold administrators or teachers accountable for the quality of their performance in being able to generate teacher or student performance.

DEFINITIONS AND NORMS OF APPROPRIATE OUTCOMES

The problem of defining outcomes, or of examining alternative definitions of outcomes, is a critical one. Outcomes of the schooling process are in no way accidental. Schools are purposive systems that reflect and implement a variety of societal values, beliefs, and priorities. These values and beliefs are operationalized in the specific context of the institution designed to help achieve them. Therefore, as in any purposive social institution, school outcomes have been planned far in the future, and people as well as organizational rules and regulations focus on attaining these outcomes. Outcomes of profit for industrial corporations, health service for hospitals, and educational gains for schools are examples of attempts to implement social goals and priorities with the power of organizational purpose. There also are unintended or covert outcomes of schooling that are not planned for, but which may occur nevertheless. One example might be that a tracking system which was originally designed for what was thought to be sound pedagogical reasons, or to maintain economic class distinctions, may be used to maintain racial segregation in integrated schools. Still another example might be the rhetoric of student independence, so often stated as an educational objective, yielding to the covert outcomes of student obedience and docility to peers and to authorities.

Broad political, economic, and cultural priorities are often supported or contested differently in each local school or community. For instance, to the extent that the characteristics of a local community mirror the demographic and political/economic characteristics of the larger society of the United States, there is likely to be local support for general societal priorities regarding outcomes of schooling. To the extent, however, that a particular local community is poor or contains a large number of minority people, it is quite reasonable that the priorities of such subcommunities may take precedence in the definition of local schooling outcomes. The same possibility may occur when strong local subcommunities of very affluent people exist; they also may press for schooling outcomes that are somewhat different from the general societal values. In most cases, these local and subcommunity pluralisms are muted and even suppressed in the name of an overarching consensus and the hope of a universally oriented system of mass public education. As has been previously noted, however, such an apparent consensus may or may not be real, and may mask substantial local and community differences in schooling.

What are some of the specific outcomes of schooling with which we should be familiar? The following discussion considers (1) tenure or length of time in school; (2) academic or intellectual achievement; (3) technical and social skill attainment; (4) attitudes toward school and society; and (5) satisfaction with schooling. Although these outcomes are treated as individual outcomes of schooling, it is possible also to view them differently—as societal, community, and organizational outcomes.

Outcome No. 1: Tenure or Length of Time in School

One important and easily standardized index of schooling outcomes is the length of time a student spends in school. Regardless of more specific performances, students can be graded and sorted on the basis of whether they have spent eight years in school, twelve years with a high school diploma, sixteen years with a college degree, or more than sixteen years with an advanced professional or human service degree of one kind or another. In some of these categories, colleges and manpower consumers (employers) look beyond tenure to specific skill performance, but for many others the length of time spent in school, per se, is the appropriate credential, and represents an effective outcome measure and an effective criterion for future sorting. On the basis of this outcome criterion, future educational and employment opportunities can be made available to students.

The length of time students spend in school can be attributed either to students' individual qualities or to qualities of the school. The ability of the school to "hold" its client population, to attract them and maintain their interest and attention over time, can be seen as a measure of the quality of the school organization. However, as with many other outcome measures, the predominant research orientation has been to see this measure as a reflection of individual and personal choices and options, and, therefore, as a reflection of students' motivation—ability and interest—rather than as an outcome of the organization processes of schooling.

For most school systems, the outcome of student tenure has serious economic and political implications. Public schools are generally financed through a combination of local and state support. The local basis of support historically has been the property tax, and wealthy school districts consistently have been able to afford better facilities and higher salary schedules than poorer systems. School retention has generally not been a problem in these districts, because parental expectations for their children often support the completion of high school and a college education. Regardless of the legitimacy of their reasons, early school leavers were not supported, either by their parents, peers, or the community; such behavior could tarnish the image of the school and deprecate the value of education. Schools that are able to retain their students and channel them into college attract prospective homeowners whose values and social origins closely parallel those of existing residents.

For those communities whose economic base has been seriously impaired by demographic transitions, industrial relocations, or general urban decline, the problem of school retention or tenure takes on a different character. Because their ability to generate revenue for the schools is hampered by low property value assessment, these school systems invariably are more dependent on aid from state and federal sources. Although the precise formula governing state aid to schools varies from state to state, most states incorporate as part of their formula for financial aid the number of students that are present in school on a given date. Two factors then emerge which are crucial to the system's ability to maintain a minimum educational program. First is the system's success at retaining students long enough in the school environs to qualify for state aid. This alone has proven to be a formidable task in some large urban systems where the retention rates in the middle and upper school levels commonly dip below the fiftieth percentile. The second factor is the establishment of a favorable public image and level of credibility so as to assure continued local support for the schools. Again, in the midst of increasing conflict in city schools, public financial support for schools is clearly on the wane. The genesis of this conflict is complex and obscured by a multiplicity of interrelated social problems and issues. The public often attributes this open conflict to the impotence of the school in not being able to control reputed troublemakers and provide a safe environment for learning, or in not being sensitive to, or effective with, poor and minority students, or young people with unique backgrounds and/or educational goals. School leaders, on the other hand, often point to the unruly or unprepared character of their students as the major contributors to these problems. Regardless of the merits of these perceptions, a school's image is an important factor in the ability of large city school systems to generate financial support for education.

The tenure outcome thus can become a crucial political and economic issue, since it reflects the schools' inability to retain their middle school and high school populations, and their inability to command the respect and support of local constituencies. Further, it lends credence to the widely held societal view that students (generally poor and black) who frequent our large urban public schools lack the motivation, ability, and personal discipline required to achieve in school and are, therefore, disinterested in acquiring an education. The question as to the appropriateness of school for the individual never seems to enter the discussion. The assumption that school somehow is good for all seldom gets challenged, whereas unfavorable public images of the poor and minority groups continue to be reinforced throughout the social order. This assumption clearly presupposes tenure as an individual outcome, and targets the responsibility for lack of tenure as residing in poor and minority students.

Finally, the use of the tenure outcome leaves in doubt just what it is that occurs while one is in school. But if we assume that part of the outcome of schooling is an exposure to a variety of organizing patterns that suit one for other outcomes, such as a set of cognitive and technical skills and competent and obedient performance in later roles and opportunities, then tenure in school itself is an important and appropriate outcome measure both for individuals and the organization. If employers and institutions of higher learning are more concerned with the credential of school completion than with the particular skills that may have gone into it, then tenure is in itself critical.

Outcome No. 2: Student Intellectual Achievement

One of the most commonly agreed-upon outcomes of the schooling process is student mastery of intellectual material and achievement of academic skills. In its most basic sense we can think of student achievement in terms of reading, writing, and arithmetic, and in the various social studies. It is relatively easy to gain apparent consensus among all sectors of the community on this outcome of schooling, because we all have been trained to believe that schools should provide basic literacy and communicative as well as computational skills. Student achievement patterns are sometimes assessed directly on a local basis, by means of classroom tests or local school graduation examinations. The current priority on standardized achievement tests represents an attempt to measure agreed-upon outcomes across a wide variety of different schools, communities, and regions of the country.

Achievement outcomes also can be assessed indirectly. Teachers and principals often are asked for their views of the skills and achievement patterns of their students; outcomes are then based upon these professionals' "grades," or assessments of student performance. It is always problematic to assess student outcomes by the reports of teachers or principals, because educators' own jobs and respect are predicated upon their ability to produce desired outcomes in their students, and to control deviants or failures. It is reasonable to assume that educators' self-interest may bias their assessments of student outcomes in a positive manner, or, that they may "explain" negative outcomes as a function of student inadequacy rather than as a reflection on their own performance as educators. Since teachers and principals have a professional interest in maintaining their own roles and self-respect, their evaluative efforts may stress one set of preferred outcomes (ones they are good at producing) to the exclusion or diminution of others.

Both direct or indirect attempts at assessment must confront the problem of separating student performance per se from the cultural biases that any testing or assessment procedure carrries. For instance, a Hispanic youngster may be competent in mathematical computations, but fail a test because the instructions are in English. Or, tests of students' reading ability may be based on stories or concepts that are familiar to white youngsters, but are strange or unknown to blacks or other minorities. Often, the linguistic patterns of different cultures and language variations of certain subcultures provide barriers leading to subpar performances on tests requiring verbal skills and language manipulation. An example of such a variation is provided by Langston Hughes, the famous black poet, in a selection taken from his classic work *The Book of Negro Folklore* [2]. In this selection, Hughes attempts to portray the rich and imaginative quality of what he terms the "Harlem Jive Talk," the street language of Harlem. Translation of this selection (William Cool Surveys the Situation) into the so-called "King's" English is provided in the footnote at the bottom of the next page.

Willie Cool Digs the Scene
Harlem Jive Talk with Translation

My Man:—The freeze has really set in on the turf, champ, and a kiddie has the toughest kind of time trying to get hold to some long bread so that he can have a ball and come on with frantic plays all up and down the line. Home, it's so bad that a lot of the cats on the stroll can't even get to their grits half the time. There used to be a few hustles that you could always fall back on for your twos and fews but nothing is happening at all. Even the soft shoe or gumshoe plays are cold. It used to be that a man could lay down a real hype by tomming to some grey but most of them plays got nixed by the hard beef laid down by some of the equal rights kinds. You can still get some fast action on the single action kick because most of the pickups carry the staff in their head and pass the scribe. This tricks the bluecoats and bulls trying to pickup on the action for a break job. It's a little tough copping any bread on the straight digit action because the boys from the ace law and order pad have been whaling like mad at the turnin' points. The heavy iron boys who didn't get snagged in the crummy play are blowing the burg if they're straight waiting for the chill to set in or they're just cooling it until somebody gets the contact straight so that the brass will hold still for an arrangement. Con plays are out, too, cause everybody is so hip, there ain't no fools to drop a shuck on. You move in one lane or square with the smooth tongue action and half the time he's got a riffle of his own that he drops on you behind a sob story so you wind up giving up some iron to him or her and then blow your stack when you see the action that plays behind it for the next time you eyeball the turkey, he running them around at a giggle juice joint. It is the craziest action, Jim, so it's best to go on the desperate tip and cop a slave for your ends. Later daddy.°

Another example of the ways in which different cultures and linguistic styles affect people's lives is expressed in the following version of the I.Q. test. The Dove Test (See Exercise 8—1) was created and standardized from the experiences of blacks in America and reflects their unique cultural background. Youngsters not acquainted with this background will have difficulty performing well on this test; by the same token, youngsters not brought up within the white and middle class traditions reflected in many other standardized intelligence or achievement tests will have difficulty performing well on them. The result is a pattern of unequal performance among various groups exacerbated by the problem of cultural conflict and test bias.

Exercise 8—1. **Testing your "Ghetto" IQ: The Dove Counterbalance Intelligence Test.** [3]

Standardized IQ tests have been severely criticized as reflecting a strong upper middle-class bias and generally measuring the verbal aptitude and cultural knowledge of that particular strata of North American society. The following selection is a test that was specifically designed to offset that bias by attempting to measure intelligence or IQ as those terms apply to lower-class black Americans.

Test your cultural knowledge and verbal skills with respect to this segment of society and compute your "Ghetto IQ." The correct answers to the test are found in the footnote at the end.

The Dove Counterbalance Intelligence Test

This test might be useful in evaluating your verbal aptitude. The verbal aptitude tested is not slanted toward middle-class experience, however, but to nonwhite lower-class experience.

° My Friend:—I am really sick about the ways things have gotten so difficult and money so scarce a fellow can hardly hustle any easy money anymore. It is so bad that many of the fellows on the street can't even make enough to cover their meals regularly. The once fertile avenues of kowtowing to the whites has been dried up by the virile campaign for equal rights. Single action on the numbers is still a possibility because the writers carry their plays in their heads instead of in writing. But the straight numbers men are either on the lam or inactive because of raids and other difficulties with the law. But things will change when the proper contacts are made with the higher ups. Confidence games are out now, too, because there are no unwary people to use as victims. In fact, you try such tricks and you may wind up falling for the other fellow's story yourself, only to be humiliated when you see the person enjoying himself with your money at a bar. Things are so difficult, Jim, that in desperation it's best to make the most drastic of all moves and go and get yourself a regular job. I'll see you later, pal.

People from a nonwhite, lower-class background are required to do well on aptitude tests keyed to white, middle-class culture, before they are allowed to perform in that culture. By the same standard, it seems only fair that people of white middle-class culture do well on this test before they be allowed to perform in such a milieu.

The following test was developed by Watts social worker Adrian Dove to measure intelligence as the term applies in lower-class black America.

If you score less than 20 (67 per cent) on the test, you are virtually failing, and might, therefore, conclude that you have a low ghetto I.Q. As white middle-class educators put it, you are "culturally deprived."

1. "T-Bond Walker" got famous for playing what?
   (a) Trombone   (b) Piano   (c) "T-Flute"   (d) Guitar
   (e) "Hambone"

2. Who did "Stagger Lee" kill (in the famous blues legend)?
   (a) His mother   (b) Frankie   (c) Johnny   (d) his girlfriend
   (e) Billy

3. A "Gas Head" is a person who has a _____.
   (a) Fast moving car   (b) Stable of "lace"   (c) "Process"
   (d) Habit of stealing cars   (e) Long jail record for arson

4. If a man is called "Blood," then he is a _____.
   (a) fighter   (b) Mexican-American   (c) Negro
   (d) Hungry hemophile   (e) Redman or Indian

5. If you throw the dice and "7" is showing on the top, what is facing down?
   (a) "Seven"   (b) "Snake eyes"   (c) "Boxcars"
   (d) "Little Joes"   (e) "Eleven"

6. Jazz pianist Ahmad Jamal took an Arabic name after becoming really famous. Previously he had some fame with what he called his "slave name." What was his previous name?
   (a) Willie Lee Jackson   (b) LeRoi Jones   (c) Wilbur McDougal
   (d) Frank Jones   (e) Andy Johnson

7. In "C. C. Rider," what does "C. C." stand for?
   (a) Civil Service   (b) Church Council
   (c) Country Circuit, preacher or an old time rambler
   (d) Country Clue   (e) "Cheatin Charlie" (the "Boxcar Gunsel")

8. Cheap "chitlings" (not the kind you purchase at a frozen-food counter) will taste rubbery unless they are cooked long enough. How soon can you quit cooking them to eat and enjoy them?
   (a) 15 minutes (b) 2 hours (c) 24 hours
   (d) 1 week (on a low flame) (e) 1 hour

9. "Down Home" (the South) today, for the average "Soul Brother" who is picking cotton (in season from sunup until sundown), what is the average earning (take home) for one full day?
   (a) $0.75 (b) $1.65 (c) $3.50 (d) $5.00 (e) $12.00

10. If a judge finds you guilty of "holding weed" (in California), what's the most he can give you?
    (a) Indeterminate (life) (b) A nickel (c) A dime
    (d) A year in country (e) $00.00

11. "Bird" or "Yardbird" was the "jacket" that jazz lovers from coast to coast hung on _____ _____.
    (a) Lester Young (b) Peggy Lee (c) Benny Goodman
    (d) Charlie Parker (e) "Birdman of Alcatraz"

12. A "Hype" is a person who _____.
    (a) Always says he feels sickly (b) Has water on the brain
    (c) Uses heroin (d) Is always ripping and running
    (e) Is always sick

13. Hattie Mae Johnson is on the County. She has four children and her husband is now in jail for nonsupport, as he was unemployed and was not able to give her any money. Her welfare check is now $286.00 per month. Last night she went out with the biggest player in town. If she got pregnant, then nine months from now, how much more will her welfare check be?
    (a) $80.00 (b) $2.00 (c) $35.00 (d) $150.00 (e) $100.00

14. "Hully Gully" came from _____.
    (a) "East Oakland" (b) Fillmore (c) Watts (d) Harlem
    (e) Motor City

15. What is Willie Mae's last name?
    (a) Schwartz (b) Matuada (c) Gomez (d) Turner
    (e) O'Flaherty

16. The opposite of square is _____.
    (a) Round (b) Up (c) Down (d) Hip (e) Lame

17. Do "Beatles" have soul?
    (a) Yes (b) No (c) Gee whiz or maybe

18. A "Handkerchief head" is _____.
    (a) A cool cat   (b) A porter   (c) An "Uncle Tom"   (d) A hoddi
    (e) A "preacher"

19. What are the "Dixie Hummingbirds"?
    (a) A part of the KKK   (b) A swamp disease
    (c) A modern Gospel Group
    (d) A Mississippi Negro paramilitary strike force   (e) Deacons

20. "Jet" is _____.
    (a) An "East Oakland" Motorcycle Club
    (b) One of the gangs in West Side Story
    (c) A news and gossip magazine
    (d) A way of life for the very rich

21. "Tell it like it _____."
    (a) Thinks I am   (b) Baby   (c) Try   (d) is   (e) Y'all

22. "You've got to get up early in the morning if you want to
    _____.
    (a) Catch   (b) Be healthy, wealthy, and wise   (c) Try to fool me
    (d) Fare well   (e) Be the first one on the street

23. And Jesus said, "Walk together children _____."
    (a) Don't you get weary. There's a great camp meeting
    (b) For we shall overcome
    (c) For the family that walks together talks together
    (d) By your patience you will win your souls
    (e) Find the things that are above, not the things that are on
    Earth

24. "Money don't get everything it's true _____."
    (a) But I don't have none and I'm so blue
    (b) But what it don't get I can't use
    (c) So make with what you've got
    (d) But I don't know that and neither do you

25. "Bo-Diddley" is a _____.
    (a) Camp for children   (b) Cheap wine   (c) Singer
    (d) New Dance   (e) Mojo call

26. Which word is not out of place here?
    (a) Splib   (b) Blood   (c) Grey   (d) Spook   (e) Black

27. How much does a "short-dog" cost?
    (a) $0.15   (b) $2.00   (c) $0.35   (d) $0.05   (e) $0.86 + tax

28. True or False: A "Pimp" is also a young man who lays around all day.
    (a) Yes (b) No

29. If a Pimp is up tight with a woman who gets state aid, what does he mean when he talks about "Mother's Pay?"
    (a) Second Sunday in May (b) Third Sunday in June
    (c) First of every month (d) None of these
    (e) First and fifteenth of every month

30. Many people say that "Juneteenth" (June 19) should be made a legal holiday because this was the day when _____.
    (a) The slaves were freed in the U.S.A.
    (b) The slaves were freed in Texas
    (c) The slaves were freed in Jamaica
    (d) The slaves were freed in California
    (e) Martin Luther King was born
    (f) Booker T. Washington died

° 1. d, 2. e, 3. c, 4. c, 5. a, 6. d, 7. c, 8. c, 9. d, 10. c, 11. d, 12. c, 13. c, 14. c, 15. d, 16. d, 17. b, 18. c, 19. c, 20. c, 21. d, 22. d, 23. a, 24. b, 25. c, 26. c, 27. c, 28. a, 29. c, 30. b.

Test bias reflects the reality that different groups in this country have different experiences, both in and out of school. Moreover, some groups have more power than others, and thus can press their definitions of achievement and school outcomes. Rather than stating this boldly and directly as a problem of cultural conflict, it is couched in the language of *technical bias*. Different experiences and realities are overlooked, a consensus is assumed, and technical measurement problems are seen to be paramount instead. Thus, educators and researchers search for "bias-free" or "culture-free" tests. No one and no thing can be culture-free; the problem is to be fair to all cultures. The problem of bias does not, however, exist solely in the tests; rather it exists in the society's basic structure and in the operations of the schools. Even the best tests will not correct this situation, although they may permit more pluralistic definitions of culturally acceptable achievement outcomes.

Perhaps the most important aspect of achievement as an outcome is that it does seem to be measurable. As such, it has garnered the overwhelming attention of most researchers and students of schools, not because it necessarily is the most important outcome, but precisely because it is measurable. Jencks notes that other outcomes might be even more important to assess than achievement patterns, per se, but that achievement patterns are the ones he uses in his study, primarily because they are measurable [4]. The priority on measuring the "measurable" is a bias supported by the professional class of educators and research scholars in education. It is also advanced by policymakers who want an allegedly objective base on which to make or evaluate educational policies and programs. It has raised to an undeserved priority the concern for achievement patterns, and has created an apparent consensus on this outcome measure.

The fact that achievement patterns are readily measurable means that they often are used as a standard and quantifiable index of student performance on marketable skills throughout the society. These patterns fit well into the credentializing apparatus that screens students for employment or future access to higher education opportunities, because of their apparent reliability and standardization. Brookover et al. in charting the historical rationale for the development and use of individual tests, from which crucial decisions affecting the lives of children ultimately would be made, offer the following interpretations:

> The accumulation of mathematically identified test scores from a number of measuring devices provides the justification for the educational decisions through which children are allocated and assigned to a wide variety of courses and careers. The underlying assumption is that both the educational and career achievement of each individual is determined by some relatively constant abilities, aptitudes, or characteristics created by forces beyond the school's realm of influence. The measurement and quantification of these fixed aptitudes, abilities, or characteristics provide the objective criteria for predicting the future of each individual and define the role which he shall play in the society. [5]

In fact, some scholars and practitioners defend such tests and testing practices precisely because they appear to work. "Fair" or not, they do predict later performance, and can be used to sort and screen students into tracks that confirm these predictions.

> Furthermore, they are not, nor are they intended to be, "culture free." Quite the reverse: they are culture bound. What they measure are the skills which are among the most important in our society for getting a good job and moving up to a better one, and for full participation in an increasingly technical world. Consequently, a pupil's test results at the end of public school provide a good measure of the range of opportunities open to him as he finishes school—a wide range of choice of jobs or colleges if these skills are very high; a very narrow range that includes only the most menial jobs if these are very low. [6]

The number and kinds of achievement tests that are administered to students at all levels of the educational system are legion. In fact, achievement outcomes from schooling have enjoyed such universal support from the more privileged sectors of society that the "business" of testing has become big business. There is not a single public (and perhaps private as well) school system in the United

States that does not administer an achievement testing program of some sort. These tests have to be purchased, administered, and evaluated—all of which require a substantial financial investment. It is highly unlikely, given the need to sort out, select, and classify young people on the basis of test scores, that such a practice will be readily discarded.

Achievement test patterns also have been utilized to assess the performance of schools as institutions rather than students as individuals. For instance, in addition to, or instead of, looking at individual student outcomes on achievement tests, one can sum or average achievement test scores for an entire school. The collective index of achievement for a school may then be utilized as a measure of the outcomes of the schooling process as implemented by that given school. We then can talk about school quality in terms of changes in overall achievement patterns that schools have been able to produce in their students over the years. We can also compare different schools' ability to create certain outcomes, or changes in outcomes.

Outcome No. 3: Technical and Social Skills

Another outcome that students may gain in schools, or that schools may produce in students, is the acquisition of technical and social skills. These skills can be distinguished from achievement patterns because they refer to patterns of behavior, rather than cognitive organizations and presentations.

One set of skill outcomes is those technical abilties to manipulate materials and objects. Examples would include things such as carpentry, automobile mechanics, computer operations, cooking, and sewing. The range of technical skills that can be elaborated upon as outcome measures is very broad. In addition, this range of skills is constantly shifting as the industrial economy moves into new forms of natural resource exploitation and productive transformation. As a consequence, needs for people with certain kinds of skills shift, and it is therefore reasonable that the school constantly adapt the curriculum to keep up with these changes.

To the degree that technical skills in manipulating materials and objects generally lead to a series of lower-status occupations, success in this skill preparation represents a way to channel young people for blue-collar and low-level white-collar job responsibilities. Higher-status and white-collar executive roles generally require the manipulation of people and symbols, rather than materials or objects. Thus, these roles require another kind of skill, as well as greater achievement in the ability to master technical mathematical and grammatical procedures.

Social skills that are either produced or acquired in schools involve the ability to work with people in a variety of social relationships. The ability to work well with peers is often stressed as an outcome of interactive processes in schools and classrooms. Less often noted, but at least as important, is the development of student ability to work well with authorities, such as teachers and principals.

Both are examples of social skills that are important for the maintenance and improvement of social relationships in this society. In some situations, passivity and compliance may work well; in other situations, aggression and dominance work well. It is hard to delineate a single set of skills that will be effective for a broad group of people in a wide range of situations.

Just as important, however, is the fact that access to the higher levels of economic status is reserved for people who have the ability to manipulate key symbols or people in assertive and even dominant ways. It is a prime skill in development of executive talent; therefore, people who do well on this skill are often screened forward to further education and higher occupational status. When we get past relatively consensual outcomes, such as achievement on cognitive tasks, tenure in school, and specific technical skills we get into an area that is clearly tied to cultural background and value preferences. Thus, we encounter problems of conflict among different subcultures and groups, with less possibility of an overarching consensus about the "appropriate way to behave and relate to others."

The range of relevant social skills is very hard to assess by conventional research and evaluation modes. Social skills are highly subjective and uniquely determined skills that may be visible in very different ways. The problems of defining and agreeing upon which skills are most appropriate has made it difficult to include social skills as a measurable outcome in many research studies.°

The development of these skills does stand as another index of one's marketability in the economic structure of a society, and as evidence of adjustment to the sociocultural and political requirements for good behavior. Development of social skills and technical skills are important aspects of the school's role as an informal socializing agent preparing people for useful attitudes toward, and roles in, a corporate economy, a welfare-oriented polity, and a community of social relationships.

Outcome No. 4: Student Attitudes Toward School and Social Systems

Another set of outcomes relating to the latent socializing functions of schools can be explored in the context of a variety of school-related attitudes. One series of examples of these attitudes are views that the student holds toward oneself, one's peers, or one's family. In some cases, these attitudes have been seen as indicators of mental health and as being related to the schools' attempt to produce and support good positive mental health on the part of the students.

° Especially difficult in research that is oriented to multiple-choice responses to prestructured questions, an inquiry/evaluative mode well suited for large quantitative studies of schools and school systems. Other research modes, which might assess these skills more effectively, are not so highly favored, either by positivist scholars or by educational managers. Among these alternative models are participant observation, life history analyses, phenomenology, and action research.

A second set of attitudinal outcome examples focuses on views regarding social issues and the broader society. For example, students' perceptions of, and trust in, political leaders, in the nature of the flag and patriotism, and in orientations toward the American economy all represent examples of an orientation toward the larger social structure. A closely related focus of societal attitudes are those directed toward current social issues such as international relations, race relations, poverty, women's rights, and the like. These attitudes become particularly poignant when such social issues begin to impinge upon the schools. Thus, an important problem in preparing for school desegregation is countering negative racial attitudes students hold. For many, one of the promises of school desegregation is that it may alter not just student achievement patterns, but student interracial attitudes as well. The attempt to desegregate schools has created a whole new set of outcome measures that remind us all of the purposes of schooling in promoting a multiracial society, and in promoting positive intergroup attitudes among students of different races.

A third major group of relevant attitudes are those that are focused on the school system itself. Examples include student attitudes toward teachers, administrators, schooling, the curriculum, particular educational processes, and the like. The school's internal functioning relies heavily on its ability to inculcate positive attitudes on the part of students toward the school system itself. Without such positive student attitudes, and the collaboration and trust they imply, the school is largely a coercive system, utilizing power and unilateral rules to engender student compliance with school policy. To the extent that the school can create or support fairly positive student attitudes toward teachers and the schooling process, then they do not have to overcome student resistance, but can build off a positive reservoir. To the extent that students may be channeled toward further schooling, positive views of education are very important as outcome measures of early schooling.

Many of these and other attitudes are derived from the formal curriculum and organization of school life. Moreover, some of these attitudes clearly can be derived from student extracurricular activities, even though these activities generally are not treated as a legitimate schooling process. There has been a reluctance on the part of both professional educators and social scientists to recognize the integral part that student activities and organizations play in the total educational complex. Studies of extracurricular activities have generally been preoccupied with determining participation rates, identifying social class bias in the activities, analyzing the clique structure, and attempting to establish a functional relationship between student activities and the formal structure of the school. Sociologists have tended to emphasize the function of these activities as a tension-reducing mechanism designed to distract the participants from the formalized, structured aspects of school life and thereby to allow for a release of energy and enthusiasm that does not pose a threat to the peace and tranquility of the formal school system. In this regard, both the professional educators and the social scientists can be faulted for the collaboration, albeit unintended, i̇n̥e systematically disregarding and deemphasing the importance of extracurricular activities as legitimate outcomes of schooling. Perhaps in no other school-related activity does the opportunity arise for the student to experience the American commitment to volunteerism as a life-style, learn the appropriate uses of leisure time, and perform some of their immediate *citizenship* responsibilities in the schools and its social environs. In this arena, the rhetoric of participation and involvement in school and community affairs could have real meaning.

Another way of interpreting these activities and orientations stresses the school's role in socializing students into more or less formal patterns of obedience and. compliance in the political and economic system. Though seldom stated so boldly, school attendance and punctuality are often utilized as measures of obedience to, and compliance with, bureaucratic rules and regulations. In that sense, student performance on these variables and the positive attitudes of students toward the hierarchical learning system are good predictors of effective adjustment to the hierarchical work scene and to employment relationships that also require compliance, obedience, punctuality, and respect for legitimate authority. Clearly the school is seen as responsible for training students in positive attitudes of patriotism and support for the capitalist economic system and the democratic American political system.

There is evidence that many of these student attitudes toward school may be related to other outcome measures, such as achievement and skill development. If the school is concerned about producing achievement or longer student tenure in school, positive student attitudes toward schooling may be related to students' putting energy into performing well on achievement patterns or staying in school. It makes a great deal of difference, however, whether these attitudes and school predispositions are treated as outcomes in themselves or as means to other outcomes. Once again, the context of school racial relations and desegregation can be used as an example. Are positive racial attitudes seen as a means of accomplishing increased black and white student achievement, or are positive racial attitudes seen as an important end or outcome in itself? There is not much evidence that schools are invested heavily in creating positive racial attitudes as goals in themselves.

Many observers note that these variables are difficult to measure. It is hard to assess just what does represent self-esteem, particularly in the context of group conflict about what self-esteem ought to be. For instance, if a black student perceives his or her fate as being controlled by impersonal social forces, is he or she to be judged as lacking in personal motivation and esteem, or to be judged as having a realistic view of an oppressed and limiting environment? The problems of conceptualization and conceptual agreement are sometimes so difficult that even scholars who respect the importance of the outcome variables fail to measure them.

Outcome No. 5: Student Satisfaction with Schooling

Student satisfaction with schooling can be interpreted as a student attitude toward schooling, although we consider it a sufficiently important outcome variable to merit attention by itself. Student satisfaction with schooling can represent an index of client or consumer evaluation of services delivered or received. Thus, it moves easily away from being a student attitude toward schooling to being a coherent evaluation of services delivered by the school. This attitude does not get caught in the ambivalent question of student performance versus school performance; it focuses explicitly on student evaluation of school performance. However, the line distinguishing between satisfaction as a separate outcome and as an attitudinal subset is a thin one.

Our concern with this outcome measure suggests that we think students ought to be satisfied with their schooling. The division of American life into work and play, and the division of the life of young people into study and play, suggests that not everyone agrees; some feel that students ought not to enjoy and be satisfied with schooling but to endure it. This is an unfortunate polarization of some of the cultural conflicts embedded in the ethics of hard work.

Students are prime and direct consumers/clients of the schooling process. Despite constitutional provisions regarding school accountability to the formal authority of the state, the state itself and parent/taxpayers are once removed from schools. They are indirect clients of the educational system; students are the primary client. Our view on students' roles in this matter is consistent with the movement in many human service systems that involve clients of lawyers, doctors and hospitals, social service systems, and mental health programs in evaluating the services they receive.

As with a number of other student attitudes discussed in this chapter, students who are satisfied with school probably seem more likely to work hard and perform well in the school environment than are students who are not satisfied with school. Students who feel that important services are not being delivered to them may feel that their own needs and orientations are not being responded to in a satisfactory manner. They probably are more likely to be alienated and to distance themselves from the school.

There are a number of basic measurement problems here, as there are in the other areas discussed. One basic question is whether and how students can be reliable judges or reporters of the quality of education they receive. Moreover, there is disagreement as to at what level of the educational process students have the ability to make these distinctions. We believe that students have this ability and have it early—certainly during the upper elementary school years. But research data on this question are not in, primarily because very few

researchers have bothered to investigate this outcome. The empirical evidenc
relating to student satisfaction is minimal, both from quantitative and qualitative perspectives. The fact that scholars and professional educators have
colluded in overlooking or ignoring this variable does not mean that we should
not treat it. We simply will have to treat it from a theoretical rather than an
empirical point of view.

A recent study attempted to measure the effects of traditional and alternative
school structure on student satisfaction and perceptions of school [7]. It revealed
a most interesting set of findings—that (1) alternative schools provided avenues
not found in the traditional school for both social and emotional growth and
feelings of satisfaction with school, while (2) clearly indicating that the
cognitive performance of the "alternative" students on achievement tests and
in grades later received in high school was equal to or higher than that of
students who had attended the traditional junior high schools. Whether the
satisfaction variable accounted for the cognitive performance or vice-versa is
not particularly crucial; more likely, these categories are correlates of one
another. The important observation is that they do not have to be seen as
separate or mutually exclusive categories. The study concluded that schools can
teach the fundamentals, emphasize the cognitive, and still be humanistic, more
tolerable, and satisfying places for learning.

More studies, such as Malin's, that relate directly to students' satisfaction
with schooling are needed since, in the final analysis, it is the client who
remains the most important and perhaps best evaluator of the worth and value
of his or her educational experiences. The standard rebuttal for educators who
decry attempts to ascertain student satisfaction with school is that "the school is
a place to learn and not a place for enjoyment or pleasure." In effect, learning
is not necessarily expected to be an enjoyable experience. Learning and
achievement in selected cognitive areas are treated synonymously, and if the
student happens to develop favorable attitudes toward school in the process, so
much the better. It should be clear, however, that in this context achievement
is the desired outcome and student satisfaction with schooling, although
desirable, is not necessarily a prime objective.

THE CHOICE OF OUTCOME IS CRITICAL

In the beginning of this chapter it was noted that the preferred outcomes
utilized by professional eduators, social scientists, and students may differ
considerably. These differences are related to views of the central purpose or
nature of educational systems. The desires of professional educators for order
and control and the rigorous standardized measurement priorities of social
scientists generally lead to a stress on the first two outcomes of tenure and
achievement, and to a treatment of these outcomes as individual student
performance measures.

Many people acknowledge the importance of other outcome possibilities, but there has not been a multiple outcome measurement program that tags enough of these variables for us to know what interactive networks are at work. Many investigators only attend to those outcomes they feel sure they can assess. Jencks makes this point, as does Coleman, in indicating that their studies are limited to variables they felt sure they could effectively assess or effectively analyze and interpret through a variety of quantitative manipulations [8]. This represents a certain bias not of the educational system, per se, but of the professional elite of information processors located in our major universities and research agencies. It is no accident, but not necessarily a product of conspiracy or conscious collusion, that this orientation matches that of professional educators and educational managers. From our point of view this represents a tremendous disservice; it limits major value debates to outcomes that are measurable, not necessarily to a variety of outcomes that all have value.

Finally, the choice of outcome measures takes us back to the starting point of this discussion. Who controls the choice among outcome measures? Are the preferred outcomes controlled by the direct, or even indirect, clients of the educational system, namely students and parental taxpayers, and their legislative representatives? Are the choices among outcome measures determined by professional educators who are responsible for implementing and executing the value priorities set by other political agencies? Are the outcome measures determined by what social researchers feel they can and cannot assess, thereby encouraging that technical elite to set the framework of discussion within which we contest important national priorities?

The determination and choice of outcome measures is a problem of moral and political values. It represents a series of choices among plural normative priorities. If measurement techniques can be developed to evaluate the full variety of these outcomes, all to the good. If measurement techniques cannot, or if scientists committed to certain measurement techniques cannot cover the range of political choices, we should consider the wider range of political choices nevertheless. To do otherwise would be to put the debate about outcomes of schooling in the hands of a politically nonresponsible elite of technical measurement experts. The right of these "experts" to make choices about research strategies should not permit research strategy to determine political choices about the preferred outcomes of schooling.

SUMMARY

This discussion of the outcomes of schooling has stressed a variety of ways of thinking about, and measuring, school outcomes. We started with an objection to the exceedingly narrow ways in which outcomes have been conceptualized previously, believing that they overstressed a highly cognitive approach to the education of the young. Moreover, it seemed to us that the measurement of these outcomes stressed a highly technical process to the exclusion of some important variables and issues. The measure of outcomes ought to be the measure of what we think is important to have happen in schools, not solely what it is that we can measure.

Five major categories of outcomes are discussed, each of which is championed by different groups as the really important things that youngsters should learn in schools, and that schools and communities ought to get out of the operations of their educational systems. Each of these outcomes can be measured, although the formalism of the measure may vary considerably.

One outcome is tenure, or the length of time students spend in school. A second is student achievement, the accomplishment of cognitive skills that is so often regarded as the only appropriate measure of school and/or student performance. A third outcome is the acquisition of various skills, especially those that are relevant to the student's technical capacity to work effectively in the society, and those that are relevant to the construction and maintenance of effective social relations. A fourth outcome is students' attitudes toward schools and the society, their orientations toward the political and economic institutions of the world in which they live. A fifth outcome is student satisfaction with the schooling they have experienced. Any and all of these outcomes are relevant for parents and educators being pleased or displeased with what students have learned. Different readers may have their preferences or their rankings among these outcomes. The choice of which to stress is crucial, as is the question of whether the same outcomes ought to be stressed, in equal degree, for all youngsters from all racial, economic, and sexual backgrounds and roles.

Most discussions of school outcomes treat them as aspects of students and stress the individual level of outcomes and the individual level of analysis of schooling operations. But school has effects on people other than youngsters, and the school's mission is not just to create change in youngsters. The school is expected to produce certain things for the entire society and for the local community. Thus, some of the outcomes of schooling must be assessed as aspects of the organization of schooling, not solely as aspects of the persons in it. One result of this focus might be the consideration of schools as being responsible for some of the things that students learn, not solely that students alone are responsible for what they learn. The latter analysis is most consistent with the themes of individual effort and responsibility writ deep into the North American ideology and character. Thus, to ask people to think differently, to think of schools as responsible for learning, is to ask for a considerable change.

It makes a great deal of difference whether these outcomes are measured at the individual or organizational level of analysis. The choice of level explicates a choice of explanation of schooling outcomes: outcomes may be explained as the products of individual effort or noneffort, or talent or nontalent; or outcomes may be explained as the products of an efficient or nonefficient school system. In the latter case, student performance on outcomes reflects the efficiency of the school and can be used to help hold the school (and its personnel) accountable for what they do with the community's resources—funds, staff, and student raw material. In the former case, student performance on outcomes reflects individual student (or groups of students') talent and energy and can be used to help hold students accountable to school people (and perhaps to the community as well) for what they do with the resources and learning opportunities the community has provided them. Our challenge to the reader is to experiment with alternative explanations and, by implication, with measurement procedures and conceptual interpretations that feed into, and flow out of, various explanatory schemes.

We now turn to the various ways in which the outcomes of schooling are reflected in providing or impeding access to power and privilege in North American society.

9

MORE OUTCOMES OF SCHOOLING:
PATTERNS OF INEQUALITY

The examination of school outcomes reveals pervasive underlying conflicts in the organization of school and society. It thrusts various people into vigorous debate and disagreement about appropriate school goals, about the priorities among those goals, and about the kind of society we wish to live in. These conflicts are not merely matters of academic interest, nor can they be resolved by technical improvements in scientific or technical assessment and analysis. They are fundamental problems of social policy and moral choice, and thus highlight varying cultural and political-economic values and priorities. Moreover, these values are highlighted and dramatized when we indicate that major outcomes of schooling represent continuing inequalities on the basis of race and sex and economic class. In a society ostensibly committed to equality and individual mobility this is a significant problem or internal contradiction. Inevitably, critical questions are raised about the evidence of such inequality, about its meaning, and about its import for policy.

One series of critical questions concerns the criteria or standards that should be used in generating concern about inequality in outcomes. For instance, we have already argued that there is substantial inequality in the society at large (see Chapter 3): in an unequal society what should be the appropriate distribution of school outcomes? Should the outcomes of schooling be different in an unequal society as compared to an equal society? How much inequality should it take for us to start to worry? Is the school an appropriate place to worry about inequality? Does educational inequality merely reflect social inequality or does it create it? Or pass it on? Or add to it? All these questions emphasize the relationship between social inequality and the operations and outcomes of schooling. They also have implications for what corrective policies or programs might follow from direct evidence of pervasive school inequality.

Another series of questions focuses on the different measures of school outcomes, and asks whether it is important to have equality on all of them. Perhaps only some of these outcomes ought to be equal in our societal value system. For instance, some scholars and philosophers argue that the North American political system requires that everyone have the same political status and rights. Therefore, equality of outcomes with regard to political knowledge and skills is critical; these skills should be distributed equally throughout the major societal groups. On the other hand, the values that underlie the economic system may not require such equality; Americans generally do not believe that everyone ought to have the same material benefits and status. Therefore, it may be appropriate for economic knowledge and job-related skills to be distributed unevenly. The question then is: on what school outcomes—political status attitudes and preparation, economic status attitudes and preparation, self-esteem, achievement, and so on—is equality important?

The third major set of questions concerns the population group we are concerned with when we address questions of equality-inequality. Should we be concerned with inequality among individuals, or inequality among major population groups? Individual differences do exist, and students do enter schools with different individual talents and resources. Thus, we think that there is little problem in accepting inequality among individuals. But we do not think that individual potential varies by race and class and sex, and when outcomes vary on these criteria serious concern is merited.

In a society marked by pervasive inequality among groups in income, occupation, and power we should not be surprised if schooling outcomes mirror these factors at work. The question addressed in this chapter is: What is the evidence and arguments about the potency of various sources of pervasive and continuing inequality in schooling? We first examine a series of outcomes for evidence of inequality. Then we explore two major explanations for this condition.

INDICATORS OF SCHOOL OUTCOMES, AND THE PROBLEMS OF INEQUALITY

This section presents data gathered from various studies that shed light on the existence of unequal outcomes of schooling. First, we consider data relevant to the question of *tenure* in school, the overall length of time students spend in school, and the highest grade levels that they attain or endure. Second, we consider a variety of definitions of academic *achievement*, and review standardized materials from several different national and/or metropolitan studies illuminating this outcome. As part of this inquiry, we consider *grades*, assuming that they are related to standardized achievement test scores. Third, we consider several indicators of student difficulty in school, *dropouts, failure,* and *suspension* rates being the most significant. Fourth, we examine students' political, economic, and social *attitudes*, relating these to learned orientations to the larger society and to useful skills. Fifth, we examine student *satisfaction* with school. And sixth, we consider data relevant to the relation between certain school outcomes, such as tenure and achievement, and *later life outcomes*, such as income and occupation.

In all these examinations, data are presented from a wide variety of studies, generally large-scale surveys with highly standardized scores and data sets. The statistical analyses that have been and could be performed on these data are beyond our concerns here, but the analytic tools of statistics have proved very helpful to scholars attempting to interpret these data.

Outcome No. 1: Tenure in School

As we have previously observed, one of the obvious and most easily recorded and understood outcomes of schooling is the extent to which students actually go to or stay in school. Across the United States, approximately 90 per cent of all students enrolled in public elementary and secondary schools attend school on an average day. But even this figure varies by state. For instance, in Maine, the average daily attendance is 92.9 per cent of enrollment, and in Vermont it is 93.5 per cent. In Maryland, the average daily attendance is 81.9 per cent of

Table 9−1. Comparative Levels of Education of the Population 25 and Over, 1950−1972 [3]

Years of Education	Nonwhite			White		
	1950	1960	1972	1950	1960	1972
Percent						
Less than 5 years	32.6	23.4	12.8[a]	8.9	6.7	3.7
Less than 1 year high school	72.5	59.6	38.2[a]	45.8	39.8	23.3
4 years high school or more	13.9	21.7	39.1[a]	36.4	41.4	60.4
4 years college or more	2.3	3.5	6.9[a]	6.6	8.1	12.6
Numbers (in thousands)						
High school graduates	1,074	2,049	4,531	28,151	38,575	60,121
Some college	414	757	1,575[a]	11,132	15,537	23,906
College graduates	176	335	797[a]	5,108	7,253	12,567

[a]1972 includes blacks only.

enrollment, and in Georgia it is 82.7 per cent. System-wide figures can be misleading, since in many of the large urban centers the average daily attendance hovers around 50 per cent of secondary school enrollment.

How long do students stay in school? How much exposure to formal schooling do people of different races and sexes and economic classes get? The length or level of education does not now appear to vary much between men and women, at least not until students reach the postgraduate level of education. Consider Figure 9–1. These data indicate men and women have just about equal educational attainment until the Ph.D. level. At that point men clearly have had dominance, and can be expected to continue this dominance in the future. According to W. Vance Grant, "In the early 1980's it is anticipated that men will still be earning more than three times as many doctorates and more than five times as many first-professional degrees as women" [2].

The data on school enrollment and tenure by race are even more challenging to traditional American notions of equal access to public schooling. The data in Table 9–1 demonstrate that as of 1972 a much greater per cent of blacks have less than five years of education than whites (12.8 v. 3.7) and less than one year of high school than whites (51% v. 27%). A much greater per cent of whites than blacks have four years of high school or more (73% v. 46%). Interestingly, differences between the 1950 data and the 1972 data indicate a lessening of these gaps, but it still remains quite evident.

Overall, as figures of median years of schooling indicate, as of 1972, blacks had completed two years less of schooling than whites. However, the differential is not constant throughout the nation. In some areas, such as the West, Northwest, and North Central areas the gap is narrowed to a year or less. In other geographic areas, such as the South and in nonmetropolitan areas generally, the gap is even larger. These data are presented in Table 9–2.

The same trends can be seen in many local community or city analyses. Data

Table 9–2. Median Years of School, 1972 [4]

Residence	Black	White
Total	10.3	12.3
Metropolitan	10.9	12.4
Central city	10.9	12.3
Outside central cities	11.0	12.4
Nonmetropolitan	8.3	12.1
Northwest	11.3	12.2
North central	11.3	12.3
South	9.1	12.2
West	12.2	12.5

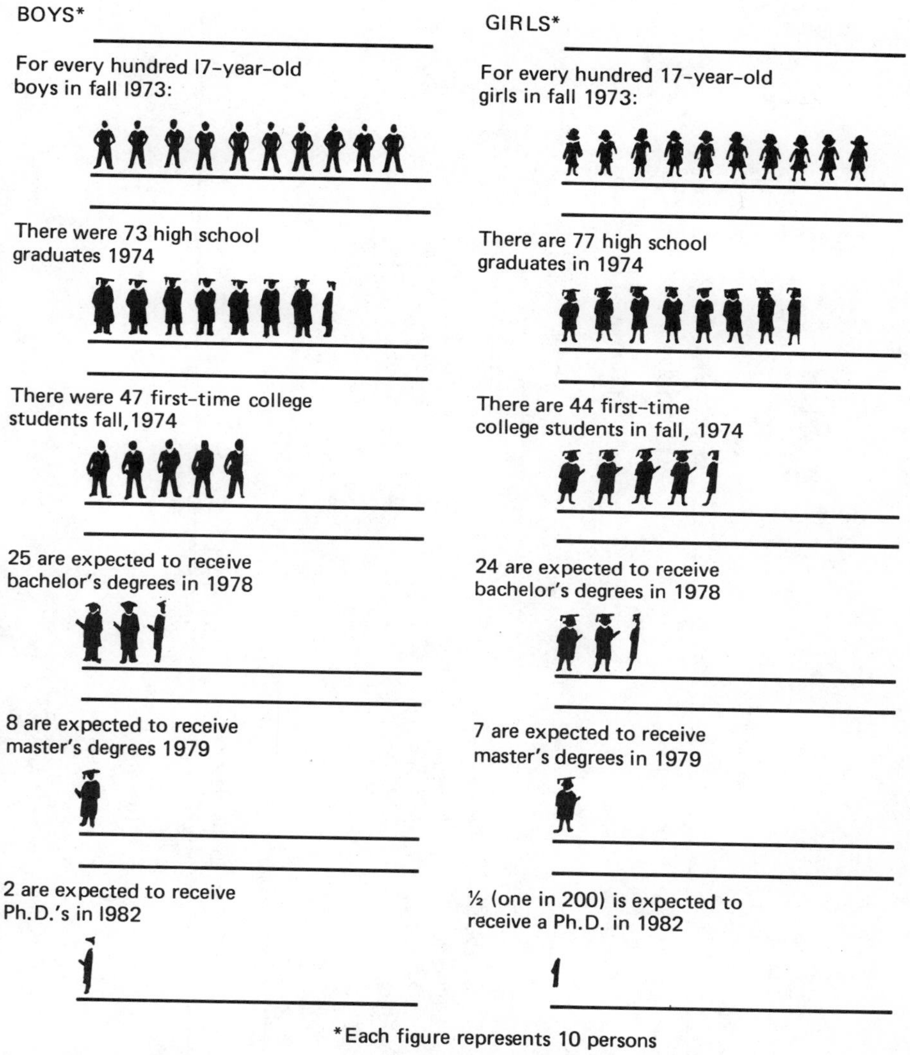

BOYS*

For every hundred 17-year-old
boys in fall 1973:

There were 73 high school
graduates 1974

There were 47 first-time college
students fall, 1974

25 are expected to receive
bachelor's degrees in 1978

8 are expected to receive
master's degrees 1979

2 are expected to receive
Ph.D.'s in 1982

GIRLS*

For every hundred 17-year-old
girls in fall 1973:

There are 77 high school
graduates in 1974

There are 44 first-time
college students in fall, 1974

24 are expected to receive
bachelor's degrees in 1978

7 are expected to receive
master's degrees in 1979

½ (one in 200) is expected to
receive a Ph.D. in 1982

*Each figure represents 10 persons

NOTE—This chart shows the years in which a person would attain various levels of education if he or she
continued in school on a full-time basis and graduated in normal progression. In actual practice, especially at
the higher education level, some students are enrolled on a part-time basis and require a longer period of
time to earn a degree. Other students return to school after an absence of 1 or more years. The figures,
therefore, should be regarded as approximations only.

FIGURE 9–1. Level of education expected for persons 17 years of age in the fall
of 1973. [1]

Table 9–3. Selected Statistics on the New York City Academic High Schools, 1970–71 [5]

Minority Students in High School	Number of Schools	Enrollment	Admissions to Class of June 1971	Avg. % Pupils Reading B.G.L.*	Avg. % Receiving Diplomas**	Distribution of Graduates by Type of Diploma by %			
						Acad.	Gen'l	Comm'l	Other
Less than 25%	21	75,141	20,868	13.6	81.2	56.3	31.1	7.3	5.4
25–50%	19	69,784	19,720	21.5	73.0	50.5	35.8	6.5	7.2
51–75%	8	35,593	9,427	40.5	60.1	37.4	44.5	7.6	1.9
76–100%	17	64,625	16,399	47.2	49.2	30.8	59.4	3.5	5.1
Total	65	245,143	66,414						

*B.G.L.: two or more years below grade level.

**Diplomas granted as a percentage of admissions to the class of June 1971.

from the New York City academic high schools further illustrate the educational completion inequality that ensues between blacks and whites. Variations in the percentages of minority students enrolled in academic high schools is demonstrated in Table 9—3.

Table 9—3 indicates that as the percentage of minority students in a high school increases, the average percentage who survive to graduate and the percentage of graduates awarded academic diplomas both decrease. As the proportion of minority students increases, a larger percentage of the diplomas granted fall in the general diploma category, a certification usually representing outcomes of manual skills rather than academic achievement. Thus, schools with different racial compositions of their student bodies achieve remarkably different outcomes.

Similar trends can be seen in the Table 9—4, representing high school graduation rates for Texas students of different racial backgrounds. These data from Texas not only indicate that black students are less likely to graduate from high school than are Anglos but that Mexican-American students are even less likely to graduate than are blacks.

In addition to, or complementary with, racial issues, economic factors also play a major role in school attendance. Table 9—5 illustrates the relationship between children not enrolled in school and the education and income of their parent(s). From Table 9—5, it can be seen readily that (1) poorer children in general are more likely to be out of school than children from higher-income families (6.8% v. 4.8% v. 2.9%), and (2) children from families with less education in general are more likely to be out of school than those from families with more education (8.0% v. 4.9% v. 3.1% v. 2.0%). The combination of low parental income and education is especially devastating.

As income level and parental education is linked to the number of children not enrolled in school, so is the occupational status of parents. Children whose

Table 9—4. Projected High School Graduates, Texas. Cumulative Per Cent Graduating by Age 21 [6]

Group	1966—67	1970—71	1974—75	1978—79
All groups	62	67	71	75
Anglo boys	66	70	74	78
Anglo girls	68	73	78	83
Negro boys	52	58	63	68
Negro girls	52	57	61	65
Latin boys*	40	45	50	55
Latin girls*	40	45	50	55

*Mexican American.

Table 9—5. Children Not Enrolled, By Education and Income
of Parent (Ages 7—17) [7]

	Income of Parent			
Education of Parent	Under $4,000	$4,000 9,999	$10,000+	Total (By Education)
Less than 8 years				
Percentage Not Enrolled	9.5	7.6	7.0	8.0
8—11 years				
Percentage Not Enrolled	6.5	5.1	4.2	4.9
12 years				
Percentage Not Enrolled	4.4	3.6	2.6	3.1
Some College				
Percentage Not Enrolled	3.6	3.1	1.7	2.0
TOTAL (By Income)				
Percentage Not Enrolled	6.8	4.8	2.9	4.0

fathers have lower-status occupations appear to be less often enrolled in school, or to be enrolled for a shorter period. Table 9—6 presents a rank ordering of the occupational statuses of fathers and the per cent of their children not enrolled in school.

In her study of Big City schools, Sexton noted that students of lower-income groups had a poorer attendance rate than students of higher-income families (90.4 v. 93.2) [9]. Interestingly, she suggests that one of the reasons for this pattern, at least at the elementary school level, may be the health-related problems common to lower-income children and their families. For instance, Sexton demonstrates that the rheumatic fever rate for lower-income families is twice that for higher-income students; diptheria rates are more than ten times as high for lower- v. higher-income students; and tuberculosis is six times more common at the low end of the income scale [10].

The influence of parental income on educational tenure, at least in terms of college attendance, is depicted in Figure 9—2. The figure shows that in 1974, only 24 per cent of college freshmen estimated their parents' income to be less than $10,000. College attendance is not necessarily the preserve of the very affluent, but neither is it readily accessible to children of poorer families.

Similar studies, conducted many years ago, tell the same general story. The analysis of the relation between parental income and college attendance for a group of Milwaukee high school seniors, demonstrated the following data in 1940. Table 9—7 is especially interesting for several reasons. It clearly represents old data; the income figures appear ludicrous to us today. But the pattern is similar today, with college attendance figures in the 20—30 per cent range at the lower-income levels and 92—100 per cent at the higher-income levels.

Table 9—6. Children Not Enrolled, By Occupation of Father
(Ages 7—17) [8]

Occupation	% Not Enrolled
Farm Laborers	7.0
Unemployed or Not in Labor Force	6.0
Laborers (excluding farm)	4.8
Operatives	3.8
Farmers and Managers	3.4
Service	3.4
Craftsmen	2.9
Managers, Administrative (excluding farm)— Self-employed	2.7
Clerical	2.3
Sales Workers	1.9
Managers, Administrative (excluding farm)—Salaried	1.7

Exercise 9—1. *Examining Family Press/Support for School Attendance*

This exercise can be done in small groups. Ask students to examine and report:

1. Their father's occupational status (using the categories in Table 9—6.
2. How their fathers (and/or mothers) felt about their school attendance?
   Would their fathers (and/or mothers) permit "skipping"?
   What excuses permitted you to stay home?
3. Did the parents of your friends handle these issues any differently?

Moreover, the sample in the Milwaukee study was controlled for IQ, allegedly a criterion for academic ability and therefore college attendance. None of these students lacked in ability, or at least not in the family socialization experiences that provide one with enough talent and drive and learned skill to score high on IQ tests. It further raises the question as to whether and how educational

Estimated Parental Income

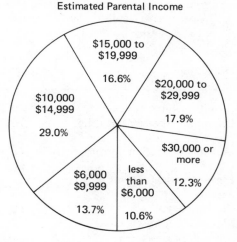

FIGURE 9—2. Characteristics of first-time college students in the fall of 1974. [11]

Table 9—7. Percentage of 1,023 Milwaukee High-School
Graduates with an I.Q. of 117 or Above Who Were in
College Full Time, in Relation to the Family Income [12]

Parental Income	Per Cent in College
$8,000 and over	100.0
5,000—7,999	92.0
3,000—4,999	72.9
2,000—2,999	44.4
1,500—1,999	28.9
1,000—1,499	25.5
500— 999	26.8
under 500	20.4
All cases	34.5

inequality has changed in the more than quarter of a century interval between
the 1940 and 1974 data sources.

Outcome No. 2: Levels of Achievement

A second series of outcome measures is school achievement. Here, too, we
find continuing evidence of sustained inequality among different racial, sexual,
and economic class groups. A nationwide standardized testing program, the

Exercise 9—2. *Examining Student Peer Group Composition*

Think back to your high school peer group(s) and try to reconstruct how and in what ways it can be compared to your college peer group.

What are some of the major differences between your high school peer group and your current college peer group?

1. In demographic characteristics (such as?)

2. In sociopolitical attitudes and values (such as?)

3. In personality (such as?)

4. In ability and/or talent (such as?)

Are these ways in which your high school peer group showed similarities to your college peer group? Explain.

National Assessment of Educational Progress, provides nationally comparative data for different groups of students in several different subject matter areas, at several different age levels [13]. A casual reading of the data indicate that the scores for males are higher than those for females in mathematics and science, whereas females' scores are higher than males' in writing and reading. The scores of white students are higher than black students' scores on every subject matter noted; other racial groups (presumably Hispanic and Asian primarily) are consistently in between. These differences are especially dramatic, and highlight the major differences in school outcomes on the basis of race. With regard to economic class, parental education often is used as one of a constellation of items indicating this variable. Actually, it is not sufficient to indicate class (occupation and income combined are more relevant), but it is a step toward that delineation. Even with this limited indication of class, the data indicate clearly that student performance increases with the increase in parental education.

Table 9—8 breaks out some of these general trends, at least for reading, at several age/grade levels. It is illustrative, and we could repeat these patterns for other subject matter areas if space permitted. The same pattern of unequal outcomes persists at all age/grade levels, both for the 1970—71 data and the 1974—75 data.

Table 9—9 presents data on mathematics achievement from a very different study of school inequality. These data continue to demonstrate the pattern of unequal outcomes, although with some different analytic devices. Using white students in the metropolitan Northeast as a norm, the table shows the number of standard deviations and grade levels at which black and white students from other regional and urban areas fall below this norm. White students in nonmetropolitan areas, and in metropolitan areas outside of the northeast did not,

Table 9–8. National Assessment of Educational Progress in Reading for Ages Nine, Thirteen, and Seventeen, by Selected Characteristics of Participants: United States, 1970–71 and 1974–75 [14]

Selected Characteristics of Participants	Age 9			Age 13			Age 17[1]		
	Mean % Correct		Mean Change	Mean % Correct		Mean Change	Mean % Correct		Mean Change
	1970–71	1974–75		1970–71	1974–75		1970–71	1974–75	
	2	3	4	5	6	7	8	9	10
1									
All participants	64.0	65.2	1.2	60.6	60.7	0.1	72.1	72.0	−0.1
Region:									
Northeast	65.8	66.8	1.0	63.2	62.1	−1.1	74.0	73.5	−0.5
Southeast	59.0	61.8	2.8	55.4	57.1	1.7	67.0	67.9	0.9
Central	66.6	67.5	0.9	63.2	63.4	0.3	74.4	74.4	(2)
West	63.3	64.1	0.7	59.9	59.8	−0.1	71.5	71.0	−0.5
Sex:									
Male	61.6	63.1	1.4	58.0	58.1	0.1	70.3	70.1	−0.1
Female	66.3	67.3	1.0	63.2	63.4	0.2	73.9	73.8	−0.1
Race:									
Black	49.7	54.5	4.8	45.6	46.4	0.8	55.2	55.4	0.2
White	66.4	67.7	1.2	63.3	63.5	0.3	74.4	74.8	0.4

Table 9–8.
(continued)

Selected Characteristics of Participants	Age 9			Age 13			Age 17[1]		
	Mean % Correct 1970–71	1974–75	Mean Change	Mean % Correct 1970–71	1974–75	Mean Change	Mean % Correct 1970–71	1974–75	Mean Change
1	2	3	4	5	6	7	8	9	10
Parental education:									
No high school	54.9	57.2	2.4	49.0	49.5	0.5	60.8	61.7	0.9
Some high school	59.0	58.9	−0.1	55.5	54.8	−0.7	65.9	65.1	−0.8
Graduated high school	64.7	66.1	1.4	61.2	60.2	−1.0	71.5	70.8	−0.7
Post high school	70.1	69.5	−0.5	67.3	67.3	(2)	77.8	77.1	−0.7
Size and type of community									
Extreme rural	60.9	63.0	2.1	56.7	56.8	(2)	69.1	70.3	1.2
Low metropolitan	52.8	55.2	2.5	51.0	48.9	−2.1	63.9	62.8	−1.1
High metropolitan	71.6	71.2	−0.4	68.3	68.7	0.3	78.9	78.7	−0.2
Main big city	65.1	62.9	−2.2	62.2	60.1	−2.1	72.2	71.9	−0.3
Urban fringe	66.5	67.3	0.9	62.6	63.1	0.5	73.4	74.2	0.8
Medium city	64.0	65.5	1.6	60.0	59.6	−0.5	73.0	71.9	−1.0
Small place	63.4	65.8	2.3	60.0	61.5	1.4	74.4	72.7	1.3

[1]All participants of this age were in school.

[2]Less than .05.

NOTE.—The mean change is equal to the difference in the mean correct for each year but may differ in the table due to rounding.

263

Table 9−9. Math Achievement: Number of Standard
Deviations Below and Number of Grade Levels Behind the
Average White in Metropolitan Northeast, for all Groups [15]

Race and Area	Standard Deviation Below			Grade Levels Behind		
	6	9	12	6	9	12
White, nonmetropolitan:						
South	0.4	0.3	0.2	0.7	0.9	1.4
Southwest	.2	.1	.1	.3	.3	.8
North	.1	.0	.1	.2	.1	.8
White, metropolitan:						
Northeast	. . . .		. . . .		. . . .		
Midwest	.0	.0	.0	.1	.0	.1
South	.2	.2	.2	.4	.6	1.2
Southwest	.3	.2	.1	.6	.7	.6
West	.1	.1	.1	.3	.3	.8
Negro, nonmetropolitan:						
South	1.4	1.3	1.4	2.6	3.7	6.2
Southwest	1.3	1.2	1.2	2.4	3.2	5.6
North	1.2	1.0	1.1	2.2	2.8	5.2
Negro, metropolitan:						
Northeast	1.1	1.0	1.1	2.0	2.8	5.2
Midwest	1.1	.9	1.0	2.1	2.5	4.7
South	1.3	1.1	1.2	2.4	3.1	5.6
Southwest	1.3	1.1	1.2	2.3	3.0	5.7
West	1.3	1.1	1.1	2.4	3.1	5.3
Mexican American	1.2	.9	.8	2.2	2.6	4.1
Puerto Rican	1.5	1.2	1.0	2.8	3.4	4.8
Indian American	1.1	.8	.7	2.0	2.4	3.9
Oriental American	.5	.1	.1	1.0	.4	.9

in the 1960s, perform up to the standards set by northeastern metropolitan whites (they scored below or behind the normed groups in both analyses shown in the table). But blacks in all parts of the country did much less well than any of these whites. Or, in the language of the organizational level of outcomes, it is clear that a lesser quality of educational services was provided to black students, in all regions.

What is perhaps most striking from these last two tables is that the inequalities in outcomes between racial groups increase as tenure in school increases. That is, longer schooling may increase the achievement of racial minorities, but it also increases the inequalities between minority achievement and white achievement. Again, these continuing disparities may be a reflection of the organizational structure's inability to respond to differences in race and

Exercise 9−3. *Explaining Increasing Racial Gaps in School Achievement Outcomes*

Note that in Tables 9−8 and 9−9 the racial differences in school achievement increase as tenure increases, or as students reach higher grade levels.

1. How do you explain these findings?
   a. What might be going on within students that could lead to such outcomes?
   b. What might be going on in the school organization (staff attitudes, procedures, norms) that could lead to such outcomes?
2. If we hypothesize that some of the students doing the poorest on these tests drop out prior to age seventeen or the twelfth grade, how does that affect your explanations?

---

social background and to provide quality educational services to minority students.

The way in which student achievement scores can differ among schools in one city is illustrated in Table 9−10. Note that the high schools with the highest percentage of minority population score lowest on reading achievement measures. This trend is consistent with other data, but is especially dramatic in this table.

Once again, a brief excursion into historic data helps confirm these images created in the standardized achievement testing "heydey" of the 1960s and 1970s. Sexton [17] reports the relation between income groups and students scores in the Iowa standard achievement test.° There is a clear difference between higher- and lower-income students on these tests of general academic skills, with the higher-income students receiving higher scores. In addition, these differences increase as students progress into higher grades, as they increase their tenure in school. Does tenure then increase inequality? Regardless of what students bring with them into school, the school experience either (1) does not help overcome preestablished inequalities in talent, orientation, skill,

---

° Only the composite scores of the Iowa test have been included in these tables. The scores in the five separate areas (language skills, work skills, arithmetic skills, reading, and vocabulary) give us valuable clues regarding the learning skills of lower-income students or the different services provided these youngsters. They also tell us something about why upper-income students are so successful in school.

Relatively speaking (relative to their composite scores, that is), lower-income groups scored well in arithmetic and work skills. Upper-income groups scored poorly in these two "non-verbal" areas, relative to their composite scores. Upper-income groups, however, scored very well on the reading section of the test, whereas lower-income groups scored worse in reading than in the other areas.

Table 9−10. Differentiation in Student Achievement Scores Among Detroit High Schools 1976 with Different Racial Populations [16]

High School	Race			Achievement		
	Per Cent				Grade 11 Reading	Per Cent
				Grade 12 Reading	Per Cent	Promoted
	White	Black	Hispanic	Percentile	above average	in June
A	17	82		55	23	73
B	0	100		19	1	41
C	21	72	6	20	3	61
D	53	46	1	34	11	56
E	0	100		18	1	43
F	53	47		41	16	60
G	42	58		25	6	53
H	30	70		33	9	62
I	0	100		14	1	49
J	0	100		14	2	43
K	0	100		19	1	43
L	0	100		22	3	54
M	1	99		13	0	63
N	3	96		17	0	36
O	1	99		15	1	53
P	0	100		20	1	43
Q	44	56		34	12	68
R	10	89		18	1	51
S	55	44		43	16	54
T	1	99		14	1	47
U	29	65	5	18	1	49
V	26	47	26	26	3	57
City Average	20	78	2	27	8	54
National Average				50	23	

or oppression; or (2) treats these students so differently that they perform even more unequally. These data are presented in Table 9−11.

School grades. One of the outcome measures that is most immediate and pertinent to the students' daily experiences in school is their grades. In the study of Elmtown's youth, for example, Hollinghead discovered a clear and systematic relationship between grades and family income, with students from higher-income families (social classes I and II) receiving significantly higher grades. Table 9−12 reproduces some of this data.

Table 9−11. Iowa Composite Scores, Major Income Groups [18]

Major Income Group	Fourth Grade	Sixth Grade	Eighth Grade
I ($3000—)	3.48	5.23	6.77
II ($5000—)	3.73	5.61	7.38
III ($7000—)	4.42	6.47	8.22
IV ($9000—)	4.84	7.05	8.67
Difference between groups I and IV	1.36	1.82	1.90

Table 9−12. Distribution of grades in Elmtown High School by Social Class of Family [19]

| Social class | Percentage with mean grade of | | |
	85−100	70−84	50−69
I and II	51.4	48.6	00.00
III	35.5	63.2	1.3
IV	18.4	69.2	12.4
V	8.3	66.7	25.0
All Classes	23.8	66.3	9.9

Outcome No. 3:
Dropouts, Failures, and Suspensions

Closely related to outcomes of both tenure and achievement, and perhaps even helping to specify and explain these outcomes, are other indications of school staying power and success/failure. For instance, Table 9−13 shows that black students of all ages tend to drop out (or be pushed out) of school almost twice as often as white students. All these rates are somewhat lower in 1975 than they were in 1970, suggesting that more students of all races are staying in rather than dropping out. The higher dropout rates among older people also suggests that fewer younger students of all races are leaving school early. But in either year, the major break in the data appears to occur in the post-seventeen-year-old grouping: that is when more students start to drop out, in general, and where twice as many blacks as whites are doing so.

Table 9–13. Per cent of High School Dropouts Among
Persons 14 to 34 years old, by Age, Race, and Sex: United
States, October 1970 and October 1975 [20]

Race and Sex	Total, 14 to 34 years	14 and 15 years	16 and 17 years	18 and 19 years	20 and 21 years	22 to 24 years	25 to 29 years	30 to 34 years
1	2	3	4	5	6	7	8	9
October 1970								
All races:								
Total	17.0	1.8	8.0	16.2	16.6	18.7	22.5	26.5
Male	16.2	1.7	7.1	16.0	16.1	17.9	21.4	26.2
Female	17.7	1.9	8.9	16.3	16.9	19.4	23.6	26.8
White:								
Total	15.2	1.7	7.3	14.1	14.6	16.3	19.9	24.6
Male	14.4	1.7	6.3	13.3	14.1	15.3	19.0	24.2
Female	16.0	1.8	8.4	14.8	15.1	17.2	20.7	24.9
Black								
Total	30.0	2.4	12.8	31.2	29.6	37.8	44.4	43.5
Male	30.4	2.0	13.3	36.4	29.6	39.5	43.1	45.9
Female	29.5	2.8	12.4	26.6	29.6	36.4	45.6	41.5
October 1975								
All races:								
Total	14.1	1.8	8.6	16.0	16.6	14.5	15.4	20.5
Male	13.2	1.6	7.6	15.5	16.4	14.0	14.4	18.9
Female	15.0	2.0	9.6	16.5	16.7	15.0	16.5	22.0
White								
Total	12.8	1.7	8.4	14.7	14.8	12.6	14.0	18.6
Male	12.1	1.4	7.3	13.7	14.5	12.6	13.2	17.4
Female	13.5	1.9	9.6	15.6	15.0	12.7	14.7	19.7
Black								
Total	23.4	2.6	10.2	25.4	28.7	27.8	27.9	36.8
Male	21.9	2.4	9.7	27.7	30.4	25.9	25.5	33.1
Female	24.7	2.8	10.7	23.4	27.3	29.2	29.9	39.6

NOTE.—Dropouts are persons who are not enrolled in school and who are not high school
graduates. Data are based upon sample surveys of the civilian noninstitutional population.

Data from Texas also indicate that not only are black students more likely to drop out of school earlier than whites (Anglos), but that Mexican-American students drop out earliest of all. Table 9—4 indicated that white students, and especially females, are more likely to graduate from Texas high schools than are blacks or Mexican-American students. Mexican-American youngsters are the least likely group to graduate, with only 55 percent expected to complete high school in 1979. Even the substantial percentage increases for each group from 1966—1979 have not narrowed the racial gap in tenure.

If we narrow our focus from the nation or state to the community or organization, we also see some of these same patterns of differential tenure in school. Table 9—14 presents other data on the senior high schools in the city of Detroit. Certain organizational and students characteristics, most particularly the racial characteristics of school, are significantly related to dropout rates in the school. For instance, Table 9—10 showed that of the six schools with the highest percentages of whites (schools D, F, G, H, Q, S), four are among the leaders in the percentage of the students promoted in June, and Table 9—14

Table 9—14. Detroit Senior High Schools: Attrition Rates by Percentages Over a Three-Year Period [21]

(1) Schools with Largest Percentages of Minority Population

Senior High School	Percentage Black	Three-year % Attrition Rate
B	100	59
E	100	60
I	100	60
J	100	59
K	100	54
L	100	48
M	99	69
N	96	74
O	99	58
P	100	59
T	99	63

(2) Schools with Largest Percentage of Whites

D	53	46
F	53	41
G	42	60
H	30	42
Q	44	29
S	55	43

shows that they are among the leaders in maintaining tenure of students. The Detroit school noted for its recruitment of middle-class blacks and the channeling of these students into higher education (School A) is noteworthy in its ability to break the pattern of racial hierarchy and to achieve high tenure in school for its students. Table 9–14 compares the attrition rates over a three-year period in high schools with the highest percentage of black and white students.

Sexton's study of schools in Big City identified a related pattern of students of lower-income groups dropping out of school more often than students of higher-income groups. As shown in Table 9–15, the evidence on school failures follows the same pattern. The data show a higher per cent of failure for lower-income students. Hollingshead's early data on Elmtown High School shows the same general picture regarding failure by the school to achieve student success [23]. In one year, 23 per cent of the youth in the lowest-income group failed at least one subject, whereas only 3 per cent of the students from the higher income-groups failed any subject.

One of the indicators of constant student failure is the number of youngsters enrolled at below their normal grade level. As shown in Figure 9–3, by age seventeen almost 20 per cent of white females are enrolled below the modal grade, and approximately 23 per cent of white males are so affected. In contrast, 45 per cent of black females and well over 50 per cent of black males are enrolled below their normal grade level. The racial differences in failure are twice as great as are the differences by sex. Moreover, for whites the number of students below normal grade level reaches its peak at about age eleven, and then stays fairly constant: thus, most white students who will be left back or who are experiencing discrimination by the school, have already done so by this age. The curves for black students, however, continue to increase: thus, as tenure in school increases, more blacks fall behind, and/or experience further discrimination. These data repeat earlier information about the relation between tenure and achievement outcomes of schooling for minorities.

Suspensions. One school outcome that indicates clearly the school's concern for administering sanctions for what it deems inappropriate behavior is disciplinary action against students, such as suspensions.

Table 9–15. Evidence on School Dropouts and Failures [22]

Income Group	Per Cent Dropouts	Per Cent of Failure in 1 or more subject
I ($5,000)	19.2	42.2
II ($6,000)	15.8	36.0
III ($7,000)	7.9	32.2
IV ($8,000)	7.2	28.8
V ($9,000)	3.6	28.6

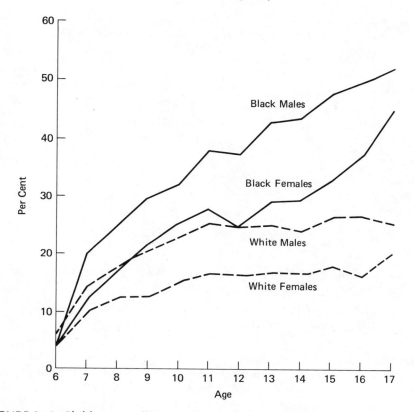

FIGURE 9—3. Children enrolled below modal grade, 1969—1971. [24]

Table 9—16. Racial Inequality Regarding Suspensions in Dallas
Schools [25]

	Suspensions	Total enrollment	Percentage
Blacks	10,050	57,174	17.5
Whites	5,973	85,485	6.0
Mexican-Americans	1,894	15,154	13.2

The data reported in Table 9—16 from Dallas schools indicate racial
inequality in this outcome measure. A more representative presentation of
racial comparisons of suspension rates among school districts in selected states
is portrayed in Table 9—17, which shows conclusively that minority students
are suspended more often than are white students.

Chapter 7 (Table 7—3) discussed data from several different schools that
showed consistently higher suspension rates for blacks than for whites. This

Table 9-17. Summary of Student Suspensions in Five Selected
States [26]

State	Number of Districts Reporting	Per Cent of Total Enrollment Reported Suspended			
		Total	White	Black	Spanish Surnamed American
Arkansas	147	3.8	2.4	6.2	1.3
Maryland	18	3.9	3.9	9.3	2.2
New Jersey	100	6.4	5.0	7.0	3.4
Ohio	46	5.3	3.7	8.0	4.3
So. Carolina	91	6.2	4.7	8.3	3.2

held true in schools with high suspension rates for all youngsters as well as those schools with generally lower suspension rates.

Outcome No. 4: Social/Political/Economic Attitudes

Another important set of outcomes of schooling is the orientations to the society and the world that youngsters develop during, and as a result of, their schooling experience. As indicated in Chapter 8, not everyone agrees that these items ought to be considered as schooling outcomes; some argue that they really are the fruits of family training and preparation, and that they mirror familial and peer group attitudes and orientations. This argument encounters at least two rebuttals. First, the same argument can be, and has been, made about all these "outcomes"; they all are probably only partly a function of schooling itself and partly a function of other factors. These outcomes can be considered as "inputs" (independent variables) or "throughputs" (intervening variables) as well as "outputs" (dependent variables), depending on the purpose and frame of analysis. In that sense, attitudinal outcomes are every bit as valid a measure of schooling as are other indicators in this section—all are subject to debate about the proportional influence of school as opposed to other factors. Second, the formal apparatus of schooling clearly is invested in, and announces itself as concerned with, goals and values such as citizenship responsibilities and the public role of socializing the young into aware and responsible workers and citizens. That role requires the inculcation of certain attitudes toward self and others, and toward the general society. Moreover, attitudes are not simply preferences of an emotional or ideological nature; they include elements of information transmitted by the formal curriculum and the informal processes of schooling. Thus, the school identifies itself as concerned

Table 9–18. Surveys of High School Youth in Ohio [27]

On the Whole, our Economic System is Just and Wise

		Agree	Undecided	Disagree
Total Sample	(1,097)	33.1%	34.8%	31.5%
Race				
White	(1,002)	34.1	35.2	30.6
Black	(62)	19.3	25.8	50.0
Sex				
Male	(551)	37.0	31.8	31.1
Female	(544)	29.0	38.1	32.2

and committed to producing "positive" outcomes on the kinds of items included in this section.

The views of students of the economic system in which they are located is one example of attitudinal outcomes that can be examined. Surveys of high school youth in Ohio resulted in the data shown in Table 9–18. Table 9–18 indicates that black youngsters have a much more negative view of our economic system than do white youngsters. If we consider the general outcomes that blacks and whites receive from the distribution of societal goods and services, jobs, and economic opportunities, it does seem logical that the views of blacks should differ from those of whites. But in a democratic society should not schooling do more than simply permit prior inequality to be replicated? Sex differences on this item are less pronounced, but do show females somewhat less positive about the economic system than males. In both cases, the schools that do not alter the social conditions cannot expect to alter these dissimilar attitudes.

Another question asks about students' attitudes toward the need for change in our form of government. The form of change is, unfortunately, unspecified, but clear differences do occur in the sample to whom the question was posed, reported in Table 9–19 [27]. Students in the college preparatory curriculum are more likely to agree that there is no need for change, as are male students. Students in largely white schools—urban, suburban, and rural—are more likely to agree that no change is needed than are students in largely black schools. Thus, in a pattern similar to the answers given to the question about the economy, black students (and females) are more likely to feel that our form of government needs to undergo major change.

With regard to other economic attitudes, two thirds of these students agreed that: "Men would *not* do their best if government owned all industry." Here there was a big difference between students in the different types of central city schools. In all-white central city schools, 72.6 per cent of students agreed, whereas, in all-black schools only 41 per cent did. A majority of students in

Table 9–19. Surveys of High School Youth in Ohio [28]

The Form of Government in This Country Needs No Major Change

		Strongly Agree	Agree	Undecided	Disagree	Strongly Disagree
Total Sample	(1,097)	5.8%	24.5%	21.0%	30.6%	17.1%
Curricula						
College preparatory	(529)	6.6	28.0	19.7	27.4	18.0
Other curricula	(568)	5.1	21.3	22.2	33.6	16.4
*Type of School**						
Rural-small city	(372)	5.6	28.5	19.9	32.3	13.2
MSA-suburban	(435)	6.4	24.8	21.4	31.0	16.1
Central city-white	(131)	6.1	25.2	23.7	26.0	17.6
Central city-mixed	(119)	5.9	13.4	21.0	27.7	31.1
Central city-black	(39)	—	15.4	15.4	35.9	23.1
Sex						
Male	(551)	7.4	27.4	20.0	26.3	18.1
Female	(544)	4.2	21.5	21.9	35.1	16.2

*Rural-small city refers to a population under 30,000; MSA refers to a city part of the metropolitan statistical area but not part of the central city; central city-white refers to schools 95% or more white; central city-black refers to schools 90% or more black.

Table 9–20. Class Distribution of Elected Representatives in Elmtown High School, Compared to the Class Distribution of the Student Body [30]

Social Class	Per cent of Student Body	Per cent of Elected Representatives
I–II	9.0	21.6
III	37.3	46.2
IV	47.0	32.3
V	6.7	00.0

central city black schools (53.8%) agreed that: "The government ought to guarantee a living to those who cannot find work," but only one third of those in other subgroups were in agreement with this proposition [29].

One school activity that relates to political activities in general, and especially to student's images of adult politics, is school elections and "play at government." The original study of Elmtown's youth generated considerable information about the ways in which students' family incomes are related to the student's degree of representation in their school's electoral politics. The higher-income classes (I, II, III) were cleary overrepresented among elected student officers, and the lower-income classes were underrepresented, as reflected in Table 9—20. Hollingshead attributes these differences to the higher-income groups' greater skills in social relations, their greater confidence, and overt forms of support from the school staff [31]. The latter variable (staff support) helps explain this outcome as an organizational process rather than an individual or community process.

Students' attitudes toward racial issues are still another example of the social outcomes of schooling. Presumably, these attitudes represent a view of society and the world that youngsters carry with them throughout their adult lives. Some of these attitudes are reflected in the views that students hold toward broad societal issues, such as racism and desegregation. Other attitudes relate to various expectations students have with respect to school experiences, such as the possibilities of good relations in school. A study of southern school desegregation provides some interesting data on 5th-grade students' attitudes, reported in Table 9—21. Black students (in 1972) had more positive attitudes toward race relations than did whites. By 1974, after two (more) years of desegregated school experience, both blacks and whites had more positive attitudes than in 1972, and had approximately equal attitudes on race relations.

Factors other than schools also play an important role in forming students' attitudes regarding social and political issues. For example, in the same study of southern schools, in communities where there has been a history of black civil rights activity, urban blacks, particularly tenth graders, reflect more pro-integration sentiment. The presence of integrated PTA's and student leadership corps appears to have had a similar effect on white students. Positive racial attitudes on the part of whites have been noted when they comprise either a very small or over 60 per cent proportion of the student body.

A key indicator of the outcome of interracial relations in desegregated schools

Table 9—21. Comparison of Race Relations Outcomes of Fifth Grade Students in 1972 and 1974 in 48 Southern Schools [32]

	1972 Mean	1974 Mean	Change	1
Student Racial Attitude				
Black Students	.96	1.08	+.12	2.00*
White Students	.66	1.06	+.40	5.71**

[1]Scale ranges from +2 (positive end) to −2 (negative end)

*p<.05   **p<.01

Table 9–22. Data on Interracial Contacts
Elicited from Tenth Graders [33]

	Per Cent Positive Responses	
	Blacks	Whites
Are the three students with whom you talk the most of the same race as you?	18.2	34.8
Have you ever called a student of a different race on the phone?	24.1	39.5
This school year, have you helped a student from another race with school work?	61.2	63.8
This school year, have you asked a student from another race to help you with your homework?	32.2	49.6

may be seen in the nature and extent of voluntary interracial contacts. One study elicited such data from tenth graders. The affirmative responses of the students are shown in Table 9–22. Voluntary contacts carried out informally (first two items) probably reflect a different set of interracial experiences than those emanating out of the more formal structures of the school. Moreover, interracial contacts and the skills required for such contacts to continue reflect a different kind of outcome than do attitudes.

Another concrete indicator of students' experiences in schools may be found in students' reports of the problems they encounter in schooling. Table 9–23 is taken from Montague's study of Washington State high school seniors, as reported in Sexton. Lower-status students report more difficulties than higher-status students on almost every item in Table 9–23. Finding it more difficult to manage a variety of interpersonal relations in school, experiencing difficulty in expressing themselves in school (an especially pronounced status difference), and engaging in greater self-criticism, lower-status students appear ready to come out of school having internalized society's conception of their inadequacies, and, in large part, blaming themselves for this situation.

Studies such as these are a constant reminder that the organizational structure of schools separates students on the basis of differences which all too often reflect their race, sex, and social class. The organization structure provides differential access to the reward systems of the school, thus making it difficult for many to engage in the school's activities where opportunities for interpersonal relations and self-expression are most frequent. Part of the reward for being in school is to be seen and affirmed as a good student, and lack of affirmation in this arena inevitably creates dilemmas for poor and minority students. Perceived inadequacies inevitably develop, and the feelings that

Table 9−23. Students Reports of Problems Encountered in Schooling [34]

	Upper Status	Middle Status	Lower Status
Difficulties in interpersonal relations in school			
Not being popular	9.0%	9.4%	16.1%
Being left out of things	13.5	11.0	21.4
Too few social activities	13.2	9.1	25.0
Too many social activities	8.9	4.5	1.8
How to make friends	10.8	13.9	17.9
Difficulties in self-expression in school situations			
Unable to express myself well	18.5	23.8	40.2
Don't like to recite	14.0	17.7	19.6
Self-criticism			
Can't seem to concentrate	26.5	27.2	35.7
Not enough time to study	15.0	12.5	21.4
Afraid I'm not passing	3.1	3.8	8.0

result from being excluded from the school's social world are directed inward toward the victim instead of outward and toward the school and social system.

Outcome No. 5: Satisfaction

Student satisfaction with their school experience is another outcome identified in Chapter 8. The data presented in Table 9−24 demonstrate a clear relationship between social status and school dissatisfaction: upper-status students are more satisfied with all three aspects of schooling.

A study of high school youth in Ohio provides some clear racial comparisons on another dimension of student satisfaction with schooling. As shown in Table 9−25, in responding to whether school helps meet the problems of real life, students in rural or mostly white schools more often disagree that school is of little help, whereas students in black or racially mixed schools more often agree with the statement, and thereby are more dissatisfied.It may be that the school provides helpful resources differently to white or black, or upper-status or lower-status students, or that these students have such different life experiences

Table 9—24. Students' Reports of Satisfaction with Schooling [35]

	Upper Social Status	Middle Social Status	Lower Social Status
School is not interesting	5.0%	7.0%	12.5%
Studies are too hard	1.9	1.3	6.2
Don't like my courses	3.7	4.1	9.8

Table 9—25. Response of High School Youth in Ohio as to Whether School Is of Little Help in Meeting the Problems of Real Life [36]

	Rural Small City	MSA Suburban	—Central City—			Total Sample
			White	Mixed	Black	
	(372)	(435)	(131)	(119)	(39)	(1,097)
Strongly agree	13.7%	16.1%	9.2%	16.8%	30.8%	15.0%
Agree	24.5	23.2	30.5	24.4	30.8	24.9
Undecided	17.7	19.5	13.7	16.8	12.8	17.7
Disagree	29.6	27.6	30.5	27.7	5.1	27.8
Strongly disagree	13.2	10.6	14.5	13.4	7.7	12.2
Don't know	1.3	3.0	1.5	.8	12.8	2.4

and needs that they need very different kinds of help, only one kind of which is forthcoming from the school. In either case, inequality in the provision of helpful resources and experiences is felt and reported, and satisfaction accordingly varies by race and status of students.

Outcome No. 6: Preparation for Later Inequality in Outcomes

The amount of education one receives has a direct relation to the average income one can expect later in life, and to the total income one can expect over a lifetime. Sexton reports just such a relationship in Figures 9—4 and 9—5. The relationship between education and income is striking; in every gradation of educational attainment, the income projection rises substantially in both

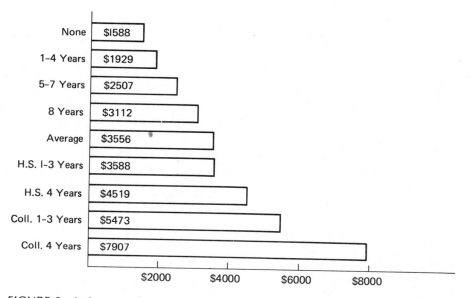

FIGURE 9—4. Average (mean) income of men 45 to 54 years old by amount of education. [37]

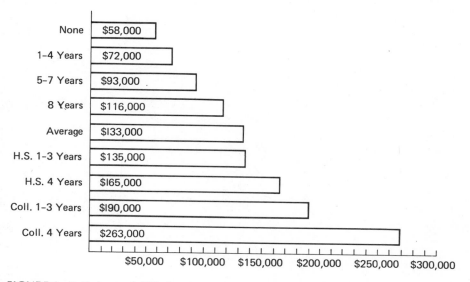

FIGURE 9—5. Estimated "lifetime" income for men by amount of education. [38]

Table 9–26. Occupation of Employed Persons 16 Years Old and Over by Sex, Race, and Years of School Completed: United States, March 1975 [39]

Sex, Race, and Occupation	Total Employed (in Thousands)	Percentage Distribution, by Years of School Completed							Median School Years Completed
		Total	Elementary School Less Than 8[1]	Elementary School 8	High School 1 to 3	High School 4	College 1 to 3	College 4 or more	
1	2	3	4	5	6	7	8	9	10
Women—White									
All occupational groups	28,996	100.0	3.2	4.8	15.6	46.0	15.9	14.4	12.6
Professional, technical, and kindred workers	4,820	100.0	.4	.4	2.6	17.9	18.5	60.3	16.5
Managers and administrators, except farm	1,626	100.0	2.5	3.6	10.3	45.1	20.3	18.3	12.7
Salesworkers	2,119	100.0	2.0	3.9	21.1	50.6	15.6	6.7	12.5
Clerical and kindred workers	10,619	100.0	.4	1.6	9.6	61.8	20.6	6.0	12.6
Craftworkers, operatives, and laborers, except farm	3,826	100.0	11.0	12.7	28.5	40.5	5.5	1.8	11.8
Private household workers	731	100.0	10.7	10.7	42.8	28.9	5.9	1.1	11.0
Service workers, except private household	4,949	100.0	5.5	9.2	26.6	44.9	11.5	2.3	12.2
Farmworkers	306	100.0	5.6	15.7	17.6	43.1	13.7	4.6	12.3
Women—Black and other races									
All occupational groups	4,032	100.0	10.0	5.9	20.6	37.7	13.9	12.0	12.4
Professional and managerial, and kindred workers[2]	669	100.0	.6	.7	4.0	18.5	19.4	56.5	16.4
Sales and clerical workers	1,120	100.0	.5	1.4	11.8	53.0	25.4	7.9	12.7
Craftworkers, operatives, and laborers, except farm	681	100.0	12.6	10.3	24.4	44.3	7.6	.6	12.1
Private household workers	486	100.0	34.2	13.6	31.3	18.5	2.1	.4	9.2
Service workers, except private household	1,063	100.0	12.8	7.2	32.8	38.2	7.9	1.0	11.7
Farmworkers	14	(3)	—	—	—	—	—	—	(3)

Men—White

All occupational groups	45,177	100.0	5.4	6.5	15.9	36.7	16.3	19.2	12.6
Professional, technical, and kindred workers	7,129	100.0	0.3	0.4	2.4	13.6	17.6	65.7	16.7
Managers and administrators, except farm	6,777	100.0	1.9	2.7	7.9	34.7	22.1	30.8	13.4
Salesworkers	2,914	100.0	1.4	1.5	10.7	34.2	26.9	25.3	13.2
Clerical and kindred workers	2,968	100.0	1.6	3.7	12.1	43.9	26.3	12.4	12.7
Craft and kindred workers	9,275	100.0	6.0	8.6	19.2	50.2	12.8	3.2	12.3
Operatives, except transport	5,008	100.0	10.2	10.2	24.6	42.9	10.2	1.8	12.1
Transport equipment operatives	2,561	100.0	8.4	11.8	25.1	42.9	9.3	2.5	12.1
Laborers, except farm	2,865	100.0	11.9	10.6	27.7	36.0	11.3	2.4	12.0
Service workers, including private household	3,575	100.0	7.7	8.8	26.3	36.7	15.9	4.6	12.2
Farmworkers	2,105	100.0	15.2	17.1	19.1	34.0	9.3	5.3	11.8

Men—Black and other races

All occupational groups	4,697	100.0	16.4	5.6	21.5	31.8	12.4	12.3	12.2
Professional, technical, and kindred workers	470	100.0	—	.2	2.6	11.1	15.3	71.1	16.9
Managers and administrators, except farm	252	100.0	4.4	2.4	2.4	33.7	20.2	36.9	14.1
Sales and clerical workers	446	100.0	2.9	.9	11.9	42.4	27.8	13.9	12.8
Craft and kindred workers	765	100.0	14.1	6.4	24.8	39.6	11.4	3.5	12.1
Operatives, except transport	689	100.0	17.7	8.0	27.1	37.2	9.1	.9	11.7
Transport equipment operatives	411	100.0	19.7	7.3	26.8	36.3	9.2	.7	11.6
Laborers, except farm	668	100.0	31.1	6.9	31.7	24.3	4.9	1.0	10.1
Service workers, including private household	839	100.0	15.9	6.2	26.7	33.3	13.3	4.8	12.0
Farmworkers	157	100.0	60.9	12.1	10.8	11.5	2.5	2.5	6.5

[1]Includes persons reporting no school years completed.
[2]Includes professional and technical workers and managers, officials, and proprietors, except farm.
[3]Per cent and median not shown where base is less than 75,000.

281

Table 9—27. Mental Disqualification of Draftees, 1950—1971 [40]

Year	Black	White
1971	33.9%	4.7%
1970	33.0	5.3
1969	38.2	8.1
1968	39.0	8.0
1967—1950	53.6	13.1
Average 1950—1971	49.8	11.5

figures. The data in Figures 9—4 and 9—5 lead us to take seriously the kinds of inequality in school tenure noted in the first set of data in this section. These outcomes matter as roads to other outcomes of future life and status and income.°

The immediate outcomes of schooling are marked by racial, sexual, and economic class inequality: the same is true of these longer-range outcomes. For instance, consider the data reported in Table 9—26. The data in Table 9—26 demonstrate the close relationship between occupation and race, sex, and years of school completed. Among both black men and women, the service worker and private household worker categories account for over 25 per cent of the occupations with over 40 per cent of these same occupations holding less than an eighth-grade education.

Information on the scores of different groups on mental tests taken for purposes of screening induction into the armed forces also reflect unequal schooling outcomes. The data in Table 9—27 indicate that blacks are rejected for military induction (on the basis of their scores on mental tests) more than four times as often as whites. As in other data on racial comparisons, the percentages of either whites and blacks rejected have decreased in recent years, but the ratios of white-to-black inequality have even increased (from fourfold in 1950—67, to sevenfold in 1971).

THEORETICAL EXPLANATIONS OF INEQUALITY IN SCHOOLING

The data discussed in the preceding sections make an impressive case for the existence of inequality in school outcomes. On variable after variable, on measure after measure, lower-class youngsters and minority youngsters (and

---

° These data, gathered and reported years ago (1960), may look ridiculous today. Certainly the mean and total income figures have risen dramatically at all levels of education. But even more importantly, the pattern demonstrated in these figures remains essentially the same.

Exercise 9—4. *Tracing Your School History*

This exercise can be done by students individually, and then shared in a group setting.

Think about your progress through the following path or chain of educational situations.

Place of Birth

↓

Family Status

↓

Nursery or Day-Care Experience

↓

Elementary School

↓

Junior High School

↓

Senior High School

↓

College (s)

At each stage of this chain, consider the following questions:

1. What was the social class composition of members of your peer group or members of your class and school?

2. Were there separate "tracks" or groups for different students?

3. What decisions did you make, if you made any, in deciding to progress further along the main path? Did you ever consider not continuing along the main path? Why? Why not?

---

often females) have a less satisfactory and effective experience with education than do more affluent and white youngsters. They consistently receive less positive outcomes from schooling. How are these pervasive differences to be explained and understood? Two contrasting ideologies or theories exist to explain these findings, both of which are reviewed briefly and applied to some of the specific data sets reported.

One of the popular conceptual frameworks for explaining these outcomes derives from a belief in individual liberty and opportunity within the American society. It suggests that people achieve according to their individual talent and merit, and are generally able to overcome inequalities of birth and location in the social structure. Within the social sciences, this belief system is rooted in paradigms of structural-functionalist analysis and is closely related to consensus theories of society and societal politics. It suggests that although social class affects the way people live their lives—especially in bringing up their children—the social class of adults can markedly differ from those of the families into which they were born. Therefore, considerable individual economic mobility is seen to exist in this society.

Not only does this view suggest that economic mobility exists, it further envisions schools as one of the chief means by which this process occurs. In school, according to this view, lower-class individuals can gain a good education and learn the skills and values that will permit them to improve their economic standing.

Given this orientation to the supportive structure of schools, the primary determinants of school outcomes, and of inequality in schooling, are individual variables such as ability, ambition, and achievement. From this point of view, which is often labeled the *meritocratic* view, individual merit counts, and will carry the day. The further assumption is made that schools operate in pluralistic ways that are tolerant and supportive of different groups of students' attempts to improve themselves.

A second equally important, but less popular view of these inequalities has its roots in beliefs about the effects of our political and economic structure, and of the power of these institutions to define and determine the place of people within the society. From this point of view, stable social structures require people to fit into them, rather than to proceed on their own, and the power of the social environment sets firm limits on what people can achieve. Economic class location is one major factor in the nature of social arrangements, and it is very hard for people to change these arrangements. In general, economic mobility is quite difficult to achieve. Although some individuals may move upward in the economic class structure, that is an exception rather than a rule, and most people remain throughout their lives in the economic class in which they begin life. Within the social sciences this view is closely allied with Marxist analyses, and is directly connected to conflict theories of societal operations and politics.

Not only does this view suggest that class structures remain quite stable and that individual achievements are rooted in, and limited by, economic origins, but that schools are one of the chief societal mechanisms that ensure this stability. Thus, students of various economic classes learn different skills and values, which force them to stay in their original locations. The primary determinants of school outcomes, and of inequality of schooling, are collective factors such as economic class (and racial group) membership and location. In general, it is argued that the ways we measure ability, ambition, and achievement are biased in ways that make them subtle derivatives of economic class and culture and racial or sexual status as well.

From this point of view, which is often labeled the *class analysis* view, class location counts, and will carry the day. The further assumption is made that schools operate in ways consistent with this process of social stability, and in ways that differentially treat and channel groups of students into programs and outcomes that are consistent with their entering economic class attributes.

The Meritocratic View. From the vantage point of the meritocratic view of schooling, schools grew out of early industrial needs to educate large numbers of the North American population. As it became clear that different kinds of industrial jobs needed to be performed, it became necessary to ensure the progress of our economy by finding and training the most talented people to take their place at the higher levels of our social and economic institutions. Consistent with American principles of democracy and equality, it was important to make sure that accidents of birth did not rule people out of this grand talent search. To do so would not only violate principles of equality and the notion that everyone could achieve what they wished for with hard work but would deprive the larger society of the resources of talented people.

Public schools were established to nurture the talents of all, to provide instruction that might bring out the best of each citizen, and to permit the society to screen, select, and allocate students to greater opportunities in accord with their individual talents and interests. The question remained, and indeed still remains: How do we identify talent? From the beginning we were convinced that talent could be understood and identified by a variety of fairly (but by no means conclusively) valid intelligence tests. Prior research and common sense that showed that people who scored higher on intelligence tests did better in school and were located in higher-status occupations seemed to be convincing evidence of the predictive power of such tests. Over time, standardized tests of ability became rather routine matters in schools; the continuing assumption was that the tests were adequate measures of individual ability. A second thrust in the identification of talent was to assess academic performance in school. The general assumption seemed to be that performance was a function of the combination of ability and some degree of motivation to learn. This motivation, or in valued terms, ambition to learn and/or to advance oneself, clearly is a key variable in taking advantage of one's natural talent and the many opportunities provided in the school for advancing one's skills and talents.

The Class Analysis View. From the vantage point of the class analysis view of schooling, schools grew out of early industrial needs to control large numbers of the new North American population. The influx of immigrants, and the aspirations of poor people to advance themselves, needed to be stabilized, so that people did not disturb the social order with their demands for change, and the prosecution of their unique life-styles and cultural values. As it became clear that different kinds of industrial jobs needed to be performed, it became necessary to ensure that children of the affluent succeeded to positions of affluence and power, and that children of lower social classes found their way into their appropriate occupations and roles. And, above all perhaps, it became necesssary to ensure that everyone felt satisfied that this was a just arrangement, and not an injustice to be challenged or objected to.

Public schools were established to socialize all the people, each according to their original social location and probable future location in the society. Thus, it was important to screen, sort, and channel students into occupational futures that were most consistent with their entering status. The question remained and indeed remains: How do we channel according to class status? One way is to generate tests of ability that are apparently universal, but that are culturally biased so that children of affluence consistently do better, and, therefore, appear to be of higher ability. On this basis, students can then be channeled on the basis of their scores on ability tests, and the true factor—power of class location—is concealed. A second pattern is for teachers and educational staffs to teach and organize in ways that ensure that students of the lower classes perform less well than do students of higher classes. If this can be done, the performance results can then be used as apparently fair-minded bases for further decisions about educational and occupational futures. Those patterns do not necessarily reflect a conscious conspiracy, but beliefs and actions consistent with American commitments to individual talent and effort.

Applying These Contrasting Explanatory Systems

Although the ways in which these two explanatory systems identify different factors as relevant in determining school outcomes, and indeed explain the history and development of public schooling in different ways have been outlined, it remains to be seen how these systems deal with some of the data sets reported. Two specific examples should make the differences clear.

As a first example, consider the mathematics achievements reported by the Coleman Report in Table 9−9. These data show that students' math achievement scores are higher when the students are from the Northeast, and when the population is predominantly male, white, and comes from families in which the parents have more than a high school education, and reside in highly metropolitan neighborhoods. Roughly the same trends, with some exceptions, are reflected in the reading scores shown in Table 9−8. We confine ourselves to the items regarding parental education, which are generally considered to be one component of the kind of socialization environment parents can provide, and are generally considered to be a key component of parental social class.

The meritocratic interpretation of these and similar data usually stresses the role that family status plays in socializing youngsters to have ambition for good performance in school. It also stresses the ways in which youngsters with certain kinds of advanced intellectual skills and talents may be concentrated in families with a higher income or, in this case, higher educational background. These youngsters enter school with a more highly developed set of cognitive skills and educational aspirations, and thus perform better throughout school. Reversal of this form of analysis stresses the existence of a "culture of poverty" or a culture of "disadvantaged minorities." Groups of poor people or minority people have suffered over the years as a result of white and affluent dominance of the society. As one result the poor have become accustomed to inferior educational performance and have depressed educational ambition as well as a lack of visible talent. Embedded in a culture that presumably does not value schooling, constrained by broken and nonsupportive family patterns, and pressed by peer and family demands for early employment, youngsters from such backgrounds simply do not perform well in school. Whereas the first set of explanations rooted low performance in the individual and his or her family setting, the second set roots it in the neighborhood or ethnic group culture or values from which the youngsters come.

The class analysis view of these data is somewhat different. It argues that schools systematically treat youngsters of different backgrounds differently. Since teachers themselves have an education beyond high school, they are most comfortable with parents of a similar background and with the children of these parents. The values and perceptions of these teachers are geared to these youngsters, and they give them every break (consciously and nonconsciously) they can. Given the assumption that talent is equally divided among the children of parents with varying educational backgrounds, the evidence that students from more highly educated parents perform better on mathematics tests suggests that the school is preparing these students for success in ways different than the students of less highly educated parents. This preparation differential did not necessarily occur at the grade level in question; rather, it probably occurred at several steps along the way, beginning with kindergarten. A variation of this class-analytic view notes that the legacy of racial and economic oppression in the United States has created differing values and expectations in different groups of the population. Youngsters from lower-class and minority background experience considerable conflict when their culture comes into contact with the culture of the school. If the school insists on implanting its own values and styles, lower-class and minority youngsters will become disaffected and alienated, and will, therefore, perform less well. If some negotiation occurs whereby mixed values can be pursued, lower-class youngsters might be able to perform well on the same or different criteria for achievement in school.

Other data that is amenable to these alternative explanations is the material on school suspensions. Although we do not have available suspension data by parental income or education, we do have racial data on this category.° Consistently, black students are suspended more often than are whites: this

---

° See Tables 7−3, 9−16, and 9−17.

occurs in schools with relatively low suspension rates as well as in schools with fairly high suspension rates. Administrative practices vary among schools, and thus school suspension rates may vary considerably, irrespective of the school's racial makeup. But regardless of general administrative practices, racial differnces still are in evidence. How do we account for this prevailing difference?

Duke suggests several different factors explaining what he calls "student misbehavior [41]." They include blaming the child, blaming the child's family background, blaming the peer group, blaming teachers, blaming the school system, blaming society, and blaming nobody. Although we may decry all the preoccupation with "blame," it does make sense to consider these different target explanations for student misbehavior, lack of discipline, school control problems, or however it is described. The terms do differ, because we are never quite sure when we examine suspension data whether we are reviewing student misbehavior or the effects of some behaviors on the rule-processing apparatus of the school. Some explanations look toward individual student variables to explain the propensity of certain students to misbehave. Other explanations locate the roots of misbehavior in the students' family upbringing, and/or in peer group relations that predispose youngsters to antisocial behavior. These explanations are similar to the meritocratic explanations for the lower achievement scores of minority and/or poor youth. Other explanations are closer to the class analytic view, and look for the role of the school in establishing certain values and discarding others, and for prosecuting people who do not conform to the prevailing culture. Moreover, some explanations stress the role of the school as acting to control classes of youth whose racial and/or class status mark them as different and/or potential problems. Racially discriminatory school discipline practices would then be a major explanation for these data.

What Should We Conclude?

The discussion of outcome measures and the evidence presented in this chapter support the proposition that schooling maintains patterns of inequality that are present in the society at large. The American society is marked by inequality among people of different social classes, sexes, races, ages, and sometimes national and geographic groupings. Schools, it is clear, produce outcomes for students and for communities that largely mirror and perhaps advance these historic and existing patterns of inequality.

Our argument that schooling mirrors and maintains patterns of inequality is not the same thing as the argument that schools do not make any difference in the organization of social inequality. That is basically the argument maintained by Jencks and others—that schools do not make any difference in the organization and maintenance of societal inequality. Our argument goes further in two ways: First, we argue that schools do make a difference; they reflect, organize, support, maintain, and rigidify the differences that exist in the society. As a result they may even increase these inequalities across time and generations—although not directly and obviously. Second, we argue that schools make it almost impossible to reduce these differences. Schools stand in the way of attempts to reach a more egalitarian society because schools are organized and operate in ways that are committed to the maintenance of inequality.

These arguments and this evidence reflect back to one's original understanding of the historic and contemporary purposes of schooling in a political, economic, and cultural system such as ours. Some people may not agree about the inequality and injustice of these schooling outcomes, and certainly some would disagree about the way different theories begin to account for different outcomes. As noted, some may argue that there is substantial economic mobility, and that over the years the gap between people of different races, sexes, and classes have narrowed. Although some of the evidence does point to a narrowing of inequalities, that narrowing is by no means substantial enough for anyone to believe that these dramatic and rigid patterns of inequality will end within the next century. For some, the maintenance of inequality is, by and large, an accidental outcome of an otherwise democratic mass public institution. It represents an occasional failure in the schools' attempts to continue to produce an egalitarian society.

From our point of view the schools are a social system managed by societal elites to prepare new members for their appropriate places in society. These places are historically assigned by the working of the corporate-capitalistic political-economic system, supported by a cultural value and belief system that justifies it. In pursuit of these objectives schools channel students into economic roles, maintaining for some conditions of privilege, for others poverty, and for others vulnerable economic existences somewhere in between. These patterns are part of the pressure of economic and political systems, and of the internal tracking and teaching that are evident in the curriculum and organization of the schools. Students are taught to support legitimate political authorities both in the political system at large and in the authoritative structure of the local schools. Schools attempt to press a monolithic political ideology and culture on groups that are indeed pluralistic and, therefore, to reduce the value conflict and value pluralism existing in various cultures or subcultures of the society.

The definition and assessment of school outcomes helps to achieve the fundamental purposes of schools and to better fit the schools to the society's dominant patterns. Testing of various sorts is used in more than schools, in industry, government, and all walks of life—to screen people for jobs, to indicate one's mental health, to demonstrate skills, and so on. With special regard to the schools, the testing apparatus is "big business," and large numbers of standardized tests are bought and sold in every sizable school system. As Cohen points out, the school testing enterprise is closely allied with

a handful of influential private agencies° that make crucial decisions regarding
the appropriate tests and how schools and students should be evaluated.

> But the expertise is not always as neutral as has been imagined, and the tests are
> hardly neutral with respect either to moral or political choices about the school
> process or about curriculum content. Nor are test materials explicit about these
> choices. The schools are presented with a simple choice—to test or not to test
> student progress and school performance using a series of unknown alternative
> conceptions about what schools do, or should do. [42]

Cohen refers to this chain of events as an example of political irresponsibility,
and views it as a

> consequence of the enormous authority of professionals, of widespread acceptance
> of the values and ideas they espouse, and of the acquiescence of public agencies,
> staffed by like-minded professionals, in the existing arrangement. But it does place
> much influence over a large number of important policy determinations outside
> public control. [43]

It also illustrates the formidable hold that the testing industry has on the public
schools who happen to be the industry's major clients and sources of revenue.

Considerable criticism has been directed toward this system in recent years,
most of it from forces external to the profession. In particular, the improper
categorization of so-called "normal" children who have become labeled as
"different" has drawn the attention of the courts. Public indignation over the
use of group tests to assign children to separate educational tracks was aroused
by recent court decisions that held that normal children are often identified as
mentally handicapped through the use of biased group tests. The overrepresen-
tation of Hispanic and black children in special education classes has long been
common knowledge; not only in California, where the problem was especially
acute, but throughout the nation, wherever large populations of minorities and
disadvantaged children swelled the public school ranks.

In the case of *Diana v. State Board of Education* (1970), it was alleged that
the placement of California children with Spanish surnames into special classes
for the mentally retarded was based upon the use of tests developed and
normed upon middle-class white samples. "Diana thus charged inherent bias
resulting not only from the use of group tests, but from individual intelligence
examinations administered by a credentialed professional psychologist" [44].
The same allegation was repeated in a later suit (*Larry v. Riles*, 1972) with
specific reference to black children [45].

Despite all the emphasis on achievement and ability testing, the mounting
evidence that behavioral, noncognitive factors may be equally decisive in
scholastic success and perhaps even more so in the world of work is accorded

° The most influential of these agencies is the Educational Testing Service, which, among other
services of educational import, administers the College Boards and Graduate Record exams.

only modest attention and very little precise measurement. As a result, much less attention is paid to what cannot be measured. The supreme irony of these observations are manifested in the following quote attributed to none other than Alfred Binet, who is often described as the "father" of modern testing:

> It seems to us that the scholastic aptitude admits of other things than intelligence; to succeed in his studies, one must have qualities which depend especially on attention, will, and character; for example a certain docility, a regularity of habits, and especially continuity of effort.

> This explains to us that our examination of intelligence can not take account of all these qualities, attention, will, regularity, continuity, docility, and courage which play so important a part in school work, and also in after-life; for life is not so much a conflict of intelligence as a combat of characters. And we must expect in fact that the children whom we judge the most intelligent, will not always be those who are the most advanced in their studies [46].

Finally, the question of how do schools sustain patterns of inequality now becomes paramount. Our analysis suggests that a number of socializing mechanisms tend to produce outcomes that serve political—economic elites. But there are other factors as well, and before launching the discussion of *Mechanism of Discrimination in Education* in the following chapter, some recognition of these factors would be appropriate. Some of these factors may be summarized as follows:

1. *Channeling* is carried out in ways that are congruent with the needs of the corporate political-economy and its culture, under a patina of democratic fair play and meritocratic individualism.

2. Schooling generates and reinforces people staying in their accustomed social statuses and roles, mainly by separating them on this basis through *curriculum differentiation, testing,* and *channeling.*

3. Schooling generates and reinforces commitments to the existing *political-economic structure*—to an obedient and docile rather than well-mobilized citizenry.

4. Schooling generates and reinforces a commitment to endure meaningless work, to respond to *technologic demands* and *credentializing needs* rather than exercising creative intelligence.

5. Deviants, failures, creative thinkers, mobilizers of protest, and ambitious climbers are often foiled, discouraged, disparaged, or otherwise *labeled* inadequate.

6. When the *priorities* of the polity and the economy change, schools change their programs to generate new (and desired) outcomes.

7. *Standardized Testing* is the basis of the school's legitimacy for *sorting* and *selecting*, since decisions based on standardized tests draw support from most quarters of the professional and political-economic elite as well as from most sectors of the social structure.

SUMMARY

In this chapter we have reviewed large amounts of data regarding the outcomes of schooling. Some readers may be overwhelmed by the sheer numbers presented, and by the many permutations and complexities in these data. But they all serve to make a point, and they point overwhelmingly to the continuing existence of inequality in schooling throughout the United States.

Any discussion of schooling outcomes, especially a discussion focused on inequality in outcomes, must address the question of which outcomes should be discussed. In Chapters 8 and 9, we discussed a wide variety of outcomes, preferring to leave the choice of emphasis to the reader. For each outcome we presented several ways of conceptualizing and/or measuring its impact on youth, and for each outcome we presented data indicating the impact on youth of different races and economic classes and sexes.

The data that was reviewed and presented indicate massive, historic, and continuing inequality on almost all outcomes measured. Tenure or length of time in school, cognitive achievement on standardized tests or in localized grades, rates of dropping out or being suspended, political and economic attitudes, student satisfaction with schooling, and the effects of education on later life achievements and opportunities all demonstrate the same general pattern. These are clear realities in the American experience, and they are not ephemeral or transitory or localized problems occurring occasionally or minimally. The data defy all efforts to speak of equality in the public arena, public in the sense that schooling is a publicly supported enterprise managed by the government and its agents.

The data indicate clearly that with regard to all categories of outcomes, the school provides unequal educational services according to racial, sexual, and economic class criteria. Put another way, with regard to all categories of outcomes there exists differential ability, by race and sex and economic class, to take advantage of offered educational services. One line of explanation, generally referred to as meritocratic, focuses on individual ability, skill, and energy (motivation) in interpreting outcomes. By this reasoning, individual responsibility for outcomes is primary. Thus, genetic, familial, or historic and cultural factors are seen as responsible for some people being able to learn more or less than others. A second line of explanation, generally referred to as class analytic, focuses on aspects of the educational delivery system as discriminating against certain groups of youngsters. By this reasoning, institutional responsibility for these outcomes is primary. Thus, irrelevant, or worse, discriminatory curricula, staffing, instructional patterns, and services in general are seen as responsible for the outcomes in which the poorer and minority students get less out of school than do whites and more affluent students.

This is a problem that begs interpretation from everyone. Whatever the interpretation, and each reader must make one, there is no way to simply read these data and then to stand apart without making a judgment. Whatever your judgment, whatever your choice of interpretative scheme (or mix of schemes), an interpretation must be made. No one explanation is complete by itself and most readers (and scholars) would combine aspects of each of the two dominant explanations. But, simply "mixing schemes" does not obliterate choices or the reality that each of us bends more one way or the other.

Exercise 9–5. *Applying Different Interpretations to Your Own School History*

This exercise can be done by students individually or in a group setting.

Refer back to your answers in exercise 9–4, page 283. Consider your answers:

1. Do your answers reflect a path consistent with the meritocratic interpretation of school performance?

2. Do your answers reflect a path consistent with the class analytic interpretation of school performance?

3. How can you explain your choice of interpretation? Would you change any of it?

10

MECHANISMS OF DISCRIMINATION IN EDUCATION: HOW DO SCHOOLS SUSTAIN PATTERNS OF INEQUALITY?

The preceeding chapter presented data supporting the argument that the outcomes of schooling are distributed unequally throughout the American society. According to some observers this is a rather systematic and/or deliberate process, one managed and carried out with the organized support of many major social institutions and actors, including schools and educational professionals. According to other observers, this is an unfortunate accident, one that occurs despite the efforts of many social actors and institutions to make room for promising young people and to create patterns of mobility for those who merit it. However, both sets of observers generally agree that schools currently do little to alter historic and continuing patterns of inequality: in fact, they may exacerbate these trends.

Chapter 9 also described the *meritocratic* and *class analytic* theories that have been offered to explain outcome inequality in schools. Meritocratic theories generally argue that individual talent and motivation accounts for students' outcomes in school and permit mobility across generations. At the same time, these theories often note the influence of family factors and economic class background on student performance. Class analytic theories generally argue that economic oppression in the society at large involves the school as an active force in denying mobility and opportuniites to poor and minority people. Thus, there is fairly limited mobility across generations, although in some circumstances individual talent is recognized and treated more potently than is class background. Theoretical arguments nonwithstanding, an adequate analysis of school operations should enable us to understand just how it is that schools fail to alter societal inequalities. Or, put another way, this analysis should help us understand how schools help sustain unequal outcomes over generations, geographies, and individuals.

295

This chapter examines some of the mechanisms that help account for these patterns. First, we review some of the *societal and community contexts* of school inequality, and consider the ways in which schools fail to influence these contexts, thereby failing to influence inequality derived from these factors. Then we review some of the *actions of school personnel*, the staffs of schools, and the ways in which their ideologies and behaviors reinforce established patterns of differential student performance and expectations, and, therefore, reinforce long-term outcomes. Finally, we review some aspects of the *school organization*, and see how they operate to sustain inequality, and/or to create it anew in each generation of students.

This chapter can constitute a summary of the theories and interpretations offered in Chapters 4, 5, 6, and 7. What we have learned about schools in those chapters is now focused on the particular problem of understanding how these factors help create and sustain the kinds of inequalities described in Chapter 9.

THE SCHOOLS' RESPONSES TO SOCIETAL/COMMUNITY CONTEXTS

We have argued throughout that schools are part of a larger societal web, part of a system of social institutions that are interdependent with one another. In particular, the school is affected by residential patterns in the local community and by prevailing centers of wealth and financial resources that are available in the community. No school can unilaterally alter the community in which it is located, and no school system can make decisions totally independent of these local forces. But at the same time, schools and school systems do have critical options at various stages, and it is these decisions that mark school priorities and help us separate educational decisions and influences from the larger set of societal forces and community factors affecting schools.

The Impact of Residential Segregation.

One example of the interplay between societal or community realities and the choices made by educational systems is evidenced in the recent history of school segregation and desegregation. It is a social fact that people of different races generally live in different neighborhoods. Such residential segregation exists throughout our society, north and south, east and west, urban and rural. Why residential segregation occurs is another matter, one that has been debated by politicians and scientists for several decades. Some scholars and decision-makers argue that residential patterns are the result of individual housing choices. Accordingly, homebuyers who have sufficient financial resources freely elect where they live, and money, cultural traditions and values cluster people who are similar to one another in common neighborhoods. Others argue that various public and private agencies (Federal Housing Authority, Federal Mortgage Acts, municipal ordinances, real estate brokers, and bank lending policies) help steer or channel people into racially and economically isolated neighborhoods. Some adherents of the latter view argue further that people often select housing on the basis of a school's reputation, and that school board decisions have a potent effect on housing choices in a community.

Residential segregation has determined patterns of school attendance, and has been directly responsible for much of the racial separation and segregation in our nation's schools. Until the 1950s there were legally sanctioned separated school systems in many southern states; thus the power of the state and the school system was added to the social fact of residential segregation to ensure that racially segregated schools were maintained. Some have argued that such legal segregation was required in the South precisely because there was less residential segregation in southern cities. In northern cities, the races were and are so severely segregated by residence that the apparently "neutral" principle of neighborhood schools was sufficient to guarantee and maintain racially separated learning environs.

Table 10−1 illustrates the impact of changing residential patterns on the racial separation and segregation of students in one of the nation's largest

Table 10−1. Numbers and Per Cents of White and Minority-Group Students* in Detroit Public Schools, 1963−1977 [1]

| Year | White Students | | Minority-Group Students | | | | Total |
| | Number | Per Cent | Black | | Other | | |
			Number	Per Cent	Number	Per Cent	
1963	141,240	48.1	150,565	51.3	1,940	0.6	293,745
1964	136,077	46.3	155,852	53.0	2.037	0.7	293,966
1965	130,957	44.4	161,487	54.8	2,378	0.8	294,822
1966	126,354	42.5	168,299	56.7	2,382	0.8	297,035
1967	120,544	40.9	171,707	58.2	2,614	0.9	294,865
1968	115,295	39.1	175,474	59.4	4,531	1.5	295,300
1969	108,264	36.8	180,630	61.5	4,965	1.7	293,859
1970	100,717	34.8	184,214	63.6	4,832	1.6	289,763
1971	96,269	33.3	187,966	64.9	5,222	1.8	289,457
1972	86,555	30.8	189,192	67.3	5,329	1.9	281,076
1973	74,965	28.2	185,359	69.8	5,254	2.0	265,578
1974	67,833	26.4	184,118	71.5	5,445	2.1	257,396
1975	56,855	22.8	187,640	75.2	5,101	2.0	249,596
1976	44,614	18.7	189,617	79.2	4,983	2.1	239,214
1977	36,227	16.0	187,498	81.8	5,046	2.2	228,771

*Including preschool students.

school systems. In a sixteen year span (from 1963—1977) the per cent of white and black students in the Detroit public schools shifted from 48.1 per cent white and 51.3 per cent black in 1963 to 16.0 per cent white and 81.8 per cent black in 1977. These changing residential patterns, aided and abetted by school system resistance, reluctance, or impotence to bring about massive desegregation have resulted in the continuation of large-scale racial segregation in our public schools. Judicial and executive pressure for southern school desegregation has resulted in tremendous gains in that area of the country. Tables 10—2 and 10—3 indicate greater amounts of racial segregation by 1972 in the northern, western, and midsouthern states than in the South itself. Table 10—2 shows that four out of five white children attended schools with at least 80 per cent white population in 1972, and only a very small percentage of white children (3.7 per cent) attended schools with 50 per cent or more minority children. Table 10—3 shows the reciprocal pattern: almost half of all black children attended schools with over 80 per cent black children, and about one third of black children attended predominantly white schools. Both tables indicate fewer whites in 80+ per cent white schools and fewer blacks in 80+ per cent minority schools in the southern states than in other parts of the country. Aside from the effects of federal pressures, the fact that most of our largest cities where minorities are concentrated are located out of the South help explain these data. Without substantial desegregation of minority-dominated central cities with white metropolitan and outlying areas, these segregated patterns will continue.

Early principles of school-community organization stressed the importance of neighborhood schools, which served families and students in close geographic proximity. This is an important feature of the American political commitment to local community control of public institutions and services. However, it came to serve as a means for justifying and consolidating racial separation in school, by building this democratic principle onto the workings of dual housing markets, racial steering in real estate marketing, different home buying and lending resources, and general segregation throughout the society.

As groups of youngsters attend racially separated schools, they appear to suffer a variety of privations. Some of these are well articulated in social research on differential achievement patterns, self-esteem, and social attitudes of youngsters. Whites as well as minority youth suffer from the lack of racial diversity and the attitudinal distortions that flow from racial isolation and separation.° People growing up in separate worlds learn separate realities, and to the distance of geography is added the cultural and psychological distance of ignorance, fear, and hostility. Moreover, the existence of state-supported racial separation is counter to basic political principles of equality under the law; it

---

° Data on minorities' experiences are detailed in Chapter 9; an interesting discussion of the losses of white children in this regard are documented in A. Meil, *The Short-Changed Children of Suburbia* [4].

Table 10–2. Geographic Distribution of White Children in Public Schools, fall 1972 [2]

Area	White School Children in Area		Attending Predominantly Minority Schools		Attending 50.0–79.9 Per Cent Majority Schools		Attending 80.0–100.0 Per Cent Majority Schools	
	Number	Per Cent	Number	Per Cent	Number	Per Cent	Number	Per Cent
United States	34,970,252	78.3	1,295,992	3.7	5,155,248	14.7	28,518,981	81.6
32 northern and western States	24,565,942	82.1	663,652	2.7	2,365,776	9.6	21,536,506	87.7
6 border States and District of Columbia	3,031,885	81.0	43,305	1.4	297,321	9.8	2,691,258	88.8
11 southern States	7,372,425	67.1	589,035	8.0	2,492,155	33.8	4,291,234	58.2

Table 10-3. Geographical Distribution of Black Children in Public Schools, fall 1972 [3]

Area	Black School-Children in Area		Attending Predominantly Majority Schools		Attending 50.0-79.9 Per Cent Minority Schools		Attending 80.0-100.0 Per Cent Minority Schools	
	Number	Per Cent	Number	Per Cent	Number	Per Cent	Number	Per Cent
United States	6,796,238	15.2	2,465,377	36.3	1,258,277	18.5	3,072,581	45.2
32 northern and western States	3,250,806	10.9	919,393	28.2	512,631	15.8	1,818,782	56.0
6 border States and District of Columbia	650,828	17.4	206,844	31.8	54,749	8.4	389,235	59.8
11 southern States	2,894,603	26.3	1,339,140	46.2	690,898	23.9	864,564	29.9

Exercise 10—1. *Identifying Racial Demography of Your Community*

This exercise can be done by students individually or in teams.

Obtain a detailed map of the city or town in which you grew up (from your local automobile association, realtors, or gas stations). Or, obtain a detailed map of the community in which the college you attend is located.

Walk, ride, or drive around parts of this city and indicate on the map where there appear to be concentration of people of different races (whites, blacks, Hispanics, Asian-Americans, American Indians).

Would you call this a racially segregated or separated community? On what basis would you decide?

violates the federal constitution, whatever its impact on youngsters and their families. The original hope of a single, unitary mass public educational system was precisely to overcome the separation of different cultures and living styles by the integration of neighborhood schools. But when neighborhoods are rigorously separated, and urban centers are largely monoracial, this agenda is easily frustrated.

In these contexts, it becomes incumbent on educational systems to help overcome school segregation based on residential patterns. But many school leaders have argued that overcoming such residential patterns is not their business; that is social reform, not education. Others have argued that the neighborhood school and a school population reflecting the cultural and racial membership of the local community are sound educational principles, which are to be revered against other goals. Still others object to any change because they fear the potential conflicts created by newly desegregated schools and classes. And, finally, some school administrators feel impotent to effect such changes, and have been reluctant to face community opposition to racial integration, and to the alteration of school-community patterns. To the extent that educational leaders follow community leaders who resist desegregation, it certainly is difficult for them to challenge well-established local norms and living patterns. Some school leaders have led desegregation efforts and have altered the contexts that create segregation, but, by and large, schools have not pursued this agenda very rigorously.

What has school resistance or caution on this agenda looked like? Schools have often supported continuing racial segregation in several ways: drawing attendance boundaries that match racial clustering in the neighborhoods, rather than deliberately trying to mix some neighborhoods of approximately equal geographic proximity; building new schools in the center of all-white or all-black neighborhoods, rather than on the margins between them; supporting different social clubs and activities for different racial groups; and so on. School support for segregation sometimes is less overt, as when schools fail to take the initiative in overcoming residential segregation, but wait for community pressure and court litigation to generate change. Even when minority parents have filed suit for the redress of segregated school facilities, schools often file countersuits and seek to sustain their current organizational patterns of racially separated schooling. And, even when the outcome of litigation demands redress and change, schools often implement desegregation in ways that continue to segregate youngsters inside schools according to different tracks, clubs, disciplinary procedures, linguistic programs, and a host of other organizational mechanisms discussed later in this chapter.

The Impact of School Funding/Resources

Another example of the interdependent relationship between the school system and the community lies in the nature of the community's resources for funding school programs and the school system's response to the resources that are available. As noted in Chapter 2, different states have or make different resources available for schooling. Chapter 4 discussed these issues at a more local level, wherein different communities often make different amounts of monies available to local schools. This occurs primarily in two ways: (1) different communities have different levels of personal wealth, so they can afford to spend more or less amounts of their wealth for the education of their young; and (2) different local communities have different values and/or

---

Exercise 10—2. *Identifying Community Racial Demography and School Composition*

This exercise can be done by students in small groups or work teams.

Begin with the map of community racial demography suggested in Exercise 10—1.

Indicate on the map the location of each elementary school.

By observation (a visit) or an examination of school system records, assess the racial composition of each of these schools.

Compare the racial composition of each elementary school with the composition of the surrounding neighborhoods.

Consider the following:

1. If the compositions of school and community are not parallel, why aren't they? What school policies can account for it?

2. Do you consider these schools racially segregated?

traditions, and, therefore, elect to spend different amounts of money on their local schools. The combination of these patterns has had some especially complex results. For instance, wealthy communities can afford to tax themselves at a lower rate and still make more money available for schooling than poorer communities, even when the latter tax themselves at a higher rate. In this context, school taxes become a regressive economic measure. Consider Table 10–4, taken from the *Serrano v. Priest* case in California, as an example.

Because community property and residential wealth (assessed value per average daily attendance) differs so markedly, poor school districts such as Newark Unified, Clovis Unified, Lamont Elementary, and Baldwin Park Unified must tax themselves at a much higher rate (at least double) to come up with even one half to one third the funds (expenditures per average daily attendance) as their neighboring, more affluent counterparts.

As argued by Zukofsky, the net effect of current tax procedures is that:

> (there is) the privilege state law now conveys upon the residents of the richest school districts, who are permitted to use their wealth for the education of their children, rather than sharing it with all taxpayers of the state for the education of all children of the state. [6]

As indicated, the problem of societal inequality concerns both the relative amounts of monies made available to support the education of rich and poor children, and the differential rates of taxation levied upon rich and poor

Table 10–4. Comparison of Selected Tax Rates and Expenditure Levels in Selected Counties 1968–1969 [5]

County and District	ADA*	Assessed Value per ADA	Tax Rate	Expenditure per ADA
Alameda				
Emery Unified	586	$100,187	$2.57	$2,223
Newark Unified	8,638	6,048	5.65	616
Fresno				
Colinga Unified	2,640	$ 33,244	$2.17	$ 963
Clovis Unified	8,144	6,480	4.28	565
Kern				
Rio Bravo Elementary	121	$136,271	$1.05	$1,545
Lamont Elementary	1,847	5,971	3.06	533
Los Angeles				
Beverly Hills Unified	5,542	$ 50,885	$2.38	$1,232
Baldwin Park Unified	13,108	3,706	5.48	577

*Average Daily Attendance

families for funds to educate their young. Both issues indicate the inequality in state support for schools, which is currently being challenged in court.

It is not solely or even primarily the school's responsibility to challenge or alter the societal distribution of wealth that makes some families rich and some poor. Nor is it necessarily the responsibility of the schools to alter state laws that make (or permit to be made) differential resources available to school districts. But the evidence suggests that within a local school district, available resources are allocated in ways that even further support greater opportunities for children of the wealthy. For instance, the facilities available in schools constitute the most general and observable evidence of resource inequality. These resources, and their accessibility to students of different classes, constitute another mechanism of differentiation. Consider Table 10—5, representing how different groups of students in one district have differential access to valued school facilities. As the author notes:

Except for library and speech, all facilities listed are much more adequate in upper-income schools. Perhaps the most unfortunate deficiency is found in science

Table 10—5. Percentage of Schools with No Facilities or Substandard Facilities [7]

Facilities	Group I $3000—	Group II $5000—	Group III $7000	Group IV $9000—	A Below $7000	B Above $7000
Science	50%	46%	3%	0%	47%	2%
Conservatory	67	50	6	6	54	6
Art room	11	11	4	0	11	4
Library	11	16	15	11	15	14
Instrumental Music & Speech	78	95	59	39	91	56
Speech	83	88	84	89	86	85
Store Room	6	18	6	6	15	6
Men's & Women's Rest Rooms	61	68	40	16	66	30
Auditorium	5	16	2	6	14	3
Auditorium Activities Room (backstage)	78	95	52	39	91	50
Office	0	11	2	0	8	2
Clinic	17	21	11	11	20	11
Kitchen	44	55	31	17	53	28
Air Raid Shelter	67	61	25	6	62	21

facilities. In the lower-income half, 47 per cent of all schools do not have proper facilities for scientific studies while only 2 per cent of schools in the upper-income half have inadequate facilities.

In some respects school facilities in group II are more deficient than in group I. This is probably attributable to the fact that slum clearance has replaced some of the oldest buildings in low-income areas with new ones. [8]

If we believe that the financial and other resources available to support education make a difference in the quality of schooling that is delivered to students, these patterns indicate school policies and procedures that support and increase the societal inequalities that already exist in the community external to the school.° A school system committed to overcoming, or at least balancing and restraining, such inequality could be making internal allocations of funds and resources that provided greater resources to poorer families and youngsters. At the very least it would disperse funds so as not to exaggerate the financial inequality that already exists.

A federal attempt to overcome these societal patterns of wealth, and the patterns of school financing that further channeled resources to support the children of the wealthy, was begun in the 1965 Elementary and Secondary Education Act (ESEA). This legislative effort at school financial reform attempted, among other things, to pay special attention to the education of our nation's poor. More specifically, it made available to local schools special

---

Exercise 10–3. *Determining the Local Economic Base of Schooling*

This exercise can be done by students individually or in groups.

How are the schools in this community financed?

1. What portion of local school funds come from federal sources, state grants, and/or local tax revenues?

2. Who pays what portion of the local funding base of schools? What is the local property tax value and school tax rate?

3. How have these figures changed over the past ten years?

° It is not absolutely clear that school finances do relate directly to youngsters' performance, as compared with the general impact of family wealth. But as some of the prior discussion illustrates, family wealth often is correlated with differential school resources. In the face of this relationship it is not clear how much difference anything but a major reallocation of resources would have. As in the discussion of racial separation, a constitutional issue currently is being faced about the legality of differential school resources, regardless of its known impacts on youngsters' performance. The school's involvement in not altering these societal trends, and in passively maintaining them, may represent a significant constitutional issue as well.

categories of funds to support the education of poor youngsters, primarily by promising extra monies to school districts that had a significant number of poor families in the community and schools.

According to Murphy, one of the initial (mis or re) interpretations of this act was to translate the concern for "poor" youngsters into those who were "educationally deprived" [9]. The meaning of this transformation, although well intended to serve a broader and needy class of youngsters, was to take the focus at least partly away from income inequality and to center on other issues, such as poor student performance. Whereas income inequality clearly can be targeted as existing prior to and outside the schools, educational deprivation may well be a mixture of family-related issues and the schools' own failure to deliver useful services to certain groups of youngsters. If we accept this analysis of educational deprivation, it is somewhat ironic to see schools receive funds to help the school correct its own failure to deliver services, under the rhetorical guise of aiding poor people.

Another (mis or re) interpretation of the act, at least as far as many educators were concerned, was to see it as general educational support for school systems rather than for poverty-stricken youngsters. The focus on educational deprivation helped make this translation possible, as did the administrative bureaucracies of local schools that were responsible for allocating funds at the local levels. Murphy reports that later studies indicated some 30 percent of the recipients of programs funded by this act were not economically disadvantaged [10]. Two kinds of things were happening: (1) the earmarked funds were funneled into the general school budget, and were allocated in ways similar to all school funds, that is, with more being allocated for more wealthy groups of youngsters; (2) the earmarked funds were funneled into special programs that primarily focused on poor youngsters, thus making available to them approximately the same amount of school financial resources as was available to more wealthy groups of youngsters. But both these patterns sustain inequality, and neither truly conforms to the intent of the act. In order to challenge and overcome societal inequality in resources, federal and local efforts must make more monies available for programming for poor youngsters than for wealthy youngsters, and not just equalize resources. Equalization of resources after several years of inequality may be a fair procedure at this time, but it does not alter historic advantage/disadvantage. ESEA's aim was for the local school system first to create financial equality within its own resource base, and then to use federal funds as an added resource for poor youngsters' programming. This seldom occurred in the early days of the program, although at later stages, with considerable federal monitoring, such procedures did begin to be adopted.

The general story here is roughly the same as in the discussion of racial segregation: (1) existing inequality in the society; (2) schools acting in ways that either passively accept that inequality, or at least do nothing to challenge it; and (3) schools acting internally in ways that increase external inequality, not only passively but actively. The result is the kinds of outcome inequality documented in Chapter 9.

Other External Societal Factors.

The discussion so far has focused on the school's response to external factors that demonstrate and create inequality, such as community residential racial segregation and community financial resources and their allocation. These certainly are not the only external forces creating inequality, nor the only ones reflected and enhanced by the current organization and operating procedures of schools. For instance, social class separation exists in the community at large and often results in patterns of racial segregation. Moreover, social class separation creates neighborhoods of differing economic resources, which result in different financial resources for different schools and school systems. Sexual inequality exists in the community at large, and it too is mirrored in the internal organization of schools.

All these external societal factors have impact on, or can be frustrated in their impact by the actions of school personnel and by organizational features of the school. The following section looks at some of the key staff components of local schools, issues that were discussed originally in Chapter 6, and provide an understanding of the potential roles of these components in sustaining educational inequality.

THE ACTIONS OF SCHOOL PERSONNEL

Chapter 6, and part of Chapter 5 as well, reviewed some characteristics of school staffs. It was indicated there that the demographic backgrounds and socialization of school staffs established the groundwork for racial, economic, and sexual inequality in the organization of schools and of school operations. Let us reconsider these issues briefly.

Although the racial, economic class, and sexual characteristics of school staffs have been changing throughout the past several decades, power in the profession of education, and power in local schools, still is maintained largely in the hands of whites, males, and relatively middle-class people. Race and sex are immutable, but even class mobility is masked by the fact that when and if people from poorer origins rise in the administrative hierarchy of schools they become middle class. In salary, role and status, and life-style they have moved into the semiprivileged category.

One result of these patterns of power concentration in the white, the affluent, and the male, is that children from other backgrounds seldom see exemplary models for their own advancement. Outside of their own family members and occasional neighborhood adults, youngsters spend most of their waking time in and with school personnel. The most prominent (nonfamily) adults in the lives of poor children usually are educators, and many of the models for their own futures are the adults they find and interact with in schools. Regardless of the character of those interactions, poor youngsters, black and Hispanic youngsters, and female youngsters find relatively few examples of people like themselves in positions of educational authority. On the other hand, these youngsters may find numerous people like themselves in school roles without authority—as bus drivers, janitors and custodians, secretaries, and paraprofessionals or class/playground aides. Girls may find models in middle-level authority positions, such as teachers, and thus become locked into these and similar visions of the limits of sex-role mobility.

The impact of these patterns goes far beyond the problem of modeling, however; let us now consider some issues in the actions of these school personnel.

Teaching for Inequality—Unobtrusive Discrimination.

Substantial research and informed discussion about the nature of the classroom experience suggests several phenomena that create arenas in which inequality is preserved and enhanced, rather than challenged and overcome. The evidence reviewed in Chapter 6 makes it clear that teachers often think about, respond to, deal with, and evaluate students on bases other than their academic traits and objective performance, per se. Some of the other factors that appear to influence teachers' perceptions and actions include the demographic characteristics of students—their race and sex and economic class, for instance. This is in no way an unnatural situation, and it is by no means limited to teachers. In a society marked by race and sex and class discrimination and prejudice, teachers are no more immune from these societal values and beliefs and expectations than other people. However, the special position of teachers, as the arbiters of students' performance and perhaps future options, makes this an especially important problem to discuss and explore.

General American values about intergroup relations and educational theories explaining the school and work performance of minorities (including poor people and women) generally focus the responsibility for poor performance on students themselves. Therefore, the characteristics of the background and preparation, style and activity, and talents and motives of minority group members are seen as the "cause" of lower achievement outcomes. This tendency reflects the way most people have accepted the meritocratic interpretation of inequality, which is fully in accord with "the American Dream." Although this is only one of the two major alternative theories discussed in Chapter 9, it is the dominant tradition and is particularly potent in professional socialization circles. Thus, it is reasonable to anticipate that teachers would hold lower expectations for black and Hispanic students than for whites, and lower expectations for lower-class youngsters than for middle-class and wealthy students. By the same token, girls are expected to be "good," to be docile and dependent, especially as compared to the acceptable aggressiveness and vigor of boys.

These educational expectations are communicated to students in several ways. First, and obviously outside the control of teachers and school personnel, the larger social environment promotes these cultural beliefs through child-rearing patterns, family experiences, church and media presentations, and the like. Second, the student peer group accepts many of these propositions and makes and enforces different conceptions about appropriate behavior for members of majority groups and minorities, affluent and poor, boys and girls. Many peer group norms mock a boy who studies "too much," a girl who plays baseball, and so on.

Into this well-established cycle of expectations and enforcements of cultural beliefs and prescriptions steps the school and schoolteachers. Teachers present a variety of informal cues and covert messages promoting differentiation, even if and when their public beliefs and rhetoric supports absolute equality. For instance, a number of research studies have shown that teachers have differing concepts of "good" female and male students. Preferred male behavior in class often is active, assertive, and independent, while preferred female student behavior often is considerate, sensitive, and obliging. Males also seem to receive more attention from teachers, perhaps as a response to their more autonomous or challenging demands. Teachers who hold such values and expectations and who behave in these ways, inevitably communicate sex-related norms to their students, promoting stereotypic self-concepts and behavior [11].

The question of teacher impartiality in desegregated schools is another case in point. One researcher reported the results of teacher-student interaction in the public schools of Austin, Texas [12]. After extensive observations in various classrooms by teams of trained observers, responses from questionnaires administered to teachers, and accounts of their classroom experiences supplied by students, the research team concluded that black children were receiving significantly fewer educational opportunities:

> Opportunities for black students' intellectual development were simply not provided to the extent made possible to white pupils . . . Blacks received more criticism and were asked questions which required less demanding complex cognitive processes. . . . Teachers generally expected white students' achievement to be higher than Blacks'. . . . Teachers gave white students answers to questions when they were unable to provide them themselves, in addition to praising and complimenting their correct responses. . . . By comparison, interaction with black students was often terminated by asking other students to give answers to questions blacks were unable to answer. [13]

These findings have been verified by other studies of classrooms using similar techniques of participant observation, teacher questionnaires, and student reporting on their experiences. Braxton and Bullock carried out a study in two poor counties in rural Georgia, interviewing 44 teachers and 208 students, prior to the desegregation of the schools and again a year later [14]. Students were probed as to whether they expected and/or experienced teachers to be impartial. Their affirmative replies are reported, in percentages, in Table 10—6.

Responses to the first pair of statements suggest that whereas only about one-half the white students expected teachers of the other race (black teachers) to be impartial, almost all felt that the ideal of teacher impartiality was possible. Black students, on the other hand, appear to be more consistent in their match of expectations of white teachers' impartiality and of the ideal of teacher impartiality toward students of other races (in this case, to whites). In neither group of students is teacher impartiality toward the other race expected by more than 60 per cent of the students. The second set of statements gathered after desegregation of students and teachers had occurred, reflect a shift, primarily in the experiences of white students. Although most felt they were allowed to participate equally in class, only 27 per cent felt they were treated impartially by the teacher. More black students felt they were treated impartially, but only 57 per cent felt they were allowed to participate equally in class. Once again, black students' reports of the experiences of impartiality and equal participation are more nearly consistent, while white students' responses to these two items markedly differ. Comparing the pre-desegregation and post desegregation responses of students, it appears that black students' experiences more nearly matched their expectations than did white students' experiences. The researchers suggest that this phenomenon may be primarily ideological in nature, reflecting white students' strong opposition to desegregation, and their unrealistic fantasies about what would happen. For black students, who appeared to have more realistic expectations, the data may "be simply another instance of the much-documented cultural fact that blacks 'know' whites more accurately than the reverse [16]." Even if they didn't experience things very

Table 10—6. Per Cent of Students Answering "Yes" to the Following Statements [15]

	White Students Per Cent	Black Students Per Cent
1. Statement: Prior to desegregation		
Teachers of the other race will be impartial	52%	59%
Teachers can be impartial to students of the other race	93	65
2. Statement: After desegregation		
You are treated impartially	27	51
You are allowed to participate equally in class	86	57

differently than they had anticipated, they still did experience unequal and differential treatment.

These studies seem to indicate that their earlier contacts and subsequent experiences with whites have provided blacks with a clearer picture of social reality. Hence, it is not surprising that blacks expect that their experiences in mixed racial schools are likely to replicate those they encounter outside the school. The black students readily learn not to expect too much from desegregated school situations and to avoid the possibility of more disappointment and disillusionment.

Youngsters pick up staff norms and often internalize these messages into their own self-definition or self-concept. This is especially likely during the elementary school years. By the time they are in junior and senior high school, students may resist such messages and resist alteration of their already formed concept and image of themselves and their academic talent. However, even when students do not believe or internalize these messages, they must still struggle against them, reinterpreting or rejecting the teacher's expectations. For the most part, it appears that students are willing to conform to the expectations for their performance that teachers present and communicate to them. The result is that different racial, economic, and sexual groups perform differently, creating outcome inequality as a function of students' differential interpretation of teachers' expectations (as well as all the other expectations they encountered before, during, and after school). The result generally is a fulfillment and reinforcement of the teacher's original expectations—partly because it's easier that way.

On those occasions when students fail to conform, and behave and perform in ways that challenge their teachers' expectations, the evidence seems to suggest that teachers simply may not reward these students. Apparently, some teachers may not "see" this positive performance, and they may fail to correctly evaluate the evidence that those students whom they expected to perform poorly actually performed quite well. Or, the teacher may indeed perceive that the student is doing better than expected, but be threatened by the experience and refuse to reward these students for their "deviance." In either case, the net effect is that these students are not rewarded for what may well be a well-done task, which can be an especially confusing and debilitating result. These students may accept the verdict, and reinterpret their good performance as bad, further adopting the teacher's initial expectation for them, and indeed, they may lose hope. Or, they may resist such redefinition, holding on to their own conception of their effective performance. In this case, the students no doubt carry a residue of suspicion and mistrust of the teacher's intent and fairness, even to the point of anger that leaks out in other forms of interaction and expression toward the teacher, the school, and social majorities. The school system responds swiftly to such expressions of anger against authority, usually defining such youngsters as troublemakers, and subjecting them to disciplinary punishment. Thus, they may be labeled as political or social problems,

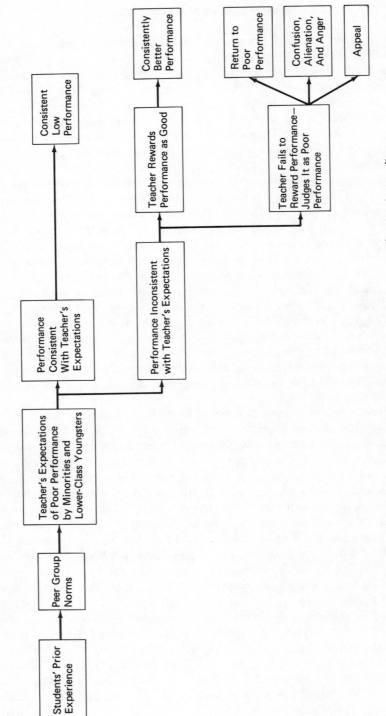

FIGURE 10—1. A path of school and classroom mechanisms confirming inequality.

compounding the intellectual or academic problems they were considered to have from the outset. Figure 10—1 illustrates this process.

Counseling for Inequality—Readjustment to Discrimination

In addition to teachers, school counselors have a great deal of close and important impact on the lives of students. Counselors often are quite active in vocational planning for students, and in safeguarding the way in which school performance is translated into occupational plans and futures for students. This may be especially important for lower-class students who may need to make vocational choices immediately after their graduation from school. Counselors are also active in the consideration and selection of colleges by middle- and upper-class youngsters and in the planning of a high school curriculum (and often extracurriculum) that will make them attractive candidates for the colleges of their choice. In planning curriculum choices, the school careers of boys and girls may be steered differently by the counselors' images of proper male and female talents and roles. Similarly, students of different economic classes and races are often channeled into formal tracks or informal course sequences that are deemed appropriate for their status and apparent talent. In addition, counselors often work with students who have deviant school careers. These are students who have broken school rules and must be disciplined or punished, and students who have behaved in ways contrary to school norms and must be counseled or treated.

Mercer has conducted considerable important research on the role of school counselors and counseling services in the control and channeling of poor, black, and Hispanic students [17]. In many schools, Spanish-speaking youngsters have been administered standardized intelligence tests that show them to be quite deficient in verbal skills. Because of their use of and commitment to their native tongue, these youngsters have a limited ability to speak and write standard English. The school typically resists bilingual instruction in classes, and would prefer to isolate these youngsters in special classes that can then focus on Spanish-speaking students specifically. Moreover, these youngsters may have a difficult time in classes managed by Anglo teachers who are not committed to multicultural teaching agendas, and who are either distressed or threatened by these youngsters' apparent "deficiencies." When the cycle of expectation and disparagement referred to previously occurs, teachers often refer these Hispanic youngsters to counselors for testing and placement as "educable mentally retarded" (EMR), a label that makes them (1) available for special classes, and (2) isolates them from the mainstream of the school and from regular classes and peers.

A number of studies have demonstrated that the probability rates for a student's being assigned to an Educable Mentally Retarded class are significantly greater for minority children than for Anglos. In reporting enrollments

Table 10–7. Summary of Enrollments in Educable Mentally Retarded (EMR) Classes in 1973–74 in Five States [18]

State	Number of Districts Analyzed	Per Cent of Total, White and Black Enrollments in EMR Classes			Number of Districts with 5 Per Cent or More of their Total White and Black Enrollments in EMR Classes		
		Total	White	Black	Total	White	Black
Alabama	112	2.3	1.5	4.0	1	2	56
Arkansas	140	2.0	1.1	3.6	5	0	26
Georgia	151	2.5	1.0	4.8	21	0	85
Mississippi	127	1.8	.8	2.6	4	1	23
South Carolina	83	2.9	1.3	5.1	17	1	43

of EMR classes in a five-state region of the South, it was estimated that black students were placed in EMR classes well in excess of the corresponding ratio for whites. A breakdown of these data is provided in Table 10–7.

Tittle has also reviewed several vocational tests utilized by counselors helping youngsters with their vocational choices, and finds them limiting in the full range of occupations that can and should be open to women [19]. The issues are quite typical. Male interests in medicine are identified with roles as optometrist, pediatrician, physician, dentist, and the like. Female interests cannot be so identified, and no such categories appear for females. Instead, what is available for them is dietician, nurse, dental assistant, and the like. Beyond the use of tests, per se, Pietrofesa and Scholossberg studied interactions between counselors and students. They indicate that:

counselors, both male and female, hold biases against female counselees entering an occupation characteristically associated with males . . . subtle pressures and influences against entering so-called "masculine" occupations by parents, as well as teachers and counselors, may do more harm than discriminatory practices by employers. [20]

This conclusion brings us full circle in our consideration of the school's role vis-à-vis the racism, sexism, and economic discrimination of the society outside the school. There is relatively little the school can do to alter the discriminatory practices of employers, but they have enough to do if they were to concentrate on the ways their personnel and programs sustain and support those discriminations by channeling students so that they may never challenge employers' prejudices.

THE SCHOOL ORGANIZATION: PRODUCING INEQUALITY IN DIFFERENTIAL PREPARATION FOR ADULT ROLES

Through its mechanisms of manufacturing outcomes that are consistent with input patterns, the school is able to channel students into certain roles on the basis of *work, politics,* and *social* relationships.° Let us examine these mechanisms or channeling systems in more detail.

Work

The character of school organization helps channel young people with regard to their work life in three ways. First, schools inculate generalized compliance to hierarchically arranged, expertise-based authority. This compliance is demanded with regard to punctuality, regularity, proper dress and appearance, deference, and the like. Such compliance fits current societal patterns, whether the young person winds up as a professional in a law office, a laborer in an automobile assembly plant, a secretary in an industrial office, or a recipient in a public welfare agency. At the same time different groups of youngsters are expected to respond differently to authority. Girls are expected to be somewhat docile, whereas boys are expected to be somewhat rebellious. Whites are expected to be compliant yet creative, as befits someone about to be part of the authority system; whereas blacks are expected to be somewhat angry and rejective, as befits those about to be oppressed by authority. The reliable socialization for compliance and for different kinds of compliance is fundamental for the maintenance of current bureaucratic forms. Once people are directed to certain hierarchically arranged statuses, established authorities control their role performance. The fact that this occurs within the school serves as a basic preparation for the students' subsequent involvement in the economic and political system.

Schools also play a major part in placing the young in their "appropriate" economic roles by sorting and tracking students for particular occupational statuses. Traditionally this is conceptualized in terms of targeting students for four-year colleges, two-year colleges, trade schools, and dropout statuses. These educational targets have their parallels in occupational targets such as professional and executive status, white-collar managerial or service roles, clerical and secretarial service jobs, blue-collar skill work, low-level labor intensive occupations, housewives, and unemployed careers. Each of these targets has its own curriculum or noncurriculum, which is composed of both formal and informal elements. Traditionally, these curricula have gone by the names college prep,

° We appreciate the assistance of Dr. James Crowfoot in collaborating to create early versions of the following materials.

Table 10—8. Percentage of Each Social Class in Yankee City
High School Enrolled in Each of Four Curricula [22]

Curriculum	Social Class				
	Lower Upper	Upper Middle	Lower Middle	Upper Lower	Lower Lower
Latin	25	68	16	21	12
Science	75	19	11	25	14
General	0	7	18	22	20
Commercial	0	5	55	32	54

Table 10—9. Curriculum Enrollments Percentage of Students
in Each School [24]

Income Group	College Preparatory	Business and Vocational	General
I ($5000—)	19	33	48
II ($6000—)	25	46	29
III ($7000—)	40	31	29
IV ($8000—)	57	21	23
V ($9000—)	79	11	10

vocational, commercial, general, special education, and remedial education. In general, their visibility, and prestige follows the order of their listing. Channeling of students by schools begins with students' assignment to particular school systems, buildings, and classrooms. Subsequently, grades, promotions, testing, attendance, deportment, and special curricula are used to facilitate and justify this channeling.

Brookover reports that research consistently "has shown that curricula are differentiated in terms of the social class of the students who enroll in each" [21]. For instance, Warner and Lunt, in *Yankee City*, report a quite clear distribution of income groupings in different curricula. The authors note that the upper-upper groups are not listed in Table 10—8 because these children were not sent to the public schools; rather they were more effectively and dramatically tracked into private high schools.

Hollingshead reported much the same relationship between income and curriculum tracking in Elmtown [23], and Sexton confirms these patterns with the following data from Big City (Table 10—9). Tables 10—8 and 10—9 both show that students from more affluent backgrounds are more often enrolled in college preparatory curricula and courses. Sexton also points out that programs

Table 10—10. Program for "Gifted" Children [25]

Income Group	Number of "Gifted" Chosen	Rate per 10,000 Students
I ($5000)	0	0
II ($5000—)	4	1.1
III ($6000—)	41	6.1
IV ($7000—)	120	20.1
V ($8000—)	123	36.0
VI ($9000)	148	78.8

By income halves, the rate per 10,000 students was:

A (under $7000)	3.7
B (over $7000)	34.4

for the gifted are concentrated for upper-income students. This is the other end of the organizational continuum that programs lower-income students into vocational, remedial, and retarded channels (Table 10—10).

Even those institutions of higher education that pride themselves on contributing to economic mobility through "open" admissions develop channeling mechanisms. The City University of New York (CUNY), for example, maintains three tracks that clearly differentiate its students, thereby exposing its economically and racially stratified character. Table 10—11 demonstrates the tracking system at CUNY in terms of student composition in each collegiate option [19]: this profile indicates that even at the college level, community colleges represent clerical and vocational tracks composed mainly of Puerto Ricans and blacks, whereas the elite senior college track is predominantly white. Since the clerical-vocational track offers a terminal degree that does not permit students access to either the preprofessional or the four-year social-services track, we once again witness the "freezing" of minorities and poor people in career lines geared toward lower-level technical, clerical, or paraprofessional jobs. This is the classic example of an institution of higher learning replicating the tracking system and channeling ideology of the public and parochial "feeder" schools, thus perpetuating the inequities of an educational system it had originally sought to reduce.

The third way schools play a major part in channeling young people for subsequent economic roles is through teaching (formally and informally) the general values and beliefs of the culture in work terms: the centrality of paying work for males and nonpaying housewife roles for females; the importance of efficiency and its reliance on technology and expertise; and the rationale for different individuals and groups winding up in particular occupational statuses. This ideological training occurs in subject matter classes (social studies, family

Table 10—11. Projected Profile of the New CUNY [26]

Elite Track	Social-Services Track	Clerical and Vocational Track
Three senior colleges	Five senior colleges Transfer program in three community colleges	Five community colleges Career programs in three community colleges
High average in high school (over 82.5)	High-school average from 75—82	Any high-school average, most under 75, many under 70
Academic diploma in high school	Mainly academic diplomas	General and vocational degrees
Mainly white	Ethnically mixed in the senior colleges; white in the transfer programs	Higher percent of blacks and Puerto Ricans but still many whites
High percent Jewish students	High per cent Catholic students	Mixed
Mainly middle class	Middle, lower-middle and working class	Mainly working and lower class
Most students aimed for graduate or professional schools	Most students aimed for careers in teaching; social work, health and public administration, or engineering	Most students geared toward lower-level technical, clerical, or paraprofessional jobs

living, history, English) and through assembly speakers, career days, honors' ceremonies, and extracurricular activities (junior achievement, nurses' club, and the like).

The creation of an ideology supporting traditional occupational choices is aided by a variety of curriculum materials. Jacobs and Eaton report a review of sex-role stereotyping in 134 books (with 2,760 stories) intended for school-children [20].

The ratio of boy-centered stories to girl-centered stories was 5 to 2; the ratio of stories with an adult male character to an adult female character was 3 to 1; the ratio of male biographies to female biographies was 6 to 1. Boys in the stories built and created things and used their wits. Girls rarely appeared in these roles. Clever girls appeared 33 times, clever boys 131. Boys showed initiative and were strong

Table 10−12. Evaluating Sexism in Readers [28]

	Male	Female
1. Number of stories where main character is:	_____	_____
2. Number of illustrations of:	_____	_____
3. Number of times children are shown:	_____	_____
(a) in active play	_____	_____
(b) using initiative	_____	_____
(c) displaying independence	_____	_____
(d) solving problems	_____	_____
(e) earning money	_____	_____
(f) receiving recognition	_____	_____
(g) being inventive	_____	_____
(h) involving in sports	_____	_____
(i) fearful or helpless	_____	_____
(j) receiving help	_____	_____
4. Number of times adults are shown:		
(a) in different occupations	_____	_____
(b) playing with children	_____	_____
(c) taking children on outings	_____	_____
(d) teaching skills	_____	_____
(e) giving tenderness	_____	_____
(f) scolding children	_____	_____
(g) biographically	_____	_____

5. In addition, ask yourself these questions: Are boys allowed to show their emotions? Are girls rewarded for intelligence rather than beauty? Are there any derogatory comments directed at girls in general? Is mother shown working outside the home? If so, in what kind of job? Are there any stories about one-parent families? Families without children? Are baby-sitters shown? Are minority and ethnic groups treated naturally?

and brave; girls were rarely depicted as having these characteristics. When a girl mastered a grown-up skill, it was usually a domestic one. Boys were competitive, girls were not. Girls did not act independently; they were smaller and more fearful than boys. [27]

They suggest the use of the checklist given in Table 10−12 to evaluate sexism in readers and other curriculum materials. The items on this list help identify the many ways in which messages about the subordinate appropriate roles of women are communicated.

The impact of this sort of ideological training and social stereotyping of the future educational and career choices of young women is quite potent. For instance, Table 10−13 presents portions of Astin's study of the career choices of college freshpersons. The data indicate that young women were much less often

Table 10—13. Career Choices of Freshman Women and Men,
1976 [29]

Career Choice	Women	Men
Artist	8	6
Businessman	12	21
Clergy and Religious Workers	0	1
College Teacher	0	0
Doctor (M.D. or D.D.S.)	3	6
Educator (secondary)	4	3
Educator (elementary)	8	1
Engineer	2	14
Farmer or Forester	1	5
Health Professional (non-M.D.)	11	4
Lawyer	3	6
Nurse	9	0
Research Scientist	2	3
Other Occupation	25	21
Undecided	11	10

planning to enter business, medicine, engineering, or the law than were young men. On the other hand, women were much more often planning to enter fields such as education (especially elementary), nursing, and non-M.D. health professions. Changes away from traditional sex-stereotyped patterns have been occurring over the past decade, as studied by Astin, but current choices still are heavily sex-typed, undoubtedly due in part to early educational experiences. Of course, in part these choices are influenced by reports and/or anticipations of discriminatory treatment of women in many of these fields. Thus, early educational experiences are not alone in the creation of expectations, stereotypes, and sexism in future roles.

The outcomes of these career plans, as well as the (discriminatory) opportunities provided college women, are reflected further in Table 10—14. In some areas very few women receive degrees of any sort, regardless of level (engineering, military science, etc.). As women progress from the baccalaureate to the doctoral level, they are represented in decreasing percentages in all disciplines. However, in some areas the drop is most marked (like business and management, computer sciences, mathematics, and theology).

The fourth way in which schools help prepare students for economic roles is in their general consumer education. Sometimes this occurs. formally in economics and family living classes, where traditional middle-class patterns of family consumption (and attendant "wise budgeting") are taught. But most of this preparation is handled by the informal culture of secondary schools that stresses clothing styles, automobiles, records, and expensive equipment-based

Table 10−14. Per Cent of Females among Degree Recipients,
by Level of Degree and Discipline, in U.S., 1977 [30]

Discipline division	Bachelor's	Master's	Doctor's
Total	46.2	47.1	24.3
Agricultural and natural resources	22.2	14.6	6.9
Architecture	21.4	22.5	15.1
Area studies	56.0	46.9	32.0
Biological sciences	36.4	33.8	21.4
Business and management	23.6	14.3	6.3
Communications	44.3	44.4	24.0
Computer and informational science	23.9	16.7	8.8
Education	72.2	65.8	34.8
Engineering	4.5	4.4	2.8
Fine and applied arts	61.4	51.2	32.5
Foreign languages	76.2	69.5	51.5
Health professions	79.2	67.9	32.0
Home economics	95.9	91.1	77.0
Law	27.5	13.2	13.3
Letters	56.7	59.5	38.2
Library science	90.9	79.6	53.3
Mathematics	41.6	35.1	13.2
Military science	.3	2.3	—
Physical sciences	20.1	16.6	9.6
Psychology	51.7	48.1	35.9
Public affairs and services	45.1	45.5	32.8
Social sciences	39.4	32.9	22.1
Theology	25.7	31.4	2.8
Interdisciplinary studies	47.0	37.1	30.6

activities. Students without new and stylish (or stylishly unstylish) clothes are frequently ostracized and the lack of a car in suburban schools may define one out of many groups and activities. The pervasive middle-class life-style stressed by the school, with its attendant materialism and consumerism, is a powerful preparation and practice for the consumer role in American society.

As has been noted, issues of economic role preparation are not solely related to economic class; they also are enormously potent with regard to racial and sexual status, and the ways in which these groups are affected by recent economic trends. As current economic pressures shrink the total economic pie, movements for women's rights and opportunities focus on gaining a greater share of the available economic rewards, and are likely to have greater impact on the attendant preparation mechanisms. For instance, as the society experiences greater conflict over sex roles, the schools are likely arenas for a more protracted struggle among the partisans of traditionally sexist work roles and groups of women (and some men) fighting for new opportunities in jobs that are traditionally closed to them. In similar ways, the concern for racial justice often appears in an escalated form in school because of the school's function in the preparation of minority students for traditional economic roles.

Politics

Schools also play a major role in channeling young people with regard to their political lives. One way is by sorting the young for different adult patterns of political activity. These different patterns include (1) political leadership and active roles in political parties and voluntary associations; (2) nominal membership in voluntary associations; (3) no membership in political parties or voluntary associations; and (4) inconsistent or sporadic voting behavior. Student political and extracurricular activities permit and encourage different levels of student participation, and thus help prepare groups of students for their "appropriate" adult patterns. This sorting process is facilitated by the kinds of student characteristics required for active participation in school political events: time availability, acceptable values, money for clothes and travel, approval and support of school and community adults, "representative" (majority) status, past experience in public speaking, academic performance, and the like.

The resultant patterns of economic differentiation in school political roles are demonstrated in the study of Elmtown's youth, as summarized in Table 10—15 and 10—16. These tables demonstrate that extracurricular activities and elected positions in school are disproportionately dominated by the most affluent student groups (social classes I and II).

A second way schools channel the young for subsequent poltical roles is through formal and informal teaching about how the American system of government functions. This teaching occurs in required courses in history and government, school-wide assemblies, and special programs celebrating citizen-

Table 10—15. Percentage of Elmtown Students Participating in all Extracurricular Activities by Social Class of Family [31]

Social Class	Per Cent with Participation	Per Cent with Nonparticipation
I—II	100	00
III	75	25
IV	57	43
V	27	73

Table 10-16. Class Distribution of Elected Representatives in Elmtown High School, compared to the Class Distribution of the Student Body [32]

Social Class	Per cent of Student body	Per cent of Elected Representatives
I-II	9.0	21.6
III	37.3	46.2
IV	47.0	32.3
V	6.7	00.0

ship. It is here that groups and individuals learn of our system's advantages to them, and most often fail to gain a sense of the system's disadvantages. Students also learn America's virtues in relation to the rest of the world, and this nation's role in advocating and protecting democracy. Here again, a very selective, and for the most part uncritical, view of history is taught.°

Critics of the curriculum materials and classroom activities that are used to teach North American history point out that our history in general is attributed to the actions of men, particularly the actions of white men, and with modest exceptions, to the actions of white men who were affluent and obviously powerful in status and rank. Little of our history discusses the key roles of women in settling the West, in creating and supporting the Revolution, and in figuring out how to manage the home front while men fought in foreign wars. The written history of our westward expansion typically casts native-Americans, Asian-Americans, and Hispanics in roles as "our" enemies, as more or less savage resisters of the Anglos' eminent domain. Only recently has any attention been focused on the roles of black people in the American Revolution, and indeed, in all our nation's wars, and on the manner in which Hispanic peoples created the southwestern portions of our nation, prior to their conquest and immersion into the new nation. The history of America's eonomic development, its industrial revolution, tells the tale as if managers and capitalists were the only positive moving force. The critical roles of working-class men and women, and of labor leaders in contributing to an industrial expansion that was somewhat humane and responsive to public needs are often left untold. Readers of these histories often come away with a positive and idealized version of North American life; perhaps with a dangerously distorted notion of past and future politics.

A third way schools channel the young for subsequent political activity is through the inculcation of traditional and limited citizenship responsibilities.

° Critical views of the uncritical teaching of North American history and politics are presented in Massialas, and in Oliver and Shaver [33].

These include the responsibilities to be informed; to vote; to comply with the laws; to respect police, judges, and elected officials; and to fight for (and sometimes defend) the country when ordered to. This is preparation for political activity that is limited with regard to roles in the formal and legitimized political system, and is further limited by not including roles in challenging social movements, protest actions, civil disobedience, revolution making, and so on.

Social

In addition to channeling young people with regard to their work and political lives, schools also channel students with regard to their social lives. Students are prepared for a particular social status and style, although in a veiled way, because of school and societal rhetoric about open social relations and democracy. The power of this myth, as with others that surround merited economic status and political values and roles, is not only in what it teaches about our society's openness. It also teaches, indirectly, that individuals who have not achieved success are themselves to blame, and that they, rather than the structure of events and power in the society or school, are the causal agents of their own status and role. Thus, young people may grow up with unrealistic assumptions about the degree to which they "merit" their privileged or oppressed status. Teaching about the openness of society, the viability of upward mobility, and the centrality of individual initiative and achievement downplays social status distinctions and mutes status conflict by directing attention about failure away from the social system to the individual. It helps to create a "false consciousness" that distracts poor and minority people and women from a clear understanding of how social status mechanisms work.

A second way by which schools channel social life is through the formal and informal approval of largely homogeneous and ranked friendship groupings. Students often enter high schools with homogeneous friendship patterns arising from racially and economically separated feeder schools, neighborhood segregation, and separate spare time activities—churches, clubs, and the like. Elementary school tracking, which reinforces separations on the basis of alleged "ability," also separates students according to race and economic class. These distinctions are maintained in junior and senior high schools through sororities and fraternities, or through their informal counterparts that operate parties which substitute for (or occur before or after) "all school parties." The effects of these patterns can be seen in the social dating patterns of Elmtown's youth, as in Figure 10—2. What is of particular significance with regard to the dating patterns of high school youth is their relative stability over the period of some thirty-seven years since the publishing of *Elmtown's Youth*. Recent studies of economic class and dating patterns also report high correlation between social status position and dating patterns. Even more revealing is the observation made by a prominent sociologist upon revisiting Muncie, Indiana (the site of

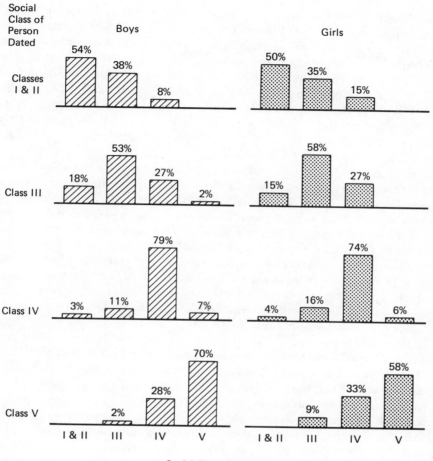

Social Class of Person Dated

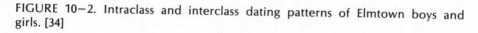

Social Class of Person Dated

FIGURE 10—2. Intraclass and interclass dating patterns of Elmtown boys and girls. [34]

Robert Lynd's classic, *Middletown*), after a time span of thirty-five years, that very little had changed. The basic values, mores, and customs of the town seemed relatively unaltered [35]. The presence of a fairly large midwestern university (Ball State), the influence of the mass media, and the mobility provided by the automobile and airplane had created more alternative life-styles; yet, the community's social institutions, churches, and schools carried on many of the same social traditions and activities as they did in the 1930s. This was particularly true of the high school.

Academic tracking also serves to channel social life by setting the limits on opportunities for contact within formal school programs. Space in schools is both formally and informally allocated to different castes; e.g., the "arista" or

A Sociology of Education

honor society meets in a classroom, "greasers" meet in the parking lot, "jocks" meet in the locker room, and so on. The channeling of social contacts within a single organization also demands certain distracting and emotional modes of integration when real political and programmatic integration is lacking. In most schools a great deal of such behavior is organized around symbols, such as athletic stars and prom queens, or through athletic events and efforts at total school "spirit." The classic example of an attempt to create school spirit is the ritual of the "pep rally," where a diverse student body comes together for a time as a collective unit and finds an enemy to "hate" that is not on the faculty [36].

A third means of channeling social status performed by the school is the legitimizing and reinforcing of middle-class norms. This formalizes the implicit societal hierarchy for status and establishes "the coin of the realm" in terms of acceptable social behavior. If youth are to enter into the formal and informal life of the school it must be in terms of white and middle-class cultural styles— their dances, music, cultural symbols, and the like. As a result, lower-status students are less involved in the social activities and functions of the school. They also seem to be more troubled than students of higher status; lower-class students appear to experience a wide range of difficulties in coping with everyday school life. The influence of social class factors on reported school social problems and relationships is shown in Table 10–17.

In the broad sense of social living the data in Table 10–17 make it clear once again that social class and economic status have an impact on that variable as well. Students of lower status find it more difficult to feel part of school situations and friendships. Although the column heading in Table 10–17 identifies difficulties in interpersonal relations that students experience, it could just as well be noted as ways in which the social status values and mechanisms of the school exclude certain students. This interpretation is also consistent in demonstrating that lower-status students are more often excluded from informal social activities than are other groups. Thus, on several dimensions reviewed,

Table 10–17. Study of Seniors in Washington State High Schools [37]

Difficulties in Inter-personal Relations in School	% Upper Social Status	% Middle Social Status	% Lower Social Status
Not being popular	9.0	9.4	16.1
Being left out of things	13.5	11.0	21.4
Too few social activities	13.2	9.1	25.0
Too many social activities	8.9	4.5	1.8
Difficulty in making friends	10.8	13.9	17.9

Exercise 10—4. *The Discovery of "channeling" in your High School*

This exercise can be done by students in small groups or in individual papers.

The materials you have just read discuss ways in which schools treat students differently on the basis of their race, economic class, and sex, and thereby channel them into future status and roles. In the following chart, list some of the differentiating mechanisms you experienced or observed in your high school.

Channeling/Differentiating Mechanisms

Work Status and Roles	Political Status and Roles	Social Status and Roles

middle-status groups are most successfully served or satisfied by the school's social activities. However, this is especially true in multiple status or racially heterogeneous schools. In economically or racially homogeneous schools, these distinctions are much less obvious or occur in other dimensions.

SUMMARY

This chapter examined some of the mechanisms of discrimination that help to account for certain patterns of societal inequality that are sustained by the schools. First, we reviewed the environmental and community contexts of school inequality, pointing out that residential segregation has been primarily responsible for much of the racial separation and segregation in the schools, and that schools generally have failed to alter this process in any substantial way. In fact, they may have reinforced and exacerbated it. Next, we discussed the ways by which the ideologies and behaviors of professional educators reinforce established patterns of differential student performances and expectations, thereby affecting long-term outcomes of schooling. And finally, we reviewed certain aspects of school organization and described how these function to sustain inequality and even assist in creating it anew in each succeeding generation. These mechanisms are integrally related to the various outcomes of schooling discussed in Chapters 8 and 9 and thus have a pronounced effect on those outcomes.

It could be argued that outcome inequality remains one of the prime latent functions of schooling in urban North America. A sizable portion of the job market requires unskilled, untrained, and undereducated laborers to fill its ranks. Our political system does not support widespread activism, especially from oppressed groups, and obviously expects that large numbers of these people will not vote or will follow the lead of more affluent and white and male leaders. Equalizing schooling outcomes would create chaos in the unskilled labor market and seriously alter the stratification system and decision-making apparatus of society. One author has referred to resultant school practices as "Strategies for Failure"—in effect, a school system's capacity to plan for the academic failure of its minorities so as to reproduce the economic and political life of the city [38]. Thus, the reproduction of societal divisions of labor by schools is an outcome essential to the maintenance of public stability.

From these *mechanisms of control* and discrimination, we now focus our attention on several of the possible *mechanisms of changes*—those strategies and approaches designed to alter the bases of inequality.

11

PROGRAMS AND PROBLEMS OF EDUCATIONAL CHANGE

This chapter discusses several different ways of creating and sustaining educational change, and examines the advantages and disadvantages of alternative strategies. In many discussions of schools and schooling, new and different programs and innovations are often suggested. But the best of new ideas are often not implemented because professionals and citizens, educators, and students or parents did not plan *how to bring about the change*. This chapter deals with the hows, with several general strategies of change. No discussion of change strategies however, can proceed usefully or realistically in the abstract; therefore the discussion is focused around the possibilities of change in several key areas of school life which have been discussed and stressed throughout this volume.

The major issues used as examples include location and exercise of power and control over educational systems; the channeling process by which educational outcomes are generated and maintained; the professional system of educational statuses and roles; the institutional and classroom technology and/or pedagogical techniques used to organize learning-teaching transactions; and the existence and impact of ideologies and practices of racism, sexism, and class discrimination. Since these issues are discussed throughout the volume, they are not elaborated on in this chapter, and we can proceed swiftly to discuss the possibilities of change. Each reader might well think about other change examples, and test out the strategies discussed in terms of their relevance to other issues that are not explicitly referred to here.

MAJOR CHANGE STRATEGIES

The major change strategies discussed include manpower retraining, classroom reorganization, organizational development or modification, client or community mobilization, social policy manipulation including actions directed toward local politico-economic systems, and the establishment of institutional alternatives. These strategies are thus distinguished by the kinds of targets that are available; each strategy focuses at a different level of the social system of education, and at a different target or arena of interaction and operation.

The first major strategy discussed is *manpower retraining*. The focus of this reeducation strategy usually is upon key aspects of individuals—teachers, administrators, students or parents, and community members. The specific retraining target might be levels of information, skill, attitudes, and values.

A second major strategy is *classroom reorganization*. The focus of this approach is on the ways the school allocates youngsters and teachers to various learning settings and the procedures utilized within those settings to create educational transactions and to facilitate teaching and learning.

A third major strategy is *organizational development* or *modification*. The focus of this strategy is the structure of roles, interpersonal relations, or programs that delineate the operating organization. Rather than concentrate on individuals, the regular and organized relationships among peoples are seen as the manipulatable aspect of school life in this approach. These targets may include cultural values, reward systems, instructional technologies, systems of communication and interaction, and decision making.

A fourth major strategy discussed is *client* or *community mobilization*. In this approach the focus is upon organizing new forms of influence among the people who are served by the educational system, whether the service is direct as with students or indirect as with parents, community members, taxpayers, and the like. Forces outside the institutional structure are mobilized in order to bring collective concern to bear on the school itself. Thus, the interface between the professional systems and the lay community system is particularly important. In addition, problems of client (student and parent or taxpayer-citizen) roles, representation in decision making, evaluation of service, and accountability are all relevant.

A fifth major strategy involves *influencing elites in the local political-economic system*. This approach starts from the premise that school and community are not only interdependent, but that powerful forces or persons in the community set the terms and limits of school life. Change must thus start, or at least focus, there. Exemplary targets might include local political elites, business and civic leaders, distribution of wealth in the local economy, and the like. Closely related to this strategy is the *manipulation of social policy*, the alteration of the formal and legal guidelines upon which schools operate. Modification of laws and policies may occur through focusing upon legislative agencies, executive offices, or judicial channels where major societal decision makers operate.

A sixth, and final strategy reviewed, is the *establishment of institutional alternatives*. In this approach, no direct attempt is made to alter traditional institutions; rather the effort is made to devlop new institutions that substitute for or complement old ones. Sometimes newer models may exist as innovations within established organizations; at other times the institutions may be built partially or completely outside the organization.

Manpower Retraining

Education is a process involving interpersonal transactions and the transformation of individuals. Sooner or later, it involves individuals relating to one another directly. The attitudes, skills, and styles of behavior of individuals all affect the way they behave with others, and more specifically, the ways they teach or otherwise partake in the teaching-learning process. There is little point in developing a new curriculum, or new educational structures, if the individuals using or staffing those innovations are not also helped to alter their behavior. Thus, one of the most popular strategies of educational reform has been to try to alter the personal attributes of those in command of the schooling system—the teachers and administrators.

The focus upon individual behavior does not mean that this strategy excludes consideration of the social context of teaching. In fact, it has recently become typical for groups of educators to be trained or retrained together, with the hope that they can support each other in their new ways of behaving. Similarly, it is not unusual to find students, administrators, and community members also undergoing training, with the assumption that all parties to the educational enterprise require new ways of dealing with one another and their common efforts. The vast majority of retraining programs, however, have focused on teachers as targets and have tried to help these front-line workers (or as some would call them, middle managers, with students as lower-level "workers") learn new ideas, skills, techniques, and the like.

One primary target of retraining strategies is the level of information that educators have about technical subjects, students, or the character of the community. For example, many college courses are available to teach teachers about the "new math," or to update their knowledge about world history or about advances in science. Some college courses also focus on changes in the American society, and the impact of these changes on youth of different races and economic classes. It is assumed that teachers who "know their students" or "know their backgrounds" will be better able to deal with students on their own terms and meet their needs more directly. Whether or not the translation is quite so direct, a number of preservice and in-service programs have been devised on this assumption. The evidence that such information transmission is the most popular approach to retrain teachers can be garnered from its preponderance in the educational programs of major universities that train teachers. The heavily rational model of "new information leads to new behavior," which dominates especially at the higher education levels, stresses information and knowledge as the prerequisites to any change in individual behavior. Inservice programs may include the use of scientists or experts to update teachers' knowledge of their fields. They may provide books and other audiovisual materials containing information about the community and about typical youngsters who live there. Teachers may also gain access to district or personal records, and/or diagnostic instruments with which they can conduct needs assessment programs with students. Principals may be given or gather similar information about their teaching staffs, new management practices, new system guidelines, and the like. As with any information-based program, data that are not placed in the proper social or explanatory context can be misleading or destructive. For instance, consideration of the evidence and issues discussed in Chapters 9 and 10 should alert us to the possibility that certain data (especially if misinterpreted) could rigidify false stereotypes, rather than free new visions and ideas.

A second major target of retraining strategies is the personal feelings educators may have about their jobs, their students, and their own lives. Greater clarification of one's own feelings of anger, fear, and joy is assumed to help a person deal with others, given the deeply personal and interpersonal nature of educational transactions. Thus, retraining programs concerned with racial desegregation often have focused on teachers' or educators' personal feelings on racial matters. The importance of this change target is supported by current research indicating that educators' judgments of the competencies of youngsters may affect their behavior with lower-class or minority students. If the unconscious or erroneous expectations of educators are communicated to students in ways that diminish their learning potential and performance, then it is indeed critical to alter these expectations and prejudgments. Consciousness raising and racial awareness programs for teachers are primarily concerned with the deeply ingrained feelings of white superiority and assumptions of black and brown incompetence that seem to pervade North American life. Some anti-racism training programs deal with a wide variety of targets, but the majority stress the unconscious feelings that many white persons, including educators of all levels, hold about racial minorities. Interpersonal exposure to minority persons of equal or similar status, exploration of whites' fantasies, open sharing of feelings of fear or threat, and feedback on evaluative judgments are all relevant components of such training programs.

A third set of targets for retraining events include educators' typical relationships and behavior with others in the school—students, teachers, and administrators. The authoritative organization of school life often reduces the amount of direct and open interpersonal contact that is possible between educators and students. At the same time, teaching and learning are deeply transactional events, which involve interpersonal exchange and reciprocity. Information is not "passed" from one inanimate or impersonal object or vessel to another; rather 2 or 10 or 20 persons are engaged in communicative acts of sharing, of giving and receiving information. In order for this sharing to be effective, the people involved must be at least somewhat open to one another.

The school and societal structures and myths that separate adults from youth, and that often make them antagonists, suggest that the development of new and effective relationships cutting across these boundaries have to overcome many traditional impediments. Therefore, it seems appropriate for both educators and youth to be participants in retraining efforts that seek to overcome these traditions, and to create more effective working relationships.

In this same context, members of the educational system who have different statuses and responsibilities also are often alienated and isolated from one another. To the extent that various persons and groups in the staff can improve their interpersonal and working relations, they may be better able to utilize their various resources and deliver higher-quality services to students.

Educational administrators who have not been specifically trained for their roles may also enter retraining programs to develop more effective working relationships. The socially unskilled manager often creates organizational systems full of rigid rules and organizational requirements but short on interpersonal networks and linkages that tie people together in pleasant and productive ways. The alternative to distant manager-worker (principal-teacher) relationships is a shared system of responsibility that can be aided by highly developed interpersonal communications and interaction systems.

A fourth set of targets in retraining efforts is the practical skills, or technology, of instruction and administration. There is considerable slip between intention and practice, and between rhetoric and reality, and many educators simply do not know how to innovate in their classroom or school—they do not know how to act upon cherished principles. For instance, principals who are newly committed to democratic staff meetings may not know how to help a teaching staff take the initiative in solving school problems. A teacher who is committed to autonomous student group work also may not know how to proceed, such as on what basis to form groups, how much latitude to permit, how to deal with neighbors' complaints about noise, and how to help students improve their group operations. By the same token, parents wishing to change the schools may not know how to organize, including who to approach and who not to, how to call a meeting, how to plan an exciting meeting, and with whom to form coalitions. Observation, role playing, and classroom practice may be essential elements in a training program devoted to the understanding and employment of new managerial or instructional technologies.

One of the first steps in any skill retraining program is to assess the needs of personnel to be retrained. The list in Exercise 11−1 is one example of such an assessment device for teachers: prospective teachers or lay citizens can also use it to assess their own leadership skills.

The responses to these questions could provide direction for a retraining program; they suggest those issues with which teachers feel they need help. The responses also identify some positive resources that can be used as aids in the retraining process, such as teachers who can handle problems other teachers

Exercise 11−1. *An Assessment Device for Teachers* [1]

The following are some typical *problems* teachers face *in the classroom.* Which of these problems might present some difficulties for you? Check the appropriate box.

	Not a problem (1)	A Problem But One I Can Handle (2)	A Problem With Which I'd Like Some Help (3)
Teaching youngsters whose abilities are very different from one another.	___	___	___
Racial or ethnic hostilities among students	___	___	___
Getting student to do assignments.	___	___	___
Dealing with defiance	___	___	___
Trying to help students with their problems.	___	___	___
Getting subject matter across effectively.	___	___	___
Raising academic achievement of students.	___	___	___
Maintaining interest of students.	___	___	___
Physical facilities in classroom.	___	___	___
Tension felt between me and a youngster of another race.	___	___	___
Getting students to pay attention.	___	___	___

would like some help with. The use of peer resources in retraining programs often has the positive side effects of increasing the level of conversation and support among the staff.

A final target of retraining efforts is the various images of the future that any member of a school or school system may have. Change is based upon some conception of alternative futures and some effort to avoid an unpleasant or unsatisfactory present. To the extent that more informed futures can be examined, or more hopeful futures imagined, changes can be directed to even more cherished goals. But for those of us who live in a harried present, there often is not enough time to conceptualize the future. Special training events may permit us that necessary luxury.

This discussion can be summarized by considering the ways different retraining targets can be utilized to work on a key issue in school change. For instance, consider the problems teachers experience when a previously all-white school is desegregated by the busing in of black and hispanic students to these classes. What issues do teachers have to deal with? What kinds of retraining would assist them to deal effectively with this situation? What do they need to know about these new students and about the probable reactions of white students? What elements of the teachers' feelings, relational behaviors, technical/instructional skills, and images of the future might have to be altered? Exercise 11-2 presents a sample list of variables in each category.

The discussion of futures brings us again to a potential drawback, or at least a major concern, in all retraining efforts. All too often retraining programs are developed with a focus upon skills or techniques, with little attention to the ends of education or to the goals that teachers and administrators elect to pursue. Matters of power and control; of racism, class discrimination, and sexism; and of organized roles of educational professionals ought to be part of any retraining effort. Whether these issues are dealt with at the level of information, attitudinal and emotional exploration, skills in implementation, future images, and so on is a matter of local design. But no training effort is free of these educational and social issues, and the problems of ends are as vital as matters of technique and social relations. "Better qualified" teachers are not just teachers who are skilled in classroom process or peer conversation. Rather, they are teachers who knowingly and skillfully are committed to antiracist education and youth's freedom from inappropriately constraining rules and regulations.

Another drawback to the use of retraining techniques is that they may be misused as devices to take the pressure off other necessary changes. The handy solution to all educational ills is often pictured as a better trained staff, and thus staff retraining is a popular strategy. But this may also be a distraction, a way of drawing energy and concern away from fundamental organizational failures, from basic racial or sexual oppression, from serious school-community cleavage, and the like. As one example, our national concern with racism and economic injustice never took the form, until lately, of dealing with community account-

Exercise 11—2. *Linking Retraining Foci and Targets to a Particular Problem*

Students can work alone or in groups to

1. Add to the beginning list some other variables or retraining foci you think are important, including filling in foci for the two targets that were left blank:

2. Place an asterisk next to those three foci you think are most important. Then several students could get together in small groups to discuss the different options they each prefer or feel are important.

Targets	Retraining Foci to Cope with Newly Interracial Classrooms
Informational	What are the new students' skill levels? What are the new students' needs? Goals? How are the white students' likely to respond to the new students?
Feelings	What racist views do I harbor? Do I feel competent to deal with this situation? What expectations do I hold for new students? Do I fear racial conflict in class?
Behaviors —social	.
Behaviors —skills	
Future imagery	What would a truly nonracist school look like? What would my classroom look like if interracial relations were very positive? How does integration look different from desegregation?
Other targets	

ability and control of schools. Rather, the "problems of the disadvantaged" were dealt with by training teachers to know them better and to relate better to such youngsters. At one level this training made sense, but by itself this approach did little except to delay a more wholesome and structural approach to our basic conception of education in a plural society and to pluralistic educational organizations. Problems that are organizational in character cannot be effectively dealt with by altering the mind states or behavior patterns of individual educators or educational consumers. If retraining is not effective, or is resisted, "unqualified" teachers and administrators may have to be replaced. The collaborative and optimistic approach to educator change should not overlook that more painful but potentially necessary reality.

Classroom Reorganization

A second strategy of change takes as its target the classroom itself, and the organization of personnel, teaching-learning resources, and materials that occurs in the classroom. The bulk of direct efforts to teach take place in this environment, and the major portion of the time that students and teachers

---

Exercise 11–3. *Planning a Retraining Program.*

This activity can be done in a small group. Several large groups can do the same task or can focus on different goals. In either case, the plans of different groups can be shared and compared.

Goal: To help teachers discover and implement new ways of dealing with sexism in the school and classroom.

Task no. 1: Select and specify some *targets* of change and some *foci* for this retraining program.

Task no. 2: Identify some resources you might use, such as lectures, books, small-group discussions, and opportunities for practice.

Task no. 3: How would you plan to evaluate this program?

---

spend in school is spent in this setting. Therefore, attempts to alter the nature of classroom structures and activities could have enormous impact on school life and on student outcomes.

Classrooms are generally organized so that 25 to 30 students (or more) engage directly with one teacher. In order to coordinate the efforts of this many students, teachers are often forced into forms of control that, by and large, diminish the possibilities for individual attention, for student creativity in moving in different directions, for pluralistic responses to varied student styles, and for the use of peer learning by students. Our view is that this is not necessary and that with new ideas and classroom skills teachers could proceed in different ways. One target of classroom reorganization efforts could be precisely this: the broadening of instructional resources/personnel to transcend assumptions that locate all teaching expertise and responsibility (and therefore power and control) in the hands of teachers. For instance, some schools have experimented with students as teachers, or at least as facilitators of other students' learning. In some cases this effort has involved older students instructing younger students, and in some cases it has involved like-age students working together in ways that share their resources, expertise, and inquiry agendas. Further, to the extent that students are involved in the creation and implementation of learning settings, knowledge gained in this process is divested of its authoritarian character and linked to the exploration and discoveries made by the learners themselves.

Thus, one series of attempts to change traditional classroom patterns involves groups of students working together. As peers collaborate in learning activities, knowledge can be shared rather than hoarded. As evaluations and grades are provided on the basis of group effort, students must learn ways of collaborating rather than solely learning how to compete. The competitive and hoarding life-style that is so omnipresent in capitalist society can be buffered by efforts that multiply student knowledge within a framework of collaborative peer relations. To implement such a program of group learning activities by students requires that teachers and students acquire the skills in managing and implementing such an instructional device, one for which neither student nor teacher has been prepared. The prior discussion of retraining efforts indicates how this agenda of skill development might fit within the target system of teachers' classroom techniques.

Team teaching programs also have been tried in various schools, in an effort to increase the educational resource base available for classroom instruction. This innovation also requires teachers to invent and develop new ways of working together, sharing power and attention in the classroom, and collaborating on what traditionally has been an individualistic enterprise.

Another major target of classroom reorganization efforts concerns the high degree of power and autonomy concentrated in the teachers. This concentration of power inevitably provides teachers with substantial evaluation responsibility as well. All too often these issues become confused, and grading becomes a

Exercise 11−4. *Examining Classroom Task Structures*

Consider the classroom you currently are in—this college classroom. Is the structure of social relations and academic performance organized around principles of individual achievement or group achievement? What might the classroom look and feel like if it were organized around group criteria? Presumably three major components of the classroom might be different; consider them each in turn.

1. The system of social interaction in a group-oriented classroom would revolve around intense interersonal relations among students, not primarily around student-teacher interactions.

2. The reward structure in a group-oriented classroom would be based upon collective performances of groups of students, rather than individual performances on papers, exams, presentations, and the like.

3. Power and control in a group-oriented classroom would be shared, or at least negotiated, between students and teacher, or among students, not unilaterally and completely located in the teacher role.

Try to identify the specific indicators of each major component. Then engage in a reflective or shared discussion of your performances, and the reasons you, the teacher, or anyone else might prefer one or another of the group-oriented or individual-oriented classroom modes.

device for maintaining control and for shaping individual obedience to prescribed behavior patterns and mastery objectives. Alternative inquiry agendas and alternative learning desires are often negated by the dominant power of the single educational professional in the classroom. When power that has been heavily centralized can be shared among classroom members, plural learning activities that speak to many individuals or several groups of students can be undertaken, and students can be involved directly in evaluating their own work. The insistence on adult feedback to students on the quality of their schoolwork is entirely consistent with the principles of good learning—the need for corrective input. The insistence on adult grading of students' schoolwork is not necessarily so consistent; it often indicates adults' commitment to control devices rather than learning devices per se.

One way in which social scientists have investigated ways to change power and influence in the classroom has been to use the assessment device shown in Table 11−1. Then, on the basis of student reported data of this sort, changes could be made in the structure of the classroom to permit more student

Table 11–1. Actual-Ideal Sources of Influence Over Classroom Matters*

How your class is run depends a lot on who decides about plans, budgets, rules, courses, hiring, student activities, and the like.

(A) Actual Influence: How much influence do you think each of the following really has in your class?

(B) Ideal Influence: How much influence do you think each of the following should have?

	(A) Actual Influence					(B) Ideal Influence				
	Has/Have Little or No Influence (1)	Has/Have Some Influence (2)	Has/Have Moderate Influence (3)	Has/Have Considerable Influence (4)	Has/Have a Great Deal of Influence (5)	Should Have Little or No Influence (1)	Some Influence (2)	Moderate Influence (3)	Considerable Influence (4)	A Great Deal of Influence (5)
a. School Board	|	|	|	|	|	|	|	|	|	|
b. Superintendent	|	|	|	|	|	|	|	|	|	|
c. Principal	|	|	|	|	|	|	|	|	|	|
d. Teachers	|	|	|	|	|	|	|	|	|	|
e. Students	|	|	|	|	|	|	|	|	|	|
f. Parents	|	|	|	|	|	|	|	|	|	|

*Data collected from students and teachers with this instrument, focusing on the school rather than the classroom, has been presented in Chapter 5 (See Tables 5–4 and 5–5, and Figures 5–1 and 5–2).

influence. It can also be used to assess, and lead to changes in, the structure of power and influence in the total school building.

Some schools have experimented with classroom structures marked by greater diffusion of teacher power and increased student autonomy. These "open classrooms" represent one recent venture in the direction of creating new patterns of initiative, power, and ultimately coordination in the classroom. The individualization of personal agendas and the response to collective agendas of subgroups of youngsters mark the major outlines of the open classroom system.

The content of the classroom generally is set by cultural values and political-economic priorities. It reflects the organizational priorities of state and local school systems, as well as the local building's norms. But at the same time, local classroom options are available and teachers often experiment with new curricula in class. For instance, one popular target of curricular and classroom reorganization efforts involves the exploration of the ways students experience their existence in the families, neighborhoods, schools and communities in which they live. Efforts to study the power structure of the local board of education, for instance, may be far more instructive for social studies classes than reading abstract texts on societal problems and governance. So may understanding the bases of community resistance and/or advocacy of a desegregation plan, or the planning efforts required to make a success of local desegregation efforts.

The major problem with the strategy of classroom reorganization is that it may ignore the extent to which the classroom is simply an organizational convenience. The classroom is one way of organizing students and teachers to carry out the overall pattern of education within the local school organization. Despite our history, the classroom is neither sacred nor always an effective device. Moreover, any attempt to create change in this arena sooner or later must attend to the pressures for maintaining the status quo, pressures often rooted in the larger structure of the school system.

Organizational Development or Modification

Both retraining efforts and classroom reorganization efforts take place within the environment of the school building itself. Both require support or corollary change in the organizational structure and operations of the local school to be implemented and maintained over time. In addition, changes in the organization itself may have far-reaching impact on the lives and working relations, as well as educational opportunities and outcomes, of all people within the school. Organizations are not merely the sum of all individuals in the school; organizations have lasting goals, decisional structures, boundaries, and norms or values that exist before and after any specific individual or set of individuals enter or leave the school. Altering these pervasive and lasting aspects of school organizations is an appropriate strategy in educational change efforts.

One of the major targets of organizational change is the structure of goals and norms that reflect the cultural beliefs of school members and/or the surrounding community. All schools try to state their goals in vague and attractive terms; thus, there seldom is debate over the general goals of education. However, more specific goals are visible in the choices of programs and policies that outline expected and appropriate behavior in schools. When goals are tied overtly to their programmatic choices and operational objectives, debates can begin. And when goals are institutionalized in a set of rules and regulations that guide the behavior of students and adults, we are more likely to see conflict and resistance on some people's part, and obedience and conformity on others'. For instance, the continuing confusion and debate over ways of implementing desegregation is linked to its possible implications for the goals and interests of various groups in the local community. There seldom is debate about the general goals of equal education and racial justice that underlie desegregation. But when these general goals are specified, and tied to specific means and programs, substantial debate ensues. Each group is quite concerned with its own goals, its own interpretation of general goals, and the ways a specific implementation plan may affect its own values and interests.

Educational goals and cultural values or beliefs also direct the structure of rewards and reward allocation among adult and student members of the school. The criteria for allocation of rewards reflect the organization's priorities, and the teacher who is rewarded for having a quiet classroom well understands the major values of the profession. Likewise, students who are rewarded for obedient and studious behavior are adapting well to what is expected of them in a mass education system. If innovative and creative students and teachers violate expected standards of behavior, they will not receive high rewards. Thus, any attempt to alter the behavior of school members must attend to the rewards that are incumbent upon organizational behavior, and seek to alter the current criteria for allocating rewards—whether these rewards are merit increases, collegial respect, good grades, outstanding recommendations, peer approval, and the like. If we want people to behave differently we must reward them for their new behavior—and that requires altering the organization's reward process.

The content of the educational enterprise, the curriculum, is another representation of major goals and values in practice. Many recent efforts have been made to increase the curriculum's relevance and appeal to contemporary youth, and especially to Third World groups, to women, and to lower-class youngsters. Courses in Black History and Women's Rights along with programs relating to biculturalism and bilingualism are examples of attempts to expand the curricular offerings and increase the relevance of contemporary education to these groups. Efforts of this sort have begun to deal with the demand for pluralism and an increased quality of educational offerings. Parallel efforts oriented toward changing instructional and classroom techniques help advance this agenda. Obviously this approach has much in common with changing the staff members' attitudes and skills. But whereas one strategy focuses on personal characteristics and behaviors, the other focuses upon the value systems and rewards that surround, constrain, and help guide individual behavior.

Another major characteristic of organizations is their membership system. Three major aspects of the collective membership of the school draw our attention as potential targets of change: First, members come from defined geographical areas, and sometimes these areas are segregated by racial and economic status. On the basis of these demographic drawing systems, students of various races and classes attend different schools. Even when students attend racially desegregated schools, they are often accorded different privileges and opportunities on the basis of their race and class. Differential tracking, classroom assignments, disciplinary actions, teachers' expectations, and the like are now referred to as "second generation problems" incident to desegregation and/or attempts to create pluralism in school membership. Second, female students and female teachers often are accorded "second-class citizenship" in school. As noted in Chapters 9 and 10, females often have less power, fewer opportunities, and more meager educational rewards and responsibilities than men. Third, schools create dramatically different membership rights and privileges for older and younger students, for adults and youth, and for teachers and students. There is no compelling evidence that this is a good educational design, but it certainly suits the needs of adults for higher-status rewards and privileges. Attempts to restructure the meaning of these demographic characteristics, student opportunities and privileges, and adult-youth role relationships represents three major targets for change in the membership of the school.

Social relations and interactions among persons, which closely resemble these membership patterns, represent another feature of all social organizations. Sharp divisions are often found in schools in communication patterns between teachers and students. Each group may engage in substantial communication and interaction internally, but it may experience minimal direct communication across these age/status boundaries. The culture of professionalism mitigates against intimacy between educators and students; it suggests that distance and impersonality are prime requisites for the ability to make impersonal and fair judgments. This very impersonal style often denies to both students and teachers some of the joys of close social interaction. Students, then, develop similar intragroup values and beliefs with appropriate peer penalties and jibes for spending too much time in interaction with adults.

Closely related to these issues in teacher-student relations are similar problems in the relationships between the faculty and administration of a school. Chapters 5 and 6 indicated that the divisions of influence and responsibility within the staff often lead to distance and even antagonisms between a principal and the teaching faculty. A staff is more likely to be effective if the various members can support one another and can learn from each others' experience. Thus, it is in the interest of improving education to consider changes that might increase the level of trust and cooperation among teachers and between teachers and the school administration.

One device that is often used to help plan how to make changes in school is the *force field*. The purpose of this device is to identify or map the various personal, organizational, and community factors that impinge on a situation and that might be considered as barriers to change or as resources to draw upon in an attempt to make change. The development of a coherent and complete list of barriers and resources that are relevant to any change effort represents a diagnosis of the situation; it may help indicate what must be done and who or what might help get it done. On the basis of a well-developed force field, specific strategies for change and actions can be planned. One example of the way a force field may be used to help plan organizational change of the sort discussed in the preceding paragraph is presented in Table 11–2.

Differences in the amount of influence people have in school also can have great impact. The staff exerts influence on students in a variety of formal and informal ways, in the classroom and outside as well. Students are limited to the

Table 11–2. Force Field Diagram of Factors in Teacher-Principal Relations [2]

Goal: To create faculty trust in each other and in the principal.

Barriers	Resources
1. Personal lack of knowledge of staff's position.	1. Special meetings to determine strengths and weaknesses of various parents and ways they can contribute.
2. Teachers resistant to becoming aware that there is a problem.	
3. Teachers unaware of their own attitudes toward others.	2. Parents with previous experiences in schools, such as former teachers.
4. Teachers aware of the fact, but reluctant to change it.	3. Parents with expertise in special areas.
5. Some parents opposed to other parents working on these matters.	4. Human relations council in the community.
6. Objections of superintendent or board of education.	5. Community groups—Jaycees, religious clubs, and the like.
7. Parents who are not clear about their feelings toward the school.	6. Parent training programs.
	7. Teachers who encourage parental participation and collaboration.
	8. Personal contact with individuals already respected in the community.
	9. Other principals who have community involvement in their schools.

exercise of informal influence, and the withholding of respect or diligent attention for adults usually represents their major tactics. The net effect is that some teachers do not feel that their students willingly accept their influence. For their part, students often feel impotent to affect major portions of their daily activities in school. The barriers to mutual influence and communication take their toll in decreasing the informal channels of interaction that are necessary to provide the glue for most organizations. As a result, there is little informal processing of grievances in school, and concerns for injustice or change seethe throughout the system until they explode in some formal appeal or public outburst. Alteration of informal influence channels, to make them more accessible to more people in the school, could help ease this situation.

A related target of change efforts is the relatively formal decision-making system in the school. In a multischool system, power to make policy and most program decisions is located in the board of education and the office of the superintendent. Some local autonomy is provided for building principals, along with some further degree of autonomy for classroom instructors. But by and large most teachers feel they have little influence upon many important school decisions. Students share these feelings, indicating no formal involvement in school policy making. The community elects the board, but clearly is isolated from ongoing decisions. Many recent change efforts focus their concerns on the alteration of these decisional structures. To the extent that new representational structures are built, new kinds of people and interests may be located at or near major decisions.

The final characteristic of organizations that is relevant for change efforts is the boundary maintaining system—the system of relations that moderates input—output from the community to the school and the reverse. Who comes in, how students and teachers are selected, is but one example. Who goes out, how students are dropped or graduated—criteria, mechanisms, and the like— how teachers are terminated, are other examples. To the extent that the school exists to serve the community, efforts to change these prime interfaces consume appropriate attention.

Tactics utilized to create change in these aspects or targets of school organizations can vary considerably. One distinguishing characteristic, however, is whether change advocates elect to gain power-parity among subgroups or to accept existing power imparities or inequalities and work within them. For instance, efforts to change organizational structures, to create innovative organizational forms, often begin with some of the following tactics: opening up communications systems, increasing interpersonal trust and interaction among members, broadening the base of involvement in making input to policy issues, establishing cross-status problem-solving groups that work on organizational problems, and having lower-level members advise decision makers on their problems and needs. All of these tactics deal with organizational characteristics in that they differ markedly from tactics of manpower retraining. However, they all occur at the convenience of people with power, and they all

Exercise 11—5. *Planning Organizational Change.*

This exercise can be done by students individually or in a group.

Try to create your own force field. Take as your goal the reorganization of the decision-making structure of the high school you attended, with the specific aim of creating a student-faculty-administration cabinet that made key decisions for all parties in the school. What are the barriers to making such a change? What are the resources you might draw on in such an effort?

Goal: Creation of a student-faculty-administration cabinet that makes decisions.

Barriers   Resources

Have you considered the position of the superintendent? The support that might or might not be forthcoming from the student body? What arguments might be used to support your position, and who would agree with them? What arguments would be likely to be used against you, and who would make them?

---

occur without significant alteration of the imparities and inequalities of the existing power structure.

The importance of power as a problem can be highlighted by suggesting some other tactics: negotiations among groups that have different positions on issues, massive noncompliance (strikes, boycotts) with policy directives, spontaneous protest or confrontation, alteration of the reward structure by the establishment of new norms, and alteration of the power stucture itself. Not all, but some of these tactics clearly suggest that power parity is underway, and that new bases of power have been developed. For instance, negotiation does not occur unless the group in power cannot rule unilaterally and must bargain in order to gain voluntary compliance from other groups. Massive noncompliance generally grows out of divergent values and a sense of impotence that has reached the breaking point: for noncompliance to be massive, rather than individually deviant, a counterorganizational effort must be going on.

Power is not only an important variable in our own framework; for many people its manipulation and alteration represents the key difference between efforts at piecemeal and temporary reform and dramatic or lasting change in social systems. To highlight these issues, Exercise 11–6 is presented on the next pages.

Client or Community Mobilization

The goals of educational systems are tightly enmeshed in the major values and beliefs of the local community. Some analysts argue that community values direct the schools; others indicate the reverse. More cautious scholars argue that these systems are codeterminant and often exist in constant negotiation and interaction with one another. Except for the informal transmissions of values, most community members are involved directly in the school only through the elections of boards of education. We have already indicated the biases inherent in this process, the overloading of school governing bodies with members of white and affluent community groups who are representatives of community powers, but not of the community in its entirety. Students have even less direct influence upon the school than do parents and other members of the community. Of course, to the extent that interaction culminates in influence, students do engage others in the school every day. But they seldom exert formal influence or power over school policy and programs.

These situations have led to an increasing emphasis upon a fourth strategy for school change efforts; one that stresses the organization and expression of power on the part of clients of the educational system—students and members of the local community. "The community" always has influenced the school— the community as represented by political or economic elites. We are talking primarily about new forms of community influence and that means "new communities" and "new clients," as the previously unrepresented speak to their own concerns for the educational system and the changes they advocate in it.

The concern for new avenues of client or community power may focus on two basic targets: (1) altering the values and skills of governing groups; and (2) organizing and articulating the needs and demands of oppressed or relatively powerless groups. The first focus involves retraining powerful people and developing new systems of communication and accountability where elites can get in touch with their constituencies, and vice versa. Members of powerful community groups generally already have access to one another, sometimes in a direct format through meetings, friendships and family settings, and some- times through indirect formats such as clubs and associations, work organiza- tions, and other civic agencies. Members of relatively powerless groups

Exercise 11−6. *Understanding the Role of Power in Organizational Development Efforts*

The following is a list of relatively common tactics utilized to alter organizational aspects of schools. Try to group them on the next page according to (1) the organizational parameters to which they are relevant, and (2) whether they represent tactics of "power system maintenance" or "power system alteration."

1. Developing and using new curricula on human relations.
2. Developing and using new math curricula.
3. Involving parents in curricula development.
4. Involving students in developing new curricula.
5. Having students teach other students.
6. Having grades allocated for group achievements.
7. Giving everyone a B if they always show up to class.
8. Having students help select teachers.
9. Having students help evaluate teachers' performance.
10. Having group meetings of teachers and students to talk over school problems.
11. Having group meetings of teachers and principals to make decisions about school problems.
12. Having retreats where all teachers get to know each other better.
13. Having retreats where black and white students get to know each other better.
14. Making the rules for student behavior clear to everyone.
15. Creating a grievance system whereby student rulebreakers can appeal their punishment.
16. Having students administer the disciplinary system.
17. Asking students to make the rules for student behavior.
18. Asking the faculty to make the rules for student behavior.
19. Asking the students to make the rules for faculty behavior.
20. Making sure everyone who deserves an A really gets it.
21. Making sure everyone who gets an A really deserves it.
22. Teaching teachers how to use student groups in class.
23. Teaching teachers how to use simulation games in class.

24. Teaching administrators how to listen to students better

25. Making sure no parts of the lunchroom are for whites only or for blacks only.

26. Having students sit on the school board in an advisory capacity.

27. Having parents monitor classrooms.

28. Having teachers visit parents at home.

29. Having parents and teachers make a curriculum for each child.

30. Having students and teachers each make a learning contract for the year.

	Tactics	
Organizational Parameters	Power System Maintenance/ Consolidation	Power System Alteration/ Reorganization
Goals		
Rewards Structure/ Allocation Criteria		
Technology Pedagogy Curriculum		
Social Interaction		
Decisional Authority		
Cultural values		
Boundary Systems		
Membership		

generally have little access to governing elites. Thus, their major change efforts to work with the governing elites involve opening up new communication linkages, and making appeals for change. Since the governing of schools is often conceived of as a non-political endeavor, educational leaders are assumed to pursue the general community welfare. As such, appeals to the concern of educational leaders for all the children and the good of the entire community ought to work.

The second focus involves relatively powerless people in generating new forms of organized power with which to express and prosecute their needs and goals. People who have common concerns must get together; express their common grievances, and mobilize their resources of money, personnel, and organization to express and demand attention to their agendas. Powerless groups, as has been previously noted, generally include those who are discriminated against on the basis of their lack of financial resources, their minority racial membership, their age, their sex, or their ethnicity. Major change efforts in this context involve generating enough power to threaten the ability of ruling elites to rule effectively unless they respond to the needs of these groups. Potential takeovers of the governing apparatus by these groups, as in elections or coups, may be unreal but it is possible for them to pose enough of a threat so that elites pay attention to important issues.

In discussing various targets of community-or-client-organized change efforts in schools, it is essential to develop a clear notion of what is meant by "the community." Actually, any community is composed of several subcommunities, which may be identified on the basis of geography; the neighborhood school concept is founded on principles of a geographic definition of community. Subcommunities may also be identified on the basis of potent demographic characteristics that distinguish people according to their resources and lifestyles. Subcommunities based upon these demographic and resource groupings are perhaps more properly called *interest groups*, because people are bound together as a result of their common interests and values. In this society, subcommunities of racial minorities, lower-class class people, young people, or females are consistently in low power positions within their larger geographic communities; they usually are ruled by relatively affluent, white, male, and older groupings.

Organization and mobilization on the basis of interest groupings often focus on the target of establishing new forms of control and accountability in educational systems. This may take the form of greater citizen and student involvement in school decision making, or it may seek more formal mechanisms of accountability, wherein the school and its staff are periodically judged by the community.

Formal evaluations or community review procedures that include the possibility for the review and dismissal of incompetent teachers, principals, and supervisors are seldom implemented. Teacher probationary regulations and tenure laws and the general power of the education profession make it difficult to achieve direct citizen control over the schools. However, in some systems, major strides in this direction have been taken. A key first step in an accountability system is to gather information on the school's performance. This means deciding what to look for and how to find it. Consider the following list of things to look for in a review of elementary school reading programs [3].

Elementary School Diagnosis

1. Does this school have a prekindergarten program? If not, why not? If yes, how many children attend? How many are on a waiting list? How long has the program been in existence? How are the results of the program evaluated? Has the program helped the children learn to read?

2. How many children attend morning kindergarten? Afternoon kindergarten? How many others are on a waiting list? Are the kindergaretn children being taught to read? To recognize letters? To count?

3. How many first graders read at the end of the first grade? How many do not? If some do not, why not?

4. Are children grouped according to reading ability in this school? If so, what is the ethnic composition of the total student body? What per cent of the nonwhite students are in the top reading classes? What per cent are in the lowest reading classes?

5. Does this school have an IGC (Intellectually Gifted Children) class? Does the district have an IGC class? How many children from this school attend such a class? What per cent are black? Puerto Rican? Oriental? White? What is the reading score which a pupil must have in order to be in such a class? How are the teachers selected for these classes?

6. Does this school have CRMD (Children with Retarded Mental Development) classes? Special opportunity classes? Any other special classes for "retarded," "disturbed," or "disruptive" youngsters? How are these children selected for these classes? What per cent of these pupils are nonwhite? How are teachers selected for these classes?

7. Do children have to read on grade level in order to be promoted to the next grade? If not, how many children who were promoted last year were reading below grade level? How many who were promoted read more than one year below grade level? More than two years below? What per cent of these children were nonwhite?

8. What is the following information for each class in this school:

_____ the total number of children in each class

_____ the number of black, Puerto Rican, Oriental, and white children in each class

_____ the number of white and nonwhite children who are reading below and above level in each class

_____ the number of years of teaching experience for each teacher of each class

_____ which of these classes is on short time or double session?

Community-generated accountability systems have to utilize community or student criteria for assessing school outcomes and not merely rely on another battery of professionally controlled and oriented measures. Beyond formal accountability, it is clear that many student organizing efforts, and those in the community as well, are geared toward fuller control of the educational system by its clients. Recent efforts at community control demonstrate both the promises and problems involved in restructuring the relationship between school and community in order to redistribute professional power and help develop student and parent power.

The strategy of community or client mobilization must begin with the identification of indigenous leadership. This leadership must be legitimized and accepted by various elements of the client/constituency system at hand. Trust is vital, for without trust in the leadership undertaking an organizing effort, no client system is likely to trust itself later. And the process of building trust cannot be rushed; it must proceed from the myriad of interpersonal linkages that are the building blocks of new social systems. As people relate to new leadership, and vice versa, and as new leadership encourages persons to relate to one another in new peer arrangements, new social networks are born. In those cases in which indigenous movements seek outside organizers to help initiate activities, she or he must quickly move to help others in the local community develop their own potential and exercise initiative in organizing others. Only in this way can local groups avoid dependency on outsiders and the ultimate political stagnation of a youth movement or community campaign.

Another requirement is the development of a collectively important set of issues or concerns. Regardless of objective definitions of the existence of a community, a subcommunity, or an interest group, no politically relevant community exists until the people who are (potentially) a part of it feel welded to one another on a set of issues that they feel, care about, and are committed to working on. Issues of this kind are often plentiful. But the school, for instance, teaches rebellious students that each of them is different and perhaps inadequate, and that they are not part of a group with legitimate concerns and issues that ought to be prosecuted through a political system. Many parents are given the same message in individual conferences that stress their child's problems, not the school's failures. Therefore, it is critical that a set of issues be developed and collectivized as a means of organizing and mobilizing a community for action.

Protests or confrontation tactics may sometimes be necessary to engage the attention of those who are in power. Lurie suggests a moderate level of confrontation tactics that might be helpful in holding a New York City school accountable for what it achieves with students [4].

Other Steps to Take

1. If your school does not improve, go to your local school board and district superintendent. Demand that they hold the principal accountable for achieving results or get a new principal.

2. You may also want to take a committee of parents to the UFT to put pressure on the union to improve the performance of its teachers.

3. You may want to hire an attorney to sue in the courts or to appeal to the State Education Commissioner. Under (New York) State Education Law 3604, "proper instruction" must be given in every school. Under Regents Rule 28, state aid may be withdrawn from school districts who do not maintain an approved curriculum.

4. Release your findings to the press, your local elected leaders, the federal Department of Education, and anyone else you think may be helpful. Be sure you are always specific. Describe carefully what you have asked, and what you have found.

5. *Beware of this danger*: Principals will try to "buy off" the most articulate parents in your group by assigning their children to the top classes and best teachers, or offering to transfer them to a "better school." *Don't* attack parents who take advantage of this offer. Remember their children, too, have only one chance for an education. Find ways to include these parents in your committee so you can still work together.

Such activities should be carefully planned, because many school leaders and some parents will look for ways to discredit new political movements on the basis of the extreme tactics and "lack of good sense" used. Carefully organized protests can be very helpful in raising issues, solidifying a nascent client organization, recruiting members, and requiring ruling elites to discuss issues with client groups. Mobilization efforts by students must employ even more deliberate means to achieve desired goals, particularly the use of "arts" such as diplomacy. Students are particularly vulnerable, both as individuals and even as an organized group. Too much of American culture and even social science represents youth as volatile and irresponsible. Without evidence to the contrary, adults are not likely to see youth as reasonable wielders of power. And even with evidence, the goals and needs of youth may be so different from those of the adults with whom they work that adults may find it most offensive to accede to the demands of youth. Especially for youth, careful choices must be made between strategies of communication and appeal, and strategies of power and threat.

In this context, tactics of negotiations become vital. Negotiations are not likely to occur unless people holding power see that it is in their interest to compromise and discuss changes with those out of power. In this sense, negotiations reflect at least temporary alterations in power; people have to be approximately equal, or at least mutually vulnerable, to negotiate. When and how to negotiate, or to escalate protests and confrontations, and to go back and forth, are highly developed skills in community mobilization and change.

Finally, any mobilizing effort must seek reforms that can be implemented in ways that continue to support and reward new ways of doing things. The products of mobilizing must be realizable and visible in new ways of doing business in schools that recognize the legitimate rights of clients to share in the control of an educational system that is ultimately accountable to them. In fact, some scholars have maintained that community participation in educational decision making represents the most plausible approach to institutional reform. Beyond reform, some degree of community control over education decision making represents the most likely ingredient to any lasting change in the structure and processes of schooling.

Influencing Political-Economic Elites and Policy Makers

The organization of schooling does not exist in a vacuum, isolated within a given building separated from the community in which it resides. Similarly, patterns of local community activity are tied inevitably to the political-economic base of resources and services found in the region or city. The school is one public arena that serves many of the people in a given locale; as such it requires interaction and collective effort from groups of people who may have seldom worked together before.

As noted in Chapter 4, and again in Chapter 10, the nature of a community's economic resources generally has enormous impact on the funds that are available for the operation and support of schooling. People concerned with altering this aspect of schooling may take one of two general tacks: (1) altering the total amount of monies available for schooling, in terms of total tax or millage revenues; or (2) altering the distributive process that determines what portions of the community pay how much for common public schools. In either case, such change efforts inevitably require appeals or challenges to the local political system, and to the priorities, interests, and loyalties of political-economic elites.

The role of the political-economic elites in a community is relevant for the conduct of schooling even if those elites are not directly involved in the governance of schooling, per se. These elites often help determine the general character of the employment market, and the kinds of skills required for effective work opportunities. Thus, the elites hire the "products" of schooling, and help establish what skills these "products" should have. They also affect the general economic health of a community and, as such, determine much of the societal context for educational issues. Since these elites also help determine the appropriate actions of the active or inactive citizenry, they set the example for the kinds of politics that are effective and that can be modeled for the young.

In any sizable community these economic and political elites do not operate solely at the local level, and changes in their operation cannot focus solely on local schools. Corporate executives and elected representatives often operate at the metropolitan, regional, state, and national levels of decision making about educational policies and programs. Decisions on energy matters, for instance, which are jointly negotiated by economic managers and political representatives, have great implications for the physical operation of school buildings, but also for the employment levels of graduates and nongraduates, as well as their future taxes and economic well-being. State and federal policy with regard to education may impact more directly on schools, but no less potently than the general state of the economy.

Since many decisions relevant to local education are made beyond the local community, a major change strategy focuses on influencing those elites who make social policy. Changes in national values and commitments clearly are reflected in the organization and conduct of our schools, and changes in these national priorities sometimes occur fairly rapidly. There are three major targets for a strategy based upon the manipulation of social policy and elite decision making. One target is the legislative system, and the making of laws governing the public conduct or content of schooling. A second target is the judiciary and its role in conducting hearings or deciding cases relevant to education. The third target is executive action and the many activities of federal and state agencies that provide support and leadership for regular and special education programs.

Some examples of the operations of legislative efforts as an avenue of educational change are provided by the experiences with congressional action on new funds for education. Special passage of funds for Innovative Projects, for compensatory aid to districts with large numbers of "disadvantaged" youngsters, and for assistance to school systems trying to desegregate their schools are illustrative of this action. Further, efforts are currently underway to influence state legislatures to pass the Equal Rights Amendment, which would affect women's rights in schools as well as in other public arenas. Action has also been recently taken in city councils and state houses on marijuana initiatives, efforts to legalize or reduce the penalties for smoking or selling marijuana.

Examples of efforts to bring about school change by working through the judiciary include a number of fairly recent and potent examples. The process of school desegregation is largely the fruit of changes brought about in the judicial arena. Recent court decisions affecting many of the largest school systems in the nation have received national attention, prompting a number of large urban systems to seriously reconsider their own status regarding the shaping of school attendance zones, and racially discriminatory practices within schools. Another example of change through the judicial arena is seen in the courts' activities to alter the patterns of school financing and in the attack on local property taxes as the sole base for raising school funds. The rights of youth also have been tested in the courts and many school administrators have had to revise their managerial styles and practices as a result. Judicial appeals have energized efforts to protect the civil rights and liberties of students as a class deserving of the same rights of due process, privacy, and freedom of speech and assembly as other Americans.

The strategy of seeking changes in schools through actions of the executive branch of government may be even more widespread and visible, as is appropriate in an age of highly active and centralized executive power. Presidential and gubernatorial commissions have examined national issues relevant to education, and have come up with findings and recommendations which are often translated into new policy and program. The Koerner Commission on Violence, and the Presidential Pornography Commission, to mention only two, have been relevant for school issues and designs. The actions of the Office of Economic Opportunity in setting guidelines and policies for disadvantaged youngsters, communities, and schools have affected ghetto and barrio education, in particular. The U.S. Office of Education has created a number of programs that have been implemented on local levels. These programs range from school lunches to aid in retraining teachers, from support for voucher programs and educational alternatives to the development of new classroom curricula. Child-care programs and emphases upon vocational and career education are only a few of the more recent thrusts of these federal executive agencies. In any particular state department of education, one can find similar examples, such as the adoption of a voucher system that might free schools from restrictions which accompany their monopolistic privileges, encouraging diversity and choice within the public school system itself.

The tactics utilized to promote changes in social policy and programs are in many ways similar across legislative, judicial, and executive options. In all cases, changes at these levels require gaining access to the governing elites. Moreover, changes cannot be hurried, and any particular grievance or injustice may get buried or bypassed by the time an agency can respond. There also is many a slip between policy and action, and change at the policy level does not automatically mean that new things will happen in the local building or classroom. At the same time, changes that occur through the use of these strategies have a good chance of becoming firmly institutionalized, and being maintained over time. Such changes carry the weight of new public values and lawful order, and although they may be resisted, the moral shoe is on the other foot. The location of power, of course, varies.

One obvious set of tactics would be to present a formal appeal through proper judicial channels or through one's appropriate legislative representative. Appeals that are buttressed with visions about how these changes will fit the needs of the prevailing elites clearly make it easier for policy structures managed by these elites to respond. Long-standing relationships of an interpersonally close or functionally integrative character may also help gain attention and action. It is in this context that so many former corporate executives seek and find leadership positions in local school and community groups—they are seen as having an "in" with people in power and an appropriate set of policy-relevant skills.

On the other hand, if strategies of appeal and interpersonal connection do not appear feasible or desirable, strategies of threat and coercion can be utilized. Emerging community or student movements of a nonelite character may generate substantial power, particularly in a single legislative district, and thus be able to command rapid attention and response. In many cases, merely the threat to take judicial action or to create a new power base to challenge current representatives will unlock old commitments to policy and practice.

Exercise 11−7 can help summarize the discussion of legislative, judicial, and executive action that may be employed to change schools. In your study of this exercise, consider the various ways in which these three social policy arenas have been instrumental in efforts to alter the locus of power and control of schooling, efforts that range from debates over the power and function of states and local communities through the role of finances and financial control. Similarly, consider the various actions taken with regard to the roles and rights of professionals in schooling, ranging from certification of professionals through decisions about the nature of due process, including the recent focus upon new curriculum offerings. And, finally, consider the multifold influence of these social policy systems on efforts to alter discrimination in schools, and the schools' role in maintaining or encouraging discrimination.

Establishment of Institutional Alternatives

An increasingly popular strategy for change in schools involves leaving them more or less as they are, and setting up alternative models outside the schools. The thrust of this strategy is to go beyond the political and institutional constraints of existing systems and to imagine, invent, and try to operate with new structures for learning and teaching. Sometimes these systems are ends in themselves in that they represent new environs for teachers and students. At other times, the ends of these new systems are realized in the traditional system's efforts to renew or innovate itself by adopting some aspects of the alternative system.

Exercise 11−7. *Identifying Examples of Legislative, Executive, and Judicial Approaches to School Change*

The following list provides some examples of policy actions that seek or sought to alter schools through the use of the judicial, the legislative, or the executive branch of government; try to place each in its appropriate column and row.

1. *Brown* v. *Topeka Board of Education.*

2. *Bradley* v. *Milliken.*

3. Requirement that parent advisory councils approve plans for desegregation programs before new federal monies can be allocated.

4. Sending federal troops to Central High School, Little Rock, Arkansas.

5. Koerner Commission on Crisis in North American Cities.

6. Federal guidelines on sex discrimination.

7. State equalization programs designed to make funds available for students in varying school districts more comparable.

8. *Tinker* v. *Des Moines*

9. *Serrano* v. *Priest*

10. Sending federal troops to newly desegregated neighborhoods in Boston.

11. Federal and state financing of teacher retraining programs in newly desegregated school districts.

12. Bayh senate committee hearings on violence, crime, and vandalism in the schools.

The innovations reflected in alternative systems appears to be largely focused upon learning structures that release students from a high degree of adult, professional control. Thus, some alternative systems emphasize student autonomy and peer-directed learning as antidotes to adult-directed activities. Other alternative systems have been set up by students themselves, and are run by them, including their own hiring of any adult staff they feel they need. Attempts to escape the racism that is prevalent within traditional schools has led to the development of black- or brown-controlled alternatives in some major cities. All three experiments, whether public or private, represent major alterations in the structure of the learning activity and the content of the cultural curriculum.

The desire to generate a new curriculum, one that is more in tune with

13. Proposed constitutional amendment to prevent use of federal funds for school busing.

14. Provision of federal funds for school lunch programs in some schools.

15. Requirement that students have a written code of rights and responsibilities and conduct.

16. Programs stressing affirmative action in staff hiring.

17. Prohibition against strikes or work stoppages by public employees (including teachers).

18. Urban plans/programs for the administrative decentralization of schools.

19. Urban plans/programs of subcommunity control of schools.

20. Transfer of funding base of schools from local millage elections to state tax revenues.

Issues	*Tactics*		
	Legislative	Judicial	Executive
Power and Control of Schooling			
Professional Roles and Rights			
Discrimination			
Other			

youth's own desires for learning, seems to be another main innovation in alternative schools. Some observers have promoted alternative schooling systems as a way to avoid and counter the traditional stress upon schooling as a credentializing apparatus, a channel for the class-stagnating system of economic, racial, and sexual discrimination in the society at large.

One of the major approaches utilized in the alternative movement is the generation of an innovative subsystem within the traditional school system. The Parkway Program in Philadelphia, special academic programs in many large city systems, and the pluralistic range present in the Berkeley, California, schools are examples of this tactic. The view of the proponents of this tactic is that the public system must be maintained and that the creation of a demonstration alternative may be the way to encourage or engender change in the larger institution. Although this is a popular and often feasible tactic, it may run into trouble maintaining support from the larger system. Minor pilot programs that do not immediately spread to the larger system are notoriously shortlived. They tend to get swallowed up and to be themselves the target of change and reinclusion rather than the reverse.

A second major approach has been to leave the traditional public school system and to create new schools outside of old channels. These "free" schools may have special arrangements with the accrediting system, or they may be completely on their own. To the extent that they last, and draw more than a few students, they usually link up with some mainstream institution in order to serve as an effective accrediting ground for later college attendance or reentry to the regular school system. Sometimes these alternatives are established by students; other cases have included teachers or parents as the initiators or coinitiators in a community experiment. To the extent that these alternatives attract some of the school's "best" students, they may represent a substantial threat to the traditional school. However, to the extent that these alternative schools draw students primarily from the white and upper middle-class groups, they also help to perpetuate a separatist and elitist vision of education and educational experimentation.

A third tactical approach argues that schooling as we know it and can imagine it operating within major institutional settings is obsolete and should be abolished. Some observers assume the inevitable indefensibility of schools and thus the disestablishment of public schools. They link this inevitability to political and cultural crises in the larger society, and probe the implications of deschooling. Here, the call is not for substitutes of a more humane character but for a complete end to formal schooling. In this view, young people should move around the society, undertaking a variety of internship experiences that would benefit them more than the experiences they currently are having in schools. The focus of concern is as much on an end to societal credentializing as upon the state of affairs within given educational institutions. For those who are ready to reject major aspects of the North American society this is an attractive alternative, a way into seriously countercultural styles of life. For those who feel that they still need to live within the larger society, perhaps those without the resources to sustain a survival level of existence outside the mainstream of society, credentialized institutions remain more or less necessary.

All these alternative forms of education have certain aspects in common. Together with compatible new modes for family, work, religion, and the like, alternative schooling can be the start of a new culture that stands as a working alternative to the old. In order to lessen the functional dominance of elites it is necessary to reduce one's dependence upon them, especially for learning about future roles. People taking this approach will have to participate in developing new schools that are small, economical, governed by clients, and in areas and neighborhoods where they are needed. Moreover, these schools will have to:

1. Design the social architecture of alternative schools—ones that are humane and democratic.

2. Teach principles of societal analysis as part of its curriculum.

3. Help to form a learning community that can teach-learn itself and govern itself.

4. Learn, and help others to learn, nonexploitative and communalist ways of behaving (including, naturally enough, nonracist, nonsexist, nonclass elitist and nonageist ways of being).

5. Link to traditional or mainstream institutions to help maintain contacts, engender certification, or do public relations work for the alternative school.

ANALYSIS OF CHANGE STRATEGIES: INTEGRATING STRATEGIES AND ISSUES

This chapter has been organized in ways that separately consider a variety of change targets delineated in pursuit of a series of high priority goals or issues for change. But very seldom is one single target selected for a change program, and multiple-target, multiple-issue campaigns are common. An integrative matrix of targets and issues is conceptualized in the chart in Table 11—3.

In working with strategy 1, retraining, it is easy to see how this might be relevant to any of the major issues running across the top of the chart. Reorganization of the classroom, however, seems most appropriate for implementing changes for issues C and D; new classroom technologies and new definitions of the role of the teacher as a professional generally require new ways of organizing the classroom. In some of the classroom examples, it would also involve alteration of the organization's decision making system and new relations with certain constituencies in the community.

Client/community mobilization strategies might be relevant for a number of issues, but be undertaken quite differently in different cases. For instance, efforts by elites to mobilize in order to maintain the status quo with respect to power and control (A), stabilization of channeling systems (B), and legitimation of discrimination (E) obviously works to the advantage of affluent, white, and male groups in the community. These efforts work to the disadvantage of low-power groups. Efforts to mobilize on behalf of low-power consumer/client groups would go about the business of change on these issues quite differently.

Alteration of the political-economic elites and social policy changes are not likely to have much direct impact on issues of classroom technology (D) or professional roles (C); these issues are more often settled on the local level and within the organizational apparatus of schooling. But if the societal settings of racial and sexual and class discrimination require discrimination and channeling

Table 11–3. Integrating Strategies of Change and Major Issues in Schools

Strategies	A. Power and Control	B. Channel-ing	Issues C. Profes-sional Roles	D. Classroom Technology	E. Discrimi-nation
1. Manpower Re-training					
2. Classroom Reor-ganization					
3. Organizational Development or Modification					
4. Community/ Client Mobiliza-tion					
5. Influencing Politi-cal-Economic Elites and Social Policy Makers					
6. Establishing Insti-tutional Alerna-tives					

in schools for their support, then it is clear that work on these target arenas could significantly alter the shape of these issues in schools. The same is true of power and control issues, which are only partly alterable by changes in the school organization itself, and much more powerfully and dramatically altered by the reorganization of external target groups, such as political and economic decision-making systems.

The strategy of developing alternative systems is probably most likely to be helpful on issues of professional roles and classroom technology (C and D). Alternatives are not likely to have a major impact on other issues unless they are large-scale alternatives, involving many students, many new resource patterns, new student outcomes, and the like.

One set of problems in school change that has been addressed throughout these pages is the tactics one might use to operate any of these strategies, or for that matter with any of these issues. Generally one set of tactics can be delineated based on appeal-communication-trust, and another set can be delineated based on threat-power. These two approaches have their basic roots in some very different assumptions about the nature of societies and social change. For instance, the appeal-communication-trust tactics generally are rooted in a consensual or collaborative notion of social systems and social change, whereas the threat-power tactics are more securely rooted in a conflictual view of these systems.

The consensus approach generally assumes that various organizational and community members have similar (or complementary) interests and shared norms. The basic glue that holds organizations and communities together is trust in others and in the authorities who make binding decisions for the entire system. In this context, one can assume that a relatively rational and open problem-solving process will permit everyone to participate as they wish, and to work together to solve organizational or community problems. Thus, the basic tactic utilized to make changes is collaborative problem solving. When problem solving fails to work effectively, or misses key issues, it is assumed that this is accidental rather than conscious. Therefore, increased communication probably will provide the basic information required to broaden the elites' decision-making perspective. Groups that feel that their needs and interests are not being met should use tactics of appeal, wherein they serve up their concerns to powerful people who they expect will have goodwill toward them. In this context, these groups can expect that their needs will be responded to positively.

For many educators, concerns with social justice and social equality are not mere rhetoric but are deeply internalized values and beliefs. Thus, an outright appeal to increase social justice and educational equality may help change attitudes and practices, promote humanism in educational structures, and otherwise have a positive impact upon school policy and programs. In general, some of the following specific tactics might be utilized.

1. Documenting low-power groups' pain, failure, and sense of injustice in the current organization of systems' benefits and operations.

2. Requesting or appealing to elites' sense of social justice to alter the system to better serve other groups' needs.

3. Increasing communication about all groups' needs and activities.

4. Presenting grievances to official decision makers.

5. Helping demonstrate to elites their own involvement in networks of social oppression.

6. Aiding elites to develop new analyses of the social system and their own survival interests.

7. Aiding elites to identify new social practices that may close the gap between the "is" and the "ought."

8. Retraining elites in the practice of more democratic or humane management procedures or instructional technologies—learning new ways to teach and administer.

9. Conducting attitude change programs that seek to resocialize whites, males, and affluent people into antiracist, antisexist, anticlass-elitist ideologies.

10. Reducing adults' fears of the potentials of youth explosion and dissolution.

11. Helping elites examine themselves and the situation so as to reduce their realistic fears—hand holding.

12. Identifying the "good guys" and giving them lots of stroking and support for their own difficult work. [5]

These tactics are likley to work if elites are supportive, or somewhat supportive, of the changes desired. But, if elites are clearly, vocally, or rather irrevocably opposed to change in the direction of social justice objectives, aid to them is most likely to be counterproductive and inadvisable.

The conflict approach generally assumes that various organizational and community members have differing interests (on the basis of race and sex and class and age), and that values are not shared in common. The basic glue that holds organizations and communities together is the interdependence required for mutual survival and the ability of one group to exert enough power to rule the system. People do not necessarily trust each other, and certainly, low-power groups do not trust the authorities to make decisions in their interest. Thus, the basic tactic utilized to make changes involves bargaining and negotiations, wherein groups with fairly equal power (or at least sufficient power to hurt one another) assess each other's strengths and make decisions that will protect and compromise everyone's needs. When this process fails to work smoothly, it is assumed to be because one group has managed to gain sufficient power to get away with ignoring or disregarding another group's needs and interests. More communication would not help in this situation; in fact, it might even give away important secrets that could be used to increase the power imbalance (e.g., secrets about one's strengths or weaknesses, fallback positions, allies in "high places", and so on). Increased efforts to mobilize one's power, or to neutralize opponents' power, is the appropriate step to take. This may take the form of gathering more potent resources—money, people, organization—or threatening other groups' stability and ability to govern, by creating disorder, threatening disruption, fragmenting ruling coalitions, and the like.

Specific tactics that might challenge the well-being and continued domination of elites may be mobilized in several ways:

1. Publicizing (gathering and exposing) elites' attitudes and actions, powers and privileges—including those of community groups who control school boards or school administrators and/or teachers who control students.

2. Documenting mechanisms of control in schools and communities.

3. Publicizing information and interpretations that contradict public information myths which school systems generate about their performance, resources, and the like.

4. Developing programs that challenge the nonschool-related activities of elites.

5. Confronting elites' ability to govern schools through threats, demonstrations, crises, legal action, walkouts, and the like.

6. Developing new ways of recruiting managers (administrators and teachers) of schools that bypass traditional elite roles and socialization experiences—and that thereby flood the system with minorities, women, poor people, working-class people, and the young.

7. Identifying inequities, oppressions, or failures in the delivery of services to school clients (or to specific racial, class, and sex-role groups of clients).

8. Organizing interest groups based on peoples' subjective awareness of their alienation and the objective conditions of oppression. [6]

These challenges to elites probably are aided by complementary work mobilizing oppressed groups, so that the challenge is more than rhetorical but is backed by new forms of strategic power.

In the context of community mobilization efforts, the consensus approach might endeavor to create a broad-based community problem-solving process. Representatives would be sought from all portions of the community and from all racial and class groups. When these people are brought together, they may be asked to respond to various problems or visions and to develop programs or policies that might create solutions to these problems. Another consensus tactic could involve a professionally designed planning process. These same representatives of various groups could work together with educators or expert consultants to plan the school system's approach to reducing discrimination or making changes in professional roles. The rational basis of community planning efforts rests on the ability of all members of the community to utilize the technical skills of professional experts who are committed to the general welfare and to be able to work together, to focus on common problems, and to agree with one another on mutually satisfactory solutions. A third tactic in this same line, and one that is central to either of the other two, is widespread dissemination of information about the school system, professionals' views of the needs of various groups, the rationale for channeling, current student outcomes, and so on.

In the same context of community mobilization the conflict approach would endeavor to organize members of particular interest groups who feel they are excluded or suffering as a result of current school policy and/or program. These members would get together and try to articulate the particular needs they have in common that are different from those of other groups, and to develop a coherent vision of needed changes. Then, they would look toward allies and uncommitted groups to generate the resources required to make a credible threat to school authorities' ability to govern the system. Threatened or actually carried out demonstrations, teacher and student strikes, and parent or service group boycotts are all examples of these strategies in action. Another conflict tactic involves the development of coalitions among groups that feel aggrieved. Although this perspective primarily calls for blacks to organize among blacks, and Spanish-speaking groups to organize themselves, it also includes the possibility that both these groups could pool their particular needs, visions, and resources in a minority coalition that might be able to exert more power than either one could alone. By the same token, minority and majority group students have on occasion developed interracial coalitions to pressure school authorities to respond to their common needs as a larger group of oppressed students. The common feature of both of these examples is the attempt to exert pressure on the system of power and control as it is currently organized. It also seeks to promote school accountability to client groups and to hold educators responsible for the educational outcomes they create.

Consensus tactics designed to alter the school organization build on, and seek to extend, the assumed consensus among all members. Starting with top managerial levels and continuing to involve official decision makers in central ways, members of other groups are consulted for input or are included as collaborators in the processes of planning and implementing change. The involvement of various groups in organizational problem solving and the attendant generation and use of new information as a basis for consensus and persuasion are critical. At the same time, legitimate authority and the power of established leaders are also used as a basis of the change process, although the use of such influence is not highlighted.

Conflict tactics relevant to organizational change stress especially the inclusion of often excluded groups, such as parents and students, in decision making and in the implementation of change. Thus, the conflict perspective often starts at the bottom and develops new "grass roots" resources for change. But both powerful and powerless groups can employ strategies that have their basis in conflict, power, and self-interest. Central to this change approach are processes of interest group organization and the mobilization and control of resources that are converted to effective power. At the same time, capabilities of information retrieval and problem solving can be employed occasionally as part of the change process.

In terms of manpower retraining efforts, the consensus approach, with its stress on information and trust, generally gives priority to attitudinal retraining and skill development programs. The assumption usually is made that people of goodwill wish to change and improve their own lives and the lives of others. Professional experts, such as educators, who are seen to have the best interests of students at heart, are particularly expected to want to learn how to meet the needs of students more effectively.

The conflict approach makes no such assumption about the inherent goodwill or altruism of professional educators. Rather, it sees these persons as members of an interest group committed to the maintenance of their own power and privilege in the system. Therefore, a retraining program for them would be accountable to and maybe even monitored by lower groups. Other strategies for changing individuals might include embarrassment and harassment, such as collecting evidence of racism, sexism, or incompetence, and using those materials in dismissal hearings. Similar tactics can be utilized by teacher groups seeking to remove a principal or alter the composition of the school board. Once again, without assumptions of trust and goodwill, power needs to be exercized to protect and/or advance one's interests.

Throughout this discussion we have stressed the distinctions between consensus tactics and conflict tactics of change. In practice, however, the differences may not be that sharp. These two tactics or families of tactics are by no means mutually exclusive, and they can be "mixed" or joined in any overall program of change. They may also be combined in a sequential manner. For instance, some persons concerned with change stress beginning with consensus-based tactics, and trying communication and collaborative problem solving first. If those tactics do not work, then shift to more conflict-based tactics; even having tried to reason first may be good for public relations and may help gain support from uncommitted portions of the organization or community. On the other hand, some persons stress beginning with conflict-based tactics, and then scaring or softening up the opposition so they will respond to communicative and collaborative efforts later. Since it is important to avoid rigidity in tactical planning, it is always wise to consider the utility of any and all tactics of change. Since it is also important to avoid confusion, it is wise to consider the assumptive base of different tactics and to employ those tactics that best fit the situation and the values and resources of change groups.

The ways in which these different tactics might be utilized with various strategies are summarized in a matrix format in Table 11–4. The trust-communication-appeal approach can be compared with the conflict-power-threat approach as each might apply to the six major change strategies discussed in this chapter. The reader could fruitfully go back through this chapter, and see how other discussions and lists of change actions fit with these two approaches. The reader could also examine the other charts and matrices, and then line them up together with the one that follows. The result ought to be a richer and wider set of alternative tactics and strategies that can be utilized in pursuit of school change.

SUMMARY

What is the point of gaining knowledge if it does not affect behavior in some way? What is the point of readers knowing the successes and failures of the North American educational system if they do not use that knowledge in some way to improve that system? We are committed to the integration of knowledge and action, and to thinking through what actions might be appropriate to alter, correct, or otherwise improve the factors and variables and institutional

Table 11–4. A Summary of Change Strategies and Tactical Approaches

Strategies	Tactical Approaches	
	Consensus (appeal, communication, trust)	Conflict (threat, power)
Manpower Retraining		
Classroom Reorganization		
Organizational Development or Modification		
Community/Client Mobilization		
Influencing Political-Economic Elites and Social Policy Makers		
Establishment of Institutional Alternatives		

operations reviewed in this book. This is an essential part of our entire inquiry together with our readers.

What one does to change, or improve, a situation depends heavily on one's interpretation of the situation and why it occurs. We have, throughout this book, offered several ways of interpreting data about our school systems, and each reader has been encouraged to make her or his own interpretive choices. Now comes the time to put that to the test. In this chapter we have presented a range of ways of acting for change, ways that are more or less attractive depending upon what we each see as important problems and what we can imagine doing about these problems.

The first change strategy discussed is changing persons, altering the attitudinal or behavioral characteristics of consumers (students and/or parents) or staff members (teachers, administrators, or service personnel) of schools. This is an enormously popular strategy, one on which our entire system of education is based—as educators basically try to implement individual change strategies to change (educate) youth themselves. The same approach can be used to change others.

One of the key mechanisms in school is the utilization of groups of students in the classroom as the learning arena. For better or worse, most schools operate with a teacher and twenty to thirty students as the primary learning and interactional unit. Thus, it is appropriate to explore possible alternatives to the way in which that unit is organized and operates. What new instructional techniques, grouping procedures, curriculum, and the like appear to be interesting and appropriate for change? Some would do away with this unit completely, preferring to work with smaller and more shifting units of primary contact and interaction.

A third change strategy focuses upon changing the organizational context within which educators and educational consumers interact, and within which the classroom exists. This approach takes seriously the dictum that you cannot change individuals without (first?) altering the situation in which they are located—their working conditions. Within that general notion, many further choices are to be made about altering the structure of organizations (decision making, membership, communication patterns) or the culture (norms, styles of work). They can be altered from the inside or the outside, gently or harshly, slowly or quickly, and so on.

Since the school is a community institution, an appropriate change strategy could focus on altering the nature of that community or its systematic relationships with the school. Such alteration generally requires efforts to inform the community about school operations and to build a new sense of concern and caring about the possibilities of change. Communities that are satisfied with their schooling, or which do not know enough about what is going on in the schools not to be satisfied, will not engage in change. Thus, building and mobilizing communities of concern is a first step in the development of this strategy of community action.

Just as the local school is linked in interdependent ways to the local community, so too is it linked to the larger structures of the North American political and economic system. In fact, this linkage is so critical, some observers suggest that there is no way to alter the nature of local educational services without altering either the structure of the political economy or the policies and programs created by political and economic decision makers. We do not agree with this argument; we think that there are many albeit small but important things to do at the local level without worrying about the larger societal sphere. But the argument has merit nevertheless, and should be attended to. We agree that wholesale change in a school, or significant change in an entire system, is not likely to occur without some major changes in societal policy and program regarding our schools. Thus, it is important that all of us think carefully about those legislative, executive, and judicial battles that affect the financing, organization, management and very content of education in the United States.

Finally, we have suggested that one can alter the outcomes of schooling, if not the conduct of it, by creating alternatives to the massive public system. Inside the system, or outside, one can create new and experimental schools that may speak more clearly and effectively to the needs of individual youngsters or to special groups who have decided to try new paths.

Throughout our discussion of change strategies, we have continually returned to the choices we, and each reader, must make with regard to what the problem is, and what the way of making change should be. Thus, we have suggested two very different tactical approaches to making change, through the creation and utilization of consensus approaches and through the utilization and creation of conflict approaches. Like all other choices raised in this book, the reader may appropriately select either option, or try to integrate them in a coherent mix. But also like other choices, the reader is urged to think through the differences, and to determine which tactical approach appeals most clearly to his or her own assumptions and explanations of the reasons American education is the way it is, and the likelihood that change can be made on one basis rather than another.

CHAPTER REFERENCES

Chapter 1

1. Wallace, A. "Schools in Revolutionary and Conservative Societies." In *Anthropology and Education*. Ed. by Frederick C. Gruber. Philadelphia: University of Pennsylvania Press, 1961, pp. 26–27.
2. Cooley, C. H. *Human Nature and the Social Order*. New York: Charles Scribner's Sons, 1922.
3. Mead, G. H. *Mind, Self and Society*. Chicago: University of Chicago Press, 1934.
4. Mead, M. "Growing Up in New Guinea." In *Sociological Foundations of Education*. Ed. by J. Roucek and Associates. New York: Thomas Y. Crowell Company, 1942, pp. 57–58.
5. Ibid., pp. 58–59.
6. Lippit, R. "The Socialization Community." In W. Cave and M. Chesler. *Sociology of Education*. New York: Macmillan Publishing Co., Inc., 1974, p. 339.
7. Collier, P., and D. Horowitz. *The Rockefellers*. New York: New American Library, 1976, p. 13.
8. Ibid., p. 79.
9. Ibid., pp. 180–181.
10. Ibid., p. 523.
11. Floud, J., and A. H. Halsey. "Education and Social Structure: Theories and Methods." In *Readings on the School in Society*. Ed. by P. Sexton. Englewood Cliffs, N.J.: Prentice-Hall, Inc., 1967, p. 4.
12. Adapted from Gabriel, R. *Traditional Values in American Life*. New York: Harcourt Brace Jovanovich, Inc., 1963, pp. 17, 21–22.
13. Rugg, H., and W. Withers. *Social Foundations of Education*. Englewood Cliffs, N.J.: Prentice-Hall, Inc., 1955. Grambs, J. *School, Scholars and Society*. Englewood Cliffs, N.J.: Prentice Hall, Inc., 1965.
14. Adapted from Spindler, G. "Education in a Transforming American Culture." In

Education and Culture: Anthropological Approaches. Ed. by G. D. Spindler. New York: Holt, Rinehart and Winston, Inc., 1963, pp. 136−137.

15. Merton, R. *Social Theory and Social Structure.* New York: The Free Press, 1957, pp. 131−160.

16. Steward, G., and M. Cole. *Minorities and the American Promise.* New York: Harper & Row, Publishers, Inc., 1956, pp. 135−136.

17. Greer, C. *The Great School Legend.* New York: Basic Books, Inc., 1972, p. 64.

18. Kane, J. "The Social Structure of American Catholics." As quoted in C. Greer, op. cit., p. 78.

19. Novak, M. *The Rise of the Unmeltable Ethnics.* New York: Macmillan Publishing Co., Inc., 1972, p. 60.

20. Ibid., pp. 62−63.

21. *Bintel Brief.* Trans. by Isaac Metzker. New York: Doubleday & Co., 1971, pp. 94−94.

22. Ibid., pp. 162−163.

23. Payne, G. "Education and Cultural Pluralism." In *One America.* Ed. by F. J. Brown and J. S. Roucek. Englewood Cliffs, N.J.: Prentice-Hall, Inc., 1951.

24. See generally: Wallace, op. cit., p. 38.

25. Ibid., p. 41.

26. Kneller, G. *Educational Anthropology: An Introduction.* New York: John Wiley & Sons, Inc., 1965, p. 92.

27. As appeared in Morrison, D. R. *Education and Politics in Africa: The Tanzanian Case.* London: C. Hurst & Co., 1976, p. 258.

28. Ibid., pp. 259−260.

29. Medlin, W. K., W. M. Cave, and F. Carpenter. *Education and Development in Central Asia.* Leiden, The Netherlands: E. J. Brill Co., 1971.

30. Freire, P. "The Adult Literacy Process as Cultural Action for Freedom." *Harvard Educational Review*, **40**, no. 2 (1970), 207.

31. Friedenberg, E. Z. *Coming of Age in America.* New York: Random House, Inc., 1963, p. 49.

32. Gabriel, op. cit., pp. 15, 16.

33. Ryan, W. *Blaming the Victim.* New York: Pantheon Books, Inc., 1971.

Chapter 2

1. Adapted from Gabriel, R. *Traditional Values in American Life.* New York: Harcourt Brace Jovanovich, Inc., 1963.

2. Weber, M. *The Protestant Ethic and the Spirit of Capitalism.* Tran. by Talcott Parsons. New York: Charles Schribner's Sons, 1930.

3. Myrdal, G. *An American Dilemma: The Negro Problem and Modern Democracy.* New York: Harper & Row, Publishers, Inc., 1944.

4. This debate is framed in the works of: Edwards, R., M. Reich and T. Weisskopf. *The Capitalist System: A Radical Analysis of American Society.* Englewood Cliffs, N.J.: Prentice-Hall, Inc., 1972; Sweezy, P., and H. Magdoff. *The Dynamics of U.S. Capitalism: Corporate Structure, Credit, Gold and the Dollar.* New York: Monthly Review Press, 1972; Galbraith, J. *The New Industrial State.* Boston: Houghton Mifflin Company, 1967; Berle, A., and G. Means, *The Modern*

Corporation and Private Property. Rev. ed. New York: Harcourt Brace Jovanovich, Inc., 1968.

5. Institute for Southern Studies. "Textile Resources." *Southern Exposure*, 3, no. 4 (1976), 80–86, p. 84.

6. Domhoff, W. *The Bohemian Grove and Other Retreats*. New York: Harper & Row, Publishers, Inc. 1974.

7. *Index to Schedule of Investments*. Ann Arbor: The University of Michigan Press, 1977.

8. *Serving Two Masters: A Common Cause Study of Conflict of Interest in the Executive Branch*. Washington, D.C.: Common Cause, 1976.

9. Callahan, R. *Education and the Cult of Efficiency*. Chicago: The University of Chicago Press, 1962.

10. Spring, J. *Education and the Rise of the Corporate State*. Boston: Beacon Press, 1972; Greer, C. *The Great School Legend*. New York: Basic Books, Inc., 1972; Katz, M. *Class Bureaucracy and Schools*. New York: Praeger Publishers, Inc., 1971; Carnoy, M. *Schooling in a Corporate Society*. New York: David McKay Co., Inc., 1972.

11. *Working with Your School*. Washington, D.C.: U.S. Government Printing Office: 730-062/623, 1977, p. 2.

12. *Education Commission of the States*. Department of Research and Information Services, 1972.

13. Tumin, M. *Readings on Social Stratification*. Englewood Cliffs, N.J.: Prentice-Hall, Inc., 1970, p. 385.

14. Jencks, C., et. al. *Inequality: A Reassessment of the Effects of Family and Schooling in America*. New York: Basic Books, Inc., 1972.

15. Lasch, C. "Inequality and Education." *The New York Review of Books*, 8, no. 20 (May 17, 1973), 22.

16. Katz, op. cit., p. XIX.

Chapter 3

1. Adapted from *Historical Statistics of the United States: Colonial Times to 1970*. Washington, D.C.: U.S. Department of Commerce, Bureau of the Census, 1975. Series B107-115, p. 55.

2. Adapted from Ibid., A57-72, p. 11.

3. Ibid., Series A82-90, p. 12.

4. Ibid., Series D182-232, p. 140.

5. Reisman, D., N. Glazer, and R. Denny. *The Lonely Crowd*. New Haven, Conn.: Yale University Press, 1950; Miller, D., and G. Swanson. *The Changing American Parent*. New York: John Wiley & Sons, Inc., 1958; Whyte, W. *The Organization Man*. New York: Doubleday & Company, Inc., 1957; Slater, P. *The Pursuit of Loneliness*. Boston: Beacon Press, 1970.

6. *Current Population Reports*. Washington, D.C.: U.S. Department of Commerce, Bureau of the Census, Series P-60, no. 85.

7. Pettigrew, T. *A Profile of the Negro American*. Princeton, N.J.: D. Van Nostrand Company, 1964.

8. *Historical Statistics of the United States: Colonial Times to 1970*. Series Y272-289, op. cit., p. 1100.
9. Harrington, M. *The Other America: Poverty in the U.S.* New York: Macmillan Publishing Co., Inc., 1963.
10. *Historical Statistics of the United States: Colonial Times to 1970*. Series Y638-651, op. cit., p. 1125.
11. *Political Participation*. Washington, D.C.: U.S. Commission on Civil Rights, May 1968, p. 222.
12. *Historical Statistics of the United States: Colonial Times to 1970*. Series Y204-210, op. cit., p. 1083.
13. *Statistical Abstract of the United States*. Washington, D.C.: U.S. Department of Commerce, Bureau of the Census. 1978, p. 520.
14. *Historical Statistics of the United States: Colonial Times to 1970*. Series H793-799, op. cit., p. 391.
15. Bronfenbrenner, U. "Socialization and Social Class Through Time and Space." In M. Maccoby, T. Newcomb, and E. Hartley, eds. *Readings in Social Psychology*. 3rd ed. New York: Holt, Rinehart and Winston, Inc., 1958.
16. Reisman, op. cit.
17. Bronfenbrenner, op. cit., p. 424.
18. Miller and Swanson, op. cit.
19. Adapted from *Historical Statistics of the United States: Colonial Times to 1970*. Series H414-432, p. 368; Series H442-476, op. cit., pp. 370−371.
20. Adapted from *Historical Statistics of the United States: Colonial Times to 1970*. Series H412-432, p. 368; Series H520-530, op. cit., p. 375.
21. Chase, A. "Skipping Through College." *Atlantic Monthly* (September 1978), 33−40.
22. *Historical Statistics of the United States: Colonial Times to 1970*. Series H486-491, op. cit., p. 373.
23. Ogburn, W. *Social Change with Respect to Culture and Original Nature*. New York: The Viking Press, Inc., 1922.

Chapter 4

1. Coleman, J. "The Struggle for Control of Education." In *Education and Social Policy: Local Control of Education*. Ed. by C. Bowers and I. D. Dyke. New York: Random House, Inc., 1970; Corwin, R. *A Sociology of Education: Emerging Patterns of Class, Status and Power in the Public Schools*. Englewood Cliffs, N.J.: Prentice-Hall, Inc., 1965.
2. Coleman, op.cit.
3. Glazer, N. "For White and Black, Community Control Is the Issue." *New York Times Magazine* (April 27, 1968), 34−54.
4. Kaufman, H. "Administrative Decentralization and Political Power." *Public Administration Review*, 29 (Jan.−Feb. 1969), 3−15.; Kasperson, R. H., and M. Breibart. *Participation, Decentralization and Advocacy Planning*. Washington, D.C.: Commission on College Geography, Resource Paper, no. 25, 1974.
5. Crain, R. *The Politics of School Desegregation*. Chicago: Aldine Publishing Company, 1968.

6. *Fulfilling the Letter and Spirit of the Law.* Washington, D.C.: USCCR, 1976, p. 175.

7. Fantini, M. "Participation, Decentralization, Community Control and Quality of Education." *Teachers College Record*, **71** (1969), 93—107.

8. Case, J. "Workers' Control: Toward a North American Movement." In *Workers' Control.* Ed. by G. Hunnius, G. Garson, and J. Case. New York: Random House, Inc., 1973.

9. Moore, C., and R. Johnston. "School Decentralization, Community Control and the Politics of Public Education." *Urban Affairs Quarterly*, **6** (1971), 421—446; Grant, W. "Community Control vs. School Integration: The Case of Detroit." *The Public Interest*, **24** (1971), 62—79; Gittell, M. "The Balance of Power and the Community School." In *Community Control of Schools.* New York: Simon & Schuster, Inc., 1970.

10. Gittell, op. cit.

11. Moore and Johnston, op. cit., 423.

12. Hamilton, C. "Race and Education: A Search for Legitimacy." *Harvard Educational Review*, **38**, no. 4 (1968), 669—684; Wilcox, P. "The Community Centered School." In *The Schoolhouse in the City.* Ed. by A. Toffler. New York: Praeger Publishers, Inc., 1968; Pfautz, H. "The Black Community, the Community School, and the Socialization Process: Some Caveats." In *Community Control of Schools.* Ed. by H. Levin. New York: Simon & Schuster, Inc., 1970; Solomon, V. "An Independent Board of Education for Harlem." *Urban Affairs Quarterly*, **4** (1968), 39—43.

13. Miller, M. "Notes On Institutional Control." *Social Policy* (Nov.—Dec., Jan.—Feb., 1972—73), 38—43.

14. James, T., and H. Levin. "Financing Community Schools." In *Community Control of Schools.* Ed. by H. Levin, op. cit.

15. Miller, op. cit.

16. Ornstein, A. *Metropolitan Schools: Administrative Decentralization vs. Community Control.* Metuchen, N.J.: Scarecrow Press, 1974, p. 293.

17. Counts, G. S. "The Social Composition of Boards of Education." *Supplemental Educational Monographs*, no. 33. University of Chicago Press. (July 1927), pp. 50—54.

18. Ibid., p. 52.

19. National School Boards Association, *Survey of Public Education in the Member Cities of the Council of Big City Boards of Education*, 1975.

20. Ibid.

21. *Toward Quality Education for Mexican Americans.* Washington, D.C.: USCCR, 1974, p. 13.

22. Crain, op. cit.

23. *Desegregating the Boston City Schools: A Crisis in Civic Responsibility.* Washington, D.C.: USCCR, 1975, p. viii.

24. *Fulfilling the Letter and Spirit of the Law*, op. cit., pp. 179—180.

25. Ibid., p. 179.

26. Fantini, op. cit.

27. Gittell, op. cit.

28. Miller, op. cit.

29. Grant, op. cit.

30. Becker, H. "The Teacher in the Authority System of the Public School." *Journal of Educational Sociology*, **27**, no. 3 (1953), 128–141, p. 138.
31. Chesler, M. "Participants' Views of Disrupted Secondary Schools: A Preliminary Research Report." Appendix D in *Task force Report on Easing Educational Tensions*. Washington, D.C; Office of the Secretary, HEW., 1969.
32. Rossi, P., R. Berk, D. Boesel, B. Edison, and W. Groves. "Between White and Black: The Faces of American Institutions in the Ghetto." In *Supplemental Studies for the National Advisory Commission on Civil Disorders*. Washington, D.C.: U.S. Government Printing Office, 1968.
33. Clapp, E. *Community Schools in Action*. New York: The Viking Press Inc., 1939, p. 89.
34. Adapted from *Community School Criteria of the Michigan Curriculum Program*. Michigan State Department of Public Instruction, September 1955.
35. Hamiliton, op. cit.; Wilcox, op. cit.
36. Adapted from *Citizen Action in Education*. Institute for Responsive Education, **6**, no. 1 (1979), 8–9.

Chapter 5

1. Callahan, R. *Education and the Cult of Efficiency*. Chicago: University of Chicago Press, 1962; Siepert, A., and R. Likert. The Likert School Profile Measurements of the Human Organization. Paper presented at AERA Symposium on "Survey Feedback in Educational Organizational Development." New Orleans, 1973; Katz, F. "The School as a Complex Social Organization." *Harvard Educational Review*, **34** (1964), 428–455; Katz, I. "The Socialization of Academic Motivation in Minority Group Children." *Nebraska Symposium on Motivation*, **15** (1967), 133–191.
2. Corwin, R. *Militant Professionalism*. New York: Appleton-Century-Crofts, 1970; Miles, M. "Some Properties of Schools as Social Systems." In *Change in School Systems*. Ed. by G. Watson. Washington, D.C.: NTL-IABS, 1967.
3. Spring, J. *Education and the Rise of the Corporate State*. Boston: Beacon Press, 1972; Carnoy, M., ed. *Schooling in a Corporate Society*. New York: David McKay Co., Inc., 1972; Carnoy, M. *Education as Cultural Imperialism*. New York: David McKay Co., Inc. 1974; Katz, M. *The Irony of Early School Reform*. Boston: Beacon Press, 1970.
4. Kimbrough, R. *Political Power and Educational Decision-Making*. Chicago: Rand-McNally & Company, 1964; Crain, R. *The Politics of School Desegregation*. Chicago: Aldine Publishing Company, 1968.
5. Baldridge, V. *Power and Conflict in the University*. New York: John Wiley & Sons, Inc., 1971.
6. Lurie, E. *How to Change the Schools*. New York: Vintage, 1970; Fantini, M. "Participation, Decentralization, Community Control and Quality Education." *Teachers College Record*, **71** (1969), 94–107; Birmingham, J. *Our Time Is Now: Notes from the High School Underground*. New York: Praeger Publishers, Inc., 1970.
7. Katz, D., and R. Kahn. *The Social Psychology of Organizations*. New York: John Wiley & Sons, Inc., 1966.
8. Gamson, W. *Power and Discontent*. Homewood, Ill.: Dorsey Press, 1968.
9. Chesler, M., and J. Lohman. "Changing Schools Through Student Advocacy." In

Organizational Development in Schools. Ed. by R. Schmuck and M. Miles. Palo Alto, Cal.: National Press Books, 1971.

10. French, J., and B. Raven. "The Bases of Social Power." In *Group Dynamics.* Ed. by D. Cartwright and A. Zander. New York: Harper & Row, Publishers, Inc., 1960; Jamieson, D., and K. Thomas. "Power and Conflict in the Student-Teacher Relationship." *Journal of Applied Behavioral Sciences,* **10** no. 4 (1974), 321–337.

11. Bidwell, C. "Students and Schools: Some Observations on Client Trust in Client-Serving Organizations." In *Organizations and Clients.* Ed. by W. Rosengren and M. Lofton. Columbus, Ohio: Charles E. Merrill Publishing Company, 1970.

12. Cuban, L. "Ethnic Content and White Instruction." *Phi Delta Kappan,* **53** (1972), 270–273; Wilson, C. "Racism in Education." In *White Racism.* Ed. by B. Schwartz and R. Disch. New York: Dell Publishing Co., Inc., 1970.

13. Friedenberg, E. "Contemptuous Hairdressers: Ceremonies of Humiliation in School." *This Magazine Is About Schools* (August 1966), 9–18.

14. Haug, M., and M. Sussman. "Professional Autonomy and the Revolt of the Client." *Social Problems,* **17** (1969), 153–161; Glasser, I. "Schools for Scandal—The Bill of Rights and Public Education." *Phi Delta Kappan,* **51** (1969), 190–194; Abbott, C. "Demonstrations, Dismissals, Due Process and the High School: An Overview." *School Review,* **77** (1961), 128–143.

15. Halpin, A., ed. *Administrative Theory in Education.* Chicago: Midwest Administration Center, 1958; Getzels, J., and E. Guba. "Social Behavior and the Administrative Process." *School Review,* **55** (1957), 423–441.

16. Getzels, J. "Conflict and Role Behavior in the Educational Setting." In *Readings in the Social Psychology of Education.* Ed. by W. Charters and N. Gage. Boston: Allyn and Bacon, 1963.

17. Bidwell, C. "The School as a Formal Organization." In *Handbook of Organizations.* Ed. by J. March. Chicago: Rand-McNally & Company, 1965.

18. Tannenbaum, A. *Control in Organizations.* New York: McGraw-Hill, Inc., 1968.

19. Ibid.

20. Gross, N., and R. Herriott. *Staff Leadership in Public Schools.* New York: John Wiley & Sons, Inc., 1965.

21. Goodlad, J. "The Schools Versus Education." *Saturday Review* (April 19, 1969), 59–61, 80–82.

22. Ibid., p. 61.

23. Gross and Herriott, op. cit., p. 99.

24. Ibid., p. 314.

25. Biddle, B., J. Twyman, and E. Rankin. *The Concept of Role Conflict.* Social Studies Series no. 11, Oklahoma State University.

26. Adapted from Chesler, M. Participants' Views of Disrupted Secondary Schools: A Preliminary Research Project. Appendix D, *Task Force Report on Easing Educational Tensions.* Washington, D.C.: Department of Health, Education and Welfare, 1969, p. 4.

27. Ibid., p. 28.

28. Edgar, D., and R. Warren. "Power and Autonomy in Teacher Socialization." *Sociology of Education,* **42** (1969), 368–399.

29. Chesler, op. cit., p. 20.

30. Clark, B. *Educating the Expert Society.* San Francisco: Chandler Publishing Co., 1962, p. 159.

31. "School Management." *Administrators Forum*, **13** (November 1969), 8—12.
32. Rafky, D. "Blue Collar Power: The Social Impact of Urban School Custodians." *Urban Education*, **6**, no. 4 (January 1972), 353.
33. Chesler, op. cit., p. 21.
34. Ibid.
35. Janowitz, M. *Institution Building in Urban Education*. Hartford, Conn.: Russell Sage Foundation, 1969, p. 29.
36. From a workshop conducted by staff members of the Center for Research on the Utilization of Scientific Knowledge and Wayne State University, for Detroit public school administrators, June 18—19, 1969.

Chapter 6

1. Carlson, R. "Variations and the Myth in the Social Status of Teachers." *The Journal of Educational Sociology*, **35** (November 1951) 104—118.
2. Havighurst, R., and B. Neugarten. *Society and Education*. Boston: Allyn and Bacon, 1957.
3. Ibid., p. 359.
4. Carlson, op. cit., pp. 104—118.
5. *National Education Research Bulletin*, **50**, no. 1 (1972), 6.
6. Wattenberg, W., "Social Origins of Teachers—Facts from a Northern Industrial City." In *The Teacher's Role in American Society: John Dewey Society Fourteenth Yearbook* (1957, I). Ed. by L. Stiles. As reported in Havighurst and Neugarten, op. cit., p. 360.
7. Havighurst and Neugarten, op. cit., p. 360.
8. *Administrative Statistics*. Research and Evaluation Department; Office of Research, Planning and Evaluation: Detroit Public Schools, January 1978.
9. Adapted from: *Administrative Statistics*, op. cit., 1978.
10. Willower, D. *Schools as Organizations: Some Illustrative Strategies for Research and Practice*. West Virginia Social Science Colloquium Series, Morgantown, West Virginia, 1967.
11. Marker, G., and H. Mehlinger. "Schools, Politics, Rebellion and Other Youthful Interests." In *The School and the Democratic Environment*. Ed. by A. Westin. New York: Columbia University Press, 1970.
12. Zeigler, H. *The Political Life of American Teachers*. Englewood Cliffs, N.J.: Prentice-Hall, Inc., 1967, p. 18.
13. Bidwell, C. "The School as a Formal Organization." In *Handbook of Organizations*. Ed. by J. March. Chicago: Rand-McNally, 1965.
14. Walberg, H. "Professional Role Discontinuities in Educational Careers." *Review of Educational Research*, **40** (1970), 414.
15. Shepard, H. "Nine Dilemmas in Industrial Research." *Administrative Science Quarterly*, **1** (1956), 295—309.
16. Haug, M., and M. Sussman. "Professional Autonomy and the Revolt of the Client." *Social Problems*, **17** (1969), 153—161, p. 153.
17. Ibid.
18. Bennis, W. "A Funny Thing Happened on the Way to the Future." *American Psychologist*, **25** (1970), 599.

19. Becker, H. "The Teacher in the Authority System of the Public School." *Journal of Educational Sociology*, **27**, no. 3 (1953), 128–141.

20. *Task Force Survey of Teacher Displacement in Seventeen States*. National Education Association, December 1965.

21. Kalish, M., and N. Goldner. "The Demise of the Management Team Approach and the Birth of Collective Bargaining for Middle Management Educational Professionals." *Michigan Journal of Secondary Education*, **12**, no. 2 (1971), 45–51.

22. Doherty, R., and W. Oberer. *Teachers, School Boards and Collective Bargaining: A Changing of the Guard*. Ithaca, N.Y.: Cornell University Press, 1967; Moskow, M., and R. Doherty. "The United States." In *Teachers, Unions and Associations: A Comparative Study*. Ed. by A. Blum. Urbana: University of Illinois Press, 1969.

23. Metzler, J. "The Need for Limitation Upon the Scope of Negotiations in Public Education: I." *Journal of Law-Education*, **2**, no. 1 (1973), 139–154.

24. Gittell, M. "The Balance of Power and the Community School. In *Community Control of Schools*. Ed. by H. Levin. New York: Simon & Schuster, Inc., 1970; Doherty, R. "Collective Negotiations and Policy Making in Public School Districts." In *The Impact of Collective Negotiations on Policy Making in New Jersey Schools*. Conference at Rutgers University, 1971.

25. Lieberman, M., and M. Moskow, *Collective Negotiations for Teachers: An Approach to School Administration*. Chicago: Rand McNally and Co., 1966; Love, T. "Joint Committees: Their Role in the Development of Teacher Bargaining." *Labor Law Journal*, **20**, no. 3 (1969), 174–182; LaNoue, G., and M. Pilo, "Teachers' Unions and Educational Accountability." *Proceedings, Academy of Political Science*, **30**, no. 2 (1970), 146–158.

26. Kay, W. "The Need for Limitation Upon the Scope of Negotiations in Public Education: II." *Journal of Law-Education*, **2**, no. 1 (1973), 155–175, p. 155.

27. "Bartoc: Bay Area Radical Teachers Organizing Committee." *Socialist Revolution*, **2**, no. 2 (1972), 126.

28. Brominski, B. "Limited Right to Strike Laws—Can They Work When Applied to Public Education: From the Perspective of the Local Judge." *Journal of Law-Education*, **2**, no. 4 (1973), 677–688.

29. Sagot, L., and T. Jennings. "Limited Right to Strike Laws—Can They Work When Applied to Public Education: From the Perspective of the Union Attorney." *Journal of Law-Education*, **2**, no. 4 (1973), 715–734, p. 716.

30. Homans, G. "Group Factors in Worker Productivity." In *Readings in Social Psychology*. Ed. by E. Maccoby, T. Newcomb, and E. Hartley. New York: Holt, Rinehart and Winston, Inc., 1958; Seashore, S. *Group Cohesiveness in the Industrial Work Group*. Ann Arbor: Institute for Social Research, 1954.

31. Chesler, M., and H. Barakat. *The Innovation and Sharing of Teaching Practices: A Study of Professional Roles and Social Structures in Schools*. Ann Arbor, Mich.: Institute for Social Research, 1967; Chesler, M., and R. Fox. "Teacher Peer Relations and Educational Change." *NEA Journal*, **56**, no. 5 (1967), 25–36.

32. Janowitz, M. *Institution Building in Urban Education*. Hartford, Conn.: Russell Sage Foundation, 1969, p. 29.

33. Chesler, M., and J. Mann. *Training Teachers for New Responses to Intergenerational and Interracial Conflict*. Ann Arbor, Mich.: Institute for Social Research, 1970.

34. From the files of the project on the Development of Alternative Responses to

Interracial and Intergenerational Conflict in Schools. Institute for Social Research, 1967—1969.

35. Chesler, M. Participants' Views of Disrupted Secondary Schools: A Preliminary Research Report. Appendix D, *Task Force on Easing Educational Tensions*, Department of Health, Education and Welfare, 1969, p. 8.

36. Jennings, K., and H. Zeigler. "Political Expressivism Among High School Teachers: The Intersection of Community and Occupational Values." *Learning About Politics*. Ed. by R. S. Sigel. New York: Random House, Inc., 1970, pp. 434—453.

37. Johnson D., and R. Johnson. *Learning Together and Alone: Cooperation, Competition and Individualization.* Englewood Cliffs, N.J.: Prentice-Hall, Inc., 1975.

38. Coleman, J. *The Adolescent Society.* New York: The Free Press, 1949.

39. Mayer, M. "The Children's Crusade." *The Center Magazine, 2*, no. 5 (September 1969), 6.

40. Becker, op. cit.

41. Willower, op. cit.

42. Ibid. p. 53—54.

43. Nordstrom, C., E. Friedenberg, and H. Gold. *Society's Children.* New York: Random House, Inc., 1967.

44. Chesler, op. cit., p. 12.

45. Niemeyer, J. "Some Guidelines to Desirable Elementary School Reorganization." In *Programs for the Educationally Disadvantaged.* Washington, D.C.: U.S. Government Printing Office, 1962, p. 81.

46. See, for instance, a series of studies summarized in Rosenthal, R., and L. Jacobsen. *Pygmalion in the Classroom.* New York: Holt, Rinehart and Winston, Inc., 1968.

47. Katz, I. "Review of Evidence Relating to the Effects of Desegregation on the Intellectual Performance of Negroes." *American Psychologist, 19* (1964), 381—399.

48. Gerard, H., and N. Miller, *School Desegregation: A Long Range Study.* New York: Plenum Press, 1975.

49. Bloom, B., A. Davis, and R. Hess. *Compensatory Education for Cultural Deprivation.* New York: Holt, Rinehart and Winston, Inc., 1965.

50. Chesler, M., and P. Segal. *Characteristics of Negro Students Attending Previously All-White Schools in The Deep South.* Ann Arbor, Mich.: Institute for Social Research, 1967, pp. 43—44.

51. Adapted from Chesler, M., S. Wittes, and N. Radin. "When Northern Schools Desegregate." *American Education, 4*, no. 6 (1968), 2—4.

52. Cohen E., M. Lockheed, and M. Lohman. "The Center for Interracial Cooperation: A Field Experiment." *Sociology of Education, 49* (1976), 47—58.

53. Michaels, H. "Classroom Reward Structures and Academic Performance." *Review of Educational Research, 47* (1977), 87—98.

54. Cohen, Lockheed, and Lohman, op. cit.

55. Chesler and Segal, op. cit.

56. Kvaraceus, W., ed. *Negro Self-Concept.* New York: McGraw-Hill, Inc., 1965; Herriot, R., and N. St. John. *Social Class and The Urban School.* New York: John Wiley & Sons, Inc., 1965.

57. Kvaraceus, op. cit., p. 112.

58. Herriot and St. John, op. cit.

Chapter 7

1. Rowntree, J., and M. Rowntree, "The Political Economy of Youth." *Our Generation*, **6** (1968), 1.
2. Feuer, L. *The Conflict of Generations*. New York: Basic Books, Inc., 1969.
3. Haskell, P. "Judicial Review of School Discipline." *Case-Western Reserve Law Review*, **21** (1979), 211–245, pp. 242–243.
4. Friedenberg, E. "Our Contemptuous Hairdressers: Ceremonies of Humiliation in School." *This Magazine Is About Schools*, **1**, no. 2 (1966), 9–18, p. 14.
5. Glasser, I. "Schools for Scandal—The Bill of Rights and Public Education." *Phi Delta Kappan*, **51**, no. 4 (1969), 190–194.
6. Discussed in Abbott, C. "Demonstrations, Dismissals, Due Process and the High School: An Overview." *School Review*, **77** (1969), 128–143.
7. Westin, A. *The School and the Democratic Environment*. New York: Columbia University Press, 1970, pp. 76–77.
8. Berkman, R. "Students in Court." *Harvard Educational Review*, **40** (1970), 567–595, pp. 569–570.
9. Discussed in Abbott, op. cit.
10. Discussed in Ibid.
11. Ibid., p. 134.
12. Ibid., p. 134.
13. Tuma, E., and N. Livson. "Family Socio-economic Status and Adolescent Attitudes Toward Authority." *Child Development* **3** (1969), 387–399.
14. Douvan, E., and J. Adelson. *The Adolescent Experience*. New York: John Wiley & Sons, Inc., 1966.
15. Wasserman. M., and J. Reimann. "Student Rebels and School Defenders." *The Urban Review*, **4** (October 1964), 9–17.
16. Erikson, E. *Youth: Change and Challenge*. New York: Basic Books, Inc., 1963.
17. Stinchcombe, A. *Rebellion in a High School*. Chicago: Quadrangle Books, Inc., 1964.
18. Ibid., p. 2.
19. See, for instance: Ryan, W. *Blaming the Victim*. New York: Pantheon Books, Inc., 1971.
20. Wittes, S. *Power and People*. Ann Arbor, Mich.: Institute for Social Research, 1970.
21. Weinberg, M. *Minority Students: A Research Appraisal*. Washington, D.C.: U.S. Government Printing Office, 1977, p. 212.
22. Coulson, J. *The Third Year of the Emergency School Aid Act (ESAA) Implementation*. Santa Monica, Systems Development Corporation, 1977, p. VII–15.
23. "Collision Course in the High Schools." *Life* (May 16, 1969).
24. Weaver, D. "Primary Aims and Appropriate Activities of Michigan Public School Student Councils." Ed. D. dissertation, The University of Michigan, 1961.
25. Forehand, G., M. Ragosta, and D. Rock. *Conditions and Processes of Effective School Desegregation*. Princeton, N.J.: Educational Testing Service, 1976.
26. *Life*, op. cit., p. 29.
27. Guskin. A., P. Cunningham, J. Guskin, and M. Hoff. *High Schools in Crisis*. Ann Arbor, Mich.: Community Resources Limited, 1971, pp. 65–66.
28. Adapted from *Analysis of Suspension Data for the Ann Arbor School District, 1975–1977*. Ann Arbor, Mich.: Student Advocacy Center, 1978, p. 11.

29. Wasserman and Reimann, op. cit., p. 17.

30. Friedenberg, op. cit.

31. *Life*, op. cit.

32. Chesler, M. "Participants' Views of Disrupted Secondary Schools: A Preliminary Research Report." Appendix D. *Task Force Report on Easing Educational Tensions.* Washington, D.C.: Office of the Secretary of HEW, 1969, p. 15.

33. Brim, O. "Adolescent Personality as Self-Other Systems." *Journal of Marriage and the Family,* **37** (1965), 156–167.

34. Chesler, M., and J. Mann. *Training Teachers for New Responses to Intergenerational and Interracial Conflict.* Ann Arbor, Mich.: Institute for Social Research, 1970.

35. Coleman, J. *The Adolescent Society.* New York: The Free Press, 1949.

36. From the files of the Educational Change Team, University of Michigan, Ann Arbor, Michigan.

37. Citron, A. *The Rightness of Whiteness.* Detroit: Michigan-Ohio Regional Educational Laboratory, 1969.

38. Bailey, S. *Disruption in Urban Public Secondary Schools.* Syracuse, N.Y.: Syracuse University Research Corp., 1970.

39. Coles, R. "The Politics of Middle Class Children." *New York Review of Books,* **22** (March 6, 1975), 13–14.

40. See for example "The Courts, Social Science & School Desegregation, Parts I and II." *Law and Contemporary Problems,* **39** (1975).

41. Katzenmeyer, W. "Social Interaction and Differences in Intelligence Test Performance of Negro and White Elementary School Pupils." *Dissertation Abstracts,* **24** (1963), 1905.

42. Katz, I. "Review of Evidence Relating to Effects of Desegregation on the Intellectal Performance of Negroes." *American Psychologist,* **19** (1964), 381–399.

43. See for instance: Schmuck, R., M. Luszki, and D. Epperson. "Interpersonal Relations and Mental Health in the Classroom." *Mental Hygiene,* **47** (1963), 289–297.

44. Chesler, M., and P. Segal. "Southern Negroes' Initial Experience and Reactions in School Desegregation." *Integrated Education,* **6** (1968), 20–28.

45. Ibid., p. 21.

46. Gottlieb, D., and W. TenHouten. "Racial Composition and the Social System of the High School." *Journal of Marriage and the Family,* **27**, no.-2 (1965), 204–212, p. 206.

47. The "contact hypothesis" has a long and distinguished history in sociological and psychological studies of racial relations. See, for example, the early works of Allport, G. *The Nature of Prejudice.* New York: Doubleday & Company, Inc., 1958; Deutsch, M., and M. Collins. *Interracial Housing.* Minneapolis: University of Minnesota Press, 1951; Jahoda, M., M. Deutsch, and S. Cook. *Research Methods in Social Relations.* New York: Dryden Press, 1951; Stouffer, S. *The American Soldier.* Princeton, N.J.: Princeton University Press, 1949, vol. 11; Williams, R. "The Reduction of Intergroup Tensions." New York: *Social Science Research Council Bulletin,* **57** (1947).

48. Ashmore, R. "Prejudice: Causes and Cures." In *Social Psychology Readings.* Ed. by B. Collins. Reading, Mass.: Addison-Wesley Publishing Co., Inc., 1970.

49. Amir, Y. "The Role of Intergroup Contact in Change of Prejudice and Ethnic

Relations." In *Toward the Elimination of Racism*. Ed. by P. Katz. New York: Pergamon Press, 1961.

50. Flacks. R. "Social and Cultural Meanings of Student Revolt: Some Informal Comparative Observations." *Social Problems*, 17, no. 3 (1970), 340–357, p. 350.

51. Roszak, T. *The Making of a Counter-Culture*. New York: Doubleday & Company, Inc., 1968, p. 16.

52. Noyes, K., and G. McAndrew. "Is This What Schools Are for?" *Saturday Review* (December 21, 1968), 58–59, 65.

53. Ibid., p. 58.

54. Rhea, B. "Institutional Paternalism in High Schools." *The Urban Review* (February 13–15, 1968), 13–15, 34.

55. Merton, R. *Social Theory and Social Structure*. New York: The Free Press, 1957.

Chapter 8

1. Keniston, K. *All Our Children*. New York: Harcourt Brace Jovanovich, Inc., 1977, p. 37.

2. Hughes, L., and A. Bontemps. *The Book of Negro Folklore*. New York: Dodd, Mead & Company, 1958, pp. 490–491.

3. Dove, A. Unpublished materials.

4. Jencks, C. *Inequality: A Reassessment of the Effect of Family and Schooling in America*. New York: Harper & Row, Publishers, Inc., 1973.

5. Brookover, W., R. Gigliotti, R. Henderson, N. Lee, R. Braley, and J. Schneider. "Quality of Educational Attainment, Standardized Testing, Assessment, and Accountability." *National Society for the Study of Education*. NSSE, Chicago, 1974, p. 171.

6. Coleman, J. *Equality of Educational Opportunity*. Washington, D.C.: U.S. Government Printing Office, 1966, p. 20.

7. Malin, B. *The Effects of Alternative and Traditional School Structure on Student Satisfaction and Perceptions of School*. Published dissertation, Ann Arbor, Michigan, 1976.

8. Jencks, op. cit.; Coleman, op. cit.

Chapter 9

1. *Digest of Education Statistics: 1976 Edition*. Department of Health, Education and Welfare. National Center for Education Statistics. Washington, D.C.: U.S. Government Printing Office, 1977, p. 13.

2. Ibid.

3. Levitan, S., W. Johnston, and R. Taggart. *Still a Dream: The Changing Status of Blacks Since 1960*. Cambridge, Mass.: Harvard University Press, 1975, p. 81.

4. Ibid., p. 82.

5. *The Fleischman Report on the Quality, Cost and Financing of Elementary and Secondary Education in New York State:* vol. 3. New York: The Viking Press, Inc., 1973, p. 156.

6. Carter, T. *Mexican-Americans in School: A History of Educational Neglect.* Princeton, N.J.: College Entrance Examination Board, 1970, p. 28.
7. Adapted from: *Children Out of School in America.* Children's Defense Fund of the Washington Research Project. Cambridge, Mass.: 1974, p. 38.
8. Ibid., p. 39.
9. Sexton, P. *Education and Income.* New York: The Viking Press, Inc., 1961.
10. Ibid.
11. *Digest of Educational Statistics*, op. cit., p. 89.
12. Brookover, W. *Sociology of Education.* New York: American Book Company, 1955, p. 87.
13. *Digest of Educational Statistics*, op. cit.
14. Ibid., p. 32.
15. Coleman, J., et. al. *Equality of Educational Opportunity.* Washington, D.C.: U.S. Government Printing Office, 1966, p. 275.
16. Research and Evaluation Department. Office of Research, Planning, and Evaluation. Detroit Public Schools, January 1978.
17. Sexton, op. cit.
18. Ibid., p. 23.
19. Hollingshead, A. *Elmtown's Youth: The Impact of Social Classes on Adolescents.* New York: John Wiley & Sons, Inc., 1949, p. 172.
20. *Digest of Educational Statistics*, op. cit., p. 65.
21. Adapted from Office of Research, Planning and Evaluation, Detroit Public Schools, op. cit.
22. Adapted from Sexton, op. cit., pp. 163, 202.
23. Hollingshead, op. cit.
24. Levitan, op. cit., p. 85.
25. Adapted from: Demerest, S., and J. Jordan. "Hawkins vs. Coleman: Discriminatory Suspension in the Effect of Institutional Racism on School Discipline." *Inequality in Education*, **20** (July, 1975), 25–41.
26. Adapted from: *Children Out of School in America*, op. cit., p. 131.
27. Bryant, B. *High School Students Look at Their World.* Columbus, Ohio: R. H. Boettler and Associates, 1970, p. 33.
28. Ibid., p. 29.
29. Ibid.
30. Hollingshead, op. cit., p. 200.
31. Ibid.
32. Adapted from: Forehand, E., M. Ragosta, and D. Rock. *Conditions and Processes of Effective School Desegregation.* Princeton, N.J.: Educational Testing Service, 1976, p. 237.
33. Adapted from: *Southern Schools: An Evaluation of the Effects of the Emergency School Assistance Program and of School Desegregation.* Chicago: National Opinion Research Center, 1973, vol. 1, p. 297.
34. Sexton, op. cit., p. 207.
35. Ibid.
36. Bryant, op. cit., p. 86.
37. Sexton, op. cit., p. 14.
38. Ibid.
39. *Digest of Educational Statistics*, op. cit., p. 183.

40. Levitan, Johnson, and Taggart, op. cit., p. 86.
41. Duke, D. "The Etiology of Student Misbehavior and the Depersonalization of Blame." *Review of Educational Research*, **48** (1979), 415–437.
42. Cohen, D. "Reforming School Politics." *Harvard Educational Review*, **48**, no. 4 (1978), 434.
43. Ibid.
44. American Psychological Association. Division of School Psychology. *School Psychology Monograph*, **2**, no. 1 (Fall 1974), 7.
45. Ibid.
46. Binet, A., and T. Simon. *Development of Intelligence in Children*. Baltimore: The Williams and Wilkins Co., 1916, pp. 254–256.

Chapter 10

1. Research and Evaluation Department. Office of Research, Planning and Evaluation. Detroit Public Schools, January 1978.
2. Weinberg, M. *Minority Students: A Research Appraisal*. Washington, D.C.: U.S. Government Printing Office, 1977, p. 99.
3. Ibid.
4. Meil, A. *The Short-Changed Children of Suburbia*. New York: Institute of Human Relations Press, 1967.
5. "Serrano v. Priest: Implications for Educational Equality." *Harvard Educational Review*, **41**, no. 4 (1971), 514.
6. Zukofsky, J. "Taxes and Schools: Equalizing Educational Opportunity." *The New Republic*, **166** (June 17, 1972), 22.
7. Sexton, P. *Education and Income*. New York: The Viking Press, Inc., 1961, p. 125.
8. Ibid.
9. Murphy, J. "Title I of ESEA: The Politics of Implementing Federal Education Reform." *Harvard Educational Review*, **41**, no. 1 (1971), 35–43.
10. Ibid.
11. See several books that demonstrate how teachers promote and/or reinforce sex-role discrimination in school: Stacy, J., S. Bereaud, and J. Daniels. *Sexism in American Education*. New York: Dell Publishing Co., Inc., 1974; Frazier, N., and M. Sadker. *Sexism in School and Society*. New York: Dell Publishing Co., Inc., 1974.
12. Weinberg, op. cit., p. 232.
13. Ibid.
14. Braxton, M., and C. Bullock. "Teacher Partiality in Desegregation." *Integrated Education: A Report on Race and Schools*, **10** (July–August 1972), 42–46.
15. Ibid., pp. 43–44.
16. Weinberg, op. cit., p. 232.
17. Mercer, J. *Labelling the Mentally Retarded: Clinical and Social System Perspectives on Mental Retardation*. Berkeley, Calif.: University of California Press, 1973.
18. Adapted from *Children Out of School in America*. Children's Defense Fund of the Washington Research Project, Cambridge, 1974, p. 103.
19. Tittle, C. "The Use and Abuse of Vocational Tests." In J. Stacey, S. Bereaud, and J. Daniels. *And Jill Came Tumbling After*. New York: Dell Publishing Co., Inc., 1974.
20. Pietrofesa, J., and N. Schlossberg. "Counselor Bias and the Female Occupational

Role." In W. Cave, and M. Chesler. *Sociology of Education.* New York: Macmillan Publishing Co., Inc., 1974, p. 150.

21. Brookover, W. *A Sociology of Education.* New York: American Book Co., 1955, p. 88.

22. Ibid.

23. Hollingshead, A. *Elmtown's Youth.* New York: John Wiley & Sons, Inc., 1949.

24. Sexton, op. cit., p. 177

25. Ibid., p. 60.

26. Trimberger, E. "Open Admissions: A New Form of Tracking?" *The Insurgent Sociologist,* **4**, no. 1 (1973), 29–43, p. 36.

27. Jacobs, C., and C. Eaton. "Sexism in the Elementary School." In W. Cave and M. Chesler. *Sociology of Education.* New York: Macmillan Publishing Co., 1974, p. 324.

28. Ibid., p. 325.

29. Adapted from Astin, A. "The Undergraduate Woman." In H. Astin and W. Hirsch, eds. *The Higher Education of Women.* New York: Praeger Publishers, Inc., , 1978, p. 108.

30. Adapted from *The Condition of Education.* Washington, D.C.: National Center for Education Statistics, 1979, p. 232.

31. Hollingshead, op. cit., p. 201.

32. Ibid.

33. Massialas, B., and A. Zazamier. *Critical Issues in the Teaching of the Social Studies.* Englewood Cliffs, N.J.: Prentice-Hall, Inc., 1964; Oliver, D., and P. Shaver. *Teaching Public Issues in High School.* Boston: Houghton Mifflin Company, 1966.

34. Hollingshead, op. cit., p. 231.

35. *Ann Arbor News,* April 8, 1979, p. E-5.

36. Waller, W. *The Sociology of Teaching.* New York: John Wiley & Sons., Inc., 1932, pp. 124–125.

37. Adapted from Sexton, op. cit., p. 207.

38. Stein, A. "Strategies of Failure." *Harvard Educational Review,* **41**, no. 2 (1971), 158–205.

Chapter 11

1. Adapted from Chesler, M., and J. Mann. *Training Teachers for New Responses to International and Interracial Conflict.* Center for Research on Utilization of Scientific Knowledge, University of Michigan, 1971, p. 153.

2. "Force Field" diagram created by The Educational Change Team, The University of Michigan, Ann Arbor, Michigan, 1971.

3. Lurie, E. *How to Change the Schools.* New York: Random House, Inc., 1970, pp. 61–62.

4. Ibid., pp. 58–59.

5. Worden, O., G. Levin, and M. Chesler. "Racism, Sexism and Class Elitism: Change Agents' Dilemmas in Combating Oppression." In *Beyond Sex Roles.* Ed. by A. Sargent. St. Paul, Minn.: West Publishing Company, 1977.

6. Ibid.

INDEX